Economic Trends

No. 604, March 2004

ISSN 0013-0400
ISBN 0 11 621671 9

© Crown copyright 2004
Published with the permission of the Controller of Her Majesty's Stationery Office (HMSO).

Applications for reproduction should be submitted to HMSO under HMSO's Class licence:
www.clickanduse.hmso.gov.uk

Contacts
For enquiries about this publication, contact the Editor, Paul Dickman.
Telephone: 020 7533 5914
E-mail: paul.dickman@ons.gsi.gov.uk

For general enquiries, contact the National Statistics Customer Contact Centre on
0845 601 3034
(minicom: 01633 812399)

E-mail: info@statistics.gsi.gov.uk
Facsimile: 01633 652747
Letters: Customer Contact Centre,
Room D115,
Government Buildings,
Cardiff Road,
Newport NP10 8XG

You can also find National Statistics on the Internet at www.statistics.gov.uk

About the Office for National Statistics
The Office for National Statistics (ONS) is the government agency responsible for compiling, analysing and disseminating many of the United Kingdom's economic, social and demographic statistics, including the retail prices index, trade figures and labour market data, as well as the periodic census of the population and health statistics. The Director of ONS is also the National Statistician and the Registrar General for England and Wales, and the agency administers the registration of births, marriages and deaths there.

A National Statistics Publication
National Statistics are produced to high professional standards set out in the National Statistics Code of Practice. They undergo regular quality assurance reviews to ensure that they meet customer needs. They are produced free from any political influence.

Regulars

2 In brief
Summary from last month's economic statistics releases

5 Economic update – March 2004
Rhys Herbert
Monthly overview of latest economic statistics

11 Forecasts for the UK economy – February 2004
Monthly comparison of independent forecasts for the UK economy

12 International economic indicators – March 2004
Nicola Mai
Monthly review of international economic indicators

25 Corporate services price index (experimental) – Quarter 4 2003
Lyndsey Severn
Quarterly results of the CSPI

Features

38 Consumer price inflation since 1750
Jim O'Donoghue, Louise Goulding and Grahame Allen
A presentation of a composite price index covering the period since 1750 which can be used for analysis of consumer price inflation or the purchasing power of the pound.

47 Oil and gas sector, 1992–2001
Sanjiv Mahajan
An overview of the structure of the UK Oil and gas sector, together with statistics covering the oil and gas industries for 1992–2001, as published in the UK *Input-output Analyses*, 2003 edition.

Methods

64 Changes to methodology employed in the CPI and RPI
Adrian Ball, Kathryn Waldron, Kevin Smith and Jonathan Hughes
An outline of three methodological changes made to the official consumer price indices from February 2004.

70 Revisions information in ONS First Releases
Graham Jenkinson and Nigel Stuttard
A description of the additional information about revisions to time series that ONS will be providing to users in its First Releases.

Tables

73 List of Tables
74 Notes to Tables
75 Tables
154 Sources

Publications

160 Portfolio of ONS macro-economic publications

in brief

At a glance – economic summaries recently released on the National Statistics website.

GDP growth

Services rose by 1.0 per cent for the second quarter in a row in the fourth quarter of 2003. Business services and finance continued to grow, by 1.4 per cent in the latest quarter, with the strongest growth in banking, insurance, real estate and business activities. The distribution, hotels and catering sector rose by 0.5 per cent due to an increase of 1.5 per cent in retail output. The transport and communications sector rose by 0.9 per cent with strong growth in air transport and transport support. Elsewhere, government and other services rose by 0.8 per cent over the quarter driven by growth in health and recreation.

Output of the production industries decreased by 0.1 per cent driven by a fall in oil and gas production in the North Sea. This fall was partially offset by a rise in energy supply driven by increased electricity and gas supply. Manufacturing output rose by 0.2 per cent in 2003 Q4, with the most significant rises in chemicals and man made fibres, transport equipment and paper, printing and publishing equipment and the most significant falls in textiles, leather and clothing and electrical and optical equipment.

Construction output rose by 1.6 per cent.

Household expenditure rose by 1.1 per cent with strong growth in household goods and services and clothing and footwear. The level of government expenditure and investment both rose over the quarter. Business investment rose over the quarter with increased activity related to construction. The trade balance worsened as imports of goods rose by 3.7 per cent and exports of goods rose by 2.2 per cent.

On the income side, compensation of employees rose by 0.5 per cent driven by an increase in average earnings, with little change in employment. Corporate incomes rose by 2.9 per cent in 2003 Q4, with diverse movements across the industrial sectors.

Real GDP quarterly growth
Per cent

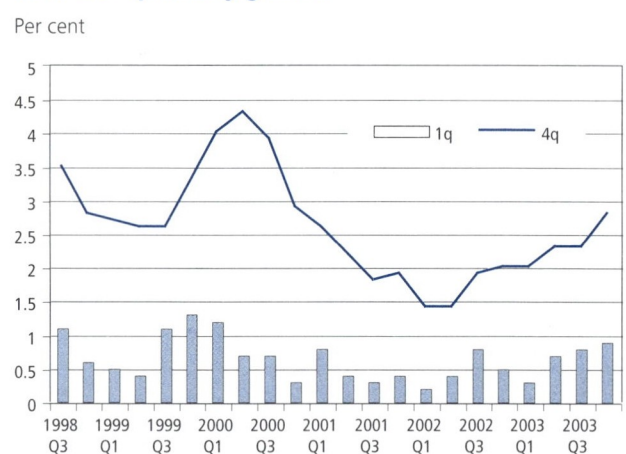

Released: **25 February 2004**

International comparisons of productivity

New estimates of purchasing power parities from the OECD mean that the UK's productivity performance relative to that in other countries was better than previously thought.

Relative to the average of all G7 countries excluding the UK, GDP per worker in 2002 was 112.8 on the new estimates compared with 116.5 on the old figures. Relative productivity measures are based on UK=100; therefore any fall in these indices is an improvement in the UK's relative productivity performance. The UK's productivity has improved significantly over the last 10 years compared with that in other countries, but the level of productivity in the UK remains below that in other G7 countries taken as a block, by around 13 percentage points.

GDP per worker, 2002

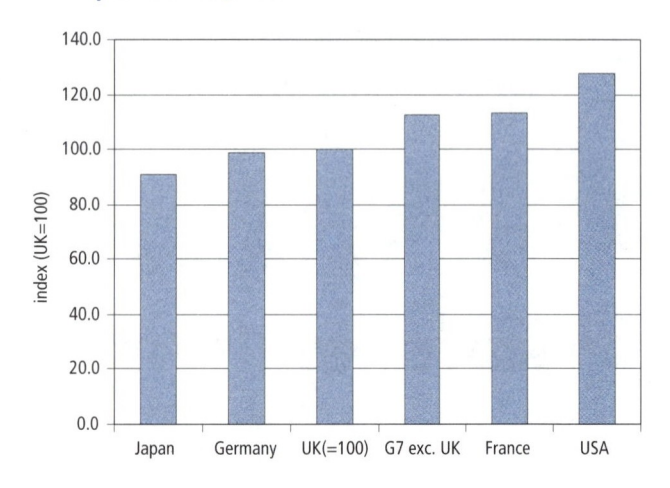

Revisions to the international price comparison data are the result of an intensive programme of work by Eurostat and the OECD. These revisions also improve the UK's relative productivity performance over time.

Relative to the G7 excluding the UK the index now shows an improvement from 117.2 in 1999 to 114.4 in 2001 and 112.8 in 2002. This compares with a deterioration in relative productivity performance between 2001 and 2002 in the September release.

Relative to the USA the recent revisions mean UK relative productivity improved marginally between 2001 and 2002 having shown a deterioration for these years in the previous release.

The UK and Germany now appear to have approximately the same level of productivity on a GDP per worker basis. In 2002 Germany's relative productivity performance with the UK was 98.8, compared with 104.6 in the previous release.

France and Japan also show a similar impact of the data revisions in 2002, changing from 113.8 to 112.9 and 93.9 to 90.6 respectively. In both cases the revised international price comparisons series are the driving force behind these changes.

Also published today are experimental international comparisons of productivity per hour worked. Output per hour worked estimates show similar movements to output per worker for Germany and the USA. In contrast, there is an improvement in France's productivity position over all years on a per hour basis due to fundamental revisions to French hours worked data.

Released: **25 February 2004**

Unemployment

This month's labour market statistics release shows a falling unemployment rate and a larger fall than for some time in the claimant count. The number of people in employment is still rising, although more slowly, and job vacancies are a little higher than a year ago. In slight contrast, the working-age employment rate is falling, with the inactivity rate up. Growth in average earnings, including bonuses, is lower.

The unemployment rate fell to 4.9 per cent. This continues to be the joint lowest unemployment rate since records began in 1984. The number of unemployed people fell by 21,000 to reach 1.46 million.

The claimant count (Job Seekers' Allowance claimants) fell by 13,400 to 892,100 in January, the lowest level since September 1975.

The employment rate for people of working age was slightly down, to 74.5 per cent, but the number of people in employment rose 5,000 over the previous three months, to 28.16 million. The fall of 22,000 full-time workers was more than offset by a rise of 27,000 part-time workers.

The inactivity rate for people of working age rose to 21.5 per cent. For men the rate was 16.3 per cent, up from 16.0 per cent three months ago, and for women it was 27.0 per cent.

Total hours worked per week fell 4.1 million hours to 901.7 million hours. This was wholly due to falls in the average hours per week worked by men.

The average number of job vacancies for the three months to January 2004 was 571,900. This was 6,600 more than a year earlier.

The annual rate of growth in average earnings (the AEI), including bonuses, was 3.4 per cent, down from last month's figure of 3.5 per cent. In the private sector, the AEI was unchanged at 3.2 per cent, but in the public sector it fell to 4.4 per cent, from 4.8 per cent last month.

Released: **16 February 2004**

Working-age employment rate
Sampling variability ±0.4 per cent

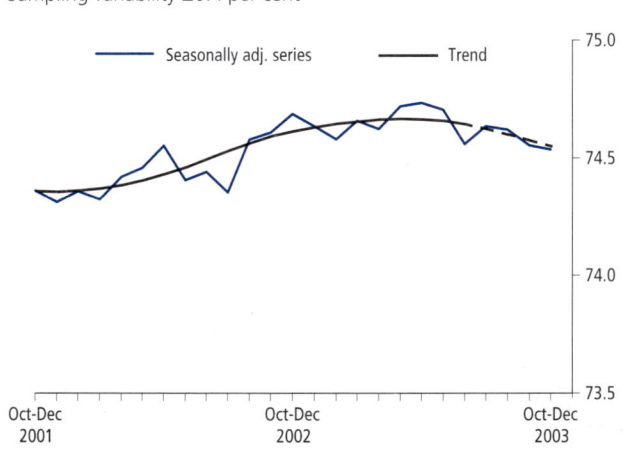

Unemployment rate
Sampling variability ±0.2 per cent

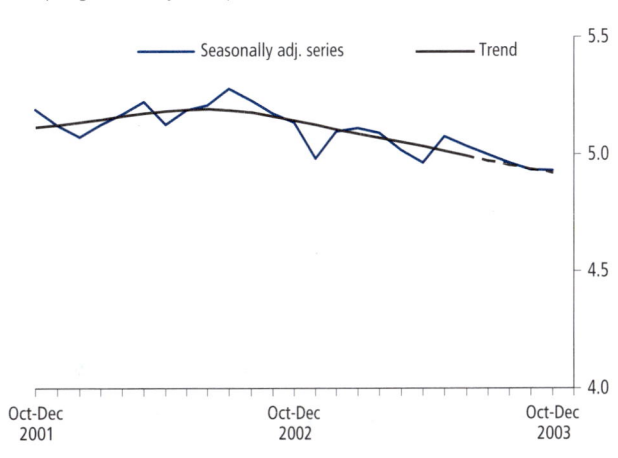

Notes

People in employment, unemployed and economically inactive make up the total household population aged 16 and over, measured through the Labour Force Survey on a consistent basis since 1984.

Working age is defined as 16-64 for men and 16-59 for women.

Average earnings growth is measured by the three-month average year-on-year growth of the Average Earnings Index (AEI).

Released: **11 February 2004**

UK debt and deficit

Government deficit as a percentage of GDP

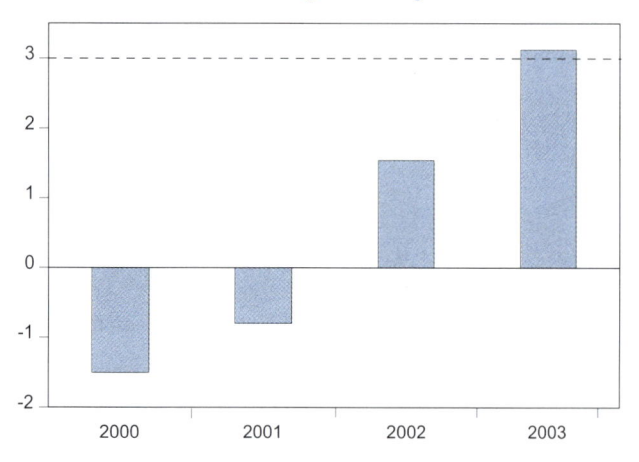

Government debt as a percentage of GDP

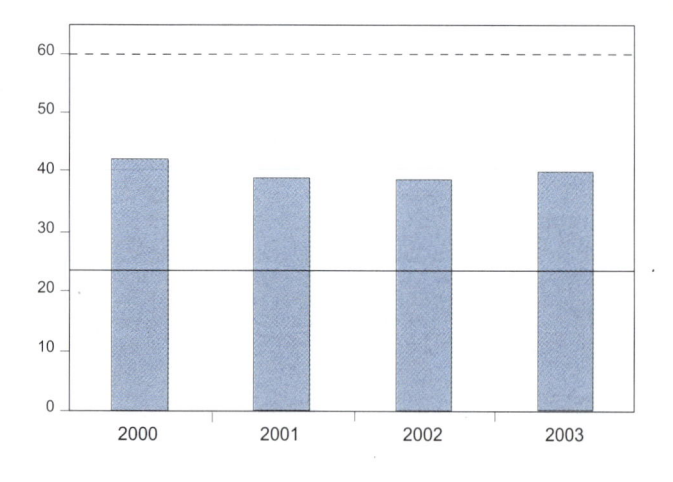

In 2003 the UK recorded a government deficit of £33.9 billion, which was equivalent to 3.1 per cent of gross domestic product (GDP).

Provisional estimates show the UK government deficit narrowly exceeded the reference value in the Maastricht Treaty's Excessive Deficit Procedure. The procedure sets deficit and debt targets of three per cent and sixty per cent respectively for all EU countries.

At the end of 2003 general government debt was £438.4 billion, equivalent to 39.8 per cent of GDP. This was the first increase in the debt percentage level since 1996, but are substantially within the reference value for excessive debt.

These data were reported to the European Commission at the end of February 2004.

General government is the total of central government and local government.

Released: **27 February 2004**

Summaries on other economic topics as well as social subjects can be found at www.statistics.gov.uk/glance

Economic update
March 2004

Rhys Herbert
Office for National Statistics

Overview

- Fourth quarter GDP growth was 0.9 per cent, slightly above the third quarter rate.

- A strong service sector continued to lead economic growth, and construction output was also buoyant.

- Consumer spending rose by 1.1 per cent in the fourth quarter, similar to its third quarter rate, while robust retail sales growth in January suggests that the consumer is continuing to spend.

- Fixed investment spending rose by 1.6 per cent in the fourth quarter but spending on capital equipment remains subdued.

- Government spending is currently a positive contributor to economic growth but the public sector finances are falling further into deficit.

- Export growth rebounded in quarter four, after a weak third quarter, led by goods exports to non-EU markets.

- Labour market aggregates remain largely stable, and private sector wage pressures are minimal.

- Producer prices figures suggest that inflationary pressures eased slightly in January.

- The CPI measure of consumer prices is below target but the inflation rate rose slightly in January.

GDP activity – overview

After the release of more detailed numbers of GDP growth in the fourth quarter of 2003, the quarterly rate was left unchanged at 0.9 per cent. However, revisions to the data for earlier quarters meant that the annual rate of growth in the fourth quarter was revised up to 2.8 per cent from the earlier estimate of 2.5 per cent. This means that the growth rate for 2003 as a whole is now judged to have been 2.3 per cent compared to the initial reading of 2.1 (figure 1). This updated fourth quarter estimate of GDP is still only based on partial information and so may be revised once again as more complete data becomes available.

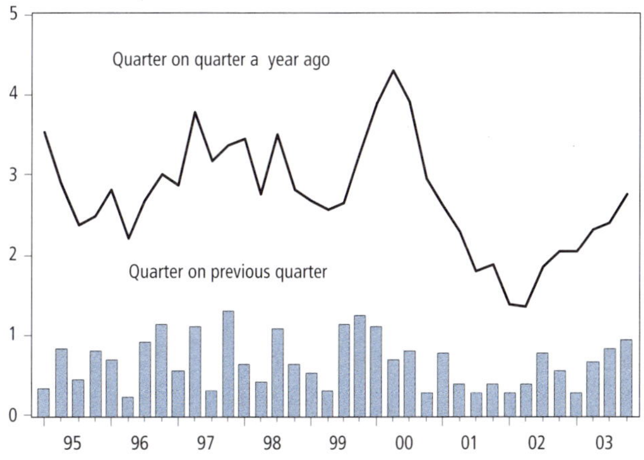

The international background became a more favourable one for growth in the second half of 2003, although the UK's largest export market, the EU, continues to be the area with the weakest growth in economic activity. GDP growth in most of the major economies accelerated in the second half of the year, although the extent and causes of this varied across countries. The US experienced very robust growth of over 2 per cent in the third quarter, this slowed to around 1 per cent in the fourth quarter but was still a considerable improvement on the first half of the year. Japanese economic growth also

Figure 1
GDP
Growth

Economic update

appears to have picked up and GDP rose by 1.7 per cent during the fourth quarter. The three biggest EMU economies France, Germany and Italy also look a little healthier, however the pace of their upturn is much more moderate. Also as much of the improvement in EU activity appears to have been accounted for by stronger exports rather than by rising domestic demand, it seems unlikely to be very favourable for UK exports. The initial indications are that these stronger international economic conditions have carried over into the early part of 2004.

Financial Market activity

Last year saw some optimism return to the stock market. After three years of negative movement the FTSE All Share Index ended 2003 up some 16 per cent. However, the recent gains still leave the FTSE All Share down by about 12 per cent compared to its level at the start of 2002. The stock market has risen further in early 2004 and at the time of writing the All Share Index was up by just over 5 per cent on the year.

2003 also saw some significant moves in sterling, although the biggest international currency movement of late has been the slide of the US dollar. In the early part of 2003 the pound fell against the euro and strengthened against the US dollar, and as a result the effective exchange rate fell by 7.2 per cent between December 2002 and May 2003. From this low the pound's effective rate rose slightly over the rest of the year as sterling's effective rate continued to be buffeted between a strong euro and a weak dollar. For 2003 as a whole the effective index ended the year down about 5.0 per cent, as a fall of over 8 per cent in the bilateral rate versus the euro was partially offset by a rise of 10 per cent against the dollar (figure 2). Early 2004 has seen the pound continue to rise, most prominently against the dollar but also recently against the euro as well and at the time of writing the effective exchange rate had climbed above its level at the start of 2003. The rebound may in part be due to the fact that the Bank of England has raised interest rates twice in recent months, by a total of 50 basis points in all, at a time when most other major central banks seem content to keep interest rates stable.

Output

Gross domestic product (GDP) in the fourth quarter of 2003 showed quarterly growth of 0.9 per cent, compared with 0.8 per cent in the previous quarter. Comparing the fourth quarter with the same quarter a year ago shows an annual growth rate of 2.8 per cent and a growth rate for 2003 as a whole of 2.3 per cent. Year on year growth over the last few years has gone from a high of 4.3 per cent in the second quarter of 2000 to a low of 1.4 per cent in the first quarter of 2002, before picking up back to the present level. This cycle is an extremely muted one when compared both with recent UK experience and with recent trends in most of the other major international economies.

For the last three years economic growth has been maintained by strength in construction and services while manufacturing and energy production declined. In contrast the first half of 2003 saw a less clear cut picture. Construction activity showed a sizeable decline in quarter one and a big pick up in the second quarter. Meanwhile, service sector growth decelerated in the first half of the year, while industrial production was roughly flat due to a combination of an improvement in manufacturing and weak energy activity. The third quarter was again different with growth being led by an accelerating service sector, continued sizeable growth in construction and flat activity in manufacturing. Finally the fourth quarter saw growth contributions that look very similar to that of the third with service sector growth again leading the way.

Construction output was responsible for much of the variable pattern in GDP in the first half of 2003. In the first quarter it fell by 1.1 per cent, while in the second quarter it rebounded by 4.4 per cent. This accounted for a difference in the GDP growth rate of around 0.3 per cent between the two quarters. In contrast construction output growth was much more stable in the second half of the year. Output grew by 2.0 in the third quarter leaving the annual growth rate at 7.3 per cent (figure 3) and is estimated to have grown by 1.6 per cent in quarter four. It should be emphasised that this last number is still very much an estimate. The figures for construction output are based on a quarterly survey conducted by the Department of Trade and Industry and only a small part of the results of this survey will have gone into the present

Figure 2
Exchange rates

£ equals

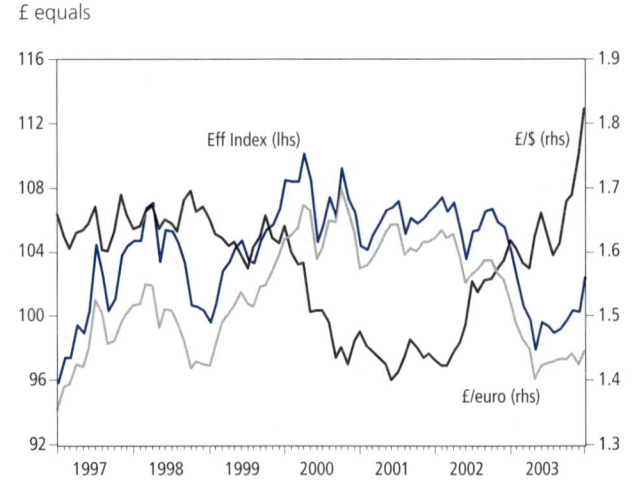

Figure 3
Construction output

Growth

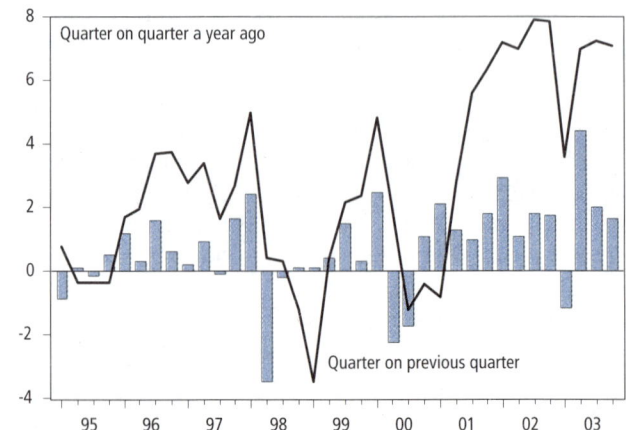

estimate of construction activity. The figure will be given a much firmer foundation in March as the full results of the survey become available.

Manufacturing output rose by 0.2 per cent in the fourth quarter of 2003 following a 0.3 per cent rise in quarter three, 0.6 per cent in quarter two and a 0.1 per cent fall in the first quarter (figure 4). The year on year rate of manufacturing output growth leapt up 1.1 per cent but this is misleading as it was impacted by unusually large quarterly fluctuations in output last year. Output first declined during the Jubilee period and then subsequently rebounded, before settling down to a more normal pattern. Other evidence of manufacturing activity was if anything weaker than official data for most of 2003 but by the end of the year pointed to a pick up in activity. The CIPS survey of purchasing managers had signalled stronger manufacturing activity as early as the third quarter and this rose even further in quarter four. The CBI and BCC surveys were considerably weaker than the CIPS numbers in the third quarter but these both picked up strongly in quarter four (figure 5).

Figure 4
Manufacturing output

Growth

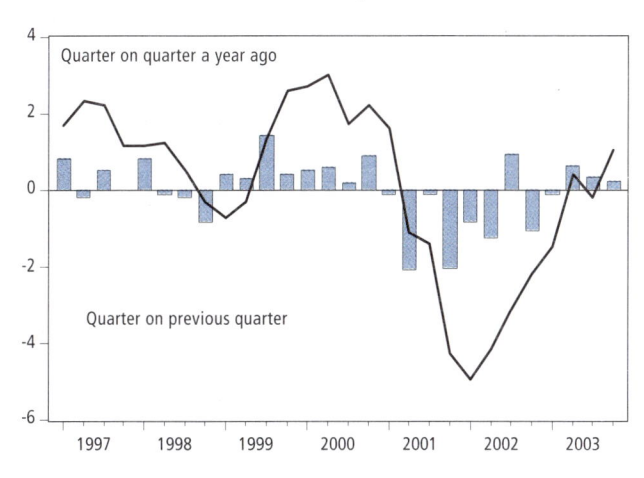

Figure 5
External manufacturing

Balances

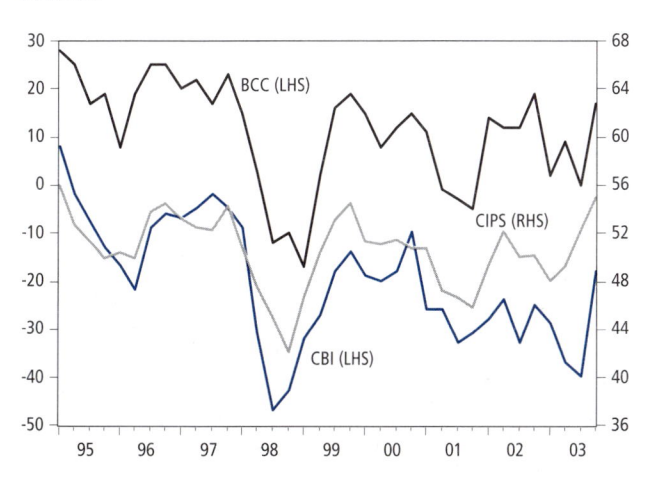

The service sector rose by 1.0 per cent in quarter four for the second quarter in a row. This confirms that activity in this area picked up appreciably in the second half of the year after a sluggish first half. The improvement seems to have been widespread and took in most areas of private sector activity as well as the public sector. For 2003 as a whole the service sector grew by 2.5 per cent, compared with 2.1 per cent in 2002. Most areas of the service sector grew strongly in quarter four for the second successive quarter (figure 6). This robust rise in activity seems to be largely confirmed by survey data. The CIPS survey of services, which has historically had a close correlation with official data, has risen sharply in recent months. Other surveys, also show some improvement and the BCC survey for instance rose sharply in the last quarter of 2003.

Figure 6
Services output

Growth

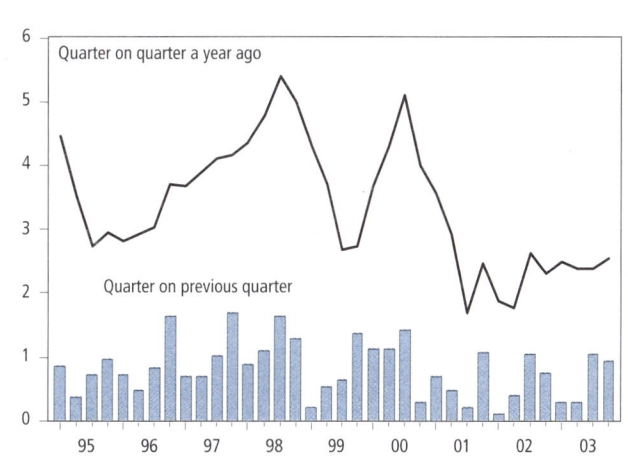

Household demand

Quarterly growth in household final consumption is initially estimated to have grown by 1.1 per cent in quarter four of 2003, the same rate as in the previous quarter. It should be noted that this is based on as yet incomplete data and so may be changed, as more information becomes available. Growth compared with the same quarter a year ago was 3.2 per cent, a slight acceleration from 3.1 per cent in the previous quarter.

Figure 7
Household demand

Growth

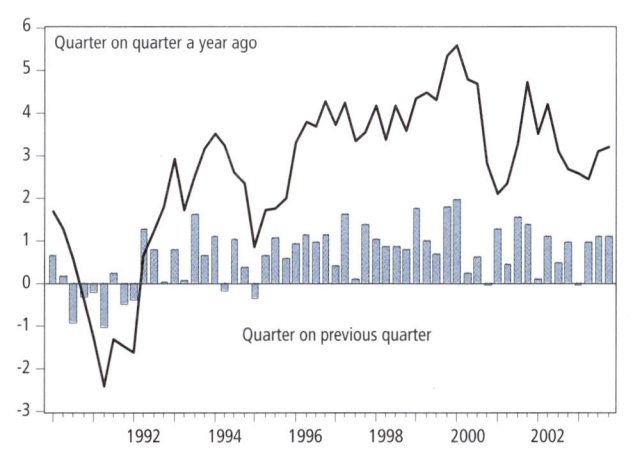

Economic update

Economic Trends 604 March 2004

Growth in consumer spending for the year as a whole was 2.8 per cent compared with 3.4 per cent in 2002, confirming that it remains one of the most robust areas of spending in the economy (figure 7).

Most of the fundamentals for consumer spending remain fairly supportive. The labour market is tight and getting tighter and while this does not seem to be having much of an upward effect on wages it should ensure that consumers remain relatively upbeat about their job prospects. Meanwhile consumer confidence is still reasonably high and the continued buoyancy of the housing market and the recovery of the stock market are further positives. There was some comment in the press following the November base rate hike that this would make consumers more cautious and anecdotal claims that the run up to Christmas was difficult for retailers but this was not backed up by any hard data.

Official retail sales certainly do not provide evidence of a pronounced slowdown. Spending rose by 1.8 per cent in the three months to the end of the year, compared with gains of 1.2 per cent in the previous three months (figure 8). The data is often difficult to seasonally adjust around year end, when it is impacted for instance by the timing of sales varying from year to year. Sometimes in the past a strong December number has given a misleading indication of the underlying strength of activity as it has been followed by a weak figure for January. This occurred for instance in December 2002 and January 2003. This does not however appear to be the case this time around as January saw another strong rise in retail sales of 0.5 per cent. External figures also suggest that consumer spending continues at a strong pace. In the run up to Christmas the evidence was admittedly mixed as the BRC survey of like-for-like retail sales showed a slowdown in sales while the CBI survey in contrast showed a rise in sales. However, both surveys rose during January (figure 9).

Figure 8
Retail sales

Growth

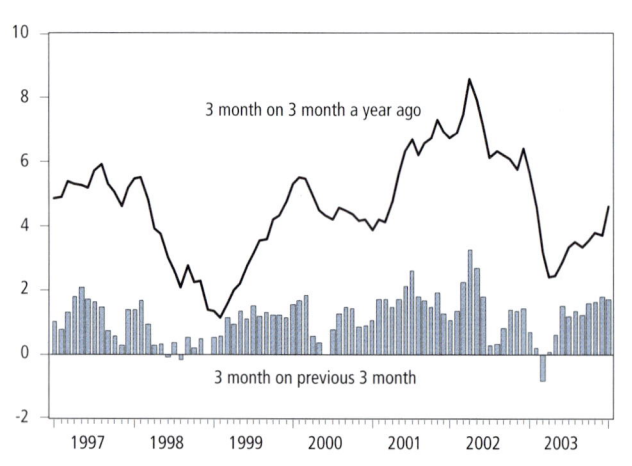

Figure 9
External retailing

Growth

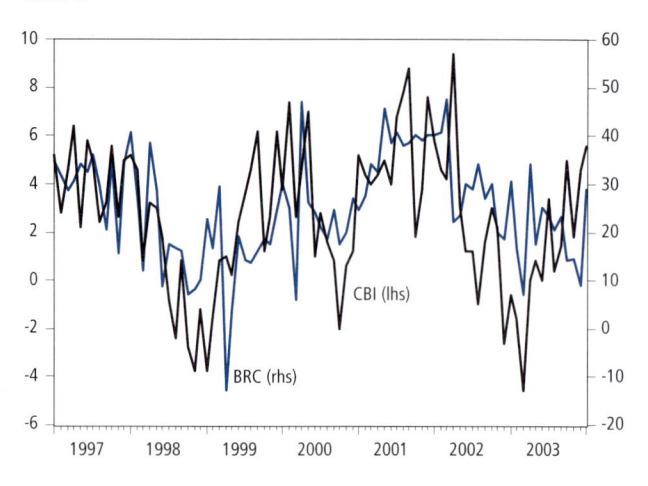

Business demand

In contrast to consumers, businesses appear to have been more reluctant to spend last year but recent data suggests that the investment climate was improving towards year end. Fixed investment for the economy as a whole rose by 1.6 per cent in the fourth quarter, following on from an upwardly revised gain of 0.9 per cent in quarter three (figure 10). For the year as a whole fixed investment was up by 2.6 per cent, compared with 1.8 per cent in 2002 and 3.6 per cent in 2001. The fourth quarter improvement was at least partly due to an upturn in business investment. This was up by 1.3 per cent in volume terms in quarter four, as for the first time in 2003 business investment climbed above its level at the end of 2002. Much of the weakness in investment over the last few years has been due to business investment, which fell sharply during 2001 before seeming to stabilise in 2002. Investment in manufacturing has been particularly weak and investment in that sector did rise slightly in quarter four but it is nevertheless still down almost 5 per cent when compared with the fourth quarter of 2002. Looking at investment by asset it is notable that expenditure on capital equipment, which has accounted for much of the fall of recent years is still weak and that much of the recent gains have been in spending on buildings.

Figure 10
Fixed Investment

Growth

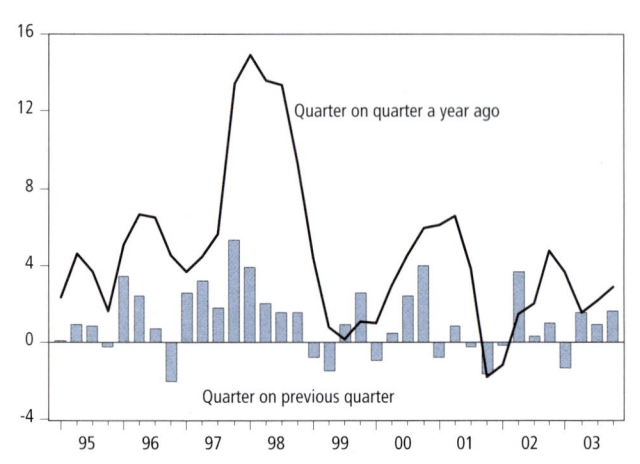

The environment remains a mixed one for investment. An increase in investment depends upon firms finding it both affordable and profitable to invest. The last few quarters have seem some improvement in profitability. Gross trading profits of non-financial corporations were up again in quarter four, although it should be emphasised that these numbers are very preliminary. Non-financial corporations have been net lenders since the first quarter of 2001, a process that has allowed them to start to repair balance sheets. However, this process still has a long way to go. The financial balance sheet shows the sector having net liabilities of £1,199 billion in the second quarter of 2003, a slight rise when compared with the previous quarter.

It is also unclear whether firms perceive this as a favourable environment in which to boost investment. They generally continue to report a lack of pricing power, and very low capacity utilisation. This combination makes it difficult to see why investment should pick up significantly without a sustained increase in demand, although the most recent surveys of investment intentions have shown an increased willingness to raise spending (figure 11).

Figure 11
Investment plans

Balances

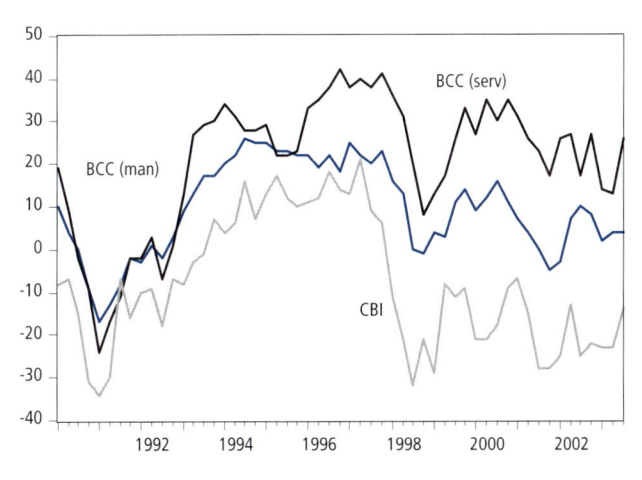

Government demand

Government final consumption expenditure in real terms grew by 1.9 per cent in the fourth quarter of 2003, a considerably faster pace of growth than in the prior two quarters. At least some of this stronger growth seems to be due to more military spending. Growth compared with the same quarter a year ago was 3.4 per cent, indicating that the underlying rate of government expenditure growth is still quite rapid, when compared to spending in much of the rest of the economy (figure 12).

The combination of faster government expenditure growth alongside weaker revenues reflecting the more subdued economic activity has led to deterioration in the public sector's finances. The data for the first ten months of fiscal year 2003–04 show a public sector net borrowing figure of £30.6 billion. This compares with a figure for £22.5 billion for the equivalent period of the previous fiscal year and a whole year total for 2002–03 of £22.9 billion.

Figure 12
Government spending

Growth

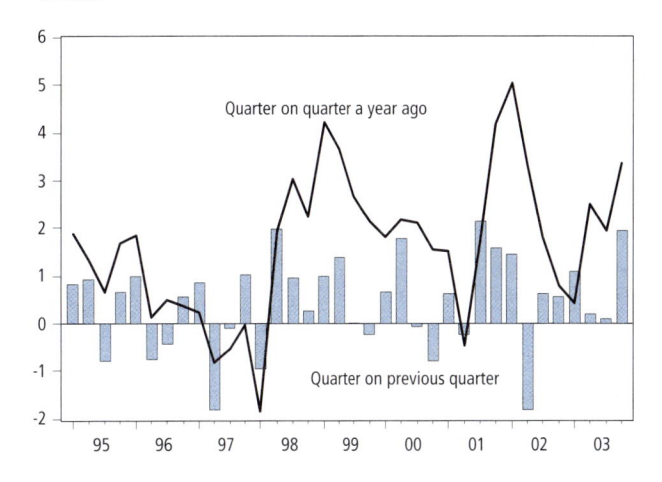

Trade and the Balance of Payments

In volume terms both import and export activity picked up in quarter four of 2003. On the quarter, exports of goods and services rose by 1.8 per cent, while imports rose slightly more quickly at 2.2 per cent. This represented faster growth in both cases than the previous quarter, when exports were almost flat, while imports rose by just over 1.0 per cent. For the year as a whole, exports fell by 0.5 per cent and imports were up by 0.8 per cent, however both of these annual rates will have been distorted by the impact of MTIC fraud. The discovery of this resulted in the import data for a number of years prior to 2003 being revised upward, but the effect on 2003 has been to reduce growth rates for both export and import numbers because of the subsequent clampdown by Customs. However, even adjusted for MTIC fraud, trade for the year, as a whole has been quite subdued (figure 13).

Figure 13
UK trade

Growth, 3 months on previous 3 months

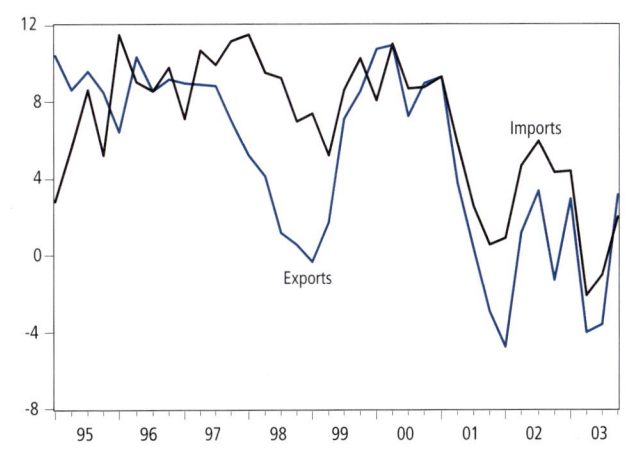

The faster rate of growth in the fourth quarter was seen in both exports and imports of goods. In contrast while exports of services rose at around the same rate as in quarter three, service imports fell sharply. Over the quarter as a whole, exports of goods were up by 2.2 per cent, while imports were up even more sharply at 3.7 per cent. The improvement in

Economic update | Economic Trends 604 March 2004

exports was almost wholly to export markets outside the EU, while in contrast exports to the EU barely rose. This may seem surprising as over the course of 2003 sterling fell against the euro but went up against the dollar and is probably at least explained by the fact that demand has been growing much more quickly outside the EU. Another factor may be the pricing behaviour of export companies. The price of goods exported to the EU rose sharply last year in sterling terms possibly suggesting that exporters used the opportunity provided by a weaker exchange rate to boost their profit margins.

Both the CBI and BCC surveys seem to confirm that export performance was subdued for much of last year. However, the survey numbers for both deliveries and orders of exports rose sharply in the fourth quarter and would be consistent with the export environment improving at the back end of the year.

Labour Market

Headline labour market statistics continue to be remarkably stable. Employment is high, with the Labour Force Survey (LFS) employment rate at 74.5 per cent in the three months to December, slightly down when compared with a month ago. Meanwhile the LFS count of employment increased by around 28,000 over the same period. The ILO unemployment rate was 4.9 per cent in the three months to December (figure 14), unchanged when compared with a month ago. The claimant count unemployment rate, at 2.9 per cent in January was down slightly on the month. All these figures point to a tight or tightening labour market but if account is also taken of those people who are officially designated as economically inactive i.e. neither employed nor unemployed but actively seeking work, then the figure does not look quite so tight (figure 14).

Figure 14
Unemployment & Economically Inactive
Per cent

Full-time employment has been falling over the last year or so as most job gains have been in part-time work. In the three months to December the number of full-time workers fell by 22,000, but was up 6,000 compared with a year ago. Meanwhile the number working part time was up by 27,000 on the three month period and by 151,000 on the year.

Another recent trend has been for job gains to be in self-employment. The number of self-employed workers in the three months to December was up 0.6 per cent compared

with the previous three months and 9.2 per cent compared with a year ago. In contrast the number in employment was slightly down on a three month basis and on the year.

Average earnings rose by a slightly slower 3.4 per cent rate in the three months to December, down by 0.1 per cent from November. This is still well below the 4.5 per cent figure that the Bank of England considers broadly consistent with their inflation target. The gap between public and private sector earnings growth remains wide by recent standards, with public sector earnings growing more quickly.

Prices

Producer output prices rose by 1.6 per cent annually in January, this compared with 1.8 per cent in December and 1.7 per cent in November. After falling back in the second quarter, output prices have since resumed the upward trend that appeared to be underway earlier in the year but last months fall marked at least a temporary interruption of this. Recent movements have been affected by fluctuations in the oil price, but underlying inflation also seems to have gone up. Output prices excluding food, beverages tobacco and petroleum products, however, were up by 1.4 per cent in January, compared with 1.5 per cent in December. Input prices were volatile in 2003. In the first quarter they rose by 1.7 per cent, then fell back by 0.5 per cent in the second quarter as the oil price declined but after that climbed once again until November before falling back ending December up 1.9 per cent. January saw a fall in input prices on the month of around 1.0 per cent.

The consumer prices index (CPI) rose slightly in December, while both the RPI and the old target measure the RPIX fell slightly. The new target for the Bank of England is to keep CPI inflation (the new term for the Harmonised Index of Consumer Prices) to 2.0. In January CPI inflation was 1.4 per cent, up by 0.1 per cent when compared with a month ago but still well below target. The rise in the CPI was due to an increase in a number of categories grouped under the heading miscellaneous goods and services. The old target measure, RPIX, fell by 0.2 per cent on the month to 2.4 per cent, slightly below the old target rate (figure 15) and the RPI also fell by 0.2 per cent to 2.6 per cent.

Figure 15
Consumer prices
Growth, month on a year ago

Forecasts for the UK economy

A comparison of independent forecasts, February 2004

The tables below are extracted from HM Treasury's Forecasts for the UK Economy and summarise the average and range of independent forecasts for 2004 and 2005, updated monthly.

Independent forecasts for 2004

	Average	Lowest	Highest
GDP growth (per cent)	2.8	1.8	3.5
Inflation rate (Q4 per cent)			
CPI	1.7	1.2	3.4
RPI	3.0	1.7	4.0
Unemployment (Q4, million)	0.90	0.78	1.09
Current account (£ billion)	−27.0	−38.0	−13.5
Public Sector Net Borrowing (2003–04, £ billion)	37.0	28.0	48.0

Independent forecasts for 2005

	Average	Lowest	Highest
GDP growth (per cent)	2.6	0.4	3.5
Inflation rate (Q4 per cent)			
CPI	1.9	1.2	2.4
RPI	3.0	1.7	3.9
Unemployment (Q4, million)	0.90	0.61	1.20
Current account (£ billion)	−28.4	−50.7	−10.0
Public Sector Net Borrowing (2004–05, £ billion)	37.7	24.0	53.0

NOTE *Forecasts for the UK Economy* gives more detailed forecasts, covering 27 variables and is published monthly by HM Treasury, available on annual subscription, price £75. Subscription enquiries should be addressed to Claire Coast-Smith, Public Enquiry Unit 2/S2, HM Treasury, 1 Horse Guards Road, London, SW1A 2HQ (tel 020 7270 4558). It is also available at the Treasury's Internet site: http://www.hm-treasury.gov.uk under 'Economic Data and Tools'.

International economic indicators
March 2004

Nicola Mai
Office for National Statistics

Overview

- Preliminary estimates for 2003 growth in all major economies are now available[1,2,3,4,5]. The country which grew most rapidly were the United States, followed in order of magnitude by Japan, UK, Italy, France and Germany.

- Growth in quarter four was particularly strong in Japan, which grew by 1.7[5] per cent in the quarter. The US and the UK economies also performed well, expanding by 1.0 and 0.9 per cent respectively. The eurozone major economies, on the other hand, still seem to struggle with Italy, France and Germany growing by 0.0[3], 0.5[2] and 0.2[1] per cent respectively in 2003 quarter four.

- The robust recovery of the US economy this year was led primarily by buoyant consumption, recovering investment and large outlays by government. Net exports on the other hand pulled growth down, although the weakness of the dollar may favour foreign trade in the coming months.

- Japanese growth seems to have been led by a balanced growth of both domestic and foreign trade components. Deflation nevertheless persists and much of recent real GDP growth is explained by falls in the GDP deflator.

- The major eurozone economies all struggled with nil or negative growth rates in the first two quarters of 2003 but experienced somewhat of an improvement in the second half of the year. The composition of growth for the German economy is not very reassuring since domestic demand is still very weak and much of the recent growth has been accounted for by inventory changes. French growth is also quite unbalanced. France has benefited from high private and public consumption but is still suffering from low or declining investment and foreign trade. Italy in the first three quarters benefited from growing consumption and inventories but suffered falling investment and negative net exports.

- After a widespread fall in industrial production in quarter two, the IOP rebounded quite strongly in quarter three in the US, Japan, France and Italy and more modestly in Germany. Figures for quarter four in the US and Japan indicate an even stronger pickup in the index. External indicators for manufacturing in the eurozone[6,7,8,9] at the start of 2004 have been mixed and did not match up with the strength of the same indicators in late 2003. In contrast, the Purchasing Managers' Index for services in the major eurozone[9] countries remains strong. In the US, the ISM manufacturing[11] and non-manufacturing (services)[12] Purchasing Managers' Indexes indicated that activity reached record levels in January.

- The Italian unemployment rate seems to be declining, the German rate is broadly flat at a high level and the French rate has been increasing since the beginning of the year according to monthly figures. Unemployment seems to be falling in the US and Japan. Inflationary pressures have been stable and fairly subdued globally. Deflation continues in Japan although more moderately than before.

EU15

The OECD discontinued production of key series needed for the production of table 1, European Union 15. This table will be replaced with other relevant data as soon as possible. We apologise to our readers for any inconvenience.

Germany

According to the latest estimates of economic activity, the German economy contracted by 0.1[1] per cent in 2003. This performance of the German economy over the year is in line with falling activity in the first two quarters of 2003, only partially offset by modest recovery in the following two quarters.

In the last quarter of 2003 German GDP grew by 0.2[1] per cent and most of the growth was due to a rise in stocks. The latest release of detailed national accounts suggests that growth would have been negative in the fourth quarter had it not been for the positive contribution of inventories, which accounted for 0.9[1] per cent of growth. Investment also contributed positively by 0.3[1] per cent although investment in machinery and equipment accounted for only 0.1[1] per cent of growth. Government expenditure made no addition to GDP growth whereas private final consumption fell, cutting –0.2[1] per cent from growth. Private consumption in Germany has fallen for three consecutive quarters. Finally, the major pullback to growth came from a sharp decrease in net exports mainly due to a rise in imports (+2.7[1] per cent), which outweighed an only modest increase in exports (+0.3[1] per cent). Overall net exports contributed by -0.7[1] per cent to growth, contrasting with the third quarter of 2003 where net exports had been the major force behind economic growth.

More generally in 2003, the German economy has been strongly affected by weak domestic demand with consumption and investment making negative contributions in almost all quarters of the year. Investment rose in the last quarter of 2003, consistent with the improvement in business confidence in the second half of the year. The IFO[6] and the ZEW[7] surveys of business confidence for February 2004, however, show a fall in confidence over the previous month. According to the IFO, the erosion in confidence came from worsening expectations on the economic situation over the next six months, affecting mainly wholesaling and manufacturing.

Net exports have also contributed negatively to GDP growth in all quarters last year with the exception of quarter three, which may reflect the weakness of neighbouring economies and the strengthening of the euro. Government expenditure contributed a little to growth in quarter two and quarter three. Inventories have been fairly volatile but generally added to growth. One interpretation of the build-up in stocks is that firms could not sell the goods they produced given the weakness of internal and external demand. This series is hard to interpret however as it may contain alignment adjustments.

Overall, there has been a lack of any appreciable momentum in the German economy over the last couple of years. GDP grew at only 1.0 and 0.2 per cent in 2001 and 2002, affected by weak domestic demand and in particular weak investment which fell over both years. It was mainly due to foreign trade that GDP grew in 2001 and 2002, with net exports contributing 1.6 and 1.7 per cent in 2001 and 2002 respectively. The slowdown in net export growth combined with the continuing weakness of the internal market led to GDP falling by 0.1 per cent overall in 2003.

Industrial production in 2003 quarter three was up 0.1 per cent on the previous quarter, growing modestly but at least recovering from the sharp slowdown of –1.2 per cent in quarter two. When compared to the same quarter a year earlier, the IOP fell by 0.6 per cent in quarter three although this is due largely to the sharp decline in the quarter two. Generally, industrial production has been weak since 2001, when it grew by only 0.6 per cent, compared to growth of 6.2 per cent in 2000 and 1.5 per cent in 1999. Overall in 2002, the index fell by 1.2 per cent.

Inflation has been very subdued in Germany in 2003, remaining well below the European average and below the ECB inflation target for the eurozone. Overall in 2003 the CPI grew by 1.0 per cent. For the last few months of 2003, CPI inflation was 1.1 per cent in the year to December, down slightly from 1.2 per cent in the year to November. Figures for the PPI show prices at the factory gate increasing by 1.7 per cent in the year to December, down from 1.9 per cent in the year to November. So far in 2003, the CPI has tended to grow more slowly than the PPI, possibly indicating deceleration of prices in the service industries and other items not included in the producer price index or some squeeze on business margins.

The unemployment rate in Germany has been high but stable recently. The rate was 9.2 per cent in December, flat on the previous month. Before this, the rate had been oscillating between 9.3 and 9.4 per cent since March 2003 posting the highest levels recorded in Germany since May 1998. Before March last year, the unemployment rate had risen gradually from a trough of 7.6 per cent in 2000 quarter four. This was at around the same when GDP growth started to fall (figure 1). Employment in 2003 fell when compared to the previous year contracting by 1.3 in the year to the third quarter. The yearly employment growth series has now declined for eight consecutive quarters, confirming the weakness of the labour market.

Figure 1
Germany: GDP growth and unemployment

Quarter on quarter a year ago growth; percentage of the workforce

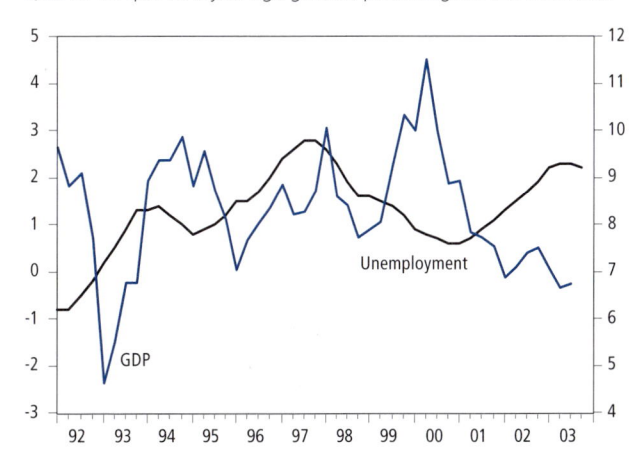

Earnings grew quite strongly in the first half of 2003 growing by 2.7 and 2.8 per cent in the year to the first and second quarters of 2003. Such strong growth however was partly due to the particularly low levels which had been reached in the same quarters a year earlier. In 2003 quarter three, earnings growth slowed to 2.1 per cent.

France

According to the latest GDP estimates produced by the French statistical office INSEE, French GDP in 2003 grew by 0.2² per cent. Growth in the year was supported by increases in household consumption and government expenditure, which grew by 1.6² and 2.4² per cent respectively. Net exports, gross capital formation and inventories on the other hand all declined, contracting by 0.9², 0.8² and 0.3² per cent respectively. In particular, net exports were associated with a sharp decline in exports (−2.1² per cent) and an increase in imports (+0.9² per cent); gross capital formation on the other hand fell mainly by declines in investment by non-financial enterprises (−2.2² per cent). Overall the economic picture for France in 2003 is similar to the one for Germany, the main difference being that household consumption has been stronger than in Germany.

The latest national accounts figures also indicate that the economy grew by 0.5² per cent for quarter four, whereas growth for quarter three was revised up to 0.4ᵇ per cent from 0.3 per cent (note that table 3 at the end of the article does not include such revision). Household consumption growth was slower than in the previous quarter but still contributed 0.2ᵇ per cent to GDP growth. Government expenditure on the other hand grew very strongly, by 1.0² per cent, outpacing growth in all other quarters. Investment grew modestly and contributed 0.1² per cent to growth and inventory changes contributed 0.2² per cent to growth. Finally, net foreign trade pulled growth down by 0.3² per cent in contrast with the last quarter when they aided growth.

Generally, GDP growth in the last two quarters of 2003 saw an improvement over the first and second quarter when growth was 0 and −0.4 in respectively. Overall in 2002, the economy grew by 1.2 per cent, the lowest growth rate since 1996. Despite the weak performance over the last two years, however, French economic growth has generally been quite strong when compared to other EU 15 members. France's performance in the recent past has been helped by tax cuts, which have underpinned growth in disposable income and consumer spending.

The INSEE monthly business survey[8] had been showing rising business confidence in the months before February. The result of the February survey however was not as positive as the previous ones with the outlook for activity in the next three months remaining stable and the balance of opinion over total order books deteriorating slightly. On the other hand, the Purchasing Managers' Index for manufacturing[i] in February showed activity is increasing. Finally, the INSEE consumer confidence indicator[j] in January showed that consumers are more optimistic about their future financial condition.

French industrial production expanded substantially in 2003 quarter three, growing by 1.1 per cent over the previous quarter. This followed from four consecutive quarters in which the IOP had fallen. Generally, industrial production has been very weak for the last couple of years, consistently showing negative annual growth rates since 2001 quarter four. The quarter on previous quarter growth rates have been more volatile but generally confirm this picture (figure 2).

Figure 2
France: Index of production

Growth

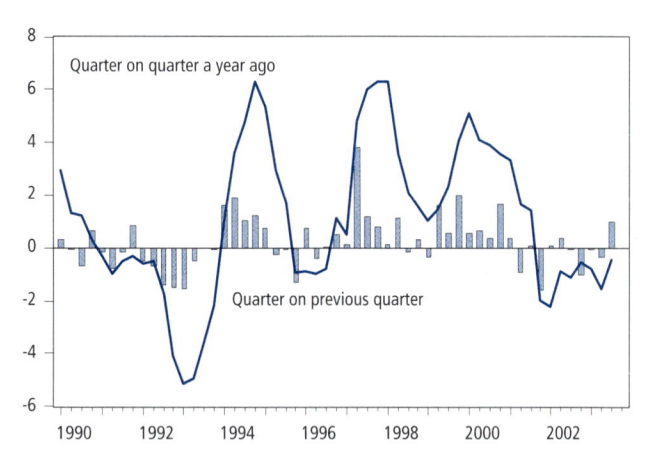

Consumer price inflation rose quite strongly in the first quarter of 2003, jumping from 1.9 per cent in the year to January to 2.6 per cent in February and March. In quarter two however inflation slowed and the rate was 1.8 and 2.0 per cent in May and June. Since quarter two, CPI inflation has again been increasing gradually and went from 1.9 in July to 2.3 in November; in the year to December, the inflation rate was 2.2 per cent. The recent increase in inflation is largely attributable to rises in food and tobacco prices and a sharp rise in agricultural prices in the summer caused by forest fires which destroyed many European crops.

Producer prices also accelerated in the first half of 2003 with growth rates of 0.6 per cent in the year to the first and second quarters. Producer price inflation, however, stalled in the third quarter and was only 0.1 per cent in the fourth quarter. In the year to December, the PPI grew by 0.1 per cent. Unlike Germany, in France CPI growth is outpacing PPI growth.

The French unemployment rate has been rising steadily over the past year, going from 9.1 per cent in January 2003 to 9.5 per cent in December. This is the highest rate since April 2000. Employment growth has been showing a steady decline since the start of 2001 when computed as growth of a quarter on the same quarter a year earlier. However, the more volatile but more timely measure of quarter on previous quarter growth suggests that employment growth has stabilised at around 0.1 per cent since 2002, with the exception of a slowdown in 2003 quarter one.

Annual earnings growth has been easing since 2000 and declined from 5.2 per cent in 2000 quarter two to 2.6 per cent in the second quarter of 2003. In the third quarter, however, there was a pick up in earnings growth which jumped to 2.9 per cent.

Italy

The preliminary estimate for economic growth in 2003 suggests that the Italian economy has grown by 0.4[3] per cent last year. The first half of the year was characterised by slightly negative growth, which was followed by quite a strong pick up in activity in quarter three and no growth in quarter four. Details on the expenditure side for quarter four growth are not yet available.

Though modest, the pickup in the economy in 2003 as estimated by the February preliminary estimate seems to indicate that Italian growth has outpaced French and German growth last year. This followed on from modest growth in 2002 of 0.4 per cent and more substantial growth of 1.7 per cent in 2001. Since 2001 the Italian economy has tended to grow more quickly than that of Germany but generally has not been as strong as the French economy, although the latest estimate for 2003 seems to imply the trend was reversed last year.

Then main component driving growth forward in the first three quarters of the year was private consumption (figure 3), which contributed 0.2, 0.3 and 0.4 respectively to growth in the first three quarters of the year. A strong pullback instead was given by investment which made negative contributions in all quarters with an especially poor performance in quarter one, where it contributed –1.3 per cent to growth. Net exports followed a similar path as in Germany and France. In particular, net exports pulled growth down in the first two quarters of the year whereas they had a sharp pickup in quarter three. The unusual pickup in quarter three seems to be linked with improving global economic conditions and increasing demand especially outside of eurozone. Finally, government consumption contributed only modestly to growth in the first three quarters, whereas inventories seem to have been fairly volatile, having made strong positive contributions to growth in the first two quarters and a highly negative contribution in the third quarter.

Industrial production has been very weak since the second quarter of 2001 showing negative annual growth in all quarters up to 2003 quarter three, with the exception of 2002 quarter four. Quarterly growth picked up in the first three quarters of 2002 but subsequently output declined. In 2003 quarter three industrial production accelerated once again and was 1.4 per cent higher than in the previous quarter but still lower than production in the same quarter a year earlier. External indicators like the Purchasing Managers' Index for manufacturing[9] at the start of 2004 point to strengthening activity in the production sector.

Consumer price inflation in recent years has been consistently higher than the EU average. From January to October 2003 inflation ranged between 2.6 and 2.8 per cent. As in France, the effect of the summer heatwave on agricultural prices has kept inflation high over the year. In November, inflation slowed to 2.5 per cent and remained at the same level in December. Producer price inflation has been slowing through the year, from 2.8 per cent in February to 0.6 per cent in October. PPI growth picked up in November when it posted 1.2 per cent but fell back down to 0.7 in December. Generally, PPI growth has been slower than CPI growth since 2001.

The unemployment rate in Italy has been declining steadily since 1998 when the rate was as high as 11.7 per cent. The rate was broadly flat at 9.0 per cent in 2002 but declined steadily in 2003 going from 9.0 per cent in January to 8.4 per cent in October. Employment growth was 0.9 per cent in the year to the fourth quarter of 2003, flat on the growth rate in the year to the third quarter.

Earnings figures are quite volatile. It is worth noting however that earnings' growth rates in the year to July, in the year to August and in the year to September 2003 were 3.2 per cent, regaining the positive momentum which had been lost between March and June. The annual growth rate for both October and November earnings was at 2.7 per cent, slower than in quarter three but still higher than earlier in the year. Earnings growth in 2002 was 2.8 per cent up from 1.8 and 2.0 per cent in 2001 and 2000 respectively.

USA

According to the preliminary GDP estimate published on 27 February 2004[4], the US economy grew by 3.1 per cent in 2003, outpacing other major OECD economies. The American economy has been showing very strong signs of recovery last year having posted positive growth in all quarters and exceptionally high growth in the second half of the year. Surveys of business activity at the start of 2004 seem to confirm the strength of the US economy. The Institute for Supply Management manufacturing and services indexes recorded record levels of activity for January with the indexes at 63.6[11] and 65.7[12] respectively (note that 50 means no change).

The main factor driving growth in 2003 was private consumption expenditure which contributed 2.2 per cent to growth last year. Estimates for investment and government consumption contributions for 2003 were not available in the OECD data set but were taken from the Bureau of Economic Analysis release. Fixed investment and government expenditure were the second biggest contributors to growth over the year adding 0.7[4] and 0.6[4] per cent respectively. Inventories did not make any contribution to growth[4], whereas

Figure 3
Italy: Consumption

Growth

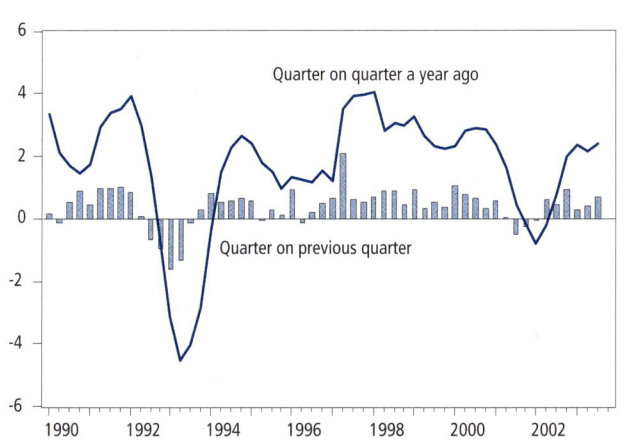

net exports took away 0.3 per cent from growth mainly thanks to an increase in imports. Overall, the data for 2003 seem to indicate that the American economy is going through a generally healthy recovery with investment finally recovering and consumer confidence at high levels. A substantial part of growth in 2003 was given by government expenditure. The trade deficit also remains quite high although the weak dollar might help trade in the coming months.

Growth in 2003 quarter four was strong (1.0 per cent) although not as strong as growth in quarter three. Consumption did not grow as fast in quarter four and contributed 0.5 per cent to growth. Investment also slowed down in the fourth quarter although growth remained sustained. Fixed investment contributed 0.3[4] per cent to growth, 0.2[4] of which was due to non-residential investment and 0.1[4] to residential investment. Government consumption did not make any contribution to growth[4] in the quarter whereas inventories added 0.2[4] per cent. Finally, net exports made a slight negative contribution of 0.1[4] per cent to growth.

The index of production has been fairly volatile but seemed to stabilise in the second half of 2003 where it increased in all months from July to December. After a decline of 1.0 per cent in 2003 quarter two, the IOP picked up in the third quarter when it grew by 1.0 per cent and was even stronger in quarter four where it grew by 1.5 per cent. Overall in 2003 the index grew by 0.3 per cent, following on from two consecutive years of contractions. In 2002 the index had contracted by 0.6 per cent and in 2001 by as much as 3.4 per cent.

Inflation rates had been low until January 2003. Since then, consumer price inflation has started to increase and reached a peak in the year to March when the rate hit 3.1 per cent. Much of this can be explained by fluctuations in the oil price and since the peak, inflation has slowed stabilising at around 2 per cent. By December, consumer price inflation was 1.9 per cent. The change in the growth rate of producer prices has followed a similar pattern to consumer price growth but have been much more volatile. PPI growth fell from a peak of 4.5 per cent in March this year to 2.2 per cent in November and 2.7 per cent in December.

The unemployment rate (figure 4) has been rising since 2000 when the rate was 4 per cent but may have turned around in the second half of 2003. From 4 per cent in 2000, the rate rose to 4.8 per cent in 2001 and 5.8 per cent in 2002. The unemployment rate reached a high of 6.3 per cent in June 2003 and since then has decreased suggesting that the recovery is being accompanied by an improvement in the labour market. By December, the unemployment rate was 5.7 per cent. Overall in 2003, the unemployment rate was 6.0 per cent. Employment in the second half of the year also picked up, growing by 0.3 and 0.4 per cent in the third and fourth quarters respectively. Overall in 2003, employment grew by 0.9 per cent, compared to a decline of 0.3 per cent in 2002.

Earnings growth has been very stable over the year up to quarter three, hovering around 3.2 and 3.3 per cent and staying at very similar levels in both 2001 and 2002 when the growth rate was 3.3 per cent. Earnings growth seems to have slowed since quarter three and the index grew by 2.4 per cent in the last three months of the year.

Figure 4
USA: Unemployment
Percentage of the workforce

Japan

The February preliminary estimate for GDP in 2003 shows that the economy grew by 2.7[5] per cent last year. 2.0[5] per cent of this growth was delivered by increases in domestic demand, while 0.7[5] per cent came from an improvement in foreign trade. It is worth noting that much of the growth in real GDP last year was due to a decline in the GDP deflator. Indeed, nominal GDP expanded by only 0.2[5] per cent over the year whereas the GDP deflator fell by 2.4[5] per cent. Contributions of individual components to 2003 growth were not published in the latest official release.

According to the latest estimates, the Japanese economy grew by 1.7[5] per cent in the last quarter of the year. The latest data suggest that 2003 has been a year of sustained economic growth in Japan with GDP rising in each quarter of the year. Estimates for the previous quarters of the year were revised up with the economy growing at 0.6[5], 0.8[5] and 0.6[5] respectively in the first three quarters of 2003 (note that table 6 does not incorporate such revisions). Japanese growth was much higher than growth in the eurozone, higher than growth in the UK but lower than growth in the US.

Quarter four was characterised by a steep rise in non-residential investment, which grew by 5.1[5] per cent in the last quarter. Private residential investment instead declined by 1.0[5] per cent. Inventories were flat whereas private consumption grew by 0.8[5] per cent compared to growth of 0.5[5] per cent in quarter three. Government consumption also increased, growing at 0.5[5] per cent in the quarter. Finally, exports expanded very robustly, growing at 4.2[5] per cent in the last quarter, while imports grew by only 1.4[5] per cent. Growth in the fourth quarter of 2003 and more generally in the last year seems to have been characterised by a healthy balance between the different expenditure components. Deflation seems to still persist however although last year it was less severe than in 2002.

Available data from the OECD suggest that industrial production was buoyant in the second half of 2003. As with all the other major economies outside the UK, the index of production contracted in 2003 quarter two by 0.8 per cent having grown by 0.4 per cent in the previous quarter. The index however saw a rebound in quarter three when it grew by 1.0 per cent and grew extremely fast in quarter four, when it expanded by 3.3 per cent. Looking at the monthly changes shows that the rise in the index in the third and fourth quarters seems to be concentrated mainly in the months from September to November. Overall in 2002, the index had declined by 1.1 per cent which, although negative, was an improvement over the previous year's contraction of 6.2 per cent. In quarter on previous quarter terms, there were strong declines in the later quarters of 2001 – which brought the index level down substantially – while in 2002, quarterly growth rates were all positive. More recently, production seems to have contracted: in December the index dropped by 1.3 per cent, although monthly figures are volatile.

Consumer and producer prices continue the deflation that began in mid-1998. Price falls had slowed since late 2002 but CPI figures for November and December seem to indicate that deflation is still quite strong. In December, CPI inflation was –0.4 per cent and PPI inflation –0.7 per cent.

The unemployment rate in December was 4.9 per cent, down from 5.2 per cent in the previous month. Unemployment declined slightly in 2003 overall (5.3 down from 5.4 per cent in 2002) although recent rates of unemployment remain high by Japanese historical standards. Such rates are unprecedented in fact since 1960 when OECD records began. Employment had picked up towards the end of the second quarter but seemed to revert back to declines since then, falling in all months from July to December. Overall in 2003 employment fell by 0.2 per cent compared to a decline of 1.3 per cent in the previous year.

Despite the current weak labour market, earnings growth, which had been in decline until late 2002, started to pick up in 2002 quarter four and was 1.8 per cent in the third quarter of 2003. This is a significant improvement from the third quarter of 2002 when earnings were 2.2 per cent lower than in the same quarter of the previous year. Figure 5 reports the movement of earnings growth calculated as month on month a year ago and the movement of the unemployment rate.

World Trade

The OECD stopped producing most series used in table 7 of this article and the data used here are the latest which were provided by the OECD when these series were produced. This section will be replaced as soon as possible.

Some data for world trade for OECD countries extends to the first quarter of 2003 and generally shows a fall back in trade from the levels seen in the first half of 2002.

Manufacturing exports of OECD countries contracted by 0.4 per cent, a deceleration from the 0.9 per cent contraction in the previous quarter. Overall in 2002, exports of manufactures in OECD countries grew by 2.5 per cent, a significant improvement over the previous year's fall of 1.0 per cent but still well below the average of the 1990s. OECD imports also increased by 2.4 per cent in 2002, up from a growth rate of –0.6 per cent in 2001 but well below the average of the 1990s. Non–OECD exports of manufactures in 2002 grew by 8.1 per cent in the same period, improving substantially from 2001 where there was a fall of 2.1 per cent. No figure is available for non-OECD imports.

Imports of goods by OECD countries also contracted, by 0.2 per cent in the first quarter of 2003 having shown growth in all quarters of 2002. In 2002 as a whole, OECD goods' imports were up 2.7 per cent compared to a contraction in the previous year of 1.1 per cent.

World trade of goods and manufactures over the past couple of years rose strongly in 2000 and fell sharply in 2001, where the rates were negative in all quarters. In 2002 growth in world trade, however, seems to have picked up again. Figure 6 shows growth rates of world trade in goods since 1990: the fall in world trade in 2001 is to be noted since it showed the largest quarterly falls since at least 1975.

Figure 5
Japan: Unemployment and earnings growth
Percentage of the workforce; Month on month a year ago growth

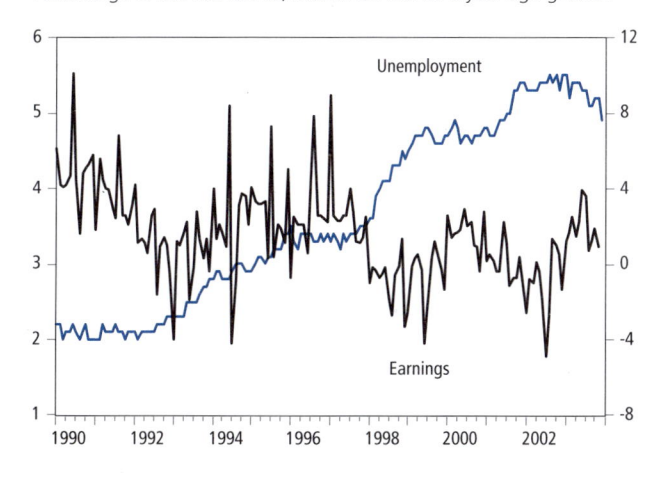

Figure 6
World trade in goods
Growth

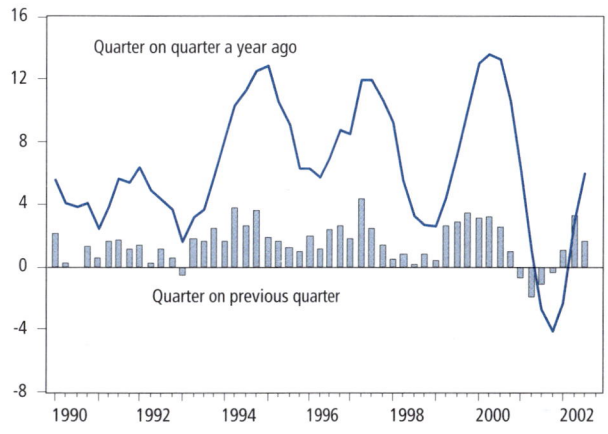

Notes

This month's International Economic Indicators uses information from OECD as well as information from other organisations. All data is from OECD Main Economic Indicators unless otherwise noted:

1. DESTATIS, Germany, http://www.destatis.de/presse/englisch/pm2004/p0790121.htm, released 19 February 2003

2. INSEE, France, hYPERLINK http://www.insee.fr/en/indicateur/cnat_trim/Pub_Meth/pr034ang.pdf http://www.insee.fr/en/indicateur/cnat_trim/Pub_Meth/pr034ang.pdf

3. ISTAT, Italy, http://www.istat.it/Comunicati/In-calenda/Allegati/Economia/Stima-prel/comunicato1.pdf

4. BEA, USA, http://www.bea.doc.gov/bea/newsrelarchive/2004/gdp403a.pdf

5. ESRI, Japan, http://www.esri.cao.go.jp/en/sna/qe034/pointe.html

6. Institute for Economic Research at the University of Munich, Germany, http://www.cesifo.de/pls/cesifo_app/CESifoFrameSet.SwitchFrame?factor=10&page=/link/gk-e.htm

7. Zentrum für Europäische Wirtschaftsforschung GmbH, Germany, http://www.zew.de/en/presse/presse.php?action=article_show&LFDNR=319

8. INSEE, France, http://www.insee.fr/en/indicateur/indic_conj/indconj_frame.asp?ind_id=11

9. REUTERS, www.reuters.com (available on subscription)

10. INSEE, France, http://www.insee.fr/en/indicateur/indic_conj/indconj_frame.asp?ind_id=20

11. Institute for Supply Management, USA, http://www.ism.ws/ISMReport/ROB022004.cfm

12. Institute for Supply Management, USA, http://www.ism.ws/ISMReport/NMROB022004.cfm

Please note that graphs do not include data coming from the above sources.

Comparisons of indicators over the same period should be treated with caution, as the length and timing of the economic cycles varies across countries. For world trade, goods includes manufactures, along with food, beverages and tobacco, basic materials and fuels.

Data for EU15, France, Germany, Italy, the USA and Japan are all available on an SNA93 basis. Cross country comparisons are now more valid.

The tables in this article are reprinted by the permission of the OECD: Main Economic Indicators (February) Copyright OECD 2004.

2 Germany

		Contribution to change in GDP											
	GDP	PFC	GFC	GFCF	ChgStk	Exports	less Imports	IoP	Sales	CPI	PPI	Earnings	Empl[1]	Unempl

Percentage change on a year earlier

	ILFY	HUBW	HUBX	HUBY	HUBZ	HUCA	HUCB	ILGS	ILHM	HVLL	ILAF	ILAO	ILIG	GABD
1999	1.9	2.0	0.2	0.8	−0.4	1.5	2.3	1.5	0.4	0.6	−1.0	2.7	−0.1	8.4
2000	3.1	1.2	0.2	0.7	−0.2	4.4	3.2	6.2	1.2	1.5	3.0	2.6	0.6	7.8
2001	1.0	0.9	0.2	−0.9	−0.8	2.0	0.4	0.6	1.1	1.9	3.1	1.6	0.3	7.8
2002	0.2	−0.6	0.3	−1.4	0.1	1.2	−0.5	−1.2	−2.2	1.5	−0.6	1.6	−0.9	8.6
2003	..	..	..	..	..	..	..	..	−0.3	1.0	1.6	..	..	9.3
2000 Q3	3.0	1.5	−	0.6	−	4.0	3.2	7.0	1.5	1.3	3.4	3.2	0.4	7.7
Q4	1.9	0.6	0.3	0.5	−	4.9	4.4	5.8	−0.5	1.8	4.2	2.3	0.8	7.6
2001 Q1	1.9	1.2	0.1	−0.2	−0.4	3.6	2.3	6.0	2.4	1.7	4.6	2.0	0.7	7.6
Q2	0.8	0.6	0.1	−0.7	−0.4	2.5	1.4	1.5	0.4	2.5	4.7	2.0	0.7	7.7
Q3	0.7	0.9	0.2	−1.3	−1.2	2.0	−0.1	−1.2	1.5	2.2	2.6	1.1	0.2	7.9
Q4	0.5	0.7	0.3	−1.4	−1.3	0.1	−2.1	−3.7	0.3	1.6	0.3	1.1	−0.3	8.1
2002 Q1	−0.1	−0.5	0.3	−1.4	−0.7	0.4	−1.9	−3.8	−4.0	1.9	−0.4	1.1	−0.5	8.3
Q2	0.1	−0.7	0.4	−1.7	0.2	1.0	−0.9	−2.0	−2.3	1.3	−1.2	1.0	−0.8	8.5
Q3	0.4	−0.7	0.6	−1.4	0.3	1.6	−	−0.4	−1.1	1.1	−1.0	2.1	−1.0	8.7
Q4	0.5	−0.4	−	−1.1	0.7	1.9	0.7	1.4	−1.2	1.2	0.3	2.4	−1.3	8.9
2003 Q1	0.1	0.4	−	−1.0	1.3	1.4	2.1	1.8	0.7	1.2	1.6	2.7	−1.6	9.2
Q2	−0.3	−	0.1	−0.4	0.7	−0.1	0.5	0.3	−	0.8	1.4	2.8	−1.3	9.3
Q3	−0.2	−0.5	−	−0.6	0.1	0.3	−0.4	−0.6	−1.9	1.0	1.8	2.1	−1.3	9.3
Q4	..	..	..	..	..	..	..	..	−0.1	1.2	1.7	..	..	9.2
2002 Dec	..	..	..	..	..	..	..	−	−1.9	1.2	0.6	..	..	9.0
2003 Jan	..	..	..	..	..	..	..	1.6	1.5	1.1	1.4	..	..	9.1
Feb	..	..	..	..	..	..	..	2.5	1.3	1.2	1.8	..	..	9.2
Mar	..	..	..	..	..	..	..	1.4	−0.7	1.2	1.6	..	..	9.3
Apr	..	..	..	..	..	..	..	0.9	−	0.9	1.6	..	..	9.4
May	..	..	..	..	..	..	..	1.3	−1.7	0.6	1.3	..	..	9.3
Jun	..	..	..	..	..	..	..	−1.3	1.7	0.9	1.3	..	..	9.3
Jul	..	..	..	..	..	..	..	2.0	−1.4	0.9	1.8	..	..	9.3
Aug	..	..	..	..	..	..	..	−2.5	−2.2	1.1	1.9	..	..	9.3
Sep	..	..	..	..	..	..	..	−1.4	−2.1	1.0	1.9	..	..	9.3
Oct	..	..	..	..	..	..	..	1.9	−0.2	1.1	1.6	..	..	9.3
Nov	..	..	..	..	..	..	..	1.4	−2.0	1.2	1.9	..	..	9.2
Dec	..	..	..	..	..	..	..	..	1.9	1.1	1.7	..	..	9.2

Percentage change on previous quarter

	ILGI	HUCC	HUCD	HUCE	HUCF	HUCG	HUCH	ILHC	ILHW				ILIQ	
2000 Q3	−0.1	−0.1	−0.1	0.2	0.2	0.6	1.0	2.0	−1.3				0.7	
Q4	−	−0.2	0.3	−0.2	0.1	1.7	1.6	0.3	0.1				1.0	
2001 Q1	0.9	0.7	−	−0.4	−0.7	−	−1.1	0.7	2.4				−1.9	
Q2	−	0.3	−0.1	−0.4	−	0.1	−	−1.5	−0.8				1.0	
Q3	−0.2	0.1	−	−0.3	−0.6	0.1	−0.5	−0.7	−0.2				0.2	
Q4	−0.1	−0.4	0.4	−0.3	−	−0.2	−0.4	−2.2	−1.0				0.5	
2002 Q1	0.2	−0.5	−	−0.4	−0.1	0.3	−0.9	0.5	−2.0				−2.2	
Q2	0.2	0.1	0.1	−0.7	0.9	0.8	1.0	0.3	1.0				0.7	
Q3	0.1	0.1	0.1	−	−0.5	0.7	0.3	0.9	1.0				−	
Q4	−	−0.1	−0.1	−	0.4	−	0.3	−0.4	−1.2				0.2	
2003 Q1	−0.2	0.2	−	−0.3	0.5	−0.1	0.5	0.9	−0.1				−2.5	
Q2	−0.2	−0.3	0.1	−0.1	0.4	−0.8	−0.6	−1.2	0.3				1.0	
Q3	0.2	−0.3	0.1	−0.2	−1.1	1.2	−0.6	0.1	−0.9				−	
Q4	..	..	..	..	..	..	..	..	0.6				..	

Percentage change on previous month

	ILKC	ILKM
2002 Dec	−2.5	−0.4
2003 Jan	2.0	0.6
Feb	0.4	0.3
Mar	−0.5	−1.4
Apr	−0.3	1.1
May	−0.7	−1.2
Jun	−0.6	2.5
Jul	2.6	−2.1
Aug	−2.9	−0.4
Sep	0.1	0.6
Oct	2.8	0.8
Nov	1.3	−2.4
Dec	..	3.6

GDP = Gross Domestic Product at constant market prices
PFC = Private Final Consumption at constant market prices
GFC = Government Final Consumption at constant market prices
GFCF = Gross Fixed Capital Formation at constant market prices
ChgStk = Change in Stocks at constant market prices
Exports = Exports of goods and services
Imports = Imports of goods and services
IoP = Industrial Production

Sales = Retail Sales volume
CPI = Consumer Prices measurement not uniform among countries
PPI = Producer Prices (manufacturing)
Earnings = Average Earnings (manufacturing), definitions of coverage and treatment vary among countries
Empl = Total Employment not seasonally adjusted
Unempl = Standardised Unemployment rates: percentage of total workforce

Source: OECD - SNA93

1 Excludes members of armed forces

3 France

	GDP	PFC	GFC	GFCF	ChgStk	Exports	less Imports	IoP	Sales	CPI	PPI[1]	Earnings	Empl[2]	Unempl
Percentage change on a year earlier	ILFZ	HUBK	HUBL	HUBM	HUBN	HUBO	HUBP	ILGT	ILHN	HXAA	ILAG	ILAP	ILIH	GABC
1999	3.2	1.9	0.3	1.6	−0.2	1.1	1.5	2.2	2.4	0.5	−1.6	2.5	2.2	10.7
2000	4.2	1.6	0.7	1.7	0.5	3.6	3.8	4.2	0.5	1.7	2.0	5.2	2.8	9.3
2001	2.1	1.5	0.6	0.4	−0.7	0.6	0.4	1.0	−0.2	1.6	1.2	4.2	1.7	8.5
2002	1.2	0.8	0.9	−0.3	−0.3	0.4	0.2	−1.2	−	1.9	−0.2	3.6	0.5	8.8
2003	..	..	..	..	..	..	..	..	..	2.1	0.3	..	..	9.4
2000 Q3	3.9	1.4	0.8	1.5	1.0	3.4	4.2	3.9	0.1	1.9	2.7	5.2	2.8	9.1
Q4	3.8	1.2	0.7	1.6	0.5	3.8	3.9	3.6	−1.3	1.9	2.4	5.0	2.7	8.8
2001 Q1	3.1	1.5	0.6	1.0	−0.3	2.7	2.4	3.4	1.1	1.2	2.4	4.3	2.3	8.6
Q2	2.2	1.5	0.6	0.5	−0.1	0.8	1.0	1.7	−0.4	2.0	1.7	4.2	1.9	8.5
Q3	2.3	1.7	0.8	0.4	−1.0	0.1	−0.3	1.4	−0.7	1.8	0.7	4.2	1.3	8.5
Q4	0.7	1.4	0.6	−0.2	−1.3	−1.4	−1.5	−2.0	−0.8	1.4	−	4.1	1.0	8.5
2002 Q1	0.8	0.8	0.9	−0.3	−0.4	−0.8	−0.6	−2.2	−1.6	2.2	−0.7	3.9	0.6	8.6
Q2	1.5	0.9	1.0	−0.1	−0.8	0.6	0.1	−0.9	−0.6	1.7	−0.5	3.9	0.5	8.7
Q3	1.3	0.7	0.9	−0.3	−0.1	0.7	0.6	−1.1	1.0	1.8	0.1	3.5	0.5	8.9
Q4	1.3	0.8	0.9	−0.4	−0.2	1.0	0.8	−0.5	1.0	2.1	0.2	3.4	0.3	9.0
2003 Q1	0.6	1.1	0.7	−0.4	−0.3	−0.1	0.4	−0.8	−0.8	2.4	0.6	2.9	−	9.2
Q2	−0.4	0.8	0.4	−0.3	−0.2	−1.1	0.1	−1.6	..	1.9	0.6	2.6	−0.1	9.3
Q3	−0.3	0.8	0.4	−0.1	−0.6	−0.9	−0.1	−0.4	..	2.0	−	2.9	..	9.4
Q4	..	..	..	..	..	..	..	..	..	2.2	0.1	..	..	9.5
2002 Dec	..	..	..	..	..	..	..	−0.2	−1.8	2.3	0.3	..	..	9.1
2003 Jan	..	..	..	..	..	..	..	−1.9	3.0	1.9	0.4	..	..	9.1
Feb	..	..	..	..	..	..	..	−	−0.7	2.6	0.7	..	..	9.2
Mar	..	..	..	..	..	..	..	−0.4	−4.6	2.6	0.7	..	..	9.3
Apr	..	..	..	..	..	..	..	−1.3	1.8	2.0	0.8	..	..	9.3
May	..	..	..	..	..	..	..	−2.6	−2.0	1.8	0.6	..	..	9.3
Jun	..	..	..	..	..	..	..	−1.0	..	2.0	0.6	..	..	9.4
Jul	..	..	..	..	..	..	..	−	..	1.9	−	..	..	9.4
Aug	..	..	..	..	..	..	..	−1.4	..	1.9	−0.1	..	..	9.4
Sep	..	..	..	..	..	..	..	0.3	..	2.1	−	..	..	9.5
Oct	..	..	..	..	..	..	..	1.9	..	2.2	..	..	..	9.5
Nov	..	..	..	..	..	..	..	1.1	..	2.3	0.2	..	..	9.5
Dec	..	..	..	..	..	..	..	..	..	2.2	0.1	..	..	9.5
Percentage change on previous quarter	ILGJ	HUBQ	HUBR	HUBS	HUBT	HUBU	HUBV	ILHD	ILHX				ILIR	
2000 Q2	0.9	0.2	0.2	0.4	−0.1	1.2	1.0	0.7	−0.7				0.7	
Q3	0.4	0.2	0.1	0.1	0.3	0.6	0.9	0.4	−				0.6	
Q4	1.3	0.3	0.2	0.5	0.2	1.0	0.8	1.7	−0.4				0.6	
2001 Q1	0.5	0.7	0.1	0.1	−0.7	−0.1	−0.5	0.4	2.3				0.4	
Q2	−	0.3	0.1	−0.2	0.1	−0.7	−0.3	−0.9	−2.2				0.3	
Q3	0.4	0.4	0.3	−	−0.6	−	−0.3	0.2	−0.3				0.1	
Q4	−0.3	−	0.1	−0.1	−0.1	−0.6	−0.4	−1.6	−0.5				0.3	
2002 Q1	0.7	0.1	0.3	−	0.2	0.5	0.4	0.2	1.4				−	
Q2	0.7	0.3	0.3	−	−0.2	0.7	0.4	0.4	−1.2				0.1	
Q3	0.2	0.3	0.1	−0.2	0.1	0.1	0.1	−0.1	1.3				0.1	
Q4	−0.3	0.1	0.1	−0.2	−0.2	−0.2	−0.1	−1.0	−0.5				0.1	
2003 Q1	−	0.4	0.1	−	0.1	−0.6	−	−0.1	−0.4				−0.3	
Q2	−0.4	−	0.1	0.1	−0.2	−0.3	0.1	−0.4	..				−	
Q3	0.3	0.3	0.1	−	−0.3	0.2	−	1.1	..				..	
Percentage change on previous month								ILKD	ILKN					
2002 Nov								0.3	−					
Dec								−0.4	−2.7					
2003 Jan								−0.8	4.1					
Feb								1.6	−1.9					
Mar								−0.4	−3.9					
Apr								0.5	4.6					
May								−2.4	−2.3					
Jun								1.3	..					
Jul								1.2	..					
Aug								−0.4	..					
Sep								0.7	..					
Oct								0.8	..					
Nov								−0.4	..					

GDP = Gross Domestic Product at constant market prices
PFC = Private Final Consumption at constant market prices
GFC = Government Final Consumption at constant market prices
GFCF = Gross Fixed Capital Formation at constant market prices
ChgStk = Change in Stocks at constant market prices
Exports = Exports of goods and services
Imports = Imports of goods and services

Sales = Retail Sales volume
CPI = Consumer Prices, measurement not uniform among countries
PPI = Producer Prices (manufacturing)
Earnings = Average Wage Earnings (manufacturing), definitions of coverage and treatment vary among countries
Empl = Total Employment not seasonally adjusted
Unempl = Standardised Unemployment rates: percentage of total workforce
IoP = Index of Production

1 Producer prices in manufactured goods
2 Excludes members of armed foces

Source: OECD - SNA93

4 Italy

	GDP	PFC	GFC	GFCF	ChgStk	Exports	less Imports	IoP	Sales	CPI	PPI	Earnings	Empl	Unempl
	\multicolumn{7}{c}{Contribution to change in GDP}							

Percentage change on a year earlier

	ILGA	HUCI	HUCJ	HUCK	HUCL	HUCM	HUCN	ILGU	ILHO	HYAA	ILAH	ILAQ	ILII	GABE
1999	1.7	1.6	0.2	0.9	0.3	–	1.4	–0.2	0.8	1.7	–0.3	2.3	1.2	11.3
2000	3.3	1.7	0.3	1.5	–1.1	3.3	2.4	4.2	–0.8	2.5	6.1	2.0	1.9	10.4
2001	1.7	0.7	0.6	0.5	–0.1	0.3	0.3	–1.1	–0.1	2.7	1.9	1.8	2.0	9.4
2002	0.4	0.3	0.3	0.1	0.4	–0.3	0.4	–1.4	–0.6	2.5	0.2	2.8	1.4	9.0
2003	..	..	..	..	..	..	..	..	..	2.7	1.5	..	1.0	..
2000 Q3	3.3	1.8	0.3	1.6	–1.2	3.6	2.8	3.6	1.3	2.6	6.7	2.0	2.1	10.3
Q4	3.0	1.7	0.3	1.0	–1.3	2.6	1.4	3.7	–2.5	2.6	6.6	1.9	2.8	9.9
2001 Q1	2.7	1.4	0.6	1.0	–0.4	1.6	1.4	3.0	1.6	2.9	4.7	1.8	3.2	9.7
Q2	2.1	1.0	0.6	0.6	–0.5	1.3	0.9	–0.4	–0.3	3.0	3.2	1.2	2.0	9.5
Q3	1.5	0.3	0.6	0.2	0.5	–0.7	–0.6	–1.9	–1.0	2.8	1.1	2.2	1.8	9.4
Q4	0.6	–0.1	0.6	0.3	–	–0.9	–0.6	–4.9	–0.6	2.5	–1.1	2.3	1.2	9.2
2002 Q1	–	–0.5	0.4	–0.5	1.5	–2.8	–1.7	–3.9	–0.3	2.4	–1.0	2.4	1.7	9.1
Q2	0.3	–0.1	0.3	–0.4	0.8	–0.7	–0.3	–2.1	–1.0	2.2	–0.6	3.4	1.9	9.0
Q3	0.4	0.5	0.3	0.3	–0.1	1.0	1.5	–0.3	–1.3	2.4	0.5	2.4	1.3	9.0
Q4	0.9	1.2	0.2	1.2	–0.5	1.2	2.3	0.9	–	2.7	1.7	2.8	0.9	8.9
2003 Q1	0.7	1.4	0.3	–	–0.6	0.3	0.8	–0.3	–0.6	2.7	2.6	2.5	0.8	8.9
Q2	0.2	1.3	0.3	–0.3	0.8	–1.4	0.4	–1.4	0.7	2.7	1.7	1.8	1.3	8.7
Q3	0.5	1.5	0.3	–0.9	0.7	–0.7	0.3	–0.3	–1.3	2.8	1.3	3.2	0.9	8.5
Q4	..	..	..	..	..	..	..	..	..	2.5	0.8	..	0.9	..
2002 Dec	..	..	..	..	..	..	..	0.5	–	2.8	2.0	2.8	..	9.0
2003 Jan	..	..	..	..	..	..	..	0.4	–1.0	2.8	2.4	2.9	..	9.0
Feb	..	..	..	..	..	..	..	–0.5	–	2.6	2.8	3.0	..	8.9
Mar	..	..	..	..	..	..	..	–0.8	–1.0	2.7	2.8	1.7	..	8.8
Apr	..	..	..	..	..	..	..	0.3	2.9	2.7	2.0	1.8	..	8.7
May	..	..	..	..	..	..	..	–2.9	1.0	2.7	1.5	1.8	..	8.7
Jun	..	..	..	..	..	..	..	–1.7	–1.9	2.7	1.4	1.6	..	8.6
Jul	..	..	..	..	..	..	..	–0.6	–1.0	2.7	1.3	3.2	..	8.6
Aug	..	..	..	..	..	..	..	0.6	–2.9	2.8	1.3	3.2	..	8.5
Sep	..	..	..	..	..	..	..	–0.9	–	2.8	1.0	3.2	..	8.5
Oct	..	..	..	..	..	..	..	0.1	–1.9	2.6	0.6	2.7	..	8.4
Nov	..	..	..	..	..	..	..	–	–2.9	2.5	1.2	2.7	..	..
Dec	..	..	..	..	..	..	..	..	..	2.5	0.7	..	..	..

Percentage change on previous quarter

	ILGK	HUCO	HUCP	HUCQ	HUCR	HUCS	HUCT	ILHE	ILHY				ILIS	
2000 Q3	0.6	0.4	0.1	0.2	–1.1	1.3	0.3	0.1	0.6				1.9	
Q4	0.7	0.2	0.1	–0.2	0.7	–0.1	–	1.5	–1.3				0.6	
2001 Q1	0.7	0.4	0.3	0.6	–0.3	1.0	1.1	–0.5	–				–0.8	
Q2	–	–	0.1	–0.1	0.2	–0.8	–0.5	–1.5	0.3				0.4	
Q3	–	–0.3	0.1	–0.2	–0.1	–0.7	–1.2	–1.5	–				1.7	
Q4	–0.1	–0.2	0.1	–	0.2	–0.3	–0.1	–1.6	–1.0				–	
2002 Q1	0.1	–	0.1	–0.2	1.1	–0.9	–	0.7	0.3				–0.4	
Q2	0.3	0.4	–	–	–0.5	1.4	1.0	0.4	–0.3				0.6	
Q3	0.2	0.3	–	0.5	–1.0	1.0	0.6	0.3	–0.3				1.1	
Q4	0.4	0.6	–	0.8	–0.2	–0.2	0.7	–0.5	0.3				–0.4	
2003 Q1	–0.2	0.2	0.2	–1.3	1.0	–1.8	–1.5	–0.5	–0.3				–0.5	
Q2	–0.2	0.3	–	–0.4	0.9	–0.3	0.6	–0.8	1.0				1.0	
Q3	0.5	0.4	–	–0.1	–1.1	1.6	0.5	1.4	–2.3				0.7	
Q4	..	..	..	..	..	..	..	..	..				–0.4	

Percentage change on previous month

								ILKE	ILKO					
2002 Nov								0.5	–					
Dec								–0.5	–					
2003 Jan								–0.2	–1.0					
Feb								–	2.0					
Mar								–0.2	–1.9					
Apr								–	3.9					
May								–1.3	–1.9					
Jun								0.7	–2.9					
Jul								1.7	1.0					
Aug								–0.1	–2.0					
Sep								–0.7	2.0					
Oct								0.2	–1.0					
Nov								0.4	–1.0					

GDP = Gross Domestic Product at constant market prices
PFC = Private Final Consumption at constant market prices
GFC = Government Final Consumption at constant market prices
GFCF = Gross Fixed Capital Formation at constant market prices
ChgStk = Change in Stocks at constant market prices
Exports = Exports of goods and services
Imports = Imports of goods and services
IoP = Industrial Production

Sales = Retail Sales volume
CPI = Consumer Prices, measurement not uniform among countries
PPI = Producer Prices (manufacturing)
Earnings = Average Wage Earnings (manufacturing), definitions of coverage and treatment vary among countries
Empl = Total Employment not seasonally adjusted
Unempl = Standardised Unemployment not seasonally adjusted

Source: OECD - SNA93

International economic indicators Economic Trends 604 March 2004

5 USA

			Contribution to change in GDP											
	GDP	PFC	GFC	GFCF	ChgStk	Exports	less Imports	IoP	Sales	CPI	PPI	Earnings	Empl[1]	Unempl

Percentage change on a year earlier

	ILGC	HUDG	HUDH	HUDI	HUDJ	HUDK	HUDL	ILGW	ILHQ	ILAA	ILAJ	ILAS	ILIK	GADO
1999	4.4	3.4	0.5	1.6	–	0.5	1.5	4.4	8.8	2.1	1.8	2.9	1.5	4.2
2000	3.7	3.2	0.3	1.2	–0.1	0.9	1.8	4.4	5.5	3.4	4.1	3.4	2.5	4.0
2001	0.5	1.7	0.4	–0.5	–0.9	–0.6	–0.4	–3.4	4.8	2.8	0.7	3.3	–	4.8
2002	2.2	2.4	0.5	–0.4	0.4	–0.3	0.5	–0.6	5.3	1.5	–0.6	3.3	–0.3	5.8
2003	3.1	2.2	..	..	–0.1	0.2	0.5	0.3	..	2.3	2.5	3.1	0.9	6.0
2000 Q3	3.5	3.1	0.2	1.0	0.1	1.1	1.9	4.3	5.2	3.5	3.9	3.2	2.3	4.0
Q4	2.2	2.8	0.1	0.8	–0.6	0.7	1.6	2.3	3.5	3.4	3.3	3.2	2.3	3.9
2001 Q1	1.9	1.8	0.4	0.3	–0.2	0.4	0.8	–0.4	2.9	3.4	2.1	2.9	0.8	4.2
Q2	0.2	1.7	0.3	–0.3	–1.3	–0.3	–0.1	–3.3	4.5	3.4	2.1	3.2	0.1	4.4
Q3	–	1.4	0.4	–0.7	–1.0	–1.1	–1.1	–4.5	3.8	2.7	0.6	3.4	–	4.8
Q4	–	1.9	0.5	–1.1	–1.2	–1.3	–1.1	–5.3	7.9	1.8	–1.5	3.7	–0.8	5.6
2002 Q1	1.2	2.5	0.4	–1.0	–0.3	–1.1	–0.6	–3.3	5.9	1.2	–1.8	3.7	–1.2	5.7
Q2	1.8	2.6	0.5	–0.7	0.2	–0.5	0.3	–1.0	5.5	1.3	–1.7	3.4	–0.5	5.8
Q3	3.0	2.6	0.5	–0.2	0.8	0.2	0.9	0.6	7.0	1.5	–0.6	3.0	0.1	5.7
Q4	2.8	1.9	0.7	0.2	1.0	0.3	1.3	1.4	3.0	2.2	1.6	3.3	0.3	5.9
2003 Q1	2.1	1.6	0.6	0.2	0.2	0.2	0.8	1.1	4.4	2.9	3.9	3.5	1.0	5.8
Q2	2.4	1.8	0.7	0.4	–	–0.1	0.5	–1.0	6.0	2.1	1.9	3.3	0.9	6.1
Q3	3.6	2.6	0.6	1.0	–0.4	0.1	0.4	–0.3	7.2	2.2	2.1	3.2	0.5	6.1
Q4	4.3	2.7	..	..	–0.1	0.6	0.5	1.6	..	1.9	2.3	2.4	1.3	5.9
2002 Dec	..	..	..	..	..	..	..	1.4	5.3	2.3	1.9	3.3	0.3	6.0
2003 Jan	..	..	..	..	..	..	..	1.3	5.5	2.6	3.0	3.3	1.3	5.8
Feb	..	..	..	..	..	..	..	1.5	2.6	3.0	4.2	4.1	0.7	5.9
Mar	..	..	..	..	..	..	..	0.4	5.2	3.1	4.5	3.3	0.9	5.8
Apr	..	..	..	..	..	..	..	–0.6	4.9	2.2	1.9	3.3	1.1	6.0
May	..	..	..	..	..	..	..	–0.9	6.9	2.0	1.7	3.3	0.7	6.1
Jun	..	..	..	..	..	..	..	–1.5	6.3	2.1	2.0	3.3	1.0	6.3
Jul	..	..	..	..	..	..	..	–0.6	6.6	2.1	2.1	3.3	0.7	6.2
Aug	..	..	..	..	..	..	..	–0.6	7.0	2.1	2.5	3.2	0.6	6.1
Sep	..	..	..	..	..	..	..	0.2	8.2	2.3	1.6	3.2	0.3	6.1
Oct	..	..	..	..	..	..	..	0.8	7.9	2.0	1.9	2.4	0.8	6.0
Nov	..	..	..	..	..	..	..	1.8	..	1.8	2.2	2.4	1.5	5.9
Dec	..	..	..	..	..	..	..	2.3	..	1.9	2.7	2.4	1.4	5.7

Percentage change on previous quarter

	ILGM	HUDM	HUDN	HUDO	HUDP	HUDQ	HUDR	ILHG	ILIA				ILIU	
2000 Q3	–0.1	0.7	–0.1	–	–0.4	0.3	0.5	–0.2	1.3				0.1	
Q4	0.5	0.6	0.1	–	–0.1	–0.1	–0.1	–0.3	0.4				0.3	
2001 Q1	–0.1	0.1	0.2	–0.1	–0.4	–0.1	–0.2	–1.5	1.6				–0.7	
Q2	–0.2	0.4	0.1	–0.3	–0.3	–0.4	–0.3	–1.3	1.2				0.5	
Q3	–0.3	0.3	–	–0.4	–0.2	–0.5	–0.4	–1.4	0.5				–	
Q4	0.5	1.1	0.2	–0.3	–0.3	–0.3	–0.1	–1.1	4.3				–0.5	
2002 Q1	1.2	0.7	0.1	–	0.5	0.1	0.3	0.5	–0.2				–1.1	
Q2	0.5	0.5	0.1	0.1	0.2	0.2	0.6	1.1	0.8				1.1	
Q3	0.8	0.3	0.1	0.1	0.4	0.1	0.2	0.2	2.0				0.6	
Q4	0.3	0.4	0.3	0.1	–0.1	–0.1	0.3	–0.4	0.4				–0.4	
2003 Q1	0.5	0.4	–	–	–0.2	–0.1	–0.3	0.2	1.1				–0.4	
Q2	0.8	0.6	0.3	0.3	–0.1	–	0.3	–1.0	2.4				1.0	
Q3	2.0	1.2	–	0.7	–	0.2	–	1.0	3.2				0.3	
Q4	1.0	0.5	..	..	0.1	0.4	0.4	1.5	..				0.4	

Percentage change on previous month

								ILKG	ILKQ				ILLA	
2002 Dec								–0.5	1.8				–	
2003 Jan								0.5	0.4				–0.5	
Feb								0.4	–2.1				0.4	
Mar								–0.7	2.2				0.3	
Apr								–0.6	0.5				0.5	
May								–0.1	1.2				0.1	
Jun								–	1.1				0.7	
Jul								0.7	1.7				–	
Aug								0.1	0.8				–0.3	
Sep								0.6	–0.4				–0.3	
Oct								0.4	–0.1				0.6	
Nov								1.0	..				–	
Dec								0.1	..				–0.1	

GDP = Gross Domestic Product at constant market prices
PFC = Private Final Consumption at constant market prices
GFC = Government Final Consumption at constant market prices
GFCF = Gross Fixed Capital Formation at constant market prices
ChgStk = Change in Stocks at constant market prices
Exports = Exports of goods and services
Imports = Imports of goods and services
IoP = Industrial Production

Sales = Retail Sales volume
CPI = Consumer Prices, measurement not uniform among countries
PPI = Producer Prices (manufacturing)
Earnings = Average Earnings (manufacturing), definitions of coverage and treatment vary among countries
Empl = Total Employment not seasonally adjusted
Unempl = Standardised Unemployment rates: percentage of total workforce

Source: OECD - SNA93

1 Excludes members of armed forces

6 Japan

		Contribution to change in GDP												
	GDP	PFC	GFC	GFCF	ChgStk	Exports	less Imports	IoP[1]	Sales	CPI	PPI	Earnings[2]	Empl	Unempl

Percentage change on a year earlier

	ILGD	HUCU	HUCV	HUCW	HUCX	HUCY	HUCZ	ILGX	ILHR	ILAB	ILAK	ILAT	ILIL	GADP
1999	0.2	0.1	0.7	−0.1	−0.4	0.1	0.3	0.6	−2.6	−0.3	−1.4	−0.7	−0.8	4.7
2000	2.8	0.5	0.8	0.8	0.3	1.3	0.8	5.1	−1.1	−0.7	0.1	1.7	−0.3	4.7
2001	0.4	1.0	0.5	−0.4	–	−0.7	–	−6.2	−1.2	−0.7	−2.4	–	−0.5	5.0
2002	−0.4	0.5	0.4	−1.6	−0.3	0.8	0.2	−1.1	−3.1	−1.0	−2.0	−1.0	−1.3	5.4
2003	..	..	..	..	..	..	..	3.1	−1.4	−0.2	−0.9	..	−0.2	5.3
2000 Q3	3.0	0.3	0.8	0.8	0.7	1.3	0.7	5.4	−0.4	−0.6	–	1.7	−0.4	4.7
Q4	3.9	0.6	0.8	1.7	0.6	1.1	0.8	5.1	−0.4	−0.8	−0.6	1.1	0.2	4.7
2001 Q1	3.2	1.1	0.6	1.1	1.0	0.2	0.7	1.5	2.3	−0.5	−1.9	0.3	0.5	4.7
Q2	1.1	1.1	0.5	0.2	0.2	−0.6	0.2	−4.4	−1.1	−0.7	−2.1	0.5	−0.4	4.9
Q3	−0.4	0.9	0.3	−0.3	−0.5	−1.0	−0.2	−9.1	−2.6	−0.8	−2.5	−0.2	−0.8	5.1
Q4	−2.2	0.8	0.4	−2.3	−0.6	−1.2	−0.6	−12.3	−3.4	−1.0	−3.0	−0.6	−1.3	5.4
2002 Q1	−3.1	0.2	0.4	−2.4	−1.5	−0.3	−0.5	−9.1	−4.4	−1.4	−2.8	−1.5	−1.5	5.3
Q2	−1.0	0.2	0.4	−2.0	−0.4	0.8	–	−3.4	−2.6	−0.9	−2.2	−0.8	−1.6	5.4
Q3	0.9	0.9	0.5	−1.7	0.5	1.1	0.4	2.9	−2.7	−0.8	−2.0	−2.2	−1.0	5.4
Q4	1.9	0.5	0.3	−0.4	0.4	1.8	0.7	6.0	−2.7	−0.5	−1.2	0.1	−1.1	5.4
2003 Q1	2.7	0.6	0.3	0.2	1.1	1.3	0.7	5.7	−1.2	−0.2	−0.8	1.8	−0.8	5.4
Q2	2.3	0.5	0.1	0.9	0.3	0.8	0.3	2.0	−2.3	−0.3	−1.1	2.6	0.1	5.4
Q3	1.8	−0.1	0.1	0.7	0.2	1.1	0.3	1.0	−2.0	−0.2	−0.7	1.8	−0.1	5.2
Q4	..	..	..	..	..	..	..	3.9	–	−0.3	−0.8	..	−0.1	5.1
2002 Dec	..	..	..	..	..	..	..	5.5	−3.5	−0.3	−1.1	−1.3	−1.1	5.5
2003 Jan	..	..	..	..	..	..	..	8.2	−2.3	−0.4	−0.9	1.2	−1.0	5.5
Feb	..	..	..	..	..	..	..	4.6	–	−0.2	−0.8	1.7	−0.9	5.2
Mar	..	..	..	..	..	..	..	4.3	−1.2	−0.1	−0.6	2.5	−0.5	5.4
Apr	..	..	..	..	..	..	..	3.3	−3.5	−0.1	−1.0	1.5	−0.4	5.4
May	..	..	..	..	..	..	..	1.3	−2.3	−0.2	−1.1	2.2	0.1	5.4
Jun	..	..	..	..	..	..	..	1.3	−1.2	−0.4	−1.2	3.9	0.6	5.3
Jul	..	..	..	..	..	..	..	0.3	−2.4	−0.2	−0.9	3.6	0.1	5.3
Aug	..	..	..	..	..	..	..	−0.2	−2.3	−0.3	−0.7	0.7	−0.2	5.1
Sep	..	..	..	..	..	..	..	2.9	−1.2	−0.2	−0.7	1.2	−0.1	5.1
Oct	..	..	..	..	..	..	..	3.6	1.2	–	−0.9	1.9	−0.3	5.2
Nov	..	..	..	..	..	..	..	4.6	−2.4	−0.5	−0.9	0.9	−0.4	5.2
Dec	..	..	..	..	..	..	..	3.4	1.2	−0.4	−0.7	..	0.3	4.9

Percentage change on previous quarter

	ILGN	HUDA	HUDB	HUDC	HUDD	HUDE	HUDF	ILHH	ILIB			ILIV		
2000 Q3	0.5	–	0.2	0.3	0.1	0.1	0.2	0.7	0.8					
Q4	1.3	0.4	0.1	0.9	0.1	0.1	0.3	1.1	−0.7			–		
2001 Q1	0.4	0.6	0.1	−0.3	0.4	−0.4	−0.1	−2.9	1.9			−1.8		
Q2	−1.1	0.1	0.2	−0.7	−0.4	−0.4	−0.2	−3.3	−2.9			1.4		
Q3	−1.0	−0.2	–	−0.2	−0.6	−0.3	−0.2	−4.3	−0.8			−0.4		
Q4	−0.5	0.3	0.2	−1.1	0.1	−0.1	−0.2	−2.5	−1.5			−0.5		
2002 Q1	−0.5	–	0.1	−0.4	−0.6	0.5	0.1	0.6	0.8			−2.0		
Q2	1.0	0.1	0.1	−0.4	0.7	0.7	0.3	2.9	−1.2			1.3		
Q3	0.9	0.5	0.1	0.1	0.4	–	0.2	2.0	−0.8			0.2		
Q4	0.4	−0.1	–	0.3	−0.1	0.5	0.1	0.4	−1.6			−0.6		
2003 Q1	0.4	0.1	0.1	0.1	0.1	0.1	0.1	0.4	2.4			−1.7		
Q2	0.6	–	–	0.4	−0.1	0.2	−0.1	−0.8	−2.3			2.3		
Q3	0.3	–	–	−0.1	0.3	0.3	0.2	1.0	−0.4			–		
Q4	..	..	..	..	..	..	..	3.3	0.4			−0.6		

Percentage change on previous month

								ILKH	ILKR			ILLB		
2002 Dec								−0.2	−3.5			−0.9		
2003 Jan								1.9	3.7			−1.3		
Feb								−2.0	2.4			−0.2		
Mar								0.1	−2.3			1.1		
Apr								−1.2	−2.4			0.7		
May								2.1	1.2			0.8		
Jun								−1.1	–			0.8		
Jul								−0.2	−2.4			−0.5		
Aug								−0.1	2.4			−0.3		
Sep								3.7	–			−0.2		
Oct								0.8	1.2			−0.2		
Nov								0.8	−2.4			−0.2		
Dec								−1.3	–			−0.2		

GDP = Gross Domestic Product at constant market prices
PFC = Private Final Consumption at constant market prices
GFC = Government Final Consumption at constant market prices
GFCF = Gross Fixed Capital Formation at constant market prices
ChgStk = Change in Stocks at constant market prices
Exports = Exports of goods and services
Imports = Imports of goods and services

Sales = Retail Sales volume
CPI = Consumer Prices, measurement not uniform among countries
PPI = Producer Prices (manufacturing)
Earnings = Average Earnings (manufacturing), definitions of coverage and treatment vary among countries
Empl = Total Employment not seasonally adjusted
Unempl = Standardised Unemployment rates: percentage of total workforce
IoP = Index of Production

1 Not adjusted for unequal number of working days in a month
2 Figures monthly and seasonally adjusted

Source: OECD - SNA93

7 World Trade in goods[1]

	Export of manufactures			Import of manufactures			Export of goods			Import of goods			Total trade	
	Total	OECD	Other	Total	OECD	Other	Total	OECD	Other	Total	OECD	Other	manufactures	goods

Percentage change on a year earlier

	ILIZ	ILJA	ILJB	ILJC	ILJD	ILJE	ILJF	ILJG	ILJH	ILJI	ILJJ	ILJK	ILJL	ILJM
1992	4.3	3.3	9.4	5.6	4.2	8.7	4.5	3.6	6.3	5.3	4.2	9.8	5.0	4.8
1993	3.7	2.1	12.1	3.8	0.8	11.0	4.1	2.2	8.1	3.3	0.7	12.8	4.0	3.5
1994	10.3	9.9	17.3	11.9	10.9	10.7	11.4	9.3	12.9	10.9	12.2	11.3	11.7	10.6
1995	9.4	10.0	11.4	10.8	9.1	12.4	10.3	9.4	9.2	10.0	10.3	12.0	10.5	9.6
1996	6.8	6.4	6.9	8.0	7.2	6.6	6.6	6.5	7.6	7.1	8.0	7.9	7.3	6.9
1997	11.2	11.9	12.9	11.7	9.7	11.9	12.1	11.0	11.7	10.3	11.3	12.8	11.9	10.8
1998	4.8	6.4	1.3	6.2	8.2	−1.1	5.2	5.8	2.3	5.6	9.6	−2.4	5.7	5.2
1999	5.6	6.1	7.2	7.9	9.0	−0.4	6.4	5.7	5.4	6.5	10.8	−0.2	7.2	6.1
2000	12.6	12.6	20.6	14.8	12.2	13.9	14.4	12.1	13.9	12.6	14.0	17.3	14.6	12.6
2001	−0.3	−1.0	−2.1	−0.1	−0.6	3.8	−1.3	−0.3	−0.1	0.5	−1.1	2.9	−0.6	0.2
2002	..	2.5	8.1	..	2.4	..	3.8	2.4	..	..	2.7	..	..	..
1996 Q3	7.1	6.7	7.3	8.1	7.7	4.6	6.9	6.6	8.3	6.8	8.8	6.3	7.5	6.9
Q4	9.2	8.2	9.7	9.0	8.5	7.8	8.5	8.9	9.9	8.3	8.9	9.4	8.8	8.7
1997 Q1	8.8	8.0	12.3	9.3	7.3	10.8	9.0	7.6	11.7	8.3	8.2	12.2	9.2	8.5
Q2	12.6	13.1	14.5	12.8	10.5	13.3	13.4	12.4	13.0	11.3	12.2	14.3	13.1	11.9
Q3	12.6	14.0	13.6	12.9	10.5	13.3	13.9	12.9	11.9	11.3	12.4	14.0	13.4	12.0
Q4	10.8	12.3	11.4	11.8	10.4	10.3	12.1	11.1	10.2	10.4	12.3	10.6	11.9	10.6
1998 Q1	9.5	11.2	6.4	10.0	11.0	4.1	10.1	10.8	6.0	9.0	12.6	3.6	10.0	9.2
Q2	5.2	6.9	1.7	6.7	8.2	0.1	5.7	6.2	2.4	6.0	9.7	−1.1	6.2	5.6
Q3	2.5	4.2	−1.3	4.2	6.9	−3.5	2.9	3.3	0.4	4.0	8.0	−5.2	3.6	3.2
Q4	2.0	3.4	−1.8	3.7	6.6	−5.2	2.2	2.7	0.2	3.3	8.0	−7.0	3.0	2.7
1999 Q1	1.7	2.9	−1.2	3.9	6.2	−4.2	2.0	1.9	1.3	3.4	7.7	−6.3	3.0	2.6
Q2	3.7	4.0	3.3	6.2	7.9	−2.5	3.9	3.7	3.7	5.2	9.6	−3.3	5.0	4.4
Q3	7.2	7.2	11.0	9.1	9.7	0.4	8.0	7.1	7.3	7.3	11.6	1.9	8.6	7.2
Q4	9.8	10.4	15.8	12.4	12.1	4.6	11.6	10.0	9.4	10.2	14.3	7.0	12.0	10.0
2000 Q1	13.5	13.5	22.5	14.7	13.3	10.2	15.5	13.4	13.7	12.5	15.0	13.7	15.1	13.0
Q2	13.8	13.9	24.2	15.7	13.2	14.0	16.2	13.1	15.7	13.4	15.1	17.8	16.0	13.6
Q3	12.7	12.6	20.3	16.1	12.9	16.9	14.3	12.0	14.6	13.9	14.7	20.3	15.2	13.3
Q4	10.5	10.4	15.3	12.6	9.5	14.7	11.5	10.1	11.6	10.8	11.1	17.4	12.1	10.6
2001 Q1	6.2	6.6	6.6	7.3	5.7	9.5	6.6	6.3	5.9	6.7	6.2	10.8	7.0	6.4
Q2	0.7	0.2	−1.0	1.0	0.2	4.9	−0.1	0.7	0.5	1.4	−0.1	4.2	0.5	1.0
Q3	−3.0	−4.4	−6.3	−3.7	−3.6	1.0	−4.8	−3.0	−2.9	−2.5	−4.5	−1.2	−4.2	−2.7
Q4	−4.9	−6.3	−7.8	−5.0	−4.5	−0.4	−6.7	−5.2	−4.0	−3.4	−5.8	−2.3	−5.8	−4.1
2002 Q1	−2.8	−4.8	−1.3	−2.6	−3.2	1.9	−4.0	−3.9	0.4	−1.9	−3.8	1.0	−3.3	−2.4
Q2	3.3	2.6	6.1	2.8	1.9	4.6	3.4	2.4	5.7	2.6	2.1	5.0	3.1	2.9
Q3	6.6	6.4	11.7	6.1	5.0	6.3	7.6	5.5	9.6	5.3	5.8	7.2	6.9	6.0
Q4	..	6.0	15.7	..	6.0	..	8.3	5.5	..	..	6.6	..	..	..
2003 Q1	..	4.0	..	..	..	..	..	..	..	..	6.1	..	..	..

Percentage change on previous quarter

	ILJN	ILJO	ILJP	ILJQ	ILJR	ILJS	ILJT	ILJU	ILJV	ILJW	ILJX	ILJY	ILJZ	ILKA
1996 Q3	2.6	2.3	3.4	2.7	2.5	2.1	2.5	2.3	3.4	2.4	2.8	2.3	2.6	2.5
Q4	2.9	2.8	3.2	2.6	2.0	3.7	2.9	3.0	2.9	2.5	2.1	3.9	2.8	2.7
1997 Q1	1.7	2.0	3.8	2.8	1.2	4.2	2.4	1.1	3.2	2.0	2.0	4.6	2.6	1.8
Q2	4.8	5.4	3.5	4.1	4.5	2.7	4.9	5.5	3.0	4.0	4.7	2.7	4.5	4.4
Q3	2.7	3.1	2.5	2.8	2.5	2.1	3.0	2.8	2.3	2.3	3.0	2.1	2.9	2.5
Q4	1.3	1.3	1.2	1.7	2.0	0.9	1.3	1.3	1.3	1.7	2.0	0.8	1.5	1.5
1998 Q1	0.4	1.0	−0.9	1.1	1.7	−1.6	0.6	0.9	−0.7	0.8	2.3	−2.0	0.9	0.6
Q2	0.7	1.3	−1.1	1.0	1.9	−1.2	0.8	1.1	−0.5	1.1	2.0	−1.8	0.9	0.9
Q3	0.1	0.5	−0.5	0.4	1.2	−1.6	0.3	−	0.3	0.4	1.4	−2.2	0.4	0.3
Q4	0.8	0.6	0.6	1.2	1.7	−0.9	0.6	0.7	1.1	1.0	2.0	−1.2	0.9	0.9
1999 Q1	0.2	0.5	−0.2	1.3	1.3	−0.6	0.4	0.1	0.4	0.8	2.1	−1.2	0.8	0.5
Q2	2.7	2.4	3.4	3.2	3.6	0.5	2.6	3.0	1.8	2.8	3.8	1.3	2.9	2.7
Q3	3.4	3.6	7.0	3.2	2.9	1.3	4.3	3.3	3.8	2.5	3.2	3.0	3.7	2.9
Q4	3.3	3.5	4.9	4.3	3.9	3.3	3.8	3.3	3.1	3.7	4.4	3.8	4.1	3.5
2000 Q1	3.5	3.4	5.6	3.3	2.4	4.7	3.9	3.2	4.3	2.9	2.8	5.0	3.6	3.2
Q2	3.0	2.7	4.8	4.1	3.5	4.0	3.2	2.7	3.7	3.6	3.9	4.9	3.7	3.3
Q3	2.4	2.4	3.7	3.4	2.6	3.9	2.7	2.2	2.7	2.9	2.9	5.2	3.1	2.6
Q4	1.3	1.5	0.5	1.2	0.8	1.4	1.3	1.6	0.5	0.9	1.2	1.3	1.2	1.1
2001 Q1	−0.5	−0.2	−2.4	−1.6	−1.2	−	−0.7	−0.3	−1.0	−0.9	−1.8	−0.9	−1.1	−0.7
Q2	−2.4	−3.5	−2.7	−2.0	−1.9	−0.4	−3.3	−2.7	−1.6	−1.5	−2.3	−1.3	−2.6	−2.0
Q3	−1.4	−2.3	−1.8	−1.3	−1.3	−	−2.2	−1.6	−0.8	−1.0	−1.7	−0.3	−1.7	−1.2
Q4	−0.7	−0.6	−1.1	−0.1	−0.1	−	−0.7	−0.7	−0.6	−0.1	−0.2	0.2	−0.4	−0.4
2002 Q1	1.7	1.5	4.5	0.9	0.1	2.3	2.2	1.0	3.4	0.7	0.3	2.5	1.5	1.2
Q2	3.7	4.0	4.6	3.4	3.2	2.3	4.1	3.7	3.7	3.0	3.7	2.5	3.8	3.3
Q3	1.8	1.3	3.4	1.9	1.7	1.6	1.8	1.3	2.9	1.7	1.9	1.8	1.8	1.7
Q4	..	−0.9	2.4	..	0.9	..	−0.1	−0.7	..	..	0.6	..	..	..
2003 Q1	..	−0.4	..	..	..	..	..	..	..	..	−0.2	..	..	..

1 Data used in the World and OECD aggregates refer to Germany after unification

Source: OECD - SNA93

Corporate services price index (experimental)
Quarter 4 2003

What is the CSPI?

The experimental Corporate Services Price Index (CSPI) measures movements in prices charged for services supplied by businesses to other businesses, local and national government. The data produced are used internally by ONS as a deflator for the Index of Services and the quarterly measurement of Gross Domestic Product (GDP). It is also used by the Treasury and Bank of England to help monitor inflation in the economy.

Results for Quarter 4, 2003

Prices of business–to–business services rose by 2.9 per cent in the year to the fourth quarter 2003, compared to 3.1 per cent in the year to the previous quarter. This is based on a comparison of the change in the top–level CSPI at the *net* sector level. (The net sector data series is the equivalent of the CSPI top–level index, *including property rentals,* shown in previous releases.)

Figure 1 shows how the percentage change for the top–level CSPI (net sector) compares with the Retail Price Index (RPI) and the Producer Price Index (PPI) for all manufactured goods (net sector).

The top–level results, on both the gross and net sector bases, are shown in Table 1. In Q4 2003, the top–level CSPI (net sector) rose by 0.6 per cent compared to the previous quarter.

Figure 2 depicts the CSPI annual growths for both the net and gross sector time series. The net CSPI growth has shown a decline from a value of 3.1 per cent in Q3 2003 to a value of 2.9 per cent in Q4 2003. The annual growth decline is similar to the CSPI gross series, which shows a decline from a value of 2.6 per cent in Q3 2003 to a value of 2.5 per cent in Q4 2003. The difference in annual growth between the gross sector and net sector CSPI is 0.4 per cent this quarter.

Corporate services price index (experimental) Quarter 4 2003

Figure 1
Experimental top–level CSPI compared with the Retail Price Index (RPI) for services and the Producer Price Index (PPI)

Percentage change on the same quarter a year ago.

Figure 2
Experimental top–level CSPI (gross and net sector)

Percentage change on the same quarter a year ago.

Table 1

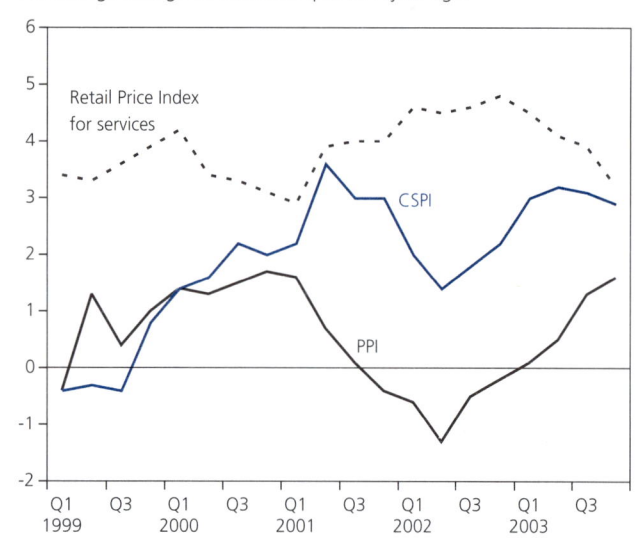

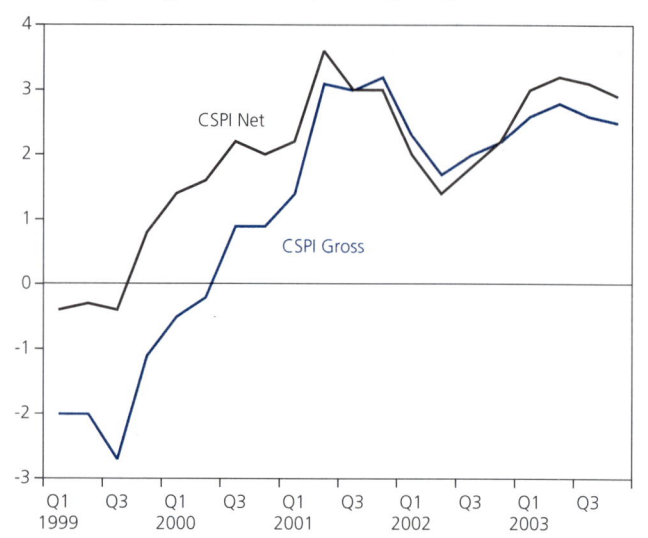

		CSPI Quarterly Index Values 2000=100		Percentage change on same quarter in previous year (per cent)	
		Gross sector	Net sector	Gross sector	Net sector
1999	Q1	100.4	98.1	−2.0	−0.4
	Q2	99.8	98.0	−2.0	−0.3
	Q3	99.3	98.1	−2.7	−0.4
	Q4	99.4	98.7	−1.1	0.8
2000	Q1	99.8	99.5	−0.5	1.4
	Q2	99.6	99.5	−0.2	1.6
	Q3	100.2	100.3	0.9	2.2
	Q4	100.3	100.7	0.9	2.0
2001	Q1	101.3	101.6	1.4	2.2
	Q2	102.7	103.1	3.1	3.6
	Q3	103.2	103.3	3.0	3.0
	Q4	103.5	103.7	3.2	3.0
2002	Q1	103.6	103.7	2.3	2.0
	Q2	104.5	104.6	1.7	1.4
	Q3	105.3	105.2	2.0	1.8
	Q4	105.8	106.0	2.2	2.2
2003	Q1	106.3	106.8	2.6	3.0
	Q2	107.4	107.9	2.8	3.2
	Q3	108.0	108.5	2.6	3.1
	Q4	108.5	109.1	2.5	2.9

Industry–specific indices

The tables attached at the end of this release contain the data for the thirty–two industries for which indices of corporate services prices are currently available. The weights for each industry index are shown at both gross and net sector levels. Some key points to note are:

- prices for the business use of *hotels* rose by 4.8 per cent this quarter (an annual increase of 8.0 per cent)

- *security services* rose by 1.5 per cent this quarter (an increase of 6.1 per cent over the year): survey respondents state that this is due, in part, to increases in the minimum wage and general price reviews

- *commercial film processing* rose by 2.5 per cent as the full impact of price increases introduced during quarter 3 2003 took effect

- *adult education* rose by 1.8 per cent (an annual increase of 5.6 per cent).

Background notes

At this release, important and substantial changes have been introduced. In summary, the key points are:

1. The experimental Corporate Service Price Index (CSPI) has been rebased to the year 2000. The rebased series was published with the Q4 2003 release on 20 February 2004. ONS has taken this opportunity to implement a number of improvements to the CSPI, which have been introduced with the rebased series.

2. For the first time, the CSPI was released as both net and gross sector time–series, aligning with the PPI release format. The net series is scoped to monitor the corporate–service activity provided to other businesses and government organisations, *outside* the corporate–services sector. The gross series is scoped to monitor the provision of corporate services to *all* businesses and government organisations. The previous practice of publishing the headline CSPI, both including and excluding *property rental payments*, arose from the high weighting this industry received in the 1995 based series. The 2000 rebasing of CSPI has assigned a smaller weight against *property rental payments* through the introduction of the Office for National Statistics (ONS) Annual Business Inquiry (ABI) data as a source for the weight.

3. Many aspects of the methods and sources used to compile the CSPI have been reviewed and updated. We have also introduced a redeveloped business–telecommunications index and new banking (loans and interest bearing deposits) index. The introduction of the new index has increased the number of published, industry–level CSPIs to thirty two, providing coverage of an estimated fifty–five per cent of net corporate service activity in the UK. ONS has also expanded substantially the survey of businesses on which the CSPI is based. We now survey 1,500 businesses, seeking price quotes for 5,000 service–products. The improvements have led to revisions from 1995, the first date for which CSPI information is available.

4. An article describing the methodology and associated impact of rebasing is available from the National Statistics website; www.statistics.gov.uk/cspi. A further two articles describe the changes to the business telecommunications index and the new banking index. We have also announced the provisional publication dates of the CSPI for a period of one year ahead of the current releases.

Note: Measurement of service sector prices is inherently difficult and challenging. When viewing the results, **it should be borne in mind that the indices shown are regarded as experimental**. This is particularly true of those that have been added to the series most recently. Therefore, some of the results will be subject to revision before the completion of the CSPI development project. The top–level index should also be viewed as **experimental**.

Next results

The next set of CSPI results will be issued on 14 May 2004 via the National Statistics website; www.statistics.gov.uk/cspi.

Further information

- Articles on the methodology and impact of rebasing the CSPI, the redevelopment of an index for business telecommunications and the introduction of an index for banking services (together with more general information on the CSPI) are available at www.statistics.gov.uk/cspi

- Inquiry Contact:
  Keith Hermiston
  Office for National Statistics
  Tel: (01633) 813493
  E–mail: cspi@ons.gsi.gov.uk

Note to the main table

There are external sources for the indices denoted by an asterisk, as follows:

Index	Source
Banking Services	Bank of England
Property rental payments (IPD)	Investment Property Databank
Car contract hire and Maintenance and repair of motor vehicles	Yewtree.com Ltd
Construction plant hire	Construction Plant–hire Association (CPA) up to Quarter 2 of 2002
Business telecommunications	Ofcom (Office of Communications)
Sewerage services	Ofwat (Office of Water Services)
National post parcels	Parcelforce
Business rail fares	Strategic Rail Authority (SRA)

TABLE 2
Corporate Services Price Indices (Experimental) (2000=100)

	Maintenance and repair of motor vehicles*	Hotels	Canteens and catering	Business rail fares*	Rail Freight	Bus and coach hire	Freight transport by road Total	International component
SIC(2003)	50.2	55.1	55.50	60.10/1	60.10/2	60.23/1	60.24	
2000 weights (per cent)								
Gross sector	2.93	3.69	3.03	0.32	0.62	0.12	12.72	
Net sector	2.08	4.08	3.36	0.16	1.03	0.20	21.15	
Annual								
1999	97.8	97.7	99.9	95.7	101.0	93.9	95.6	97.5
2000	100.0	100.0	100.0	100.0	100.0	100.0	100.0	100.0
2001	102.9	104.3	104.2	103.1	100.5	106.8	102.9	100.3
2002	106.1	104.3	105.4	106.1	102.1	114.7	103.9	99.3
2003	110.2	109.5	106.6	109.8	103.5	120.8	106.1	99.3
Percentage change, latest year on previous year								
1999	2.2	−2.2	0.2	4.9	1.4	6.5	1.8	0.9
2000	2.3	2.3	0.1	4.5	−1.0	6.5	4.6	2.6
2001	2.9	4.3	4.2	3.1	0.5	6.8	2.9	0.3
2002	3.1	0.0	1.1	2.9	1.6	7.4	1.0	−1.0
2003	3.9	5.0	1.1	3.5	1.4	5.3	2.1	0.1
Quarterly results (not seasonally adjusted)								
1999 Q1	96.7	100.0	99.9	95.7	100.5	92.3	93.9	97.7
Q2	97.6	96.8	100.4	95.7	101.2	93.1	95.2	97.4
Q3	98.0	96.8	99.8	95.7	101.2	93.8	95.8	97.4
Q4	98.7	97.1	99.4	95.7	101.2	96.5	97.6	97.4
2000 Q1	99.1	98.8	99.1	100.0	101.8	98.1	98.9	99.5
Q2	99.6	100.1	100.1	100.0	99.4	99.9	99.3	99.5
Q3	100.2	100.7	100.1	100.0	99.4	100.6	100.2	100.0
Q4	101.2	100.5	100.7	100.0	99.4	101.4	101.6	101.0
2001 Q1	102.0	102.9	103.2	103.1	100.3	103.4	102.5	100.9
Q2	102.8	104.7	104.4	103.1	101.1	105.1	103.0	100.2
Q3	103.5	104.5	104.5	103.1	100.5	108.1	103.1	99.8
Q4	103.3	104.9	104.6	103.1	100.1	110.8	103.0	100.1
2002 Q1	104.9	103.7	104.7	106.1	101.3	111.7	102.9	99.6
Q2	105.5	103.4	105.3	106.1	102.1	113.3	103.6	99.4
Q3	106.6	104.0	105.7	106.1	102.4	116.4	104.3	99.7
Q4	107.4	106.0	105.7	106.1	102.5	117.4	104.9	98.3
2003 Q1	108.9	107.2	106.1	109.8	102.7	119.2	105.6	99.3
Q2	109.8	107.2	106.4	109.8	103.4	120.8	106.1	99.3
Q3	110.4	109.1	106.7	109.8	103.6	121.6	106.3	99.5
Q4	111.7	114.4	107.0	109.8	104.2	121.5	106.6	99.1

TABLE 2 – *continued*

	Maintenance and repair of motor vehicles*	Hotels	Canteens and catering	Business rail fares*	Rail Freight	Bus and coach hire	Freight transport by road Total	International component
SIC(2003)	50.2	55.1	55.50	60.10/1	60.10/2	60.23/1	60.24	
Percentage change, latest quarter on previous quarter								
1999 Q1	0.9	−0.8	−0.3	4.9	1.1	2.5	−0.1	0.9
Q2	0.9	−3.2	0.5	0.0	0.7	0.9	1.3	−0.3
Q3	0.4	0.0	−0.6	0.0	0.0	0.8	0.6	0.0
Q4	0.7	0.4	−0.3	0.0	0.1	2.9	1.9	0.0
2000 Q1	0.3	1.7	−0.4	4.5	0.5	1.6	1.3	2.2
Q2	0.5	1.3	1.1	0.0	−2.3	1.9	0.5	0.0
Q3	0.6	0.6	0.0	0.0	0.0	0.7	0.9	0.5
Q4	1.0	−0.2	0.5	0.0	0.0	0.8	1.4	0.9
2001 Q1	0.8	2.4	2.5	3.1	0.9	1.9	0.9	−0.1
Q2	0.8	1.8	1.2	0.0	0.8	1.7	0.5	−0.6
Q3	0.6	−0.2	0.1	0.0	−0.6	2.8	0.1	−0.4
Q4	−0.2	0.3	0.1	0.0	−0.4	2.5	0.0	0.3
2002 Q1	1.5	−1.1	0.0	2.9	1.2	0.9	−0.1	−0.5
Q2	0.6	−0.3	0.6	0.0	0.8	1.4	0.7	−0.2
Q3	1.0	0.6	0.4	0.0	0.2	2.8	0.6	0.3
Q4	0.8	1.9	0.0	0.0	0.1	0.9	0.5	−1.4
2003 Q1	1.5	1.2	0.4	3.5	0.2	1.5	0.7	1.0
Q2	0.8	0.0	0.2	0.0	0.7	1.3	0.5	0.0
Q3	0.6	1.8	0.3	0.0	0.2	0.6	0.2	0.1
Q4	1.2	4.8	0.2	0.0	0.5	0.0	0.3	−0.3
Percentage change, latest quarter on corresponding quarter of previous year								
1999 Q1	1.9	1.0	1.0	4.9	0.7	6.5	−0.3	1.5
Q2	1.9	−2.8	0.7	4.9	1.1	6.0	1.8	0.7
Q3	2.2	−3.2	0.0	4.9	1.8	6.2	2.1	0.6
Q4	3.0	−3.6	−0.7	4.9	1.9	7.2	3.8	0.6
2000 Q1	2.5	−1.3	−0.8	4.5	1.3	6.3	5.2	1.9
Q2	2.0	3.3	−0.2	4.5	−1.7	7.3	4.3	2.2
Q3	2.2	4	0.4	4.5	−1.8	7.2	4.6	2.7
Q4	2.5	3.4	1.2	4.5	−1.8	5.1	4.1	3.7
2001 Q1	2.9	4.2	4.2	3.1	−1.4	5.4	3.7	1.4
Q2	3.2	4.7	4.3	3.1	1.6	5.3	3.7	0.7
Q3	3.3	3.8	4.3	3.1	1.1	7.4	2.8	−0.2
Q4	2.1	4.4	4.0	3.1	0.7	9.2	1.4	−0.9
2002 Q1	2.8	0.7	1.4	2.9	1.0	8.1	0.4	−1.2
Q2	2.6	−1.3	0.9	2.9	1.0	7.7	0.6	−0.8
Q3	3.0	−0.5	1.2	2.9	1.9	7.7	1.2	−0.2
Q4	3.9	1.0	1.0	2.9	2.4	6.0	1.8	−1.8
2003 Q1	3.9	3.3	1.4	3.5	1.3	6.7	2.6	−0.3
Q2	4.0	3.7	1.0	3.5	1.3	6.7	2.3	−0.1
Q3	3.6	5.0	1.0	3.5	1.2	4.4	1.9	−0.2
Q4	4.1	8.0	1.2	3.5	1.6	3.5	1.7	0.9

TABLE 2 – *continued*
Corporate Services Price Indices (Experimental) (2000=100)

	Commercial vehicle ferries	Sea and coastal water freight	Business air fares	Freight forwarding	National post parcels*	Courier services	Business telecomm- ications*	Banking services*
SIC(2003)	61.10/1	61.10/2	62.10/1	63.4	64.11	64.12	64.2	65.12
2000 weights (per cent)								
Gross sector	0.29	0.73	3.28	7.48	3.48	2.42	11.84	2.90
Net sector	0.37	0.92	1.59	6.20	1.81	1.26	5.39	3.23
Annual								
1999	98.1	97.3	94.7	99.1	96.0	99.8	119.1	90.8
2000	100.0	100.0	100.0	100.0	100.0	100.0	100.0	100.0
2001	98.7	100.7	115.1	100.4	103.0	102.7	92.6	108.2
2002	100.6	95.0	122.8	99.8	107.1	107.1	90.6	116.5
2003	102.8	96.2	127.3	104.1	113.3	109.2	87.9	125.3
Percentage change, latest year on previous year								
1999	11.3	−1.8	2.4	−7.1	2.9	1.4	−17.7	..
2000	1.9	2.8	5.6	0.9	4.1	0.2	−16.0	10.2
2001	−1.3	0.7	15.1	0.4	3.0	2.7	−7.4	8.2
2002	2.0	−5.7	6.7	−0.6	3.9	4.2	−2.2	7.7
2003	2.1	1.2	3.7	4.3	5.9	2.0	−3.0	7.6
Quarterly results (not seasonally adjusted)								
1999 Q1	100.6	99.9	93.8	101.6	94.6	99.4	129.7	90.1
Q2	98.7	98.6	94.8	99.1	96.5	99.9	121.3	89.0
Q3	97.7	95.9	94.8	97.5	96.5	100.2	115.0	92.0
Q4	95.5	94.8	95.4	98.3	96.5	99.5	110.5	92.0
2000 Q1	100.9	96.8	96.2	98.9	96.5	98.6	107.0	94.9
Q2	99.8	98.8	98.0	99.3	101.2	99.2	99.6	99.3
Q3	100.4	101.7	100.0	100.5	101.2	100.0	99.1	103.8
Q4	98.9	102.7	105.8	101.2	101.2	102.2	94.3	102.0
2001 Q1	101.5	103.9	111.9	102.2	101.1	100.4	93.1	101.4
Q2	99.0	101.6	113.1	100.6	103.7	101.5	92.8	109.0
Q3	97.0	99.9	116.8	99.4	103.7	104.2	93.7	106.7
Q4	97.3	97.5	118.5	99.4	103.7	104.8	90.8	115.7
2002 Q1	101.8	96.4	120.7	98.5	103.7	106.0	88.3	113.6
Q2	100.5	94.1	122.2	99.5	108.2	106.6	89.5	117.8
Q3	100.6	94.1	123.3	100.4	108.2	107.7	93.0	113.4
Q4	99.6	95.4	124.8	100.9	108.2	107.9	91.4	121.3
2003 Q1	102.6	98.8	124.9	102.2	108.2	108.6	88.2	122.5
Q2	102.8	97.4	127.1	104.4	115.0	109.4	87.3	125.8
Q3	102.8	94.5	128.5	104.7	115.0	109.3	88.2	125.7
Q4	102.8	94.0	128.6	105.1	115.0	109.4	87.8	127.4

TABLE 2 – *continued*

	Commercial vehicle ferries	Sea and coastal water freight	Business air fares	Freight forwarding	National post parcels*	Courier services	Business telecomm-unications*	Banking services*
SIC(2003)	61.10/1	61.10/2	62.10/1	63.4	64.11	64.12	64.2	65.12
Percentage change, latest quarter on previous quarter								
1999 Q1	13.7	0.3	0.4	−2.0	0.0	0.3	−1.6	..
Q2	−2.0	−1.3	1.1	−2.4	2.0	0.5	−6.5	−1.2
Q3	−1.0	−2.8	0.0	−1.6	0.0	0.3	−5.2	3.4
Q4	−2.2	−1.1	0.6	0.7	0.0	−0.6	−3.9	−0.1
2000 Q1	5.6	2.1	0.8	0.7	0.0	−0.9	−3.2	3.2
Q2	−1.0	2.1	2.0	0.4	4.8	0.6	−6.9	4.7
Q3	0.6	2.9	2.0	1.2	0.0	0.8	−0.6	4.5
Q4	−1.4	1.0	5.8	0.7	0.0	2.1	−4.8	−1.7
2001 Q1	2.6	1.2	5.8	1.0	0.0	−1.8	−1.3	−0.5
Q2	−2.5	−2.2	1.1	−1.6	2.5	1.1	−0.3	7.4
Q3	−2.0	−1.7	3.3	−1.2	0.0	2.6	1.0	−2.1
Q4	0.3	−2.4	1.4	−0.1	0.0	0.6	−3.2	8.5
2002 Q1	4.6	−1.1	1.9	−0.9	0.0	1.2	−2.7	−1.8
Q2	−1.3	−2.4	1.2	1.0	4.4	0.6	1.3	3.6
Q3	0.1	0.1	0.9	0.9	0.0	0.9	4.0	−3.7
Q4	−1.0	1.3	1.2	0.5	0.0	0.2	−1.8	6.9
2003 Q1	3.0	3.6	0.1	1.3	0.0	0.6	−3.5	1.0
Q2	0.2	−1.4	1.7	2.2	6.3	0.7	−1.0	2.7
Q3	0.0	−3.0	1.1	0.2	0.0	−0.1	1.0	−0.1
Q4	0.0	−0.5	0.1	0.4	0.0	0.1	−0.5	1.4
Percentage change, latest quarter on corresponding quarter of previous year								
1999 Q1	15.1	1.2	4.0	−6.8	5.6	2.2	−16.7	..
Q2	11.9	2.8	1.9	−8.3	2.0	1.2	−16.8	..
Q3	10.3	−6.0	1.6	−8.2	2.0	1.5	−21.1	..
Q4	8.0	−4.8	2.1	−5.2	2.0	0.5	−16.2	..
2000 Q1	0.2	−3.1	2.5	−2.6	2.0	−0.7	−17.5	5.3
Q2	1.2	0.2	3.4	0.2	4.8	−0.7	−17.8	11.6
Q3	2.8	6.1	5.5	3.0	4.8	−0.2	−13.8	12.7
Q4	3.6	8.3	10.9	3.0	4.8	2.6	−14.7	10.9
2001 Q1	0.6	7.3	16.4	3.4	4.8	1.7	−13.0	6.9
Q2	−0.9	2.8	15.4	1.3	2.5	2.3	−6.9	9.7
Q3	−3.4	−1.8	16.8	−1.1	2.5	4.1	−5.4	2.8
Q4	−1.6	−5.1	12.0	−1.8	2.5	2.6	−3.8	13.5
2002 Q1	0.3	−7.2	7.8	−3.6	2.5	5.7	−5.1	12.0
Q2	1.5	−7.5	8.0	−1.1	4.4	5.1	−3.6	8.1
Q3	3.7	−5.8	5.6	0.9	4.4	3.3	−0.7	6.3
Q4	2.4	−2.1	5.3	1.5	4.4	3.0	0.7	4.8
2003 Q1	0.8	2.5	3.5	3.7	4.4	2.4	−0.1	7.8
Q2	2.3	3.6	4.0	4.9	6.3	2.6	−2.4	6.8
Q3	2.2	0.3	4.2	4.3	6.3	1.5	−5.2	10.8
Q4	3.2	−1.5	3.1	4.2	6.3	1.4	−4.0	5.1

TABLE 2 – continued
Corporate Services Price Indices (Experimental) (2000=100)

	Property rentals*	Real estate agency activities	Car contract hire*	Construction plant hire*	Market research	Technical testing	Employment agencies
SIC(2003)	70.2	70.3	71.1	71.32	74.13	74.3	74.5
2000 weights							
Gross sector	7.88	3.71	2.54	2.38	1.15	0.77	14.39
Net sector	12.33	1.56	3.56	5.69	0.98	0.97	6.59
Annual							
1999	94.6	93.9	97.1	95.1	97.7	98.7	97.8
2000	100.0	100.0	100.0	100.0	100.0	100.0	100.0
2001	106.5	101.9	94.9	104.2	102.6	103.8	107.1
2002	111.0	102.6	94.6	102.0	107.0	107.2	112.0
2003	115.6	105.8	89.8	108.2	109.8	111.0	114.8
Percentage change, latest year on previous year							
1999	5.4	4.9	1.7	4.1	..	0.4	4.0
2000	5.7	6.5	3.0	5.1	2.4	1.3	2.3
2001	6.5	1.9	−5.1	4.2	2.6	3.8	7.1
2002	4.3	0.7	−0.3	−2.1	4.3	3.3	4.6
2003	4.1	3.1	−5.1	6.1	2.6	3.6	2.5
Quarterly results (not seasonally adjusted)							
1999 Q1	92.5	90.9	95.6	96.4	97.2	98.7	96.8
Q2	93.7	93.6	95.9	93.9	97.3	98.6	97.9
Q3	95.4	95.1	97.4	94.3	97.9	98.7	97.9
Q4	96.8	96.0	99.2	96.0	98.3	99.0	98.4
2000 Q1	98.0	98.5	100.1	96.6	99.7	99.3	99.3
Q2	99.3	99.7	100.5	100.8	100.0	99.6	99.9
Q3	100.6	100.6	100.0	101.7	100.5	100.0	100.1
Q4	102.2	101.3	99.4	100.9	99.8	101.1	100.7
2001 Q1	104.1	101.9	97.3	101.8	102.3	101.7	102.7
Q2	105.7	101.9	94.5	108.0	102.6	104.2	106.8
Q3	107.2	101.9	94.1	105.0	102.7	104.3	108.7
Q4	108.8	101.8	93.7	101.9	103.0	104.9	110.0
2002 Q1	109.6	101.5	94.1	100.3	106.4	106.0	111.6
Q2	110.7	102.0	94.3	101.4	106.5	106.3	111.9
Q3	111.3	103.0	94.5	102.9	106.9	107.6	112.4
Q4	112.5	103.8	95.5	103.3	108.3	108.9	112.2
2003 Q1	113.4	103.9	94.4	106.5	109.1	109.9	113.5
Q2	115.5	104.9	87.5	108.4	109.3	110.5	115.1
Q3	116.3	106.7	88.1	108.8	110.3	111.7	115.5
Q4	117.1	107.6	89.0	109.1	110.6	111.9	115.3

TABLE 2 – *continued*

	Property rentals*	Real estate agency activites	Car contract hire*	Construction plant hire*	Market research	Technical testing	Employment agencies
SIC(2003)	70.2	70.3	71.1	71.32	74.13	74.3	74.5
Percentage change, latest quarter on previous quarter							
1999 Q1	1.5	0.3	0.5	6.3	3.0	0.3	1.4
Q2	1.3	3.0	0.3	−2.6	0.1	−0.1	1.1
Q3	1.8	1.6	1.6	0.5	0.6	0.1	0.1
Q4	1.5	0.9	1.9	1.8	0.4	0.3	0.5
2000 Q1	1.2	2.6	0.9	0.7	1.4	0.4	0.9
Q2	1.3	1.2	0.4	4.3	0.3	0.2	0.6
Q3	1.3	0.9	−0.5	0.8	0.5	0.5	0.2
Q4	1.6	0.7	−0.6	−0.7	−0.7	1.1	0.6
2001 Q1	1.9	0.6	−2.1	0.9	2.5	0.6	2.0
Q2	1.5	0.0	−2.9	6.1	0.3	2.5	4.0
Q3	1.4	0.0	−0.4	−2.7	0.0	0.1	1.8
Q4	1.5	−0.1	−0.5	−3.0	0.4	0.6	1.2
2002 Q1	0.8	−0.3	0.5	−1.5	3.2	1.0	1.4
Q2	1.0	0.5	0.2	1.0	0.1	0.3	0.3
Q3	0.5	0.9	0.2	1.5	0.4	1.2	0.4
Q4	1.1	0.8	1.1	0.4	1.2	1.3	−0.2
2003 Q1	0.8	0.1	−1.1	3.1	0.8	0.9	1.1
Q2	1.8	1.0	−7.3	1.9	0.2	0.6	1.4
Q3	0.7	1.7	0.6	0.3	0.9	1.1	0.4
Q4	0.7	0.8	1.1	0.3	0.2	0.2	−0.2
Percentage change, latest quarter on corresponding quarter of previous year							
1999 Q1	4.7	3.5	0.2	4.0	..	0.4	5.2
Q2	5.1	4.8	−0.3	2.8	..	0.3	4.6
Q3	5.8	5.2	2.7	4.0	4.4	0.3	3.4
Q4	6.2	5.9	4.2	5.9	4.2	0.6	3.0
2000 Q1	5.9	8.3	4.7	0.3	2.6	0.7	2.5
Q2	5.9	6.5	4.8	7.4	2.8	1.0	2.1
Q3	5.4	5.7	2.6	7.8	2.7	1.3	2.2
Q4	5.5	5.6	0.2	5.1	1.5	2.1	2.4
2001 Q1	6.3	3.5	−2.8	5.4	2.6	2.4	3.5
Q2	6.5	2.3	−6.0	7.1	2.6	4.7	7.0
Q3	6.6	1.4	−5.8	3.3	2.1	4.3	8.6
Q4	6.5	0.5	−5.8	1.0	3.3	3.8	9.3
2002 Q1	5.3	−0.4	−3.2	−1.4	4.0	4.2	8.6
Q2	4.7	0.1	−0.2	−6.1	3.8	2.0	4.8
Q3	3.8	1.0	0.3	−2.0	4.2	3.1	3.4
Q4	3.4	2.0	1.9	1.4	5.1	3.8	1.9
2003 Q1	3.5	2.4	0.3	6.1	2.6	3.7	1.7
Q2	4.3	2.8	−7.2	7.0	2.6	4.0	2.8
Q3	4.6	3.6	−6.8	5.7	3.2	3.8	2.8
Q4	4.1	3.6	−6.7	5.6	2.2	2.8	2.8

TABLE 2 – *continued*
Corporate Services Price Indices (Experimental) (2000=100)

	Security services	Industrial cleaning	Commercial film processing	Conract packaging hire	Direct marketing & secretarial services	Translation & interpretation services
SIC(2003)	74.60	74.70	74.81/9	74.82	74.83(pt)	74.83(pt)
2000 weights (per cent)						
Gross sector	1.97	2.35	0.16	0.59	0.33	0.05
Net sector	2.48	2.36	0.20	1.33	0.34	0.05
Annual						
1999	97.9	99.3	99.8	98.8	98.7	100.2
2000	100.0	100.0	100.0	100.0	100.0	100.0
2001	104.4	101.1	99.9	101.8	101.2	99.6
2002	108.2	104.0	99.9	103.1	99.7	101.5
2003	113.7	106.1	103.7	109.3	100.4	102.6
Percentage change, latest year on previous year						
1999	1.7	1.0	0.2	..	0.3	0.8
2000	2.1	0.7	0.2	1.2	1.3	−0.2
2001	4.4	1.1	−0.1	1.8	1.2	−0.4
2002	3.6	2.9	0.0	1.3	−1.5	1.9
2003	5.1	2.0	3.7	6.0	0.7	1.1
Quarterly results (not seasonally adjusted)						
1999 Q1	97.3	98.8	99.8	98.9	97.8	100.2
Q2	97.7	99.1	99.9	98.8	99.4	100.2
Q3	98.1	99.5	99.9	98.8	98.9	100.2
Q4	98.6	99.7	99.9	98.8	98.8	100.2
2000 Q1	99.0	99.9	99.9	99.6	99.9	100.2
Q2	99.7	100.0	100.0	99.4	99.9	100.2
Q3	100.4	100.0	100.0	100.7	100.3	99.9
Q4	100.9	100.1	100.0	100.3	99.9	99.6
2001 Q1	102.1	99.9	100.0	101.1	100.6	99.7
Q2	103.8	100.6	100.1	101.3	101.5	99.7
Q3	105.4	100.9	99.8	102.3	101.3	99.4
Q4	106.3	103.1	99.8	102.4	101.5	99.5
2002 Q1	107.4	103.5	99.9	102.5	100.9	101.4
Q2	107.7	103.9	99.9	102.4	99.3	101.5
Q3	108.3	104.0	99.9	103.2	99.3	101.4
Q4	109.3	104.8	99.9	104.2	99.3	101.6
2003 Q1	111.8	105.6	100.6	105.0	99.7	102.3
Q2	113.0	104.8	100.4	109.7	99.6	102.7
Q3	114.2	106.7	105.5	110.9	100.9	102.7
Q4	116.0	107.4	108.1	111.6	101.3	102.7

TABLE 2 – *continued*

	Security services	Industrial cleaning	Commercial film processing	Conract packaging hire	Direct marketing & secretarial services	Translation & interpretation services
SIC(2003)	74.60	74.7	74.81/9	74.82	74.83(pt)	74.83(pt)
Percentage change, latest quarter on previous quarter						
1999 Q1	0.1	0.3	0.1	..	0.3	0.5
Q2	0.4	0.3	0.1	−0.1	1.7	0.1
Q3	0.4	0.4	0.0	0.0	−0.5	0.0
Q4	0.5	0.2	0.0	0.0	−0.1	0.0
2000 Q1	0.4	0.2	0.1	0.8	1.1	0.0
Q2	0.7	0.2	0.1	−0.2	0.0	0.0
Q3	0.7	0.0	0.0	1.3	0.5	−0.4
Q4	0.5	0.1	0.0	−0.4	−0.4	−0.2
2001 Q1	1.2	−0.2	0.0	0.8	0.7	0.0
Q2	1.7	0.7	0.0	0.2	0.9	0.0
Q3	1.5	0.3	−0.3	1.0	−0.2	−0.3
Q4	0.9	2.2	0.0	0.1	0.2	0.2
2002 Q1	1.0	0.4	0.2	0.1	−0.6	1.8
Q2	0.3	0.4	0.0	0.0	−1.6	0.1
Q3	0.5	0.1	0.0	0.8	−0.1	0.0
Q4	0.9	0.8	0.0	0.9	0.0	0.2
2003 Q1	2.3	0.8	0.7	0.8	0.4	0.7
Q2	1.0	−0.8	−0.2	4.5	−0.1	0.5
Q3	1.1	1.8	5.0	1.0	1.3	0.0
Q4	1.5	0.7	2.5	0.6	0.3	0.0
Percentage change, latest quarter on corresponding quarter of previous year						
1999 Q1	2.3	1.1	0.2	..	−0.6	0.9
Q2	2.0	1.0	0.2	..	0.1	0.9
Q3	1.3	1.0	0.1	..	0.3	0.8
Q4	1.4	1.1	0.1	..	1.4	0.6
2000 Q1	1.7	1.0	0.1	0.7	2.2	0.1
Q2	2.1	0.9	0.1	0.6	0.4	0.0
Q3	2.3	0.5	0.2	1.9	1.5	−0.3
Q4	2.3	0.4	0.2	1.5	1.1	−0.6
2001 Q1	3.1	0.0	0.1	1.5	0.7	−0.6
Q2	4.2	0.5	0.1	1.9	1.7	−0.6
Q3	5.0	0.8	−0.3	1.6	1.0	−0.5
Q4	5.3	3.0	−0.3	2.1	1.6	−0.1
2002 Q1	5.2	3.6	−0.1	1.4	0.3	1.7
Q2	3.8	3.3	−0.1	1.1	−2.1	1.8
Q3	2.8	3.1	0.2	0.9	−2.0	2.1
Q4	2.9	1.7	0.2	1.7	−2.2	2.1
2003 Q1	4.1	2.1	0.7	2.5	−1.2	0.9
Q2	4.8	0.8	0.5	7.1	0.3	1.3
Q3	5.4	2.6	5.5	7.4	1.7	1.3
Q4	6.1	2.5	8.1	7.1	2.0	1.1

TABLE 2 – *continued*
Corporate Services Price Indices (Experimental) (2000=100)

	Adult education	Sewerage services*	Waste disposal	Commercial washing & dry cleaning	TOP –LEVEL CSPI Gross sector	Net sector
SIC(2003)	80.42	90.00/1	90.00/2	93.01		
2000 weights						
Gross sector	1.53	2.27	1.43	0.67	100	
Net sector	1.54	3.99	2.52	0.68		100
Annual						
1999	97.7	109.6	95.3	100.3	99.7	98.2
2000	100.0	100.0	100.0	100.0	100.0	100.0
2001	103.9	98.3	105.3	101.2	102.7	102.9
2002	106.8	99.1	111.3	102.0	104.8	104.9
2003	111.1	102.7	118.6	102.4	107.6	108.1
Percentage change, latest year on previous year						
1999	2.0	3.2	2.6	0.9	−2.0	−0.1
2000	2.3	−8.7	4.9	−0.3	0.3	1.8
2001	3.9	−1.7	5.3	1.2	2.7	2.9
2002	2.7	0.8	5.7	0.9	2.1	1.9
2003	4.1	3.7	6.5	0.3	2.6	3.0
Quarterly results (not seasonally adjusted)						
1999 Q1	97.3	107.1	93.1	100.0	100.4	98.1
Q2	97.6	110.4	95.5	101.0	99.8	98.0
Q3	97.8	110.4	96.3	101.1	99.3	98.1
Q4	98.3	110.4	96.3	99.1	99.4	98.7
2000 Q1	99.5	110.4	99.2	99.7	99.8	99.5
Q2	99.5	96.5	100.4	100.2	99.6	99.5
Q3	100.3	96.5	100.2	100.4	100.2	100.3
Q4	100.8	96.5	100.2	99.8	100.3	100.7
2001 Q1	101.4	96.6	101.8	100.3	101.3	101.6
Q2	104.6	98.9	104.7	101.1	102.7	103.1
Q3	104.6	98.9	106.8	101.2	103.2	103.3
Q4	105.1	98.9	107.9	102.0	103.5	103.7
2002 Q1	106.0	98.9	108.0	102.4	103.6	103.7
Q2	106.3	99.1	110.9	102.1	104.5	104.6
Q3	107.3	99.1	111.3	102.5	105.3	105.2
Q4	107.4	99.1	115.0	101.1	105.8	106.0
2003 Q1	109.3	99.1	115.7	102.4	106.3	106.8
Q2	110.2	104.0	119.8	102.2	107.4	107.9
Q3	111.4	104.0	119.4	102.2	108.0	108.5
Q4	113.4	104.0	119.5	102.7	108.5	109.1

TABLE 2 – *continued*

	Adult education	Sewerage services*	Waste disposal	Commercial washing & dry cleaning	TOP –LEVEL CSPI Gross sector	Net sector
SIC(2003)	80.42	90.00/1	90.00/2	93.01		
Percentage change, latest quarter on previous quarter						
1999 Q1	1.0	0.0	0.2	0.8	−0.1	0.2
Q2	0.3	3.0	2.6	1.0	−0.6	−0.1
Q3	0.2	0.0	0.8	0.1	−0.4	0.1
Q4	0.5	0.0	0.0	−2.1	0.1	0.6
2000 Q1	1.2	0.0	3.0	0.6	0.4	0.8
Q2	0.1	−12.5	1.2	0.5	−0.2	0.1
Q3	0.8	0.0	−0.2	0.2	0.6	0.8
Q4	0.5	0.0	−0.1	−0.6	0.1	0.4
2001 Q1	0.7	0.0	1.6	0.5	0.9	1.0
Q2	3.1	2.4	2.9	0.8	1.4	1.4
Q3	0.0	0.0	2.0	0.1	0.5	0.2
Q4	0.5	0.0	1.0	0.8	0.3	0.4
2002 Q1	0.8	0.0	0.1	0.4	0.1	0.0
Q2	0.3	0.2	2.7	−0.2	0.9	0.8
Q3	0.9	0.0	0.3	0.4	0.8	0.6
Q4	0.1	0.0	3.3	−1.4	0.5	0.8
2003 Q1	1.7	0.0	0.6	1.3	0.4	0.7
Q2	0.9	4.9	3.6	−0.2	1.0	1.1
Q3	1.0	0.0	−0.3	0.0	0.6	0.5
Q4	1.8	0.0	0.1	0.4	0.5	0.6
Percentage change, latest quarter on corresponding quarter of previous year						
1999 Q1	2.5	3.5	0.5	1.6	−2.0	−0.4
Q2	2.0	3.0	2.6	1.1	−2.0	−0.3
Q3	1.7	3.0	3.8	0.9	−2.7	−0.4
Q4	2.0	3.0	3.6	−0.1	−1.1	0.8
2000 Q1	2.2	3.0	6.5	−0.3	−0.5	1.4
Q2	2.0	−12.5	5.1	−0.8	−0.2	1.6
Q3	2.5	−12.5	4.1	−0.7	0.9	2.2
Q4	2.5	−12.5	4.0	0.7	0.9	2.0
2001 Q1	2.0	−12.5	2.6	0.6	1.4	2.2
Q2	5.1	2.5	4.3	0.9	3.1	3.6
Q3	4.3	2.5	6.6	0.9	3.0	3.0
Q4	4.3	2.5	7.7	2.2	3.2	3.0
2002 Q1	4.5	2.4	6.1	2.1	2.3	2.0
Q2	1.7	0.2	5.9	1.0	1.7	1.4
Q3	2.6	0.2	4.2	1.3	2.0	1.8
Q4	2.2	0.2	6.6	−0.9	2.2	2.2
2003 Q1	3.1	0.2	7.1	0.0	2.6	3.0
Q2	3.7	4.9	7.9	0.1	2.8	3.2
Q3	3.8	4.9	7.3	−0.3	2.6	3.1
Q4	5.6	4.9	3.9	1.5	2.5	2.9

Consumer Price Inflation since 1750

Jim O'Donoghue and Louise Goulding
Office for National Statistics
Grahame Allen
House of Commons Library

This article presents a composite price index covering the period since 1750 which can be used for analysis of consumer price inflation, or the purchasing power of the pound, over long periods of time. The index is based on both official and unofficial sources and replaces previous long-run inflation indices produced by the ONS, the Bank of England and the House of Commons Library. It shows that:

- between 1750 and 2003, prices rose by around 140 times

- most of the increase in prices has occurred since the Second World War: between 1750 and 1938, a period spanning nearly two centuries, prices rose by a little over three times; since then they have increased more than forty-fold.

Put another way, the index shows that one decimal penny in 1750 would have had greater purchasing power than one pound in 2003.

Background

Researchers are often interested in knowing how consumer price inflation, or the purchasing power of the pound, has changed over a period of time. Typically, researchers want to revalue sums of money from a period in the past to today's prices, or to compare how much a pound could buy at different periods in time, often spanning a century or more. This type of question can be answered by reference to an appropriate price index. Unfortunately, there is no single source available for making comparisons over long periods of time, and a composite index has to be specially constructed for this purpose. This will often involve choices. For instance, in recent periods, the ONS has published two direct measures of consumer price inflation – the retail prices index and the consumer prices index (which was published as the harmonised index of consumer prices until December 2003, when it became the basis for the Government's target measure of inflation) – and one indirect measure, a household expenditure deflator derived from the National Accounts.

This article presents a composite price index covering the period since 1750, which allows long-run comparisons to be made of consumer price inflation and the purchasing power of the pound. It replaces similar indices that have been published in the past by the Office for National Statistics, the Bank of England and the House of Commons Library. The article describes and assesses the sources which make up this composite price index, and explains why some sources are preferred over others for the purpose of long-run comparisons.

Changes in the purchasing power of a currency are the inverse of changes in the levels of prices: when prices go up, the amount that can be purchased with a given sum of money goes down. If prices double, for example, any given amount of currency will buy only half the quantity of goods and services it previously did. Questions about changes in the purchasing power of the pound are usually framed in terms of what the domestic consumer can buy. The price index presented in this article therefore reflects movements in the prices of goods and services purchased by the private domestic consumer, that is, ordinary households, rather than those purchased by businesses or public authorities. It shows the change in the internal purchasing power of the pound for goods and services purchased in the UK; no attempt is made to measure changes in the external value of the currency arising as a result of movements in exchange rates.

It should be noted that in general the relevance and quality of the primary sources diminishes the further one goes back in time. This means that comparisons further back in time and over long periods should be regarded as more approximate than comparisons over short periods in more recent years. In addition, there have been continual changes in the pattern of household expenditure over time. These changes can be accommodated in a price index, such as the retail prices index or the consumer prices index, by regularly updating the commodities for which prices are collected, and the expenditure weights associated with them. However, over a period of time these changes build up, with the result that the commodities for which we measure prices now are very different from 50 years ago, let alone 250 years ago. As a result, it is not possible to compare the cost of exactly the same fixed basket of goods and services over an extended time period (for example, to answer questions such as how much a basket of goods and services costing £100 today would have cost 100 years ago).

Sources

The composite price index is obtained by linking together indices from several different published sources. When there is a choice between different sources, the decision about which one is to be preferred is not always clear-cut. The criteria used to assess the alternative sources include the form of the index and whether it is a direct or derived measure: for example, all other things being equal, a directly constructed price index is preferable to an implied deflator. Continuity is also important, as are breadth and representativeness of the coverage of goods and services and the quality of the expenditure weights used to combine the component indices. The preferred sources are described below in reverse chronological order, together with brief comments on their quality and, where appropriate, how they compare against alternative sources.

1947 to current day

The decision is clear-cut. The retail prices index (RPI) is the preferred index over this period. It is of the correct index form; it is available monthly back to June 1947; and it is the most familiar measure of inflation in the UK. More information about the RPI can be found on the National Statistics website, www.statistics.gov.uk/rpi, and in the *Retail Prices Index Technical Manual*.

1870–1947

During this period, the implied deflator for consumers' expenditure is used, derived from estimates of consumers' expenditure valued at current and constant prices. These are taken from the unofficial national accounts of the United Kingdom, prepared by the Department of Applied Economics at Cambridge University (Feinstein, 1972). These results were put together in a form which was as nearly as possible consistent in concept and definition with the then Central Statistical Office's (post-1947) official estimates of the National Accounts.

Feinstein assesses the quality of the figures for *levels* of consumers' expenditure as shown below. It should be noted that there is no assessment of the quality of the implied deflator, but this is likely to be substantially lower:[1]

- 1914–1938: firm estimates: margin of error: = < 5 per cent
- 1890–1913: good estimates: margin of error = +/– 5 per cent to 15 per cent
- 1870–1889: rough estimates: margin of error = +/– 15 per cent to 25 per cent.

Feinstein comments that there was a heavy reliance on interpolation during the two wartime periods. The year to year movements in prices during the First and Second World Wars should therefore be treated with caution. He also notes that in the period to 1920, the data includes Southern Ireland (comprising roughly 2 per cent of total consumers' expenditure), although this is unlikely to have had a significant effect on the implied deflator. From that date, the geographical coverage is the UK.

During the period 1914–1947, an alternative index, the Cost of Living Index (COLI) produced by the former Ministry of Labour, also exists. The implied consumers' expenditure deflator is preferred to the COLI, mainly due to the latter's relatively limited coverage in terms of both products and population, together with concern about the quality of the weights used to produce the aggregate index. This concern is recognised in the report of the first RPI Advisory Committee, *Interim Report of the Cost of Living Advisory Committee*. The COLI uses the same fixed weights during the entire period, based on a survey of expenditure patterns of urban working class households conducted in 1904. The weights were influenced by a highly subjective assessment of what constituted legitimate expenditure for a working-class family; beer was completely excluded and the weight used for tobacco was much less than the actual proportion of expenditure on tobacco. By the 1930s, the COLI's weights were very out of date and unrepresentative.

1850–1870

For 1850–1870 a retail price index produced by G H Wood is used. This is constructed partly from statistics in the Board of Trade's Report on Wholesale and Retail Prices, and partly from data collected by Wood himself from Co-operative Society records (Layton and Crowther).

Wood's index extends further, up to 1910, but this later period is not used in the composite long-run index. Layton and Crowther comment that "the basis for Wood's figures is comparatively slight, many of the figures being contract rather than genuine retail prices; hence too much reliance should not be placed on the details of the calculation, which is rather in the nature of an intelligent guess than an authoritative statement of the course of retail prices."

1750–1850

For the years up to 1850, the price index used is one compiled by Phelps-Brown and Hopkins. There is no suitable alternative index available for this period. Phelps-Brown and Hopkins' index covers the prices of consumables, drawn from a variety of sources: until the early 19th century, prices are generally based on records from a few local markets, the accounts of colleges and hospitals in the South East of England, and from records of the Navy Victualling service. Subsequent to that, some of the sources cease and are replaced by wholesale prices from the organised produce markets (for example, Smithfield's wholesale meat market in London). The price index is built up from six main categories of expenditure, each of which has a constant weight during the entire course of the index. Within these main categories, the weights of the components were allowed to vary to take account of the changing pattern of consumption, and the availability of data sources.

Phelps-Brown and Hopkins' price index extends further into the 20th century, but is not preferred to the other sources listed above because its coverage is restricted to consumables. Their index also extends back to the 13th century.

Results

Trends in inflation

Table 1 shows for each year the level of the price index, based on January 1974 equal to 100. January 1974 was chosen so the index numbers at the start or the end of the period are not inconveniently large or small. Table 2 shows the percentage change in the index over the previous year – that is, the annual rate of inflation (see also Figure 1). The figures in this table are derived from the primary sources used to construct the composite index shown in Table 1. This ensures that the annual rates of change are consistent with those published elsewhere. It should be noted that because the index levels of the primary sources are different from those shown in Table 1 (reflecting the different reference dates), rates calculated from these primary sources may differ slightly from those derived from the data in Table 1.

The tables show that over the period as a whole, prices have risen by around 140 times. Prices roughly doubled between 1750 and the end of the 18th century, but were at about the same level over 100 years later, prior to the start of the First World War. The fluctuations prior to 1914 partly reflect harvest quality and wars, with European Wars having the most marked impact on UK inflation. Prices increased by 50 per cent over the first ten years of the Napoleonic Wars (1803–1815), and doubled over the four years of the First World War and two succeeding years. Prices fell in most years between 1921 and 1936, or showed very small year-on-year increases of less than one per cent, reflecting the falls in profits and wage costs associated with rising unemployment during the Depression. Prices have risen in every year since.

Taken as a whole, in the period between 1750 and 1938, before the start of the Second World War, prices rose by a little more than three times. Since then prices have increased more than forty-fold. The most rapid increases in prices occurred in the early years of the Second World War, and more particularly between 1973 and 1981. Over this latter eight-year period, prices more than tripled, with inflation reaching 24 per cent in 1975, and exceeding 10 per cent in each year except 1978. The situation in Britain reflected the experience of the entire industrial world, which was struck by a series of supply shocks during the 1970s, including a quadrupling in the world price of crude oil in 1973. Internationally, the effect of these supply shocks was most evident in 1974 when consumer price inflation exceeded 10 per cent in the US, Italy, France and Japan, while German inflation peaked at 7 per cent. In the UK, in the ten years from 1982 to 1991, inflation was above 4 per cent in most years, but has been below that in every year since.

These results are also presented graphically. Figure 2 plots the price index on a linear scale. It clearly shows the rapid increase in prices that has occurred since the Second World War, though over-emphasises the rate at which this change has taken place, since the level of prices was already much higher compared to the 18th and 19th centuries. For instance, a doubling in the price index from 10 to 20 appears as a much smaller vertical distance on the scale than a doubling from 100 to 200. This problem can be overcome by the use of a logarithmic scale as in Figure 3. In this chart, a given proportional increase in the index (that is, the same inflation rate) appears as the same vertical distance on the index axis, regardless of the actual starting value of the index.

Figure 1
Composite Price Index: annual percentage change: 1751 to 2003

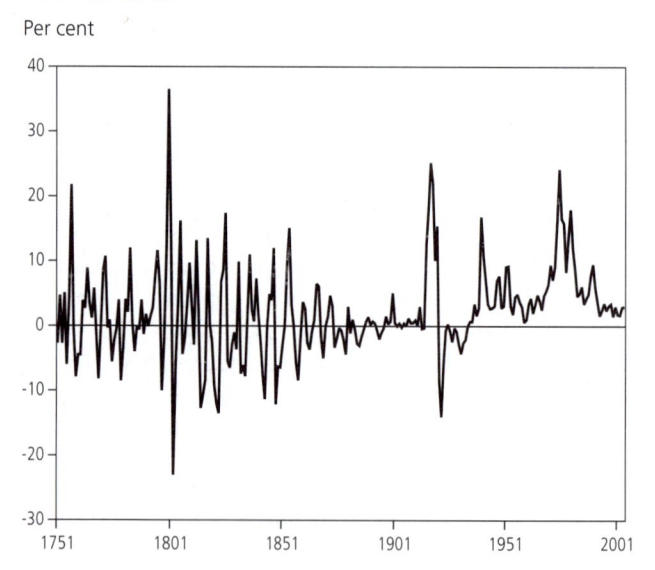

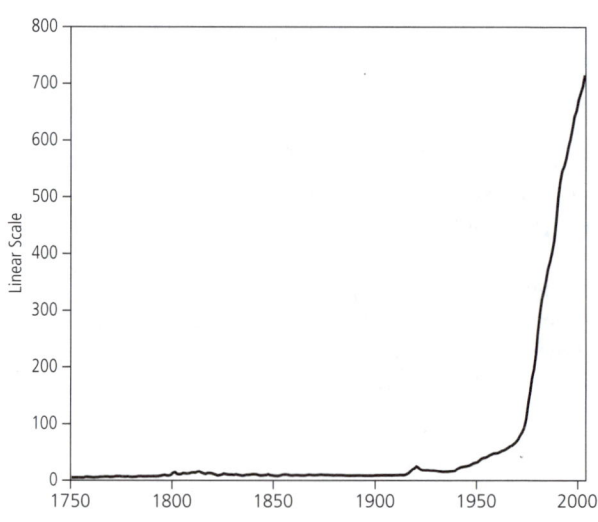

Figure 2
Composite Price Index 1750 to 2003, January 1974 = 100 (linear scale)

Figure 3
Composite Price Index 1750 to 2003, January 1974 = 100 (logarithmic scale)

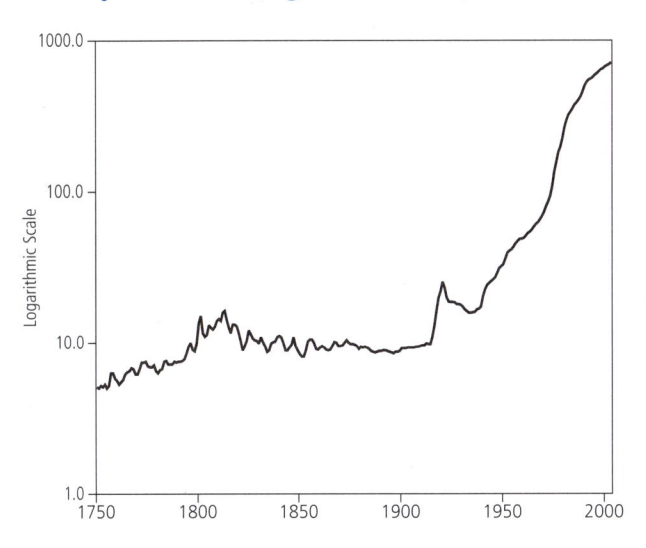

Calculating changes in the purchasing power of the pound

The results in Table 1 can also be used to calculate changes in the purchasing power of the pound. Two examples of how to do this are given below.

Example 1: what is the equivalent sum of money in 2003 prices of £50 in 1850?

This question is answered by determining by how much prices have risen over this period. The calculation is:

$$\text{amount to be revalued} \times \frac{\text{later year's index}}{\text{earlier year's index}}$$

Inserting the relevant index values from Table 1 gives:

$$£50 \times \frac{715.2}{8.4} = £4,257$$

Example 2: what was the purchasing power of the pound in 1995, compared with 100p in 1965?

In other words, if one pound could buy one hundred pence worth of goods and services in 1965, what would the same pound buy in 1995 in view of the general rise in the prices of those goods and services in the intervening period? The calculation to answer this question is:

$$100 \times \frac{\text{earlier year's index}}{\text{later year's index}}$$

Inserting the relevant index values from Table 1 gives:

$$100p \times \frac{58.4}{588.2} = 9.9p$$

In other words, the purchasing power of the pound fell by 90.1 per cent during the period in question. By inverting the numerator and denominator in the above equation, one could also say that it required £10.07 in 1995 to buy what a pound could purchase in 1965.

Other tables

Table 3 shows the purchasing power of the pound, based on January 1974 equal to 100 – this is simply the inverse of the results presented in Table 1. That is, an increase in the general level of prices appears as an increase in the index level in Table 1, but as a fall in the purchasing power of the pound in Table 3.

Table 4 presents similar results to Tables 1, but on a monthly basis, back to June 1947. The figures in this table can be used in conjunction with those in Table 1 to obtain estimates of change in prices or the purchasing power of the pound up to a particular month. For instance, in example 1 above, if we wanted to revalue £50 from 1850 to March 2003, the calculation would be:

$$£50 \times \frac{709.7 \; \textit{(from Table 4)}}{8.4 \; \textit{(from Table 1)}} = £4,224$$

Publication

Tables 1, 2 and 4 will be published monthly in the *Focus on Consumer Price Indices* on the National Statistics website. It should be noted that because of the limitations of some of the primary sources, particularly before 1947, the results shown in Tables 1, 2 and 3 are not within the scope of National Statistics.

The results presented in this article also appear in the House of Commons Library Research Paper *Inflation: the value of the pound 1750–2002*.

Note

1. The consumers' expenditure deflator is calculated as the ratio of indices of current price and constant price expenditure:

$$I_t = \frac{CP_t / CP_0}{KP_t / KP_0} \times 100$$

where CP_t is current price expenditure in period t and KP_t is the corresponding constant price expenditure.

The implied deflator, I_t, is likely to be subject to a smaller margin of error than the underlying expenditure data as it is based on relative, rather than absolute, levels; furthermore, errors in the level of current price expenditure are likely to be reflected in the constant prices values, since the two are closely linked.

References

Feinstein C H (1972). *National Income, Expenditure and Output of the United Kingdom 1855–1965*, Tables 2, 5, 24 and 25.

House of Commons Library Research Paper 03/82. *Inflation: the value of the pound 1750–2002*. http://www.parliament.uk/commons/lib/research/rp2003/rp03-082.pdf.

Layton and Crowther *An Introduction to the Study of Prices*, Appendix E. Table I, p 265.

Office for National Statistics (1998) *Retail Prices Index Technical Manual 1998*.
http://www.statistics.gov.uk/statbase/Product.asp?vlnk=2328&More=N

Phelps-Brown and Hopkins (1956) Seven Centuries Of The Prices Of Consumables, *Economica*, November 1956, pp 311–314.

RPI Advisory Committee, March 1947. *Interim Report of the Cost of Living Advisory Committee*, Cmd. 7077.

Economic Trends 604 March 2004 | Consumer Price Inflation since 1750

Table 1
Composite Price Index, 1750 to 2003

January 1974 = 100

Year	Index CDKO	Year	Index CDKO	Year	Index CDKO	Year	Index CDKO	Year	Index CDKO
1750	5.1	1801	15.1	1852	8.1	1903	9.3	1954	41.3
1751	5.0	1802	11.6	1853	8.9	1904	9.3		
1752	5.2	1803	11.0	1854	10.2			1955	43.1
1753	5.1	1804	11.3			1905	9.3	1956	45.3
1754	5.3			1855	10.5	1906	9.3	1957	46.9
		1805	13.1	1856	10.5	1907	9.4	1958	48.4
1755	5.0	1806	12.6	1857	10.0	1908	9.4	1959	48.6
1756	5.2	1807	12.3	1858	9.1	1909	9.5		
1757	6.3	1808	12.8	1859	9.0			1960	49.1
1758	6.3	1809	14.0			1910	9.6	1961	50.8
1759	5.8			1860	9.3	1911	9.6	1962	53.0
		1810	14.4	1861	9.5	1912	9.9	1963	54.0
1760	5.6	1811	14.0	1862	9.3	1913	9.8	1964	55.8
1761	5.3	1812	15.9	1863	9.0	1914	9.8		
1762	5.5	1813	16.3	1864	8.9			1965	58.4
1763	5.7	1814	14.2			1915	11.0	1966	60.7
1764	6.2			1865	9.0	1916	13.0	1967	62.3
		1815	12.7	1866	9.5	1917	16.3	1968	65.2
1765	6.4	1816	11.6	1867	10.1	1918	19.9	1969	68.7
1766	6.5	1817	13.2	1868	10.0	1919	21.9		
1767	6.8	1818	13.2	1869	9.5			1970	73.1
1768	6.7	1819	12.9			1920	25.3	1971	80.0
1769	6.2			1870	9.5	1921	23.1	1972	85.7
		1820	11.7	1871	9.6	1922	19.9	1973	93.5
1770	6.2	1821	10.3	1872	10.0	1923	18.7	1974	108.5
1771	6.7	1822	8.9	1873	10.4	1924	18.6		
1772	7.4	1823	9.5	1874	10.0			1975	134.8
1773	7.4	1824	10.3			1925	18.6	1976	157.1
1774	7.5			1875	9.8	1926	18.5	1977	182.0
		1825	12.1	1876	9.8	1927	18.0	1978	197.1
1775	7.0	1826	11.4	1877	9.7	1928	18.0	1979	223.5
1776	6.9	1827	10.7	1878	9.5	1929	17.8		
1777	6.9	1828	10.4	1879	9.1			1980	263.7
1778	7.1	1829	10.3			1930	17.3	1981	295.0
1779	6.5			1880	9.4	1931	16.6	1982	320.4
		1830	9.9	1881	9.3	1932	16.2	1983	335.1
1780	6.3	1831	10.9	1882	9.4	1933	15.8	1984	351.8
1781	6.6	1832	10.1	1883	9.3	1934	15.8		
1782	6.7	1833	9.5	1884	9.1			1985	373.2
1783	7.5	1834	8.7			1935	15.9	1986	385.9
1784	7.6			1885	8.8	1936	16.0	1987	402.0
		1835	8.9	1886	8.7	1937	16.6	1988	421.7
1785	7.2	1836	9.9	1887	8.6	1938	16.8	1989	454.5
1786	7.2	1837	10.1	1888	8.7	1939	17.3		
1787	7.2	1838	10.2	1889	8.8			1990	497.5
1788	7.5	1839	10.9			1940	20.2	1991	526.7
1789	7.4			1890	8.8	1941	22.4	1992	546.4
		1840	11.1	1891	8.9	1942	24.0	1993	555.1
1790	7.5	1841	10.9	1892	8.9	1943	24.8	1994	568.5
1791	7.5	1842	10.0	1893	8.8	1944	25.5		
1792	7.6	1843	8.9	1894	8.7			1995	588.2
1793	7.8	1844	8.9			1945	26.2	1996	602.4
1794	8.5			1895	8.6	1946	27.0	1997	621.3
		1845	9.3	1896	8.5	1947	28.9	1998	642.6
1795	9.4	1846	9.7	1897	8.7	1948	31.1	1999	652.5
1796	10.0	1847	10.9	1898	8.7	1949	32.0		
1797	9.0	1848	9.5	1899	8.8			2000	671.8
1798	8.8	1849	8.9			1950	33.0	2001	683.7
1799	9.9			1900	9.2	1951	36.0	2002	695.1
		1850	8.4	1901	9.2	1952	39.3	2003	715.2
1800	13.5	1851	8.1	1902	9.2	1953	40.5		

Note: The results in this table do not fall within the scope of National Statistics, due to the limitations of some of the primary sources, particularly pre-1947, used to construct the index.

Source: Office for National Statistics

Table 2
Composite Price Index: annual percentage change: 1751 to 2003

Year	Per cent CDSI	Year	Per cent CDSI	Year	Per cent CDSI	Year	Per cent CDSI	Year	Per cent CDSI
1750	..	1801	11.7	1852	–	1903	0.4	1954	1.8
1751	-2.7	1802	-23.0	1853	9.3	1904	-0.2		
1752	4.7	1803	-5.9	1854	15.1			1955	4.5
1753	-2.7	1804	3.2			1905	0.4	1956	4.9
1754	5.1			1855	3.3	1906	–	1957	3.7
		1805	16.2	1856	–	1907	1.2	1958	3.0
1755	-6.0	1806	-4.4	1857	-5.6	1908	0.5	1959	0.6
1756	4.2	1807	-1.9	1858	-8.4	1909	0.5		
1757	21.8	1808	3.4	1859	-1.8			1960	1.0
1758	-0.3	1809	9.7			1910	0.9	1961	3.4
1759	-7.9			1860	3.7	1911	0.1	1962	4.3
		1810	3.2	1861	2.7	1912	3.0	1963	2.0
1760	-4.5	1811	-2.9	1862	-2.6	1913	-0.4	1964	3.3
1761	-4.5	1812	13.2	1863	-3.6	1914	-0.3		
1762	3.9	1813	2.5	1864	-0.9			1965	4.8
1763	2.7	1814	-12.7			1915	12.5	1966	3.9
1764	8.9			1865	0.9	1916	18.1	1967	2.5
		1815	-10.7	1866	6.5	1917	25.2	1968	4.7
1765	3.5	1816	-8.4	1867	6.1	1918	22.0	1969	5.4
1766	1.2	1817	13.5	1868	-1.7	1919	10.1		
1767	5.8	1818	0.3	1869	-5.0			1970	6.4
1768	-1.1	1819	-2.5			1920	15.4	1971	9.4
1769	-8.2			1870	–	1921	-8.6	1972	7.1
		1820	-9.3	1871	1.4	1922	-14.0	1973	9.2
1770	-0.4	1821	-12.0	1872	4.7	1923	-6.0	1974	16.0
1771	8.5	1822	-13.5	1873	3.1	1924	-0.7		
1772	10.7	1823	6.8	1874	-3.3			1975	24.2
1773	-0.3	1824	8.6			1925	0.3	1976	16.5
1774	0.9			1875	-1.9	1926	-0.8	1977	15.8
		1825	17.4	1876	-0.3	1927	-2.4	1978	8.3
1775	-5.6	1826	-5.5	1877	-0.7	1928	-0.3	1979	13.4
1776	-2.2	1827	-6.5	1878	-2.2	1929	-0.9		
1777	-0.4	1828	-2.9	1879	-4.4			1980	18.0
1778	4.0	1829	-1.0			1930	-2.8	1981	11.9
1779	-8.5			1880	3.0	1931	-4.3	1982	8.6
		1830	-3.6	1881	-1.1	1932	-2.6	1983	4.6
1780	-3.4	1831	9.9	1882	1.0	1933	-2.1	1984	5.0
1781	4.1	1832	-7.4	1883	-0.5	1934	–		
1782	2.1	1833	-6.1	1884	-2.7			1985	6.1
1783	12.0	1834	-7.8			1935	0.7	1986	3.4
1784	0.6			1885	-3.0	1936	0.7	1987	4.2
		1835	1.7	1886	-1.6	1937	3.4	1988	4.9
1785	-4.0	1836	11.0	1887	-0.5	1938	1.6	1989	7.8
1786	0.0	1837	2.5	1888	0.7	1939	2.8		
1787	-0.6	1838	0.7	1889	1.4			1990	9.5
1788	4.0	1839	7.3			1940	16.8	1991	5.9
1789	-1.3			1890	0.2	1941	10.8	1992	3.7
		1840	1.8	1891	0.7	1942	7.1	1993	1.6
1790	1.8	1841	-2.3	1892	0.4	1943	3.4	1994	2.4
1791	-0.1	1842	-7.6	1893	-0.7	1944	2.7		
1792	1.5	1843	-11.3	1894	-2.0			1995	3.5
1793	2.8	1844	-0.1			1945	2.8	1996	2.4
1794	7.7			1895	-1.0	1946	3.1	1997	3.1
		1845	4.9	1896	-0.3	1947	7.0	1998	3.4
1795	11.6	1846	4.0	1897	1.5	1948	7.7	1999	1.5
1796	6.4	1847	12.0	1898	0.3	1949	2.8		
1797	-10.0	1848	-12.1	1899	0.7			2000	3.0
1798	-2.2	1849	-6.3			1950	3.1	2001	1.8
1799	12.3			1900	5.1	1951	9.1	2002	1.7
		1850	-6.4	1901	0.5	1952	9.2	2003	2.9
1800	36.5	1851	-3.0	1902	–	1953	3.1		

Note: The results in this table do not fall within the scope of National Statistics, due to the limitations of some of the primary sources, particularly pre-1947, used to construct the index.

Source: Office for National Statistics

Table 3
Purchasing power of the pound: 1750 to 2003

January 1974 = 100 pence

	Purchasing power CHVF		Purchasing power CHVF		Purchasing power CHVF		Purchasing power CHVF		Purchasing power CHVF
1750	1,961.6	1801	661.0	1852	1,231.3	1903	1,077.6	1954	242.3
1751	2,016.3	1802	858.6	1853	1,126.8	1904	1,080.3	1955	231.8
1752	1,925.7	1803	912.7	1854	979.0	1905	1,075.9	1956	220.9
1753	1,978.4	1804	884.1	1855	947.9	1906	1,076.1	1957	213.0
1754	1,881.9	1805	760.9	1856	947.9	1907	1,063.2	1958	206.8
1755	2,002.3	1806	796.0	1857	1,003.7	1908	1,058.4	1959	205.6
1756	1,922.5	1807	811.0	1858	1,095.8	1909	1,052.8	1960	203.6
1757	1,578.9	1808	784.1	1859	1,116.2	1910	1,043.7	1961	196.8
1758	1,583.2	1809	714.9	1860	1,076.0	1911	1,042.2	1962	188.8
1759	1,719.7	1810	693.0	1861	1,047.7	1912	1,012.4	1963	185.1
1760	1,799.9	1811	713.5	1862	1,076.0	1913	1,016.8	1964	179.3
1761	1,884.9	1812	630.4	1863	1,116.2	1914	1,019.4	1965	171.1
1762	1,814.0	1813	615.3	1864	1,126.8	1915	906.0	1966	164.6
1763	1,766.9	1814	704.8	1865	1,116.2	1916	767.4	1967	160.6
1764	1,623.2	1815	788.9	1866	1,047.7	1917	612.8	1968	153.4
1765	1,568.2	1816	861.1	1867	987.1	1918	502.3	1969	145.5
1766	1,549.3	1817	758.4	1868	1,003.7	1919	456.4	1970	136.8
1767	1,465.0	1818	756.4	1869	1,057.0	1920	395.4	1971	125.0
1768	1,481.9	1819	775.7	1870	1,057.0	1921	432.5	1972	116.7
1769	1,614.2	1820	855.4	1871	1,042.2	1922	502.9	1973	106.9
1770	1,620.9	1821	972.6	1872	995.8	1923	535.0	1974	92.2
1771	1,493.4	1822	1,124.7	1873	965.6	1924	538.9	1975	74.2
1772	1,348.9	1823	1,053.1	1874	998.5	1925	537.1	1976	63.7
1773	1,353.6	1824	970.1	1875	1,017.6	1926	541.6	1977	54.9
1774	1,341.1	1825	826.7	1876	1,021.0	1927	554.7	1978	50.7
1775	1,420.1	1826	874.8	1877	1,028.1	1928	556.3	1979	44.7
1776	1,452.1	1827	935.6	1878	1,051.7	1929	561.3	1980	37.9
1777	1,457.6	1828	963.7	1879	1,099.9	1930	577.2	1981	33.9
1778	1,401.2	1829	973.4	1880	1,067.6	1931	602.8	1982	31.2
1779	1,530.9	1830	1,009.9	1881	1,079.8	1932	618.9	1983	29.8
1780	1,585.4	1831	918.5	1882	1,068.7	1933	632.5	1984	28.4
1781	1,522.8	1832	991.7	1883	1,073.8	1934	632.7	1985	26.8
1782	1,491.4	1833	1,056.0	1884	1,103.4	1935	628.2	1986	25.9
1783	1,331.8	1834	1,144.8	1885	1,137.2	1936	623.6	1987	24.9
1784	1,324.2	1835	1,125.8	1886	1,156.1	1937	603.2	1988	23.7
1785	1,379.4	1836	1,014.3	1887	1,162.3	1938	593.8	1989	22.0
1786	1,379.4	1837	990.0	1888	1,154.4	1939	577.7	1990	20.1
1787	1,387.7	1838	983.3	1889	1,138.8	1940	494.8	1991	19.0
1788	1,334.9	1839	916.4	1890	1,136.0	1941	446.4	1992	18.3
1789	1,352.0	1840	900.0	1891	1,127.9	1942	416.6	1993	18.0
1790	1,328.8	1841	921.5	1892	1,123.8	1943	403.1	1994	17.6
1791	1,330.3	1842	996.9	1893	1,132.2	1944	392.5	1995	17.0
1792	1,310.7	1843	1,123.6	1894	1,154.9	1945	381.7	1996	16.6
1793	1,274.6	1844	1,124.7	1895	1,166.8	1946	370.1	1997	16.1
1794	1,183.4	1845	1,072.6	1896	1,170.8	1947	345.8	1998	15.6
1795	1,060.8	1846	1,031.5	1897	1,154.0	1948	321.1	1999	15.3
1796	996.9	1847	920.7	1898	1,150.3	1949	312.4	2000	14.9
1797	1,107.5	1848	1,047.4	1899	1,142.3	1950	303.1	2001	14.6
1798	1,132.4	1849	1,118.2	1900	1,086.6	1951	277.7	2002	14.4
1799	1,008.1	1850	1,194.4	1901	1,081.4	1952	254.4	2003	14.0
1800	738.6	1851	1,231.3	1902	1,081.4	1953	246.7		

Note: The results in this table do not fall within the scope of National Statistics, due to the limitations of some of the primary sources, particularly pre-1947, used to construct the index.

Source: Office for National Statistics

Table 4
Retail Prices Index: Long run series

January 1974 = 100

	Annual average	Jan	Feb	Mar	Apr	May	Jun	Jul	Aug	Sep	Oct	Nov	Dec
	CDKO												
1947	..	..	..	..	..	..	28.9	29.1	28.9	29.1	29.3	29.9	30.0
1948	31.1	30.1	30.7	30.8	31.2	31.2	31.7	31.2	31.2	31.3	31.3	31.4	31.5
1949	32.0	31.5	31.6	31.5	31.4	32.0	32.1	32.2	32.2	32.3	32.5	32.5	32.6
1950	33.0	32.6	32.7	32.8	32.9	33.0	32.9	32.9	32.7	32.9	33.3	33.4	33.6
1951	36.0	33.9	34.2	34.5	35.0	35.9	36.0	36.6	36.7	37.0	37.2	37.4	37.7
1952	39.3	38.3	38.4	38.5	39.2	39.2	39.8	39.8	39.5	39.5	39.8	39.8	40.0
1953	40.5	40.0	40.1	40.4	40.8	40.6	40.8	40.8	40.6	40.5	40.5	40.6	40.5
1954	41.3	40.5	40.5	40.8	41.0	40.9	41.1	41.8	41.5	41.5	41.7	41.8	42.1
1955	43.1	42.2	42.2	42.2	42.5	42.4	43.3	43.4	43.1	43.4	43.8	44.5	44.5
1956	45.3	44.4	44.4	44.9	45.6	45.5	45.4	45.3	45.4	45.3	45.6	45.7	45.9
1957	46.9	46.3	46.3	46.2	46.4	46.4	46.9	47.3	47.2	47.1	47.5	47.8	48.0
1958	48.4	48.0	47.7	48.1	48.6	48.5	48.9	48.1	48.1	48.1	48.5	48.7	48.9
1959	48.6	49.0	48.9	48.9	48.6	48.4	48.5	48.4	48.5	48.2	48.5	48.8	48.9
1960	49.1	48.8	48.8	48.7	48.9	48.9	49.2	49.3	49.0	49.0	49.4	49.7	49.8
1961	50.8	49.8	49.8	50.0	50.3	50.4	50.9	50.9	51.3	51.3	51.3	51.9	52.0
1962	53.0	52.1	52.2	52.4	53.1	53.3	53.6	53.4	53.0	52.9	52.9	53.1	53.3
1963	54.0	53.5	54.0	54.1	54.2	54.2	54.2	53.9	53.7	53.9	54.1	54.2	54.3
1964	55.8	54.6	54.6	54.8	55.3	55.8	56.0	56.0	56.2	56.2	56.3	56.7	56.9
1965	58.4	57.1	57.1	57.3	58.4	58.6	58.8	58.8	58.9	58.9	59.0	59.2	59.5
1966	60.7	59.6	59.6	59.7	60.5	60.9	61.1	60.8	61.2	61.1	61.2	61.6	61.7
1967	62.3	61.8	61.8	61.8	62.3	62.3	62.5	62.1	62.0	61.9	62.4	62.8	63.2
1968	65.2	63.4	63.7	63.9	65.1	65.1	65.4	65.4	65.5	65.6	65.9	66.1	66.9
1969	68.7	67.3	67.7	67.9	68.7	68.6	68.9	68.9	68.7	68.9	69.4	69.6	70.1
1970	73.1	70.6	71.0	71.4	72.5	72.7	72.9	73.5	73.4	73.8	74.6	75.1	75.6
1971	80.0	76.6	77.1	77.7	79.4	79.9	80.4	80.9	81.0	81.1	81.5	82.0	82.4
1972	85.7	82.9	83.3	83.6	84.4	84.8	85.3	85.6	86.3	86.8	88.0	88.3	88.7
1973	93.5	89.3	89.9	90.4	92.1	92.8	93.3	93.7	94.0	94.8	96.7	97.4	98.1
1974	108.5	100.0	101.7	102.6	106.1	107.6	108.7	109.7	109.8	111.0	113.2	115.2	116.9
1975	134.8	119.9	121.9	124.3	129.1	134.5	137.1	138.5	139.3	140.5	142.5	144.2	146.0
1976	157.1	147.9	149.8	150.6	153.5	155.2	156.0	156.3	158.5	160.6	163.5	165.8	168.0
1977	182.0	172.4	174.1	175.8	180.3	181.7	183.6	183.8	184.7	185.7	186.5	187.4	188.4
1978	197.1	189.5	190.6	191.8	194.6	195.7	197.2	198.1	199.4	200.2	201.1	202.5	204.2
1979	223.5	207.2	208.9	210.6	214.2	215.9	219.6	229.1	230.9	233.2	235.6	237.7	239.4
1980	263.7	245.3	248.8	252.2	260.8	263.2	265.7	267.9	268.5	270.2	271.9	274.1	275.6
1981	295.0	277.3	279.8	284.0	292.2	294.1	295.8	297.1	299.3	301.0	303.7	306.9	308.8
1982	320.4	310.6	310.7	313.4	319.7	322.0	322.9	323.0	323.1	322.9	324.5	326.1	325.5
1983	335.1	325.9	327.3	327.9	332.5	333.9	334.7	336.5	338.0	339.5	340.7	341.9	342.8
1984	351.8	342.6	344.0	345.1	349.7	351.0	351.9	351.5	354.8	355.5	357.7	358.8	358.5
1985	373.2	359.8	362.7	366.1	373.9	375.6	376.4	375.7	376.7	376.5	377.1	378.4	378.9
1986	385.9	379.7	381.1	381.6	385.3	386.0	385.8	384.7	385.9	387.8	388.4	391.7	393.0
1987	402.0	394.5	396.1	396.9	401.6	402.0	402.0	401.6	402.8	404.0	405.9	407.9	407.5
1988	421.7	407.5	409.1	410.7	417.4	419.0	420.5	420.9	425.7	427.6	432.0	434.0	435.1
1989	454.5	437.9	441.1	443.0	450.9	453.7	455.3	455.6	456.8	460.0	463.5	467.5	468.7
1990	497.5	471.4	474.2	478.9	493.5	497.9	499.8	500.2	505.4	510.1	514.0	512.9	512.5
1991	526.7	513.6	516.4	518.4	525.1	526.7	529.0	527.8	529.0	531.0	533.0	534.9	535.3
1992	546.4	534.9	537.7	539.3	547.6	549.5	549.5	547.6	548.0	549.9	551.9	551.1	549.1
1993	555.1	544.0	547.6	549.5	554.7	556.6	556.2	555.1	557.4	559.8	559.4	558.6	559.8
1994	568.5	557.4	560.6	562.2	568.9	570.8	570.8	568.1	570.8	572.0	572.8	573.2	576.0
1995	588.2	576.0	579.5	581.9	587.8	590.2	591.0	588.2	591.4	594.1	591.0	591.0	594.5
1996	602.4	592.5	595.3	597.7	602.0	603.2	603.6	601.2	604.0	606.7	606.7	607.1	609.1
1997	621.3	609.1	611.5	613.1	616.6	619.0	621.3	621.3	625.3	628.4	629.2	629.6	631.2
1998	642.6	629.2	632.4	634.4	641.5	645.0	644.6	643.0	645.8	648.6	649.0	648.6	648.6
1999	652.5	644.6	645.8	647.4	651.7	653.3	653.3	651.3	652.9	655.7	656.8	657.6	660.0
2000	671.8	657.2	660.8	664.3	671.0	673.4	675.0	672.6	672.6	677.4	677.0	678.9	679.3
2001	683.7	675.0	678.5	679.3	682.9	687.2	688.0	683.7	686.4	688.8	687.6	684.9	684.1
2002	695.1	683.7	685.6	688.4	693.1	695.1	695.1	693.9	695.9	700.6	701.8	703.0	704.2
2003	715.2	703.8	707.3	709.7	714.8	716.0	715.2	715.2	716.4	720.0	720.4	720.8	723.9

Source: National Statistics

Oil and gas sector, 1992–2001

Sanjiv Mahajan
Office for National Statistics

This article presents an overview of the structure of the UK Oil and gas sector together with statistics produced by the Office for National Statistics (ONS) covering the oil and gas industries for 1992 to 2001 as published in the *UK Input-Output Analyses*, 2003 Edition on 24 October 2003. These estimates are consistent with those published in the 2003 *Blue Book* and 2003 *Pink Book*.

The estimates show that in 2001, the contribution of the Oil and gas sector to UK Gross Value Added (GVA) at current basic prices accounted for £28.2 billion out of a total of £880.9 billion (3.2 per cent of the total). GVA for the oil and gas sector grew by 64.2 per cent between 1992 and 2001, compared with the growth of GVA for the whole economy of 61.2 per cent over this period.

Introduction

Outputs from the oil and gas extraction and petroleum related industries are inputs into most economic goods and services, whether for use in the home, for business or for leisure.

These industries enable the production of fuel for cars and heating for homes, industry and commerce but are also vital for production of plastics, paints, cleaning products, clothing, furniture, pharmaceuticals, synthetic rubber, electricity generation and many more products essential to the economy.

This article provides information and statistics produced by the ONS covering the oil and gas industries. In this article, we only consider the direct effect on the economy of these sectors, and not the indirect effect of these sectors on gross value added at current basic prices of the oil and gas consuming industries.

The data for these analyses have been derived from the 1992–2001 Input-Output Annual Supply and Use Tables published by the ONS in October 2003. In some cases, where parts of I-O groups are covered, proportions have been obtained from the ONS Annual Business Inquiry, a key input in producing the Input-Output Annual Supply and Use Tables.

Figure 1 shows the growth of the oil and gas sector compared to the whole UK economy. Tables 3 and 4 provide a chronology of key events and further statistics covering this sector.

Figure 1
GVA: Oil and gas sector growth relative to whole economy

Per cent growth (Rebased to 1992)

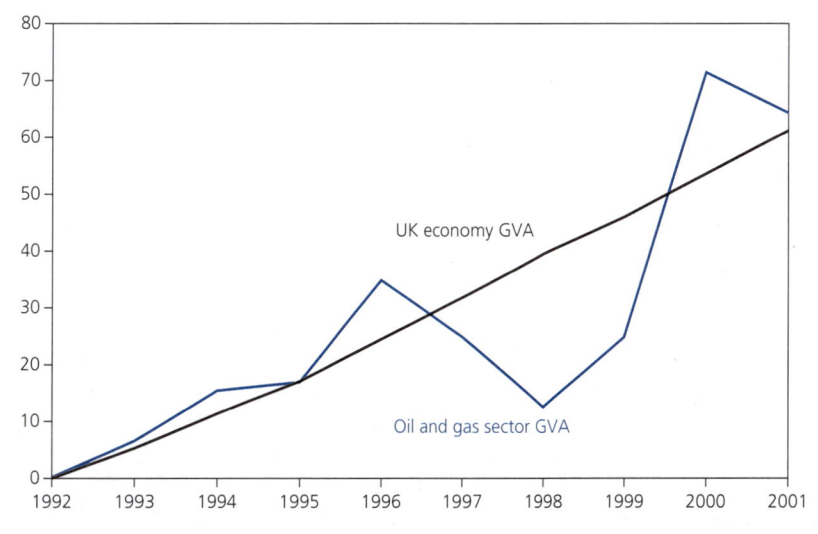

Table 1
Oil and gas sector coverage by I-O industry

SIC (92) class	I-O number	I-O group name
11.00	5	Extraction of crude petroleum and natural gas; service activities incidental to oil and gas extraction
23.20	35 (part)	Refined petroleum products
40.20	86 (part)	Manufacture of gas; distribution of gaseous fuels through mains
50.50	89 (part)	Retail sale of automotive fuel

Oil and gas sector coverage by industry

The oil and gas sector covers the industries shown in Table 1. These industries cover the direct activity of the oil and gas extraction industries and petroleum related industries. The main focus of this section is on I-O groups 5, 35 (part) and 86 (part).

The classification of the 123 I-O groups is based on the 1992 version of the *Standard Industrial Classification* (SIC(92)). All UK businesses are split into separate reporting units, and classified on the Inter Departmental Business Register (IDBR) to industries according to the product which forms the greatest part of their output.

In the oil and gas related industries, there are a number of major multinational businesses carrying out a wide range of activities, from extraction to retail. Where possible, reporting units carrying out narrow types of activity are identified within the business structure, which are then classified to the appropriate industry grouping.

Overview of the industry structure

Upstream – extraction and exploration of oil and gas

The UK oil and gas extraction industry, referred to as 'upstream' or as the UK Continental Shelf (UKCS), also includes all related exploration activity but excludes seismic surveying. These activities together with services incidental to oil and gas extraction, form I-O industry group 5. In 2001, there were 312 reporting units held on the IDBR in this industry group.

The main products of the 'upstream' industry are crude oil and natural gas. In their natural state, crude oil and natural gas have little practical use and need to be converted into products for consumption, for example: liquefied petroleum gas, petrol, diesel, jet fuel, bitumen, gas oil, naptha and methane gas.

Crude oil is a mixture of many different oily substances which boil at different temperatures, allowing for separation through a distillation process. Crude oil is not held at the oil rig for long before it is sent on to the refinery and is usually moved either by sea tankers or pipelines. The crude oil is then held in an oil terminal for processing.

Downstream

The UK petroleum industry, also referred to as 'downstream', involves refining, distribution, marketing and exporting of petroleum products. These businesses range from large multinational oil companies, independent retail groups and supermarket chains to single-site independent retailers.

Refining of crude oil

The main products of the refining part of the 'downstream' industry covered by I-O industry group 35, are fuel and lubricants for transport to be consumed by industry, commerce and retail sectors. Industry and commerce sectors include agriculture, manufacturing, energy generation, construction, distribution, transport and service sectors including government. The retail sector includes petrol filling stations' sales of fuels and lubricants.

The refining process also produces petrochemicals, which are major inputs for I-O product groups 40 (synthetics), 42 (paints), 44 (detergents), 45 (adhesives), 47 (synthetic rubber) and 48 (plastics).

Storage and transportation of fuels

Another key element of the 'downstream' activity is the storage, transportation and delivery of fuel to the end user through pipeline networks, rail, ship or road. Large storage terminals exist around the country that are supplied from the refineries by pipeline, rail and sea. Connected to these terminals is a network of pipelines across the UK owned by individual oil companies, joint ventures and government. These pipelines are used to move refined products such as petrol, diesel and jet fuel on behalf of major oil companies. Distribution of jet fuel to major airports is mainly via pipelines linking storage at the airport to the wider network.

Transportation using rail or road tankers has relatively higher costs compared with the use of pipelines, and therefore land tankers comprise only a small proportion of oil products transported. Specialist transport operators classified to I-O group 97 (auxiliary transport services) tend to be contracted-in to deliver products to the end user, whether direct to businesses or to a petrol filling station.

Ships are also used to move crude oil across the North Sea to refineries, as well as for transporting large volumes of petroleum products from the refinery to coastal ports within the UK and abroad.

Retailing of fuels

Demand for transport fuels and retail fuels continues to grow steadily other than for jet fuel. However, Figure 2 shows since 1992, petrol sales (motor spirit) have declined by 12.9 per cent while sales of diesel (DERV) have increased by 47.5 per cent (see www.dti.gov.uk).

Over the past ten years, the structure of retail provision has undergone continual change. The number of filling stations, mostly classified to I-O industry group 89, has declined from 18,549 sites in 1992 to 12,201 sites in 2001,

Figure 2
Petrol and diesel sales

Million tonnes

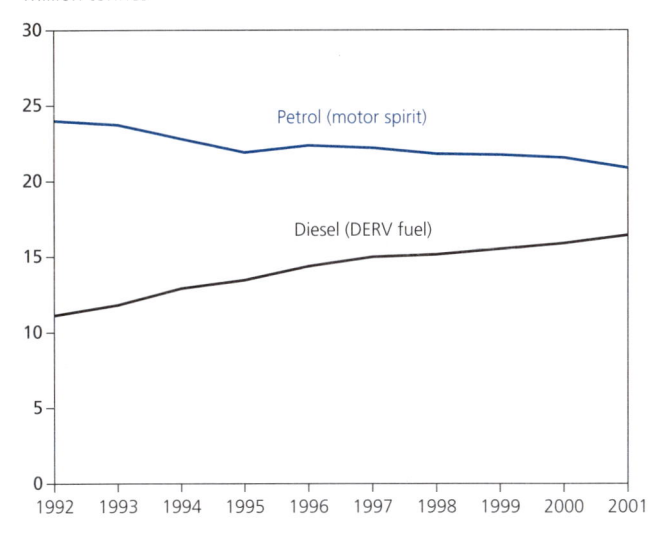

[Line chart showing Petrol (motor spirit) declining from ~24 to ~21 million tonnes, and Diesel (DERV fuel) rising from ~11 to ~16 million tonnes, 1992–2001]

as shown in Figure 3 (data from Retail Marketing Survey). This restructuring of retail has been led by the entry into the market of supermarket groups and the development of the out-of-town store with petrol filling stations (hypermarkets). These supermarkets and out-of-town businesses have increased their market share from 11 per cent in 1992 to 28 per cent in 2001. This new form of competition has encouraged existing fuel retailers to sell using large volume throughput sites with a wide-range of shopping facilities, serving consumers doing their regular weekly shopping.

Fuel retailers not part of the out-of-town phenomenon include independent fuel retailers, and the refiners' own distribution network to small companies and the agricultural sector. Independent retailers have agreements with oil companies to sell fuel under the brand name of the company.

Figure 3
Petrol filling stations in the UK

Number

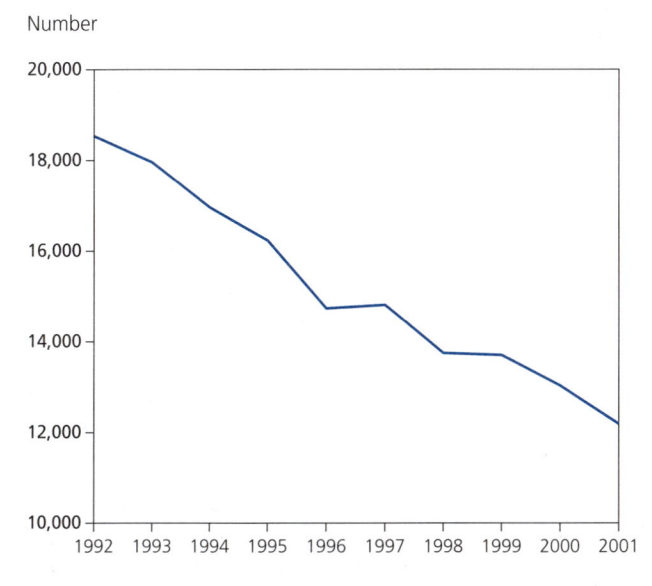

[Line chart showing number of petrol filling stations declining from ~18,500 in 1992 to ~12,000 in 2001]

Gas – manufacture, distribution and supply

The manufacture, distribution and supply (including transmission) of gas is all covered by I-O group 86, whereas oil extraction, refining, distribution and supply cuts across several I-O groups beyond the oil and gas extraction activity covered by I-O group 5.

Since 1986 the gas industry has been undergoing continual change. There was one vertically integrated monopoly supplier, whose business involved activities from extraction to monopoly purchasing of gas at the beach and supply of gas to final consumers. Privatisation arrangements created an independent regulator, Ofgas, to administer price controls and promote competition. The Gas Act 1995 paved the way for opening the Great Britain (GB) gas market to full competition, which included the legal separation of gas pipelines from gas shipping and gas supply. The industrial gas market was fully competitive by the mid-1990s; the household market was opened to full competition by 1998. The industry is now very much non-consolidated with separate businesses carrying out the different extraction, distribution and supply activities. The Office for Gas and Electricity regulates both gas and electricity markets, and is responsible for protecting the interests of consumers.

Manufacture and transportation of gas in Great Britain

Gas comes from producers' operating rigs in about one hundred dry gas fields, and associated gas from condensates and oil fields beneath the sea around the British Isles. Gas is moved onshore through terminals where a single company takes over responsibility for transporting it. The National Transmission System (NTS) is the network used to transport gas in GB. Compressor stations then push the gas through the NTS into eight regional networks, which make up the UK's local gas distribution system.

This distribution system comprises over 170,000 miles of distribution pipelines and transports gas to third party pipeline systems and consumers. These third-party pipeline systems reduce the gas pressure for delivery through low-pressure pipes to consumers.

Storage of gas

Gas demand varies, within the day and from season to season. This requires gas storage capacity, to enable gas supply to be matched to demand. Gas can be stored in a number of ways: notably in underground pipelines, a depleted gas field offshore, underground in salt cavities or depleted gas fields, and as liquefied natural gas.

In 2001, over 40 reporting units on the IDBR were classified to this industry. The increase in the number of competitors and associated regulation has led to a reduction in retail prices (apart from a blip caused by pre-paid contracts) and bundling of energy supply with other products. For example, there are now single businesses supplying both gas and electricity together with other products such as financial and telecommunication services.

Impact of changes in the oil price

Oil is a key raw material in the production of various goods and services, so a rise or fall in the price has a direct effect on a company's cost base. They may decide to pass on the change to customers, and the price change will naturally feed through to inflation. Figure 4 shows the profile of the spot price for Brent crude oil between 1992 and 2001.

As the oil price rises, companies may absorb some of the increase in costs in order to avoid raising prices and losing customers. If the oil price falls, companies are given a choice between higher profits from the lower costs of production and cutting prices to gain, or maintain, market share.

In general, pump prices follow the trend of crude oil and refined product prices although there is less of a direct correlation to pump prices because of exchange rate movements, and excise duties and VAT which account for a large proportion of the price. For example, in 2000, prices at the pump actually fell although the price of crude oil rose to $29.0 per barrel.

Statistical overview of UK oil and gas activity

In 2001, the contribution of the oil and gas sector as defined in Table 1 to UK GVA at current basic prices accounted for £28.2 billion out of a total of £880.9 billion (3.2 per cent of the total). Figure 1 shows that GVA at current basic prices for this sector grew by 64.2 per cent between 1992 and 2001, compared with the growth of GVA at current basic prices for the whole economy of 61.2 per cent over this period. However, the growth rates of UK GVA and the oil sector GVA clearly differ between 1996 and 2000.

Figure 5 shows the factor income composition of GVA at current basic prices generated by the oil and gas sector. Compensation of employees contributed £5.6 billion in 2001 (growth of 15.7 per cent over 1992). Gross operating surplus (which includes gross operating profits and rental income) for the oil and gas sector in 2001 amounted to £22.1 billion (growth of 89.6 per cent over 1992) and gross operating surplus peaked in 2000 at £23.5 billion. Taxes (*less* subsidies) on production in 2001 amounts to £0.5 billion falling by 26.9 per cent from £0.7 billion in 1992.

I-O industry group 5

GVA at current basic prices for this industry grew by 122.2 per cent between 1992 and 2001 from £9.7 billion to £21.6 billion, as shown in Figure 6.

Gross operating surplus (which includes profits) formed the largest contribution to GVA at current basic prices for this industry for all years between 1992 to 2001. Gross operating surplus grew from £8.5 billion in 1992 to £20.0 billion in 2001.

The contribution of compensation of employees to GVA at current basic prices grew from £1.2 billion in 1992 to £1.5 billion in 2001. Taxes (*less* subsidies) on production have contributed less than £0.1 billion in each year over this period.

Figure 4
Brent crude oil spot price
$ per barrel

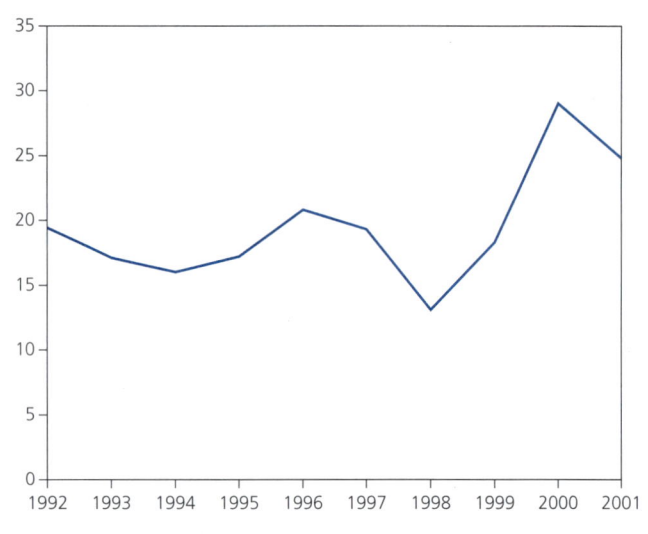

Figure 5
Factor incomes generated by oil and gas sector in 2001
Per cent

- Taxes (less subsidies) on production (1.7%)
- Compensation Employees (19.8%)
- Gross Operating Surplus (78.4%)

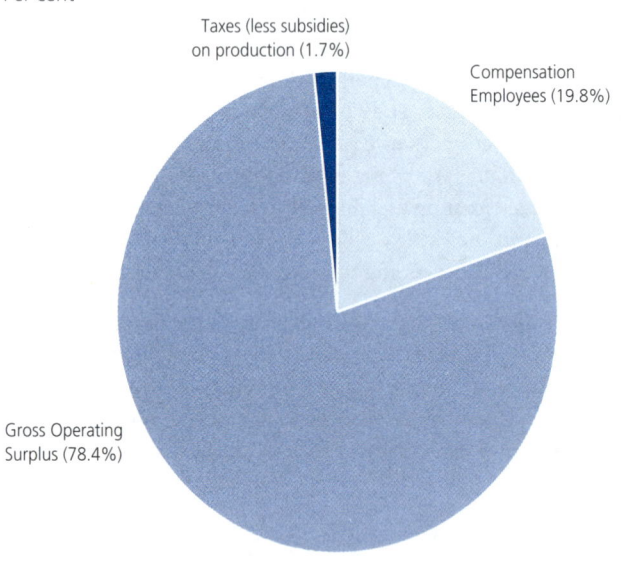

Figure 6
Oil and gas sector GVA by industry group
£ billion

Figure 7
Gross operating surplus (I-O industry 5) growth relative to Brent crude oil price

Per cent growth (Rebased to 1992)

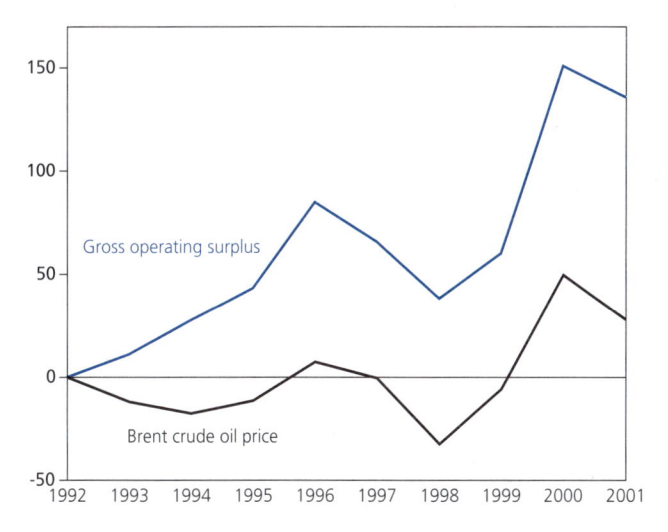

Figure 7 shows the profile of gross operating surplus for this industry matched against the movements in the price of crude oil. For many periods, the movements correlate well.

I-O industry group 35

Between 1992 and 2001, GVA at current basic prices for this industry has fluctuated between £1.9 billion and £2.3 billion, and in 2001 amounted to £2.1 billion, as shown in Figure 6.

In all years between 1992 and 2001, compensation of employees accounts for the largest contribution to GVA at current basic prices for this industry, growing from £1.1 billion in 1992 to £1.7 billion in 2001. Over this period, the contribution of gross operating surplus to GVA at current basic prices has been more erratic, falling from £0.9 billion to £0.4 billion. Similar to I-O industry group 5, taxes (*less* subsidies) on production have contributed less than £0.1 billion in each year between 1992 and 2001.

I-O industry group 86

GVA at current basic prices for this industry fell by 19.9 per cent between 1992 and 2001 from £4.0 billion to £3.2 billion, as shown in Figure 6.

Gross operating surplus formed the largest contribution to GVA at current basic prices for this industry for all years between 1992 to 2001. Gross operating surplus fell from £1.9 billion in 1992 to £1.5 billion in 2001.

The contribution of compensation of employees to GVA at current basic prices fell from £1.7 billion in 1992 to £1.5 billion in 2001.

Taxes (*less* subsidies) on production have fallen from £0.5 billion in 1992 to £0.3 billion in 2001. A large property portfolio owned by the industry was sold to the property industry between 1995 and 1996, prompting a large drop in payments of national non-domestic rates (business rates). This sale was also recorded as a disposal of fixed assets, which in turn resulted in a fall in gross fixed capital formation (acquisitions *less* disposals of fixed assets) for the industry in 1996.

Oil and gas sector, product supply and demand

Table 2 shows a summary oil and gas sector product supply and demand balance struck at purchasers' prices for the year 2001, and the changes since 1992.

The UK supply of products is composed of domestic output, imports of goods and services, distributors' trading margins and taxes (*less* subsidies) on products.

Table 2
Oil and gas sector Supply and Demand product balances in 2001

Product group	I-O group 5 £m	Per cent change since 1992	I-O group 35 (part) £m	Per cent change since 1992	I-O group 86 (part) £m	Per cent change since 1992	I-O group 89 (part) £m	Per cent change since 1992
Supply								
Domestic output	26,296	112.8	12,389	39.2	13,472	57.7	2,332	2.4
Imports of goods and services	5,373	27.9	4,473	110.0	18	−10.0	8	25.5
Distributors' trading margins	−812	n/a	1,431	90.0	-	n/a	−1,183	4.4
Taxes (less subsidies) on products	78	−42.7	19,932	93.8	405	0.4	95	−9.8
Total supply	30,935	85.1	38,225	73.2	13,895	55.0	1,252	−0.2
Demand								
Intermediate demand	19,093	81.2	19,571	97.8	7,930	134.7	482	−6.6
HHFCe	-	n/a	13,916	49.4	5,948	5.0	763	4.6
Gross capital formation	356	−76.8	72	24.5	−4	−96.1	-	n/a
Exports of goods and services	11,485	147.7	4,667	66.1	21	23.5	6	−29.3
Total demand	30,935	85.1	38,225	73.2	13,895	55.0	1,252	−0.2

The UK demand for products is composed of intermediate demand, final consumption expenditure (by households, non-profit institutions, and general government), gross capital formation (gross fixed capital formation, changes in inventories and valuables) and exports of goods and services.

I-O product group 5

Table 2 and Figure 8 show that the UK supply of extraction of oil and gas products between 1992 to 2001 grew by 85.1 per cent from £16.7 billion to £30.1 billion.

The supply of extraction of oil and gas is mainly composed of domestic output and imports. Between 1992 and 2001, domestic output grew by 112.8 per cent from £12.4 billion to £26.3 billion and imports grew by 27.9 per cent from £4.2 billion to £5.4 billion.

Most of the supply of this product is either used up as intermediate consumption or exported. In terms of intermediate consumption, there are very few industries that consume this product. Figure 9 shows the intermediate consumption of this product in 2001, the main players being I-O industry group 5 (oil and gas extraction) using £1.7 billion, 35 (refined petroleum products) using £10.3 billion, 85 (electricity) using £2.6 billion and 86 (gas) using £4.5 billion.

I-O product group 35

Figure 8 and Table 2 show that the total UK supply of refined petroleum products between 1992 to 2001 grew by 73.2 per cent from £22.1 billion to £38.2 billion.

Over this period, domestic output grew by 39.2 per cent from £8.9 billion to £12.4 billion; imports grew by 110.0 per cent from £2.1 billion to £4.5 billion; and distributors' trading margins on refined petroleum products grew by 90.0 per cent from £0.8 billion to £1.4 billion.

Taxes (*less* subsidies) on products, which include both excise duties and VAT, grew by 93.8 per cent from £10.3 billion to £20.0 billion. Figure 10 shows that in 1992 these taxes formed 46.6 per cent of the total supply, steadily rising to 62.3 per cent in 1998 before falling back to 52.1 per cent in 2001.

Figure 11 shows the consumption of petroleum products by category of demand.

In 2001, sales to industry, commerce, business and government accounted for about 51.2 per cent of total demand. Many of these sectors include high volume consumers whose purchases of this product form a large proportion of their operating costs, and whose input costs are therefore very sensitive to price changes. Examples include manufacturers, airlines, energy generators and distributors, shipping and road transport.

Figure 9
Intermediate consumption of I-O product 5 (by industry)

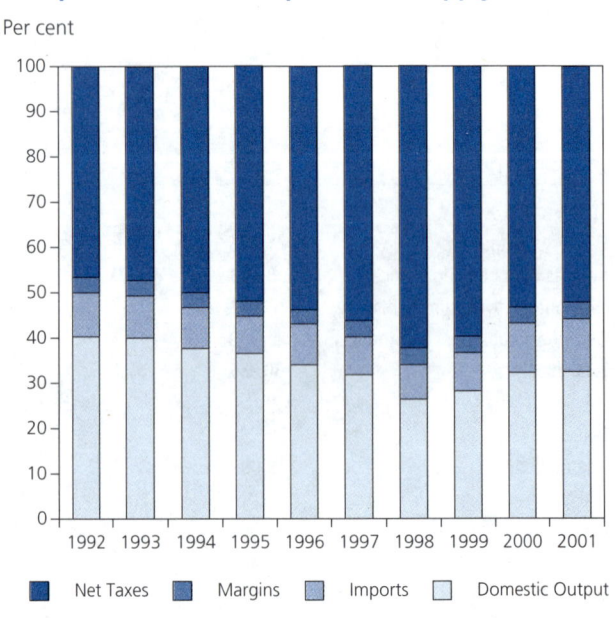

Figure 8
Supply of oil and gas sector by product

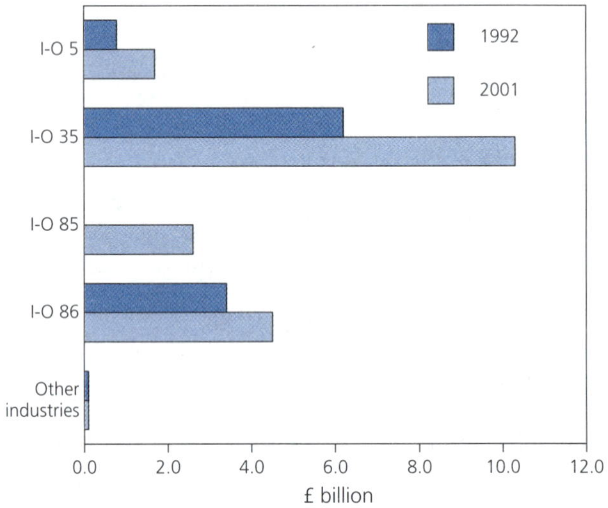

Figure 10
Composition of refined petroleum supply

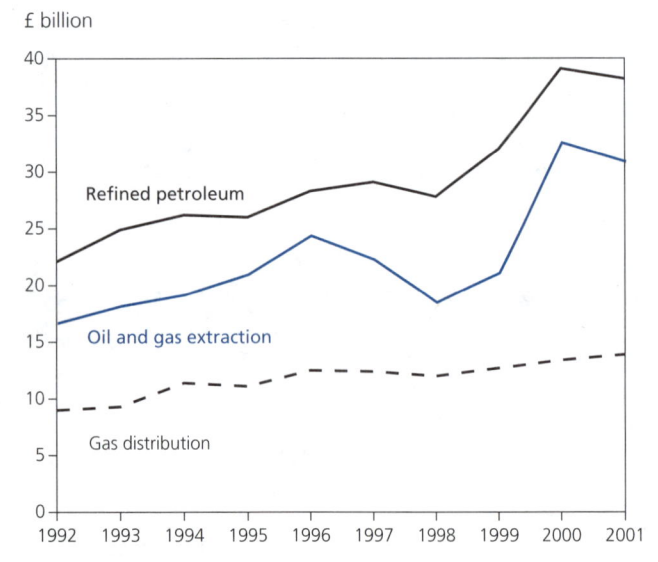

Households accounted for 36.4 per cent of total demand in 2001, and exports accounted for 12.2 per cent.

Figure 12 shows the intermediate consumption of I-O product group 35 by the eleven broad industrial sectors for the years 1992 and 2001. In all years from 1992 to 2001, the largest consuming sector was transport and telecommunications. This sector consumed £2.6 billion in 1992 growing to £6.0 billion in 2001.

I-O product group 86

Figure 8 and Table 2 show that the UK supply of gas products between 1992 to 2001 grew by 55.0 per cent from £9.0 billion to £13.9 billion.

The supply of gas is mainly composed of domestic output, which between 1992 and 2001, grew by 57.7 per cent from £8.5 billion to £13.5 billion.

Of the supply of gas in 2001, 57.0 per cent is used up as intermediate consumption by UK industries and 42.8 per cent consumed by households.

Figure 13 shows the intermediate consumption of I-O product group 86 by the eleven broad industrial sectors for the years 1992 and 2001. In 1992, the manufacturing sector was the largest consuming sector at £1.0 billion rising to £1.7 billion in 2001. In 2001, the energy sector was the largest consuming sector and consumed £0.9 billion in 1992 growing to £4.6 billion in 2001. This increase reflects a number of structural changes, for example, non-consolidation of the gas industry and greater purchases of gas for resale by energy suppliers.

Electricity industry

The electricity product is generated using key inputs such as coal, gas, nuclear fuel and renewables, such as wind power. The intermediate inputs to the electricity industry have changed rapidly through the 1990s when, for example, the use of coal and oil has been substituted by greater use of gas.

Figure 14 shows the electricity industry's intermediate consumption by product in 1992 and 2001. The intermediate consumption of the coal product in 1992 was £3.6 billion, forming 19.7 per cent of the total intermediate consumption, falling to £1.5 billion and 6.4 per cent in 2001. The intermediate consumption of gas in 1992 was £0.5 billion (2.6 per cent of the total) moving to £3.4 billion (14.6 per cent of

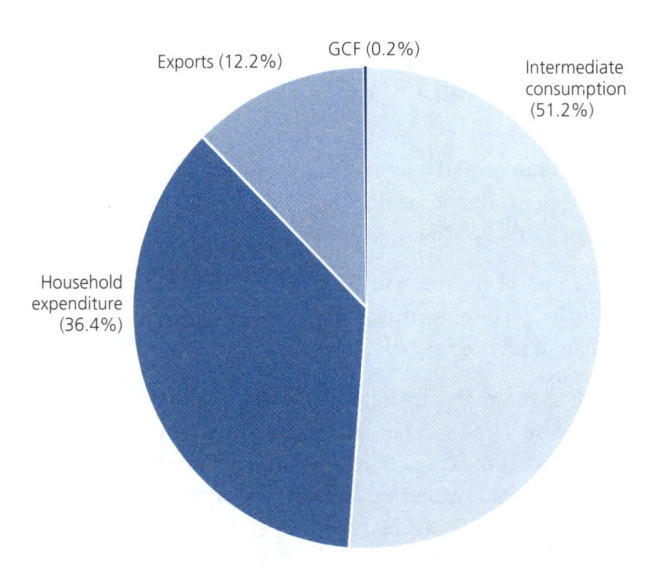

Figure 12
Intermediate consumption of I-O product 35 (part)
£ billion

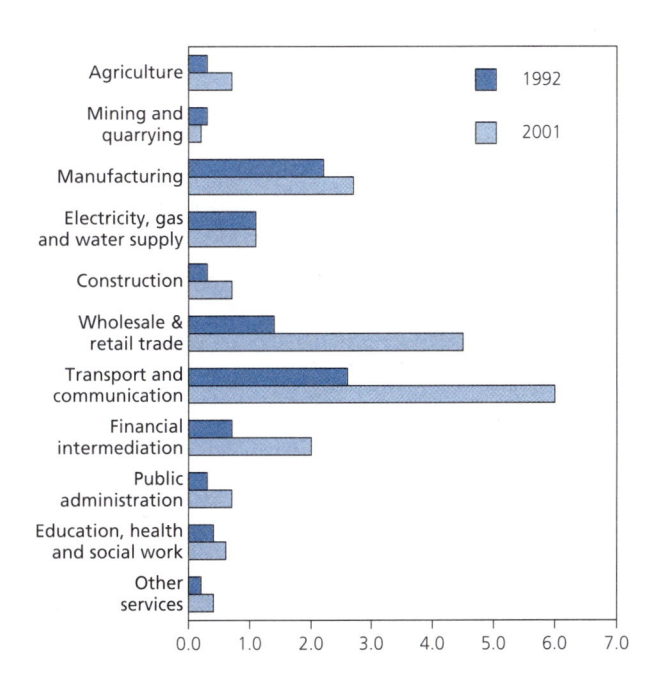

Figure 13
Intermediate consumption of I-O product 86
£ million

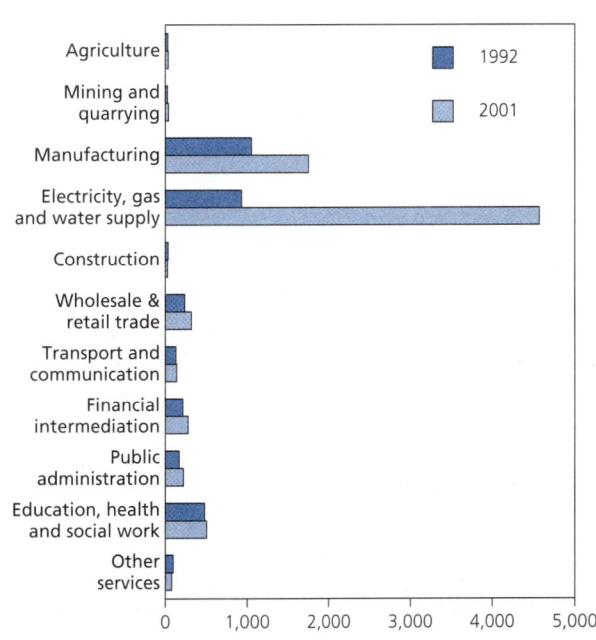

Figure 11
Consumption of refined petroleum in 2001
Per cent

- Exports (12.2%)
- GCF (0.2%)
- Intermediate consumption (51.2%)
- Household expenditure (36.4%)

Figure 14
Electricity industry's intermediate consumption by product
£ billion

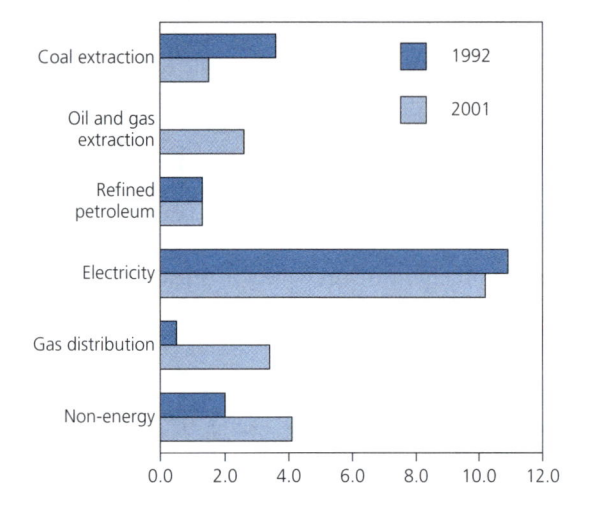

Figure 15
Relative shares of energy consumption by households in 2001
Per cent

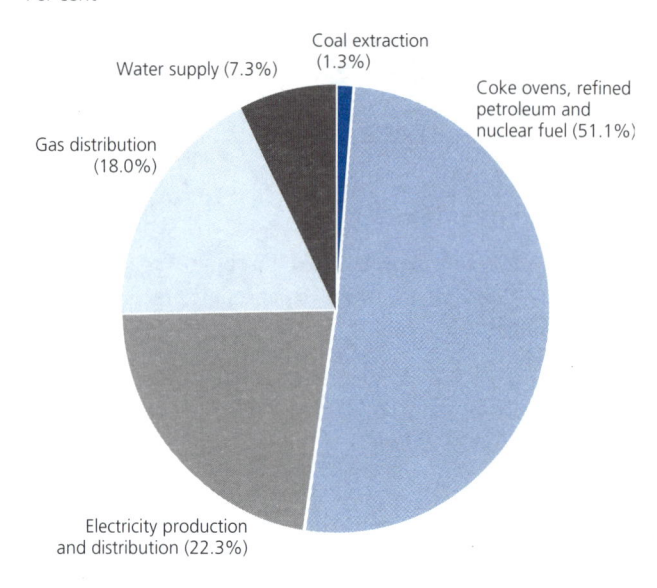

Figure 16
Retail prices of electricity, gas and oil
Index numbers (1987=100)

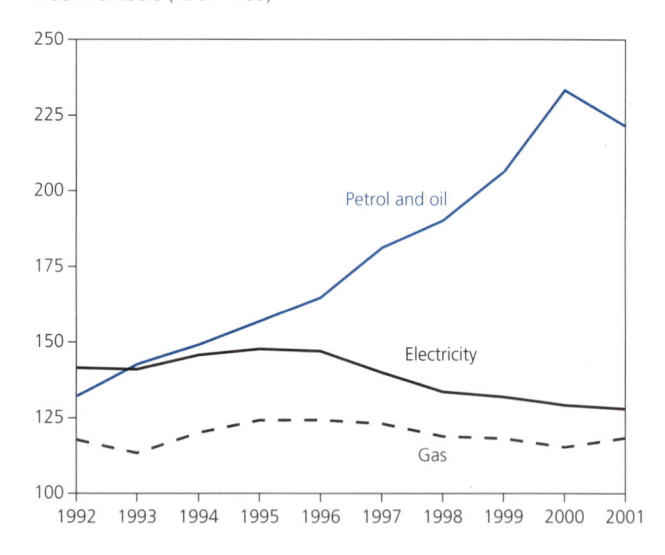

the total) in 2001. This increase reflects both the greater use for own consumption and the purchases of gas for resale to the industrial and household sectors.

Household final consumption expenditure

Figure 15 shows the split of energy products consumed by households. In 2001, refined petroleum products account for the largest proportion of the total at 51.1 per cent which amounts to £16.9 billion compared to 43.3 per cent and £11.8 billion in 1992.

The supermarkets' move into non-food related products, together with the expansion of out-of-town stores has taken place through a period when the number of roadside filling stations has fallen from 18,549 sites in 1992 to 12,201 sites in 2001, as shown in Figure 3. This, together with the slim margin on fuel retailing, has prompted the redevelopment of many sites to provide various other facilities, for example, by diversifying into shops, cafes and restaurants. The role of the forecourt shop has also expanded, from dealing in a limited range of vehicle related products to a more convenience type store selling a much wider range of goods.

With high volumes and low margins, changes in the crude oil price, whether caused by scarcity or the exchange rate, tend to be reflected in pump prices as these fluctuations cannot be ignored for any length of time.

Figure 16 shows that changes in the retail prices of energy consumed by households vary by type of product. In 2001 compared with 1992, the retail price paid for electricity has fallen by 13.5 per cent, the retail price paid for gas has risen by less than 1 per cent and the retail price paid for petrol and oil has increased by 89.2 per cent.

A large proportion of the retail price paid for petrol and oil is formed by the excise duty and VAT component. The excise duty itself varies on the type of fuel. Figure 17 shows the proportion that excise duty comprises of the full retail price on 4 star, unleaded and diesel fuels (data from the Institute of Petroleum).

Exports and imports

I-O product group 5

Exports of oil and gas grew from £4.6 billion in 1992 to £11.5 billion in 2001, contributing to 4.2 per cent of total UK exports of goods and services, and 1.2 per cent of GDP at current market prices in 2001.

Imports of oil and gas grew from £4.2 billion in 1992 to £5.4 billion in 2001, comprising 1.8 per cent of total UK imports of goods and services in 2001.

Figure 18 shows that for all years between 1992 and 2001, the UK has run a trade surplus on this product, growing over this period from £0.4 billion to £6.1 billion. In 2001, this I-O product formed the second largest trade surplus after I-O product group 102 (auxiliary financial services).

I-O product group 35

Exports of refined petroleum products grew from £2.8 billion in 1992 to £4.7 billion in 2001, contributing 1.7 per cent of total UK exports of goods and services, and 0.5 per cent of GDP at current market prices in 2001.

Imports of refined petroleum products grew from £2.1 billion in 1992 to £4.5 billion in 2001, comprising 1.5 per cent of total UK imports of goods and services in 2001.

Figure 18 shows that for all years between 1992 and 2001, the UK has run a trade surplus on this product. In 1992, this was £0.7 billion falling to £0.2 billion in 2001.

I-O product group 86

Imports and exports of this product are negligible.

Gross fixed capital formation

Figure 19 shows the gross fixed capital formation (GFCF) for the three main I-O industry groups covered in this section. GFCF for I-O group 5 has fallen from £6.9 billion in 1992 to £3.9 billion in 2001. The level of GFCF for I-O group 35 has remained broadly unchanged over the same period, whereas GFCF for I-O group 86 has fallen from £1.3 billion to £0.9 billion.

For I-O industry group 5 (oil and gas extraction), GFCF includes the cost of mineral exploration undertaken (successful or not) in order to discover new deposits of minerals or fuels. The costs cover actual test drilling and borings, aerial or other surveys and transportation costs, whether undertaken on own account or contracted-in from another business. Figure 20 shows GFCF for this industry separating out the mineral exploration investment.

Figure 18
Net trade balance (by product)
£ million

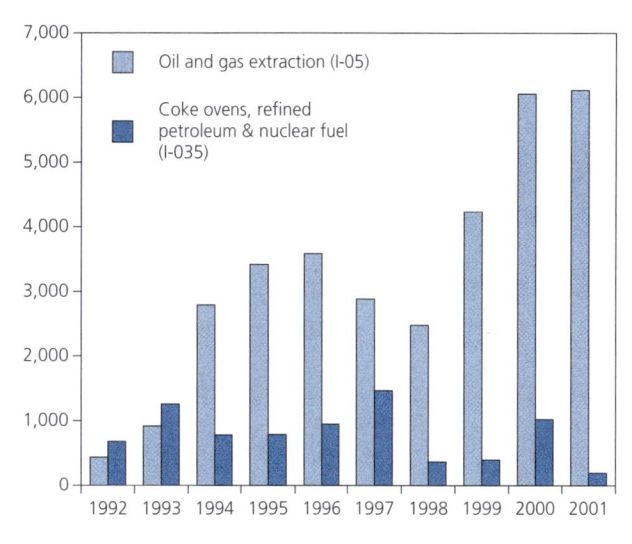

Figure 19
GFCF by industry
£ million

Figure 17
4 star, unleaded and diesel, average UK duty paid as a proportion of retail price
Per cent per litre

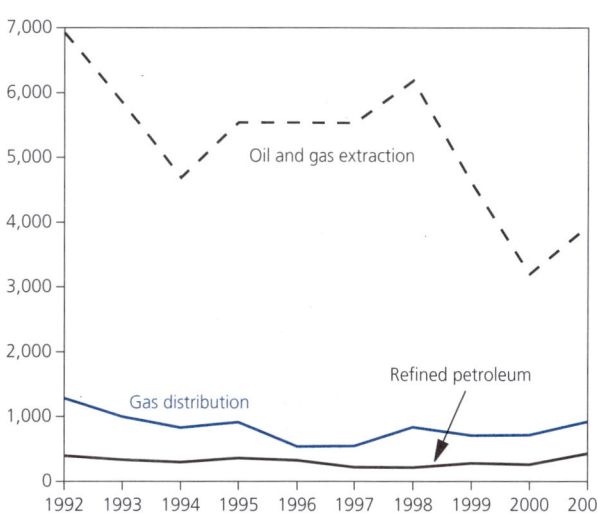

Figure 20
Oil and gas industry: GFCF split between exploration and other assets
£ million

Table 3
Chronology of events affecting the oil and gas industries

Year	Month	Event
1964		First exploration licences granted offshore UK.
1965		First gas field discovered by BP at West Sole.
1969		First oil found in UK waters by Amoco – Arbroath field.
1981		UK oil production exceeded consumption.
1988		Piper Alpha oil platform tragedy occurred in North Sea.
1992	Jan	Landmark reached with 100 fields in production in the UK.
	Mar	Libya threatened with sanctions for its refusal to extradite suspected terrorists.
	May	Saudi Arabia supported an increase in crude oil price during a meeting of the Organisation of Petroleum Exporting Countries (OPEC).
	Aug	Hurricane Andrew swept across the Gulf of Mexico forcing Gulf coast refineries to shut down.
	Sep	Exchange Rate Mechanism (ERM) collapsed – 'Black Wednesday'. Ecuador said it would withdraw from OPEC to avoid production quotas and membership costs. Russian President Yeltsin signed decree lifting state controls on energy prices and imposed steep, graduated taxes on domestic oil companies to prevent rapid price hikes.
	Nov	OPEC agreement failed to halt the oil price slide. Bill Clinton appointed US President.
	Dec	Cuts in production and in refinery runs introduced by several key OPEC members to maintain the New York Mercantile Exchange (NYMEX) oil price level at $19.40 per barrel.
1993	Mar	VAT imposed on domestic fuel following UK budget.
	May	Canadian House of Commons approved the North American Free Trade Agreement (NAFTA), lowering trade barriers within North America.
	Jul	Oil price in US fell to below $18 per barrel.
	Nov	US House and Senate approved NAFTA.
	Dec	Fall in oil prices continued.
1994	Mar	Crude prices fell and quickly recovered to meet the OPEC group quota.
	Apr	International Energy Agency (IEA) claimed world energy demand would grow 50 per cent by 2010, mostly in South-East Asia.
	May	Enterprise Oil of London made a bid to acquire Lasmo. Civil war erupted in Yemen. China banned imports of most crude oil and refined products and tightened control on oil prices and trading in an effort to help struggling state companies.
	Jul–Sep	Strike by oil workers in Nigeria hit oil production.
	Oct	North Sea production reached a record high of 5.76 million barrels per day over the month.
	Dec	Nine companies led by British Gas announced plans to lay a 240 km subsea pipeline from UK to Belgium.
		UK coal industry privatised.
1995	Mar	Crude prices rose on the expectation that US would embargo purchases of Iranian oil.
	Jun	European Commission (EC) approved the 240 km pipeline between UK and Belgium to provide the first UK exports of gas to continental Europe.
	Aug	North Sea production dragged oil prices down. Hurricane Opal hit the Gulf of Mexico, forcing down production and briefly lifting prices.
	Nov	British Gas split into two businesses: supply and shipping under British Gas Trading Ltd and transportation (Transco) under British Gas plc.
	Dec	Winter storms in the US lifted oil and gas demand and prices.
1996	Jan	EC agreed guidelines for a unified energy policy for European Union members.
	Feb	Development activity in the North Sea reached new record levels with 261 wells started.
	May	United Nations and Iraq agreed to resume oil exports to raise as much as $2bn for humanitarian purposes. The move raised the OPEC group quota.
	Jul	EC agreed to tighten vehicle emission standards and fuel specifications in a program to reduce emissions from road transport.
	Sep	UK Office of Gas Supply revealed plans to provide 1.5 million customers across Avon, Kent, Dorset, East and West Sussex with a choice of gas suppliers.
	Dec	Start of the Asian Economic Crisis in Thailand prompted falls in the stock market.

Year	Month	Event
1997	Feb	British Gas plc split into two companies: BGplc, handling UK gas supply and worldwide exploration and production; and Centrica plc, handling UK gas sales, trading and retail operations.
	May	New Labour government, headed by Tony Blair, elected in the UK.
	Aug	Economic and financial crisis hits Russia.
	Oct	Crude oil prices jumped as tensions rose in Iraq. Saddam Hussein banned American members of the UN inspection team in Iraq, raising questions over Iraq's state of military armament and readiness.
	Dec	EU agrees to deregulate one third of Europe's natural gas market in three phases over 10 years. First instalment of Windfall Tax collected from UK Utilities (£2.6 billion).
1998	Jan	Asian economic crisis ended.
	Jun	Second phase of the Asian Economic Crisis (Asia II) started, with the crisis spreading to Russia, Brazil and the West. Iran sought to increase its world oil production capacity.
	Sep	OPEC cut production and North Sea output steadied to stop oil price slide, but underlying growth in oil demand remained weak.
	Nov	US Energy Information Administration stated that Asia II would continue to depress oil prices.
	Dec	Exxon and Mobil Corporation merged to form the largest private oil company in the world. Second instalment of Windfall Tax collected from UK Utilities (£2.6 billion).
1999	Jan	Euro currency introduced across Europe. Asia II economic crisis ended. Merger of British Petroleum and Amoco Group completed.
	Mar	OPEC agreed to cut oil output for a year.
	Apr	National minimum wage introduced in UK.
	Aug	Oil and gas prices increased. NYMEX offered to buy 70 per cent of International Petroleum Exchange (IPE).
	Dec	Vladimir Putin replaced Boris Yeltsin as President of Russia.
2000	May	BP Amoco received EU approval to acquire Burmah Castrol for $4.7 billion.
	Jul	BP Amoco changed its name to BP.
	Sep	Hauliers and farmers staged large-scale protests over price of UK fuel and prompted UK petrol crisis. NYMEX crude price climbed past $37 per barrel, then dropped to $31 per barrel at the end of the month.
	Oct	BG plc demerged into two separate listed companies, of which Lattice Group plc was the holding company for Transco and BG group plc included the international and gas storage businesses. Chevron agreed to acquire Texaco for $35.1 billion.
2001	Jan	George W. Bush became US President.
	Mar	Kashagan field in the Caspian Sea declared the world's largest oil find in three decades.
	Apr	IEA lowered global oil demand forecast. UK government introduced the Climate Change Levy (CCL). German energy provider E.ON placed to take over Powergen in UK.
	May	Brent crude futures price peaked near $30.
	Jun	Discovery of the large Buzzard Oil Field in the North Sea changed the accepted view that there were no more large fields to be discovered in the North Sea. International Petroleum Exchange announced plans to merge with Intercontinental Exchange.
	Sep	Terrorists attack and destroy World Trade Centre in New York.
2002	Apr	Shell UK's Goldeneye contract with Foster Wheeler opened the way to new onshore gas processing facilities at St Fergus.
	Jun	Revised oil recovery forecasts for the Buzzard field suggested it was the largest North Sea oil discovery in the last 25 years, with over 1 billion barrels of oil in place.
	Oct	National Grid company and Transco merged to form National Grid Transco plc.
	Nov	UK and Norway co-operated to maximise cross-border oil and gas production in the North Sea.

Acknowledgements

The members of the Current Price Input-Output Branch listed below have developed the Oil and gas sector analyses based on the 2003 Edition of the *United Kingdom Input-Output Analyses* and the underlying I-O Annual Supply and Use Tables. We are very grateful to the many individuals, both inside and outside the ONS, who provided data, analyses and a wide-range of assistance and co-operation in producing these tables. The Current Price Input-Output Branch members: Bob Cuthbert, Daniel Mistry, Ian Gouldson, Neil O'Driscoll, Sharon Kaur, Jeremy Okai, James Lockerbie, Joanne Penn, Sanjiv Mahajan and Richard Tanguy.

References

The Institute of Petroleum (www.petroleum.co.uk) [Average UK retail price and duty paid on fuel].

International Petroleum Encyclopaedia (1992–2001) by Pennwell Publishing.[Chronology of events].

Office for National Statistics (2003) *United Kingdom Input-Output Analyses, 2003 Edition*. Available at www.statistics.gov.uk/inputoutput

Office for National Statistics (2003) *United Kingdom National Accounts – the Blue Book 2003*. TSO: London.

Platts (www.platts.com) [Brent crude oil spot price].

Retail Marketing Survey [Number of petrol stations in the UK].

www.dti.gov.uk [Chronology for 2002 and 2003] and [Inland deliveries of petroleum].

Oil and gas sector, 1992–2001 — Economic Trends 604 March 2004

Table 4
Oil and gas sector statistics at a glance

	\multicolumn{10}{c}{All estimates are in £ million or proportions as appropriate}	\multicolumn{2}{c}{Growth rates (per cent)}
	1992	1993	1994	1995	1996	1997	1998	1999	2000	2001	*2000–2001*	*1992–2001*
Oil and gas sector Supply and Demand product balances												
Supply of I–O product group 5												
Domestic output of products at basic prices	12 358	13 546	15 541	17 444	20 057	18 282	16 159	18 496	27 484	26 296	–4.3	112.8
Imports of goods and services	4 202	4 481	3 540	3 393	4 204	3 863	2 272	2 390	5 332	5 373	0.8	27.9
Distributors' trading margins	14	16	19	21	25	22	20	165	–342	–812	n/a	n/a
Taxes (*less* subsidies) on products	136	139	103	104	103	86	45	41	81	78	–3.5	–42.7
Total supply of products at purchasers' prices	16 710	18 182	19 203	20 962	24 389	22 253	18 495	21 091	32 555	30 935	–5.0	85.1
Demand for I–O product group 5												
Total intermediate demand (including NPISHs and GG)	10 538	11 517	11 949	13 086	15 605	14 307	12 947	14 285	21 053	19 093	–9.3	81.2
Households final consumption expenditure (HHFCe)	–	–	–	–	–	–	–	–	–	–	n/a	n/a
Gross capital formation	1 535	1 267	922	1 068	995	1 199	797	184	114	356	211.5	–76.8
Exports of goods and services	4 637	5 398	6 333	6 808	7 788	6 746	4 751	6 622	11 387	11 485	0.9	147.7
Total demand for products at purchasers' prices	16 711	18 182	19 203	20 962	24 388	22 252	18 495	21 091	32 555	30 935	–5.0	85.1
Supply of I–O product group 35 (part)												
Domestic output of products at basic prices	8 902	9 991	9 893	9 509	9 634	9 247	7 326	9 050	12 595	12 389	–1.6	39.2
Imports of goods and services	2 130	2 319	2 361	2 118	2 590	2 427	2 102	2 719	4 280	4 473	4.5	110.0
Distributors' trading margins	753	856	877	844	866	1 040	1 042	1 160	1 382	1 431	n/a	n/a
Taxes (*less* subsidies) on products	10 287	11 782	13 116	13 487	15 222	16 349	17 288	19 118	20 814	19 932	–4.2	93.8
Total supply of products at purchasers' prices	22 073	24 948	26 247	25 958	28 312	29 064	27 757	32 047	39 071	38 225	–2.2	73.2
Demand for I–O product group 35 (part)												
Total intermediate demand (including NPISHs and GG)	9 894	11 154	12 455	12 856	13 577	13 149	13 822	16 240	19 016	19 571	2.9	97.8
Households final consumption expenditure (HHFCe)	9 313	10 186	10 615	10 101	11 176	11 806	11 516	12 593	14 745	13 916	–5.6	49.4
Gross capital formation	58	35	36	98	25	218	–48	101	10	72	592.0	24.5
Exports of goods and services	2 809	3 574	3 140	2 904	3 534	3 891	2 467	3 114	5 300	4 667	–12.0	66.1
Total demand for products at purchasers' prices	22 073	24 948	26 247	25 958	28 312	29 064	27 757	32 047	39 071	38 225	–2.2	73.2
Supply of I–O product group 86 all (part)												
Domestic output of products at basic prices	8 542	8 936	10 825	10 351	11 708	11 663	11 576	12 277	12 965	13 472	3.9	57.7
Imports of goods and services	20	18	20	19	23	17	13	23	18	18	0.0	–10.0
Distributors' trading margins	–	–	–	–	–	–	–	–	–	–	n/a	n/a
Taxes (*less* subsidies) on products	404	346	576	688	768	675	391	352	384	405	5.6	0.4
Total supply of products at purchasers' prices	8 966	9 299	11 421	11 059	12 499	12 355	11 980	12 652	13 367	13 895	4.0	55.0
Demand for I–O product group 86 (part)												
Total intermediate demand (including NPISHs and GG)	3 378	3 627	5 704	5 197	6 095	6 238	6 420	7 384	7 354	7 930	7.8	134.7
Households final consumption expenditure (HHFCe)	5 666	5 697	5 726	5 885	6 404	6 105	5 536	5 304	5 839	5 948	1.9	5.0
Gross capital formation	–95	–44	–28	–46	–22	–10	–	–59	151	–4	–102.4	–96.1
Exports of goods and services	17	19	19	23	22	22	23	23	23	21	–8.7	23.5
Total demand for products at purchasers' prices	8 966	9 299	11 421	11 059	12 499	12 355	11 980	12 652	13 367	13 895	4.0	55.0
Supply of I–O product group 89 (part)												
Domestic output of products at basic prices	2 277	2 019	2 019	1 658	1 499	1 823	1 787	1 837	2 144	2 332	8.8	2.4
Imports of goods and services	7	6	7	5	5	6	6	6	8	8	5.4	25.5
Distributors' trading margins	–1 133	–1 015	–1 009	–828	–737	–906	–928	–953	–1 089	–1 183	n/a	n/a
Taxes (*less* subsidies) on products	105	88	86	70	64	81	70	72	87	95	8.9	–9.8
Total supply of products at purchasers' prices	1 255	1 098	1 103	905	831	1 003	935	963	1 150	1 252	8.9	–0.2
Demand for I–O product group 89 (part)												
Total intermediate demand (including NPISHs and GG)	516	463	483	396	366	435	392	417	464	482	3.9	–6.6
Households final consumption expenditure (HHFCe)	730	627	612	503	459	562	537	540	679	763	12.5	4.6
Gross capital formation	–	–	–	–	–	–	–	–	–	–	n/a	n/a
Exports of goods and services	9	8	8	7	6	6	6	6	7	6	–9.1	–29.3
Total demand for products at purchasers' prices	1 255	1 098	1 103	905	831	1 003	935	963	1 150	1 252	8.9	–0.2

Table 4 - *continued*
Oil and gas sector statistics at a glance

	All estimates are in £ million or proportions as appropriate											Growth rates (per cent)	
	1992	1993	1994	1995	1996	1997	1998	1999	2000	2001	*2000–2001*	*1992–2001*
Analysis of oil and gas sector (by industry)												
Total output												
5 Oil and gas extraction	14 190	15 630	17 992	20 177	23 209	21 113	18 344	20 293	28 661	27 374	-4.5	92.9
part of 35 Coke ovens, refined petroleum and nuclear fuel	9 219	10 300	10 176	9 886	9 869	9 544	7 704	9 404	13 136	13 106	-0.2	42.2
part of 86 Gas distribution	8 897	9 364	11 432	11 260	11 859	11 440	11 057	10 711	11 439	11 458	0.2	28.8
part of 89 Motor vehicle distribution and repair	2 475	2 165	2 163	1 764	1 613	1 945	1 870	1 905	2 251	2 390	6.1	-3.4
Total output at basic prices	**34 781**	**37 459**	**41 763**	**43 087**	**46 550**	**44 041**	**38 975**	**42 313**	**55 488**	**54 328**	**-2.1**	**56.2**
Total intermediate consumption												
5 Oil and gas extraction	4 465	4 738	5 499	6 474	6 085	5 678	5 140	5 249	5 828	5 766	-1.1	29.1
part of 35 Coke ovens, refined petroleum and nuclear fuel	7 129	8 198	7 944	7 584	7 819	7 641	5 764	7 326	11 071	10 959	-1.0	53.7
part of 86 Gas distribution	4 871	5 238	7 521	8 143	8 711	8 308	7 826	7 387	8 062	8 233	2.1	69.0
part of 89 Motor vehicle distribution and repair	1 150	1 015	1 005	829	811	981	957	944	1 118	1 182	5.7	2.8
Total intermediate consumption	**17 614**	**19 190**	**21 969**	**23 030**	**23 426**	**22 608**	**19 687**	**20 906**	**26 079**	**26 139**	**0.2**	**48.4**
Gross value added at basic prices												
5 Oil and gas extraction	9 725	10 892	12 493	13 703	17 124	15 435	13 204	15 044	22 833	21 608	-5.4	122.2
part of 35 Coke ovens, refined petroleum and nuclear fuel	2 091	2 101	2 233	2 302	2 050	1 902	1 941	2 078	2 065	2 147	4.0	2.7
part of 86 Gas distribution	4 026	4 126	3 911	3 117	3 148	3 132	3 231	3 324	3 377	3 225	-4.5	-19.9
part of 89 Motor vehicle distribution and repair	1 325	1 150	1 158	936	803	964	913	961	1 134	1 208	6.6	-8.8
Total GVA at basic prices	**17 167**	**18 269**	**19 794**	**20 057**	**23 125**	**21 433**	**19 289**	**21 407**	**29 409**	**28 189**	**-4.1**	**64.2**
Gross fixed capital formation												
5 Oil and gas extraction	6 924	5 846	4 687	5 536	5 536	5 530	6 186	4 605	3 197	3 938	23.2	-43.1
part of 35 Coke ovens, refined petroleum and nuclear fuel	395	334	298	359	325	219	215	279	259	429	65.3	8.7
part of 86 Gas distribution	1 281	997	827	912	536	543	835	706	713	917	28.6	-28.4
part of 89 Motor vehicle distribution and repair	103	147	129	74	29	39	119	73	157	120	-23.7	16.0
Total GFCF	**8 703**	**7 324**	**5 941**	**6 881**	**6 425**	**6 330**	**7 355**	**5 663**	**4 327**	**5 404**	**24.9**	**-37.9**

GFCF represents Gross Fixed Capital Formation.
NPISHs represents Non-Profit Institutions Serving Households
ToP represents taxes (*less* subsidies) on production.

GG represents General Government Final Consumption Expenditure.
Balance of trade is recorded as exports *less* imports.
Differences between totals and sums of components are due to rounding.

Table 4 - *continued*
Oil and gas sector statistics at a glance

	All estimates are in £ million or proportions as appropriate										Growth rates (per cent)	
	1992	1993	1994	1995	1996	1997	1998	1999	2000	2001	*2000–2001*	*1992–2001*
Intermediate consumption of oil and gas sector products (by industry)												
I–O product group 5												
1 Agriculture [1–3]	–	–	–	–	–	–	–	–	–	–	n/a	n/a
2 Mining and quarrying [4–7]	832	893	1 164	1 528	1 777	1 483	1 667	1 605	2 128	1 675	-21.3	101.3
3 Manufacturing [8–84]	6 262	6 789	6 440	6 609	7 954	7 429	5 123	6 662	11 127	10 317	-7.3	64.7
4 Electricity, gas and water supply [85–87]	3 444	3 834	4 345	4 950	5 875	5 395	6 157	6 018	7 798	7 102	-8.9	106.2
5 Construction [88]	–	–	–	–	–	–	–	–	–	–	n/a	n/a
6 Wholesale & retail trade [89–92]	–	–	–	–	–	–	–	–	–	–	n/a	n/a
7 Transport and communication [93–99]	–	–	–	–	–	–	–	–	–	–	n/a	n/a
8 Financial intermediation [100–114]	–	–	–	–	–	–	–	–	–	–	n/a	n/a
9 Public administration [115]	–	–	–	–	–	–	–	–	–	–	n/a	n/a
10 Education, health and social work [116–118]	–	–	–	–	–	–	–	–	–	–	n/a	n/a
11 Other services [119–123]	–	–	–	–	–	–	–	–	–	–	n/a	n/a
Total intermediate consumption	10 538	11 517	11 949	13 086	15 605	14 307	12 947	14 285	21 053	19 093	-9.3	81.2
I–O product group 35 (*part*)												
1 Agriculture [1–3]	343	358	356	401	453	579	557	612	686	741	8.1	116.3
2 Mining and quarrying [4–7]	307	302	343	285	288	241	199	236	268	234	-12.6	-23.7
3 Manufacturing [8–84]	2 214	2 439	2 719	2 968	2 520	2 596	2 586	2 617	2 621	2 687	2.5	21.4
4 Electricity, gas and water supply [85–87]	1 082	1 140	1 105	1 100	887	983	955	1 122	1 237	1 130	-8.7	4.5
5 Construction [88]	269	298	349	318	353	354	424	494	629	651	3.5	142.2
6 Wholesale & retail trade [89–92]	1 379	1 639	1 953	2 076	2 531	2 414	2 715	3 437	4 217	4 468	6.0	224.0
7 Transport and communication [93–99]	2 615	3 099	3 546	3 573	4 111	3 796	4 060	4 897	5 842	5 989	2.5	129.1
8 Financial intermediation [100–114]	743	843	992	1 013	1 187	1 065	1 216	1 543	1 931	2 016	4.4	171.3
9 Public administration [115]	331	369	370	412	415	406	408	474	643	679	5.5	105.1
10 Education, health and social work [116–118]	394	412	445	421	503	439	418	479	553	580	4.8	47.0
11 Other services [119–123]	217	255	279	290	329	277	284	328	388	395	1.8	81.9
Total intermediate consumption	9 894	11 154	12 455	12 856	13 577	13 149	13 822	16 240	19 016	19 571	2.9	97.8
I–O product group 86 (*part*)												
1 Agriculture [1–3]	30	25	32	27	36	38	39	32	29	35	20.5	18.0
2 Mining and quarrying [4–7]	26	16	21	20	28	26	27	32	38	38	-0.9	43.2
3 Manufacturing [8–84]	1 051	1 158	1 512	1 300	1 759	1 810	1 798	1 681	1 571	1 744	11.1	66.0
4 Electricity, gas and water supply [85–87]	933	1 092	2 915	2 866	3 060	3 106	3 099	4 210	4 302	4 573	6.3	390.2
5 Construction [88]	34	38	30	19	24	27	36	32	28	27	-0.8	-20.4
6 Wholesale & retail trade [89–92]	232	259	222	154	219	247	327	312	305	313	2.6	34.7
7 Transport and communication [93–99]	127	145	124	83	114	125	158	145	134	136	1.5	6.6
8 Financial intermediation [100–114]	210	228	199	139	192	211	282	276	268	273	1.9	30.1
9 Public administration [115]	166	168	179	190	173	159	150	165	180	216	20.0	30.1
10 Education, health and social work [116–118]	474	408	397	345	421	420	425	422	426	500	17.3	5.3
11 Other services [119–123]	94	92	74	54	69	69	80	77	74	76	1.5	-20.0
Total intermediate consumption	3 378	3 627	5 704	5 197	6 095	6 238	6 420	7 384	7 354	7 930	7.8	134.7
I–O product group 89 (*part*)												
1 Agriculture [1–3]	74	64	58	52	45	48	41	41	42	42	-0.3	-42.7
2 Mining and quarrying [4–7]	–	–	–	–	–	–	1	1	2	1	-12.3	n/a
3 Manufacturing [8–84]	24	23	23	17	15	15	15	18	24	27	11.9	12.8
4 Electricity, gas and water supply [85–87]	2	2	2	2	2	2	1	3	4	5	39.4	142.9
5 Construction [88]	–	–	–	–	–	–	–	–	–	–	n/a	n/a
6 Wholesale & retail trade [89–92]	125	111	116	95	91	116	105	112	124	130	4.3	3.9
7 Transport and communication [93–99]	104	95	102	78	71	86	75	77	82	84	2.4	-18.6
8 Financial intermediation [100–114]	113	99	111	92	85	102	96	104	117	122	4.4	7.3
9 Public administration [115]	–	–	–	–	–	–	–	–	–	–	n/a	n/a
10 Education, health and social work [116–118]	29	28	28	24	26	32	27	28	32	33	3.7	16.6
11 Other services [119–123]	17	15	15	14	13	14	12	12	13	13	4.1	-21.5
Total intermediate consumption	488	438	455	373	347	413	373	396	440	459	4.1	-6.0

Table 4 - *continued*
Oil and gas sector statistics at a glance

	All estimates are in £ million or proportions as appropriate											Growth rates (per cent)	
	1992	1993	1994	1995	1996	1997	1998	1999	2000	2001	*2000–2001*	*1992–2001*
Household final consumption on energy (by product)												
4 Coal extraction	451	448	450	464	483	440	396	410	350	442	26.3	-1.8
35 Coke ovens, refined petroleum and nuclear fuel	11 760	12 322	12 780	12 832	13 793	14 778	15 287	16 149	17 949	16 913	-5.8	43.8
85 Electricity production and distribution	7 648	7 811	8 056	8 163	8 347	7 943	7 734	7 387	7 420	7 381	-0.5	-3.5
86 Gas distribution	5 666	5 697	5 726	5 885	6 404	6 105	5 536	5 304	5 839	5 948	1.9	5.0
87 Water supply	1 612	1 776	1 964	2 078	2 206	2 312	2 402	2 516	2 406	2 425	0.8	50.5
Total HHFCe consumption on energy	27 137	28 053	28 976	29 422	31 233	31 577	31 355	31 765	33 965	33 110	-2.5	22.0
Relative shares of energy consumption by households (per cent)												
4 Coal extraction	1.7	1.6	1.6	1.6	1.5	1.4	1.3	1.3	1.0	1.3	29.6	-19.5
35 Coke ovens, refined petroleum and nuclear fuel	43.3	43.9	44.1	43.6	44.2	46.8	48.8	50.8	52.8	51.1	-3.3	17.9
85 Electricity production and distribution	28.2	27.8	27.8	27.7	26.7	25.2	24.7	23.3	21.8	22.3	2.0	-20.9
86 Gas distribution	20.9	20.3	19.8	20.0	20.5	19.3	17.7	16.7	17.2	18.0	4.5	-14.0
87 Water supply	5.9	6.3	6.8	7.1	7.1	7.3	7.7	7.9	7.1	7.3	3.4	23.3
Total	100	100	100	100	100	100	100	100	100	100	n/a	n/a
Electricity industry consumption of energy (by product)												
4 Coal extraction	3 608	2 552	2 490	2 615	2 260	1 925	1 701	1 365	1 217	1 474	21.1	-59.1
5 Oil and gas extraction	–	–	–	–	–	443	1 324	1 892	2 780	2 641	-5.0	n/a
35 Coke ovens, refined petroleum and nuclear fuel	1 346	1 361	1 310	1 364	1 073	1 207	1 242	1 409	1 480	1 350	-8.8	0.3
85 Electricity production and distribution	10 873	10 360	10 107	9 879	9 322	10 056	10 579	11 610	12 122	10 197	-15.9	-6.2
86 Gas distribution	483	712	1 101	1 051	1 642	1 739	1 655	2 591	3 170	3 376	6.5	599.6
(Other non-energy)	2 017	2 005	2 138	2 116	2 412	2 853	3 035	2 983	3 234	4 060	25.5	101.2
Total intermediate consumption	18 326	16 990	17 146	17 025	16 710	18 224	19 536	21 851	24 002	23 098	-3.8	26.0
Balance of trade in goods and services (by product)												
5 Oil and gas extraction	435	917	2 793	3 415	3 584	2 883	2 479	4 232	6 055	6 112	n/a	n/a
part of 35 Coke ovens, refined petroleum and nuclear fuel	679	1 256	779	786	945	1 464	365	395	1 020	193	n/a	n/a
part of 86 Gas distribution	-3	1	-1	4	-1	5	10	0	5	3	n/a	n/a
part of 89 Motor vehicle distribution and repair	2	2	1	2	1	1	0	-1	-1	-2	n/a	n/a

GFCF represents Gross Fixed Capital Formation.
NPISHs represents Non-Profit Institutions Serving Households
ToP represents taxes (less subsidies) on production.

GG represents General Government Final Consumption Expenditure.
Balance of trade is recorded as exports *less* imports.
Differences between totals and sums of components are due to rounding.

Table 4 - continued
Oil and gas sector statistics at a glance

	All estimates are in £ million or proportions as appropriate											Growth rates (per cent)	
	1992	1993	1994	1995	1996	1997	1998	1999	2000	2001	2000–2001	1992–2001
Contribution to oil and gas sector GVA by type of factor income												
I–O industry group 5												
Compensation of employees	1 213	1 444	1 638	1 536	1 413	1 339	1 458	1 426	1 518	1 544	1.7	27.3
Gross operating surplus	8 464	9 402	10 808	12 121	15 653	14 033	11 700	13 548	21 234	19 957	-6.0	135.8
Taxes (*less* subsidies) on production	48	46	47	46	58	63	46	70	81	107	32.1	122.9
Total GVA at current basic prices	**9 725**	**10 892**	**12 493**	**13 703**	**17 124**	**15 435**	**13 204**	**15 044**	**22 833**	**21 608**	**-5.4**	**122.2**
I–O industry group 35 (*part*)												
Compensation of employees	1 088	1 171	1 202	1 259	1 382	1 381	1 350	1 578	1 682	1 682	0.0	54.6
Gross operating surplus	940	866	966	975	603	457	538	459	333	408	22.7	-56.6
Taxes (*less* subsidies) on production	63	65	65	68	65	64	53	41	51	58	13.1	-7.9
Total GVA at current basic prices	**2 091**	**2 101**	**2 233**	**2 302**	**2 050**	**1 902**	**1 941**	**2 078**	**2 065**	**2 147**	**4.0**	**2.7**
I–O industry group 86 (*part*)												
Compensation of employees	1 656	1 812	1 870	1 698	1 711	1 646	1 662	1 590	1 562	1 493	-4.4	-9.8
Gross operating surplus	1 898	1 835	1 558	935	1 209	1 260	1 333	1 486	1 587	1 456	-8.3	-23.3
Taxes (*less* subsidies) on production	472	479	483	484	228	226	236	248	228	276	21.1	-41.5
Total GVA at current basic prices	**4 026**	**4 126**	**3 911**	**3 117**	**3 148**	**3 132**	**3 231**	**3 324**	**3 377**	**3 225**	**-4.5**	**-19.9**
I–O industry group 89 (*part*)												
Compensation of employees	874	782	782	637	540	624	589	642	784	870	11.0	-0.4
Gross operating surplus	361	289	303	240	208	285	277	276	300	287	-4.6	-20.6
Taxes (*less* subsidies) on production	91	79	73	59	55	55	46	43	49	51	4.7	-43.3
Total GVA at current basic prices	**1 325**	**1 150**	**1 158**	**936**	**803**	**964**	**913**	**961**	**1 134**	**1 208**	**6.6**	**-8.8**
Total of oil and gas sector												
Compensation of employees	4 831	5 209	5 492	5 130	5 046	4 990	5 059	5 236	5 546	5 589	0.8	15.7
Gross operating surplus	11 663	12 392	13 635	14 270	17 673	16 035	13 848	15 770	23 454	22 108	-5.7	89.6
Taxes (*less* subsidies) on production	673	669	667	657	406	408	381	401	409	492	20.3	-26.9
Total GVA at current basic prices	**17 167**	**18 269**	**19 794**	**20 057**	**23 125**	**21 433**	**19 289**	**21 407**	**29 409**	**28 189**	**-4.1**	**64.2**
Whole economy indicators												
GDP at current market prices	610 854	642 327	681 327	719 176	763 290	810 944	859 436	903 865	951 265	994 037	4.5	62.7
GVA at current basic prices	546 434	575 461	608 740	639 908	680 206	720 371	762 359	797 814	839 194	880 904	5.0	61.2
Households final consumption expenditure (HHFCe)	379 758	401 970	422 397	443 367	474 311	503 813	536 933	570 440	603 349	635 704	5.4	67.4
Gross fixed capital formation	100 583	101 027	108 314	117 448	126 291	133 776	150 540	154 647	161 210	166 691	3.4	65.7
Exports of goods and services	144 091	163 640	180 508	203 509	223 969	233 027	230 334	238 794	267 007	271 708	1.8	88.6
Imports of goods and services	151 659	170 125	185 255	207 051	227 419	231 951	238 838	254 711	286 557	299 328	4.5	97.4
Compensation of employees	347 713	357 662	369 645	386 718	405 835	433 306	465 854	495 596	532 518	564 067	5.9	62.2
Gross operating surplus	184 139	203 863	225 401	239 034	260 315	272 798	281 676	286 753	290 586	300 074	3.3	63.0
Taxes (*less* subsidies) on production	14 582	13 936	13 694	14 156	14 056	14 267	14 829	15 465	16 090	16 763	4.2	15.0
Oil and gas sector contribution related to whole economy variables												
Oil and gas GVA as a proportion of whole economy GVA	3.1	3.2	3.3	3.1	3.4	3.0	2.5	2.7	3.5	3.2	-8.7	1.9
Oil and gas GVA as a proportion of Oil and gas total output	49.4	48.8	47.4	46.6	49.7	48.7	49.5	50.6	53.0	51.9	-2.1	5.1
Oil and gas CoE as a proportion of Oil and gas GVA	28.1	28.5	27.7	25.6	21.8	23.3	26.2	24.5	18.9	19.8	5.1	-29.5
Oil and gas GOS as a proportion of Oil and gas GVA	67.9	67.8	68.9	71.1	76.4	74.8	71.8	73.7	79.8	78.4	-1.7	15.4
Oil and gas ToP as a proportion of Oil and gas GVA	3.9	3.7	3.4	3.3	1.8	1.9	2.0	1.9	1.4	1.7	25.5	-55.5
Oil and gas GFCF as a proportion of whole economy GFCF	8.7	7.2	5.5	5.9	5.1	4.7	4.9	3.7	2.7	3.2	20.8	-62.5
HHFCe on energy as a proportion of total HHFCe	7.1	7.0	6.9	6.6	6.6	6.3	5.8	5.6	5.6	5.2	-7.5	-27.1
I–O product 35 (*part*):												
ToP as a proportion of total domestic demand	53.4	55.1	56.8	58.5	61.4	64.9	68.4	66.1	61.6	59.4	-3.6	11.2

Table 4 - *continued*
Oil and gas sector statistics at a glance

	\multicolumn{10}{c}{All estimates are in £ million or proportions as appropriate}	\multicolumn{2}{c}{Growth rates (per cent)}
	1992	1993	1994	1995	1996	1997	1998	1999	2000	2001	*2000–2001*	*1992–2001*
Supplementary information												
Oil and gas exploration expenditure (£m)	1 507	1 213	939	1 086	1 096	1 195	762	458	348	371	*6.6*	*–75.4*
Spot price for oil ($ per barrel):												
Brent crude	19.37	17.07	15.98	17.18	20.80	19.30	13.11	18.25	28.98	24.77	*–14.5*	*27.9*
Producer price indices (2000=100):												
Petrol and oil	57.1	61.6	63.6	67.1	71.8	76.1	77.6	85.2	100.0	94.9	*–5.1*	*37.8*
Electricity	118.6	123.2	123.3	118.7	114.7	107.7	107.5	107.5	100.0	96.2	*–3.8*	*–22.4*
Gas	125.9	121.2	118.8	110.9	84.8	87.8	92.4	91.9	100.0	140.7	*40.7*	*14.8*
Retail price indices (1987=100):												
Petrol and oil	132.1	142.6	149.1	156.8	164.7	181.1	190.1	206.1	233.2	221.3	*–11.9*	*89.2*
Electricity	141.5	141.0	145.7	147.7	147.0	140.0	133.6	131.9	129.2	128.0	*–1.2*	*–13.5*
Gas	117.8	113.3	120.1	124.2	124.3	123.1	118.9	118.2	115.3	118.4	*3.1*	*0.6*
Average UK retail price of petrol (pence per litre):												
4 star	50.1	53.7	56.1	59.1	61.4	67.1	71.2	77.0	85.3	79.5	*–6.8*	*58.6*
Unleaded	46.2	49.3	50.8	53.5	56.4	61.9	64.8	70.4	80.7	75.1	*–6.9*	*62.7*
Diesel	45.4	49.2	50.9	53.7	57.4	62.4	65.9	72.5	82.2	77.7	*–5.5*	*71.4*
Average UK duty paid on petrol (pence per litre):												
4 star	27.3	30.3	33.3	36.4	39.3	43.4	48.6	52.3	51.2	47.5	*–7.3*	*73.9*
Unleaded	23.2	25.6	28.5	31.6	34.5	38.6	43.4	46.7	48.6	47.2	*–2.9*	*103.5*
Diesel	22.6	25.0	27.9	31.6	34.5	38.6	44.2	49.3	51.6	54.2	*5.1*	*139.7*
Average UK duty paid as a proportion of retail price (per cent):												
4 star	*54.5*	*56.5*	*59.4*	*61.6*	*64.1*	*64.6*	*68.3*	*67.9*	*60.0*	*59.8*	*–0.5*	*9.6*
Unleaded	*50.2*	*51.9*	*56.2*	*59.1*	*61.2*	*62.3*	*66.9*	*66.3*	*60.1*	*62.8*	*4.4*	*25.1*
Diesel	*49.8*	*50.8*	*54.9*	*58.8*	*60.2*	*61.8*	*67.1*	*68.0*	*62.7*	*69.7*	*11.2*	*39.9*
Number of petrol stations in the UK	18 549	17 969	16 971	16 244	14 748	14 824	13 758	13 716	13 043	12 201	*–6.5*	*–34.2*
Inland deliveries (sales million tonnes)												
Petrol (motor spirit)	24.04	23.77	22.84	21.95	22.41	22.25	21.85	21.79	21.60	20.93	*–3.1*	*–12.9*
Diesel (DERV fuel)	11.13	11.81	12.91	13.46	14.37	14.98	15.14	15.51	15.88	16.42	*3.4*	*47.5*

GFCF represents Gross Fixed Capital Formation.
NPISHs represents Non-Profit Institutions Serving Households
ToP represents taxes (*less* subsidies) on production.

GG represents General Government Final Consumption Expenditure.
Balance of trade is recorded as exports *less* imports.
Differences between totals and sums of components are due to rounding.

Changes to methodology employed in the CPI and RPI from February 2004

Adrian Ball, Kathryn Waldron, Kevin Smith and Jonathan Hughes
Office for National Statistics

This article outlines three methodological changes to be made to the official consumer price indices from February 2004. The first, local probability sampling, will increase the representivity of items priced for selected durable goods. The other changes concern the introduction of hedonic quality adjustment for digitial cameras in both the CPI and RPI and the extension of hedonic quality adjustment to the RPI for personal computers.

Introduction

As part of an ongoing programme of work to apply the best available statistical methodology in the calculation of official consumer price indices three changes will be made to the February indices published in March 2004:

- the introduction of local probability sampling for the selection within retail outlets of some high turnover, high technology goods

- the introduction of digital cameras into the basket of goods priced for both the CPI and RPI. Hedonic regression will be used to produce valuations of changes in quality

- the extension of the hedonic regression method of quality adjustment for PCs from the CPI to the RPI.

This article explains the decision to implement and describes each methodology in turn.

All of the changes explained in this article will be introduced into the CPI and RPI for February 2004, published in March. Research will continue to look for ways to improve our official consumer price indices, including identifying other items that may benefit from Local Probability Sampling or hedonic quality adjustment.

Local Probability Sampling

It is important when constructing a consumer price index that the items being priced are representative of consumer spending. The use of random sampling procedures can help to achieve this. The Office for National Statistics (ONS) uses random sampling to select which shops price collectors visit to collect prices (ONS, 1998). However, full random sampling is not always cost effective or possible to achieve, and it requires detailed data on sales values to be fully effective. This is the case for the selection of items within shops, where the selection of products and varieties is currently purposive (or judgmental) and is carried out by collectors.

Under current methods, collectors are sent to shops with a generic item description, for example a 24"–32" widescreen television or freestanding, 12 place setting, dishwasher. It is then up to the collector to choose the particular model selected for price collection. If there is more than one model available to the collector, the model most representative of customers' purchases in terms of sales is selected. Where possible, this is done in conjunction with store managers, who know what sells well. However, this is not always the case and, as collectors do not have detailed knowledge of each of the items collected, this can result in non-representative goods being selected.

Market sales data indicate that this is a particular problem with high technology goods, where initial selection problems are compounded by a high rate of change in the market which limits the life of the sample. For instance, collectors will often price well-known brands, in the belief that their sales are high, ignoring budget and 'own' brands. Also, collectors will be less inclined to select new models that have entered the market. These problems most often arise when dealing with durable electronic goods, such as widescreen televisions, dishwashers, washing machines and vacuum cleaners, so research on new methods of sampling has focussed on these goods.

Several alternative methods were tested and subsequently rejected – such as asking collectors to list all models available in a shop, and then randomly selecting from the list (a technique used by the Bureau of Labor Statistics in the US), or using scanner data[1] to produce a random sample by giving each collector a prioritised list of model numbers to select from. The former was rejected because the method demanded an unrealistic level of statistical expertise from the price collectors, the latter because it yielded a low coverage rate when piloted in the field and therefore was not cost effective.

A variant of the second method, based on groups of models rather than individual models, has been developed as a practical and efficient way of ensuring the items priced in consumer price indices are representative of consumer spending.

What is Local Probability Sampling?

The principle behind the methodology of Local Probability Sampling is to use the selling patterns of a combination of attributes (for example, for televisions these are screen size, sound quality, picture frequency, etc.) to create a representative sample. Scanner data is stratified by attributes, giving us a matrix of the proportion of total sales represented by each combination of attributes. For example, in the case of televisions a matrix could look like:

Brand	Screen size	Teletext	Sound	Frequency	Expenditure (per cent)
High	28–29	Fastext	Stereo	50	16
High	28–29	Fastext	Dolby	100	4
Medium	28–29	Fastext	Stereo	100	20
Low	28–29	Fastext	Stereo	50	8
Low	28–29	No	Stereo	50	2
High	30–32	Fastext	Stereo	50	10
High	30–32	Fastext	Dolby	100	5
Medium	30–32	Fastext	Stereo	50	6
Low	30–32	Fastext	Stereo	50	8

Where brands are grouped together into price categories based on analyses from hedonic regressions.

This matrix is then used as the reference for a Probability Proportional to Sales (PPS) scheme to select the combinations of attributes that each collector will search for. PPS gives each combination of attributes a chance of being included proportional to its total expenditure. The final sampling produces a list of six prioritised attribute groupings for each price collector. Each collector is asked to find an item matching the first attribute group on the list in their outlet, if this is not possible they move on to the second etc. They have six choices and if the sixth is not found they revert to the current method of looking for the best sold in the outlet. The appropriate attributes are identified by hedonic regression techniques which identify price determining characteristics.

Which items will we apply the method to?

Initially the ONS investigated this method of sampling for five items: vacuum cleaners; dishwashers; washing machines; 14" televisions and widescreen televisions. Scanner data had shown, by revealing differences between the consumer prices indices samples and sales patterns, that the current method of purposive sampling was not fully adequate. Pilot collections were carried out for these items in November 2002, March 2003 and July 2003. Subsequent analyses of the outcomes centred on two areas:

- How successful the collectors were in applying the method. We examined the proportion of times the collector was able to find a model that fitted into one of the six groups of attributes provided to them in the prioritised list. With the exception of 14" televisions, the results showed a steady improvement over time in the proportions being observed. The overall success rate, equating to the percentage of locations where Local Probability Sampling was successful, was around 80 per cent.

- Whether the sample achieved through the selection in the field was more representative of purchasing patterns. In order to do this the achieved sample was tested statistically using the x^2 test (chi-squared test), comparing achieved frequencies with expected frequencies derived from scanner data. The results showed that the new methodology yielded a sample not significantly different from that expected, and significantly better than under purposive sampling.

Figure 1 shows the comparison between the expected percentage of specific dishwasher models, numbered one to

Figure 1
Observed versus expected models for dishwashers

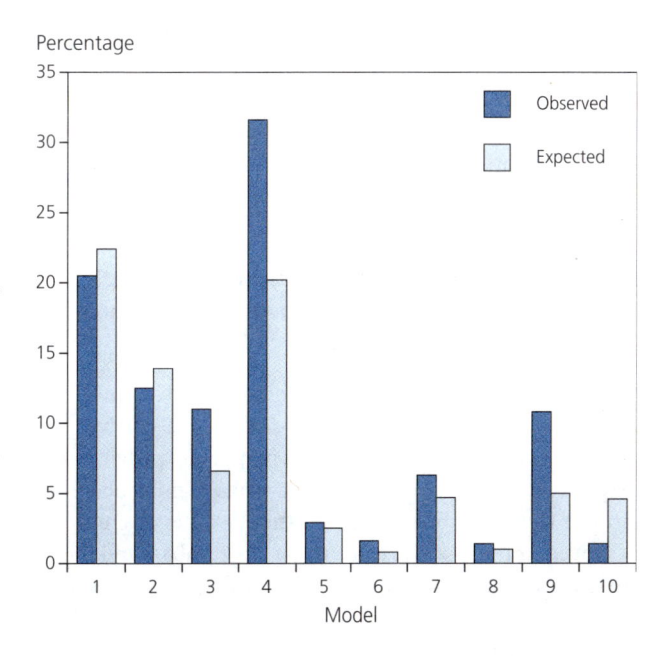

ten, and the percentage that were actually collected under the proposed sampling scheme. This shows that the expected and observed frequencies are very similar, confirming the two datasets are not significantly different.

Local probablity sampling proved unsuccessful for 14" televisions. Shops have not been replacing 14" televisions with comparable models. Rather, stores are filling the space freed up with combined televisions and video. Collectors therefore were unable to find models meeting the selection criteria, as so few were available. It was therefore decided to implement Local Probability Sampling only for the other four items (vacuum cleaners, dishwashers, washing machines and widescreen televisions). In addition, Local Probability Sampling will be implemented for digital cameras, which is a new basket item and for which prices are collected centrally by ONS.

How does Local Probability Sampling work in the field?

As already stated the collectors are given a list of six prioritised attribute groupings from which to select an item. An example of this for widescreen televisions can be seen below.

Choice	Brand	Screen size	Teletext	Sound
1	Panasonic, Sony, Toshiba	32"	Fastext	Stereo
2	Hitachi, Goodmans, Orion	28"	Fastext	Stereo
3	Panasonic, Sony, Toshiba	32"	Fastext	Dolby
4	Samsung, JVC, Sharp	32"	Fastext	Stereo
5	Samsung, JVC, Sharp	24"	No	Stereo
6	Panasonic, Sony, Toshiba	28"	Fastext	Stereo

The collector searches for a model that matches the first attribute group on the list and selects this if it is available. If not, the collector moves on to the second attribute group on the list. This continues until one is selected or until the list is exhausted, in which case the collector makes their own selection using the current guidelines.

The following month the collector attempts to price the same model as the previous month. If this is not possible the collector searches for a comparable model from the same group. If no such model can be found the collector searches for a model fitting the first attribute group, and the process begins again. A flow chart of this process can be seen in Appendix A.

A complete resample of goods will be carried out annually, ensuring the items in the basket of goods for our consumer price indices remain representative.

Collectors are assisted in their selection by improvements to the handheld PC that collectors ordinarily use. When a collector enters the brand and model number of an item they have selected, the PC compares the brand and model number with a database containing the attributes of a number of models. If the model is contained in the database and the attributes do not match, the collector is asked to confirm any values that do not match, alerting the collector to possible errors.[2]

More items are to be reviewed in the forthcoming year for possible introduction to the Local Probability Sampling scheme for 2005.

Other methodological developments in the CPI and RPI

Hedonic quality adjustment of digital cameras

Digital cameras will be a new item introduced into the CPI and RPI baskets from 2004. The digital camera market has experienced high levels of growth over the last three years, with expenditure reaching levels where the inclusion of digital cameras in the consumer price indices is warranted. Due to the high degree of quality change of this product, and the rapid rate of change in the models available, it has been decided to introduce digital cameras with hedonic quality adjustment.

As both the CPI and RPI use a fixed basket, when an item is replaced, prices have to be adjusted to take account of any significant quality change. This ensures that the index only reflects underlying price changes.

Two factors lead to the decision to use hedonic quality adjustment: the large technological improvements in digital cameras, and the speed of replacement of models in the RPI sample. An experimental sample for 2003 indicated a high number of technological improvements over a twelve-month period, mainly involving a higher resolution (represented by an increase in the number of mega pixels) and more powerful zooms. In addition we found that, on average, 10 per cent of the sample needed to be replaced each month.

The estimation method used in the hedonic technique is an ordinary least squares regression that relates the log of the price of an item to its measurable characteristics. This provides hedonic regression's key advantage compared with other methods of quality adjustment in that each individual specification change can be valued.

There are two main methods of application; indirect and time dummy approach. We use the indirect method as opposed to the time dummy approach. A more detailed explanation of the methodology and the decisions behind its use are given in a previous article (Ball and Allen, 2003).

The hedonic regression is calculated on the basis of a single month's data, using unweighted price data which is obtained from retailer websites. Brand, model, and both in-store and web site prices, where available, are collected for all models available. This is then linked to the relevant model in the attribute data set, that contains a wide range of variables:

- megapixels
- optical zoom
- digital zoom
- macro mode

- manual focus
- EV compensation
- flash / red-eye reduction / fill-in / external socket
- burst mode
- movie mode
- LCD screen size
- storage media
- dimensions
- weight.

When a quality change occurs, the regressions are used to estimate the prices of the original and replacement models. These are compared, and used to compute base prices adjusted for changes in quality. An illustrative example can be found in Appendix B.

The hedonic regression will be updated at least every six months to allow for changes in the market.

Hedonic quality adjustment of PCs

Since February 2003, hedonic regression techniques have been used to quality adjust the personal computers (PCs) index within the CPI (Ball and Allen, 2003).

This change was not made to the PC index within the RPI, which continued to use the previous method of 50 per cent option costing. This is because the National Statistician considered it appropriate to be more reserved about introducing methodological changes into the RPI given its widespread use and the fact that, uniquely amongst National Statistics, it cannot be revised. However, it was also stated that the practice would be kept under review in light of our experiences of using hedonic quality adjustment in the CPI and PPI.

A parallel run of the CPI and RPI PC indices during 2003, as well as continued research into hedonic techniques, such as for digital cameras, has lead us to conclude that we can now introduce hedonic quality adjustment into the RPI PC index. This methodological change, from the previous option cost method, will be introduced from the February 2004 index, published in March.

Notes

1. Based on Electronic Point of Sale (EPOS) data, recorded by barcode readers.

2. It also needs to be noted that some items are priced by the head office of the ONS. This has meant that the method has been adapted to the needs of this sampling regime. The program works in much the same way, though in this case items and prices are recorded in a specially designed spreadsheet.

References

Ball A and Allen A (2003) The introduction of hedonic regression techniques for the quality adjustment of computing equipment in the Producer Prices Index (PPI) and the Harmonised Index of Consumer Prices (HICP). Economic Trends No. 592, pp 30–36.

Office for National Statistics (2004). Consumer Price Indices First Release, February 2004. Published 16 March 2004. www.statistics.gov.uk/statbase/product.asp?vlnk=868

Office for National Statistics (1998). The RPI Technical Manual 1998, chapter 3. The Stationery Office: London.

Appendix A

A flowchart showing the process of selecting and pricing an item using the Local Probability Sampling technique.

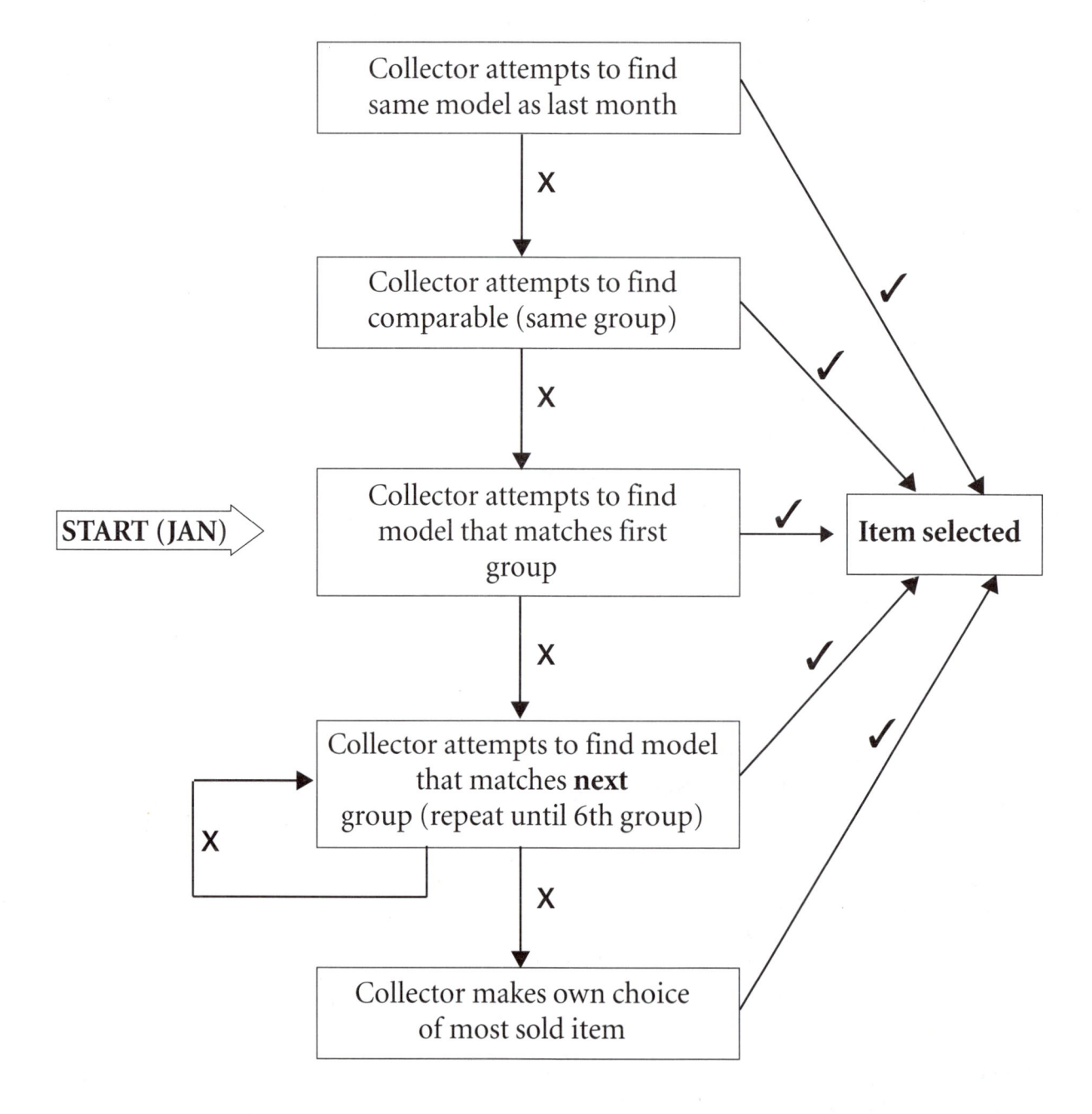

```
                          ┌─────────────────────────────┐
                          │ Collector attempts to find  │ ────✓────┐
                          │ same model as last month    │          │
                          └─────────────────────────────┘          │
                                        │ X                         │
                                        ▼                           │
                          ┌─────────────────────────────┐           │
                          │ Collector attempts to find  │ ────✓───┐ │
                          │ comparable (same group)     │         │ │
                          └─────────────────────────────┘         │ │
                                        │ X                       │ │
                                        ▼                         ▼ ▼
                          ┌─────────────────────────────┐     ┌──────────────┐
    START (JAN) ─────▶    │ Collector attempts to find  │─✓──▶│ Item selected │
                          │ model that matches first    │     └──────────────┘
                          │ group                       │         ▲ ▲
                          └─────────────────────────────┘         │ │
                                        │ X                       │ │
                                        ▼                         │ │
                          ┌─────────────────────────────┐ ────✓───┘ │
                  ┌─────▶ │ Collector attempts to find model │       │
                  │       │ that matches **next**            │       │
                  │ X     │ group (repeat until 6th group)   │ ──✓───┘
                  └──────┤                                  │
                          └─────────────────────────────┘
                                        │ X
                                        ▼
                          ┌─────────────────────────────┐
                          │ Collector makes own choice  │
                          │ of most sold item           │
                          └─────────────────────────────┘
```

Appendix B

Producing a quality adjusted index

Step 1: Produce regression model

Step 2: Predict old and new price

Attribute	Co-efficient	January level	Model effect on price	February level	Model effect on price
Brand		DC company		DC company	
Intercept	3.94619	1	£51.74	1	£51.74
Megapixels	0.25395	2	X1.66	3	X2.14
Optical zoom	0.04789	3	X1.15	3	X1.15
Flash	0.4983	1	X1.65	1	X1.65
Macro	−0.00214	5	X0.99	5	X0.99
Manual focus mode	0.04949	1	X1.05	1	X1.05
Predicted price			£169.84		£218.94
Actual price			£189.99		£235.00

(Only change is increase in megapixels)

Note: Predicted price = Intercept x effect of megapixels x effect of optical zoom x effect of flash x …

Step 3: Adjust base price to reflect new attributes

Change to January due to changes in quality = $\dfrac{\text{Predicted price new model}}{\text{Predicted price old model}}$

= £218.94 / £169.84

= 1.289

New base price = Base price old model x quality change

= £189.99 x 1.289

= £244.92

Step 4: Compare current price with new

Hedonic digital camera index = (£235.00 / £244.92) x 100

= 95.9

Unadjusted index = (£235.00 / £189.99) x 100

= 124

Revisions information in ONS First Releases

Graham Jenkinson and Nigel Stuttard
Office for National Statistics

The Office for National Statistics (ONS) has started to provide users with more information about revisions to time series in its First Releases. The changes will help users see the statistics in context to aid their interpretation. In addition to clearer identification of revisions and the reasons for them, the main change will be a new table in the background notes to releases giving summary information about past revisions to key indicators.

Introduction

Starting with the UK Output, Income and Expenditure First Release (25 February 2004), ONS will be providing users with more information in its First Releases about revisions to time series. This will help users interpret and use the latest estimates as they will know how estimates have been revised in the past. The new information will appear in a standard form in each First Release, accompanied by explanations of any special features if necessary.

These changes will contribute towards the implementation of the National Statistics Protocol on Revisions. Principle 3 of the Protocol says "A statement explaining the normal effect of revisions will accompany the release of all key outputs subject to regular revisions." The changes will put the revisions to key series in an historical context, will clearly identify revisions being made, and will explain the status of the figures and identify any planned future revisions.

Summary of changes

The main change will be a new table in the background notes to releases giving information about past revisions to key indicators. The table will usually be in this form for releases giving quarterly series. There will be a slightly different form for releases of monthly series.

	Revisions between first publication and estimates three years later	
Value in latest period	Average over the last 5 years (bias)	Average over the last 5 years without regard to sign (average absolute revision)

Key indicator 'a'
Key indicator 'b'
Key indicator 'c'

The second column shows the bias over the last five years – revisions are biased if they are consistently different from zero in either direction. The information in this column will be tested using a modified t-statistic to see whether there is statistical evidence that the bias is significantly different from zero for any of the indicators. (If the test is not significant this implies that the observed bias might have occurred by chance when there is no bias in the revisions.) The third column in the table shows the average absolute revision to the key variables over this period – this gives the average size of revisions over the last five years as an indication of the reliability of the latest figures.

The ONS recognises that revisions are only one indicator of statistical quality and revisions do not capture the complete picture. The revised data may itself, be subject to sampling or other sources of error. Other aspects of quality in statistics are set out in the Eurostat framework and include accuracy, timeliness, and robustness.

Other developments to implement the protocol on revisions include:

- a table, or tables, of revisions to the main series published in the release with an explanation of the reasons for them. These tables appear after the other tables and are designated with an R in their numbering

- in most cases, identification of the periods subject to revision in the current edition of the release

- an extra note to explain the status of the figures and planned future revisions

- in some cases a periodic article about the revisions performance of the indicators. For example an article about GDP revisions appeared in *Economic Trends*, December 2003.

When will the new material appear?

It is being introduced over the next four months and should be in all releases published after the end of June 2004.

Which releases will carry the new information?

All those which carry long runs of time series information.

Will the information be in other ONS publications?

The immediate priority will be its inclusion in First Releases. But other publications giving long run time series will follow where appropriate.

What is the modified t-statistic?

Revisions are considered to be biased if the mean revision is statistically significantly different from zero. A t-test compares the calculated bias in the series (that is, the mean revision) with the variability of the revisions to test whether the bias is significant. However, the standard t-test is based on the assumption that the revisions are independent of each other. This is not true for a time series as revisions made for one period may be associated with revisions made to previous periods. The modified t-test corrects for this lack of independence by adjusting the estimate of the variability of the revisions to take into account the serial correlation, that is the extent of the association between successive revisions. A technical description of the modified t-statistic and its calculation is given in the Appendix.

Appendix A

The modified t-statistic

For the purpose of the revisions information contained in the First Releases, the revision to a economic series, r_t, is defined as the difference between the initial estimate of that series and the updated estimate, made twelve months later (for monthly series) or 3 years later (for a quarterly series). The revisions to a series are considered to be biased if the mean revision is statistically different from zero. A modified t-test is used to test the significance of the mean revisions. The rationale for using a modified t-test is that successive revisions in a series may not be independent. If they are not independent (i.e. there is serial (or auto-) correlation in the revisions) the standard t-test would overstate the significance of the results.

We assume that the revisions fit a regression model of the form:

$$r_t = \mu + \varepsilon_t \quad \text{for } t=1 \text{ to } n \quad \text{i.e. with no explanatory variable.}$$

If the errors are thought to be serially correlated, they follow an autoregressive model of order one, AR(1):

$$\varepsilon_t = \alpha \varepsilon_{t-1} + u_t$$

where the u_t are independent and the auto-correlation coefficient, α, is between -1 and 1.

The standard t-statistic is:

$$t = \frac{\bar{r} - \mu}{\sqrt{\sigma^2 / n}}$$

where $\bar{r}$ is our sample mean revision, μ is the population mean revision (which we will assume is zero and test for as our null hypothesis), σ^2 is the variance and n is the number of observations.

Priestly (1981) has suggested that, where auto-correlation is present, the equivalent number of independent observations for estimating the mean should be reduced to:

$$n \frac{(1-\alpha)}{(1+\alpha)}$$

and thus the variance of the mean should be adjusted by increasing it to:

$$\frac{\sigma^2 (1+\alpha)}{n (1-\alpha)}$$

Under these circumstances, our modified t-adjusted statistic will be:

$$t\text{-adj} = \frac{\bar{r}}{\sqrt{\text{adjusted variance}}} \quad \text{[using } n^* \text{ degrees of freedom]}$$

with the null hypothesis that the population mean is zero and n^*, the equivalent number of independent observations for estimating the variance, is:

$$n \frac{(1-\alpha^2)}{(1+\alpha^2)}$$

The calculation follows the steps below:

1. **Calculate the sample mean**

$$\bar{r} = \frac{\sum_{t=1}^{n} r_t}{n}$$

2. **The coefficient α is estimated by $\hat{\alpha}$ where**

$$\hat{\alpha} = \frac{\text{Cov}(r_{t-1}, r_t)}{\sqrt{\text{Var}(r_{t-1}) \text{Var}(r_t)}}$$

$$= \frac{\sum_{i=2}^{n} (r_{i-1} - \bar{r}_{t-1})(r_i - \bar{r}_t)}{\sqrt{\sum_{i=2}^{n-1} (r_i - \bar{r}_{t-1})^2 \sum_{i=2}^{n} (r_i - \bar{r}_t)^2}}$$

Where $\bar{r}_{t-1} = \dfrac{\sum_{i=1}^{n-1} r_i}{n-1}$ and $\bar{r}_t = \dfrac{\sum_{i=2}^{n} r_i}{n-1}$

3. **The estimate for the variance of the sample mean is s where**

$$s^2 = \frac{\sum_{t=1}^{n} (r_t - \bar{r})^2}{n}$$

4. **The estimate of the adjusted sample variance is s^* where**

$$s^{*2} = \frac{s^2 (1 + \hat{\alpha})}{n (1 - \hat{\alpha})}$$

5. **The adjusted degrees of freedom is n^* where:**

$$n^* = n \frac{(1 - \hat{\alpha}^2)}{(1 + \hat{\alpha}^2)}$$

6. **Calculate modified t-statistic, t-adj**

$$t\text{-adj} = \frac{\bar{r}}{s^*} \quad \text{[using } n^* \text{ degrees of freedom]}$$

7. **Compare the t-adjusted value with the critical t-value**

Compare the absolute t-adjusted value against the critical t value at 95 per cent significance (2-tailed) and reject the null hypothesis if $|t\text{-adj}| > t\text{-critical}$, i.e. if rejected the test statistic is statistically significant.

Tables

1. Summary
1.1 Selected monthly indicators — 75

2. UK Economic Accounts
2.1 National accounts aggregates — 76
2.2 Gross domestic product: by category of expenditure — 78
2.3 Gross domestic product and shares of income and expenditure — 80
2.4 Income, product and spending per head — 80
2.5 Households' disposable income and consumption — 82
2.6 Households' final consumption expenditure, chained volume measures — 82
2.7 Gross fixed capital formation — 84
2.8 Gross value added, chained volume indices at basic prices, by category of output — 86
2.9 Gross value added chained volume indices at basic prices, by category of output service industries — 88
2.10 Summary capital accounts and net lending/net borrowing — 90
2.11 Private non-financial corporations: allocation of primary income account — 92
2.12 Private non-financial corporations: secondary distribution of income account and capital account — 94
2.13 Balance of payments: current account — 96
2.14 Trade in goods (on a balance of payments basis) — 98
2.15 Measures of UK competitiveness in trade in manufactures — 100

3. Prices
3.1 Prices — 102

4. Labour market
4.1 Labour market activity: seasonally adjusted — 104
4.2 Labour market activity: not seasonally adjusted — 106
4.3 Labour market activity by age: seasonally adjusted — 110
4.4 Jobs and claimant count — 112
4.5 Regional claimant count rates — 114
4.5A Unemployment rates — 116
4.6 Average earnings (including bonuses) — 118
4.7 Productivity and unit wage costs — 120

5. Selected output and demand indicators
5.1 Output of production industries — 122
5.2 Engineering and construction: output and orders — 124
5.3 Motor vehicle and steel production — 126
5.4 Indicators of fixed investment in dwellings — 128
5.5 Number of property transactions — 130
5.6 Change in inventories: chained volume measures — 132
5.7 Inventory ratios — 132
5.8 Retail sales, new registrations of cars and credit business (Great Britain) — 134
5.9 Inland energy consumption: primary fuel input basis — 136

6. Selected financial statistics
6.1 Sterling exchange rates and UK reserves — 138
6.2 Monetary aggregates — 140
6.3 Counterparts to changes in money stock M4 — 142
6.4 Public sector receipts and expenditure — 144
6.5 Public sector key fiscal indicators — 144
6.6 Consumer credit and other household sector borrowing — 146
6.7 Analysis of bank lending to UK residents, amounts outstanding — 148
6.8 Interest rates, security prices and yields — 150
6.9 A selection of asset prices — 152
Measures of variability of selected economic series — 153

Notes to tables

Identification codes

The four-letter identification code at the top of each data column is the ONS reference for this series of data on our database. Please quote the relevant code if you contact us requiring any further information about the data.

Currency of data

All data in the tables and accompanying charts are current, as far as possible, to 5 March 2004.

Some data, particularly for the latest time period, are provisional and may be subject to revision in later editions.

Geographic coverage

Statistics relate mainly to the United Kingdom. Where figures are for Great Britain only, this is shown on the table.

Seasonal adjustments

Almost all quarterly data are seaonally adjusted; those not seasonally adjusted are indicated by the abbreviation NSA.

Money

There is no single correct definition of money. The most widely used measures are:

M0
This is the narrowest measure and consists of notes and coins in circulation outside the Bank of England and bankers' operational deposits at the Bank.

M4
This comprises notes and coin in circulation with the public, together with all sterling deposits (including certificates of deposit) held with UK banks and building societies by the rest of the private sector.

The Bank of England also publish data for liquid assets outside M4.

Conventions

Rounding may lead to inconsistencies between the constituent parts and the total in some tables.

A horizontal line between two consecutive figures indicates that the figures above and below the line have been compiled on different bases and are not strictly comparable. Footnotes explain the differences.

Billion denotes one thousand million.

Symbols used

.. not available

-   nil or less than half the final digit shown

+   a series for which measures of variability are given on page 153

†   data have been revised since the last edition; the period marked is the earliest in the table to have been revised

*   average (or total) of five weeks

National Statistics Online

www.statistics.gov.uk

Users can download time series, cross-sectional data and metadata from across the Government Statistical Service (GSS), using the site search and index functions from the homepage. Many datasets can be downloaded, in whole or in part, and directory information for all GSS statistical resources can be consulted, including censuses, surveys, journals and enquiry services. Information is posted as PDF electronic documents, or in XLS and CSV formats, compatible with most spreadsheet packages.

Time Series Data

The time series data facility on the website provide access to around 40,000 time series, of primarily macro-economic data, drawn from the main tables in our major economic and labour market publications. Users can download complete releases or view and download customised selections of individual time series.

Complete copies of *Economic Trends* can be downloaded from the following webpage:

www.statistics.gov.uk/statbase/product.asp?vlnk=308

1.1 Selected monthly indicators

seasonally adjusted unless otherwise stated

		2002	2003	2003 Q2	2003 Q3	2003 Q4	2003 Nov	2003 Dec	2004 Jan	%Change Latest 3 months avg over previous 3 months
Output -chained volume measures (CVM) (2000 = 100 unless otherwise stated)										
Gross value added at basic prices	CGCE	103.2	105.2	104.7	105.6	106.4	..	..	..	0.8
Industrial production	CKYW	95.7	95.0	95.1	95.1	95.0	94.7	94.6	..	-0.1
Oil and gas extraction	CKZO	93.4	87.4	88.7	86.1	83.1	82.8	82.0	..	-3.5
Manufacturing	CKYY	95.1	95.0	95.0	95.3	95.5	95.3	95.2	..	0.2
Construction	GDQB	111.2	118.2	117.7	120.1	122.1	..	..	..	1.6
Car production (thousands)	FFAO	135.8	138.1	138.9	143.6	138.3	137.9	140.1	140.2	-1.2
Domestic demand										
Retail sales volume (2000 = 100)	EAPS	112.7	116.6	116.1	117.5	119.6	119.4	120.4	121.0	1.7
GB new registrations of cars ('000s)[1]	BCGT	2 682.0	2 646.2	642.7	742.8	523.1	175.7	160.8	..	-29.6
Manufacturing:change in inventories (£m,CVM, reference year 2000)	DHBM	-1 967	-231	-234	501	-327	..	..	..	
Prices (12 monthly % change) and earnings (headline rate)										
Consumer prices index	CJYR	1.3	1.4	1.3	1.4	1.3	1.3	1.3	1.4	
Retail prices index[1]	CZBH	1.7	2.9	3.0	2.9	2.6	2.5	2.8	2.6	
Retail prices index[1] (less MIPS)[2]	CDKQ	2.2	2.8	2.9	2.8	2.6	2.5	2.6	2.4	
Producer output prices (less FBTP)[3]	EUAA	-0.1	1.3	1.2	1.2	1.4	1.4	1.5	1.4	
Producer input prices[4]	EUAB	-4.5	1.3	-0.5	1.2	2.8	4.3	1.9	-	
GB average earnings -whole economy[5]	LNNC	..	..	3.0	3.6	3.4	3.5	3.4	..	
Foreign trade[6] (2000 = 100 volumes unless otherwise stated)										
UK balance on trade in goods (£ million)	BOKI	-46 630	-46 385	-10 934	-11 700	-12 748	-4 356	-4 159	..	
Non EU balance on trade in goods (£ million)	ENRX	-25 935	-22 626	-5 512	-5 818	-5 809	-2 177	-1 406	..	
Non EU exports of goods (excl oil & erratics)	ENUA	96.2	105.0	102.8	104.2	111.1	108.1	117.1	..	6.6
Non EU imports of goods (excl oil & erratics)	ENTS	98.5	104.6	103.0	103.5	110.8	112.1	109.8	..	7.0
Non EU import & price index (excl oil)[7]	ENXR	-5.8	-3.3	-4.5	-0.6	-1.7	-1.5	-2.5	..	
Non EU export & price index (excl oil)[7]	ENXS	0.2	-2.3	-3.5	-0.4	-1.4	-1.1	-2.2	..	
Labour market and productivity (2000 = 100 unless otherwise stated)										
UK claimant unemployment (thousands)	BCJD	946.8	933.0	946.5	933.2	915.9	916.5	905.5	892.1	-2.6
UK employees in manufacturing (thousands)	YEJA	3 628	3 503	3 503	3 475	3 456	3 461	3 456	..	-0.5
Whole economy productivity[8]	LNNN	102.5	..	103.7	104.3	..	..	..	..	0.6
Manufacturing productivity[8]	LNNX	104.8	109.9	109.4	111.0	112.3	112.1	112.3	..	1.1
Unit wage costs - whole economy	LNNK	106.3	..	108.3	108.9	..	..	..	..	0.6
Unit wage costs - manufacturing	LNNQ	103.0	101.8	101.3	100.9	100.9	101.1	101.2	..	-0.1
Financial markets[1]										
Sterling ERI (1990=100)	AGBG	106.0	100.2	99.1	99.2	100.2	100.4	100.3	102.4	1.7
Average exchange rate /US $	AUSS	1.50	1.63	1.62	1.61	1.71	1.69	1.75	1.82	7.6
Average exchange rate /Euro[9]	THAP	1.59	1.45	1.43	1.43	1.43	1.44	1.42	1.44	0.2
3 month inter-bank rate[10]	HSAJ	3.94	3.95	3.55	3.66	3.95	3.90	3.95	4.05	
3 month interest on US Treasury bills[11]	LUST	1.20	0.93	0.89	0.94	0.93	0.92	0.93	0.90	
Monetary conditions/government finances										
M0 (year on year percentage growth)	VQMX	7.9	7.3	7.7	7.9	7.5	8.0	7.2	7.7	
M4 (year on year percentage growth)	VQJW	6.2	7.2	8.1	6.6	6.7	6.9	6.9	8.4	
Public sector net borrowing (£ million)[1,12]	ANNX	-22 889	..	-15 047	-6 268	-13 661	-8 019	-5 219	4 358	
Net lending to consumers (£ million)(broader)	RLMH	21 050	19 055	5 251	4 855	3 921	1 467	873	1 928	-14.1

		2003 Jan	2003 Feb	2003 Mar	2003 Apr	2003 May	2003 Jun	2003 Jul	2003 Aug	2003 Sep	2003 Oct	2003 Nov	2003 Dec	2004 Jan	2004 Feb
Activity and expectations															
CBI output expectations balance[1]	ETCU	2	-1	-5	-10	-3	-6	-4	-3	-3	-4	-2	5	21	14
CBI optimism balance[1]	ETBV	-19	..	..	-27	..	..	-13	..	-7	..	..	..	17	..
CBI price expectations balance	ETDQ	-14	-14	-18	-8	-13	-15	-14	-15	-10	-9	-10	-4	-1	-2
New engineering orders (2000 = 100)	JIQH	77.0	79.6	75.9	93.2	76.2	76.6	84.0	78.8	77.9	84.1	85.6	72.8	..	..

1 Not seasonally adjusted
2 MIPS: mortgage interest payments
3 FBTP : food, beverages, tobacco and petroleum
4 See footnote 2 on Table 3.1.
5 See footnote 2 on Table 4.6
6 All Non EU figures exclude Austria, Finland & Sweden
7 12 monthly percentage change
8 Output per filled job.
9 Prior to January 1999, a synthetic Euro has been calculated by geometrically averaging the bilateral exchange rate of the 11 Euro-area countries using "internal weights" based on each country's share of the extra Euro-area trade
10 Last Friday of the period
11 Last working day
12 Annual figure is for the financial year

2.1 National accounts aggregates

	£ million		Indices (2000 = 100)						
	At current prices		Value indices at current prices		Chained volume indices (2000=100)			Implied deflators[2]	
	Gross domestic product at market prices	Gross value added (GVA) at basic prices	Gross domestic product at market prices[1]	Gross Value added (GVA) at basic prices	Gross national disposable income at market prices	Gross domestic product at market prices	Gross value added (GVA) at basic prices+	GDP at market prices	GVA at basic prices
	YBHA	ABML	YBEU	YBEX	YBFP	YBEZ	CGCE	YBGB	CGBV
Annual								
1998	859 436	762 359	90.3	90.8	94.5	93.7	93.9	96.4	96.7
1999	903 865	797 814	95.0	95.1	95.8	96.4	96.3	98.6	98.7
2000	951 265	839 194	100.0	100.0	100.0	100.0	100.0	100.0	100.0
2001	994 037	880 904	104.5	105.0	103.4	102.1	101.9	102.3	103.0
2002	1 042 908	924 745	109.6	110.2	106.4	103.9	103.2	105.6	106.8
2003	1 100 462	976 180	115.7	116.3	..	106.3†	105.2	108.8	110.6
Quarterly								
1998 Q1	209 840	186 227	88.2	88.8	92.5	92.8	92.8	95.1	95.6
Q2	212 891	189 021	89.5	90.1	93.9	93.2	93.4	96.1	96.5
Q3	217 418	192 771	91.4	91.9	95.9	94.2	94.4	97.0	97.4
Q4	219 287	194 340	92.2	92.6	95.5	94.8	95.1	97.3	97.4
1999 Q1	221 178	195 352	93.0	93.1	93.8	95.3	95.3	97.6	97.7
Q2	224 190	198 440	94.3	94.6	95.2	95.6	95.7	98.6	98.8
Q3	227 870	201 045	95.8	95.8	96.3	96.7	96.6	99.1	99.2
Q4	230 627	202 977	97.0	96.7	97.8	97.9	97.6	99.1	99.1
2000 Q1	235 050	207 339	98.8	98.8	99.2	99.0	98.9	99.8	99.9
Q2	236 352	208 160	99.4	99.2	99.5	99.7	99.7	99.7	99.6
Q3	239 182	211 135	100.6	100.6	101.0	100.5	100.6	100.1	100.1
Q4	240 681	212 560	101.2	101.3	100.3	100.8	100.9	100.4	100.5
2001 Q1	245 227	217 171	103.1	103.5	102.6	101.6	101.7	101.5	101.8
Q2	247 908	219 657	104.2	104.7	103.0	102.0	101.7	102.2	102.9
Q3	248 578	220 099	104.5	104.9	103.8	102.3	101.8	102.2	103.1
Q4	252 324	223 977	106.1	106.8	104.3	102.7	102.3	103.3	104.4
2002 Q1	255 864	226 863	107.6	108.1	104.6	103.0	102.5	104.5	105.5
Q2	258 634	229 239	108.8	109.3	105.1	103.4	102.8	105.2	106.3
Q3	262 476	232 769	110.4	110.9	107.4	104.2	103.5	105.9	107.1
Q4	265 934	235 874	111.8	112.4	108.4	104.8	104.0	106.7	108.1
2003 Q1	269 771†	239 522†	113.4	114.2	108.8	105.1†	104.2†	108.0	109.6†
Q2	273 027	242 473	114.8	115.6	107.4	105.8	104.7	108.5†	110.4
Q3	276 879	245 477	116.4†	117.0†	108.2	106.7	105.6	109.2	110.8
Q4	280 785	248 708	118.1	118.5	..	107.7	106.4	109.7	111.4

Percentage change, quarter on corresponding quarter of previous year[3]

Quarterly

1998 Q1	5.6	4.9	5.6	4.9	4.2	3.5	3.5	2.1	1.4
Q2	5.6	5.5	5.6	5.5	3.4	2.8	3.5	2.8	1.9
Q3	6.9	6.9	6.9	6.9	5.6	3.5	3.8	3.2	3.1
Q4	5.8	5.9	5.8	5.9	4.4	2.8	3.4	3.0	2.5
1999 Q1	5.4	4.9	5.4	4.9	1.4	2.7	2.7	2.6	2.2
Q2	5.3	5.0	5.3	5.0	1.4	2.6	2.5	2.6	2.4
Q3	4.8	4.3	4.8	4.3	0.4	2.7	2.3	2.2	1.8
Q4	5.2	4.4	5.2	4.4	2.4	3.3	2.6	1.8	1.7
2000 Q1	6.3	6.1	6.3	6.1	5.8	3.9	3.8	2.3	2.3
Q2	5.4	4.9	5.4	4.9	4.5	4.3	4.1	1.1	0.8
Q3	5.0	5.0	5.0	5.0	4.9	3.9	4.1	1.0	0.9
Q4	4.4	4.7	4.4	4.7	2.6	3.0	3.3	1.3	1.4
2001 Q1	4.3	4.7	4.3	4.7	3.4	2.6	2.8	1.7	1.9
Q2	4.9	5.5	4.9	5.5	3.5	2.3	2.1	2.5	3.3
Q3	3.9	4.2	3.9	4.2	2.8	1.8	1.2	2.1	3.0
Q4	4.8	5.4	4.8	5.4	4.0	1.9	1.4	2.9	3.9
2002 Q1	4.3	4.5	4.3	4.5	1.9	1.4	0.8	3.0	3.6
Q2	4.3	4.4	4.3	4.4	2.0	1.4	1.0	2.9	3.3
Q3	5.6	5.8	5.6	5.8	3.5	1.9	1.7	3.6	3.9
Q4	5.4	5.3	5.4	5.3	3.9	2.0	1.7	3.3	3.5
2003 Q1	5.4†	5.6	5.4†	5.6	4.0	2.0†	1.6†	3.3	3.9†
Q2	5.6	5.8	5.6	5.8	2.2	2.3	1.9	3.1†	3.9
Q3	5.5	5.5†	5.5	5.5†	0.7	2.4	1.9	3.1	3.5
Q4	5.6	5.4	5.6	5.4	..	2.8	2.3	2.8	3.1

1 "Money GDP."
2 Based on chained volume measures and current price estimates of expenditure components of GDP.
3 These estimates of change are based in some cases on less rounded figures than in the table.

Source: Office for National Statistics; Enquiries 020 7533 6031

Economic Trends **604** March 2004 — Tables section

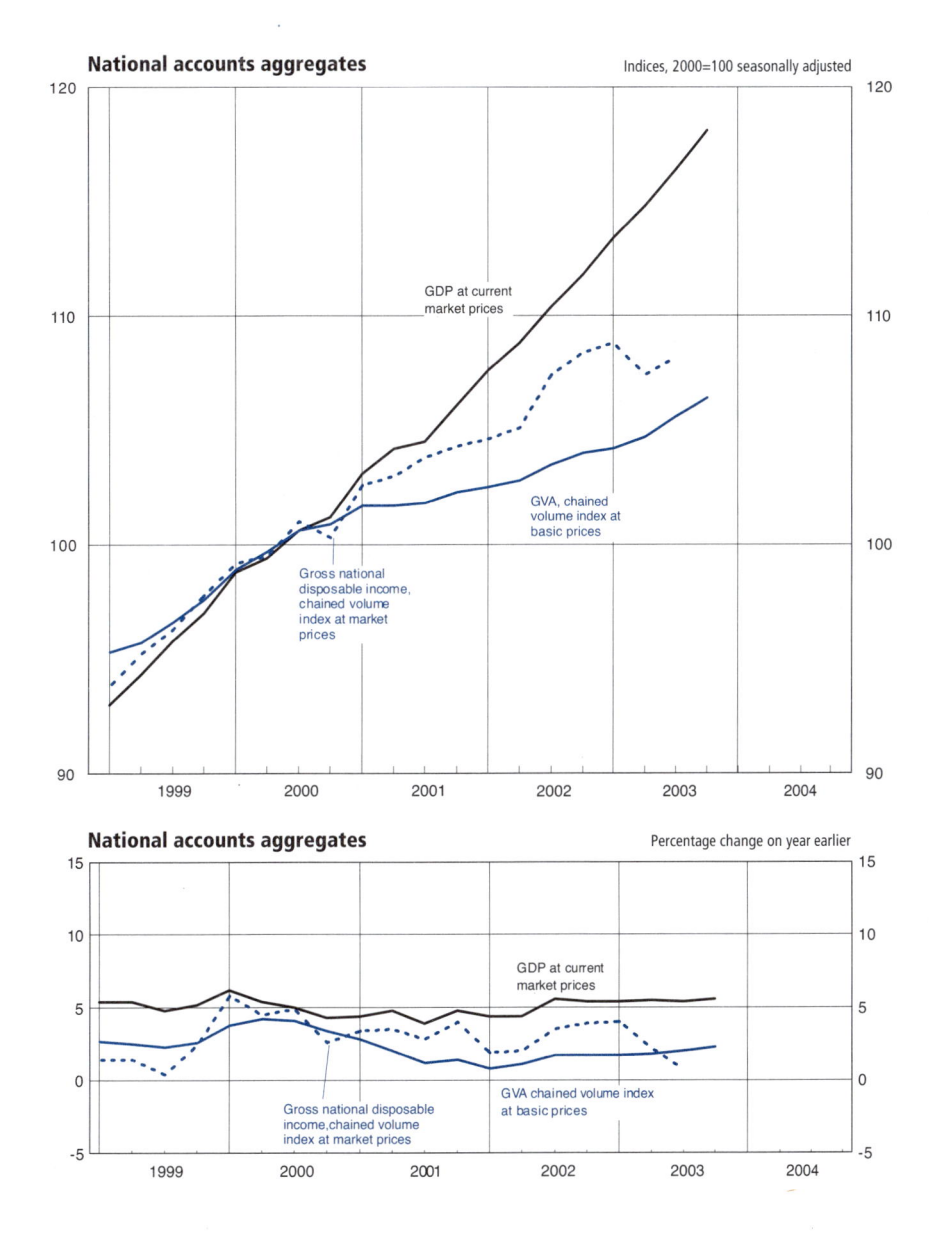

National accounts aggregates — Indices, 2000=100 seasonally adjusted

- GDP at current market prices
- GVA, chained volume index at basic prices
- Gross national disposable income, chained volume index at market prices

National accounts aggregates — Percentage change on year earlier

- GDP at current market prices
- GVA chained volume index at basic prices
- Gross national disposable income, chained volume index at market prices

2.2 Gross domestic product: by category of expenditure
Chained volume measures

Reference year 2000, £ million

	Households	Non-profit institutions[2]	General government	Gross fixed capital formation+	Changes in inventories[3]	Acquisitions less disposals of valuables	Total	Exports of goods and services+	Gross final expenditure	less Imports of goods and services+	Statistical discrepancy (expenditure)	Gross domestic product at market prices
	ABJR	HAYO	NMRY	NPQT	CAFU	NPJR	YBIM	IKBK	ABMG	IKBL	GIXS	ABMI
Annual												
1998	552 186	21 713	169 085	153 148	4 913	57	901 069	233 982	1 135 080	243 400	–	891 684
1999	577 665	21 543	174 445	155 576	6 426	28	935 377	243 985	1 179 410	262 601	–	916 639
2000	603 349	23 188	177 794	161 210	5 271	3	970 815	267 007	1 237 822	286 557	–	951 265
2001	622 136	23 845	180 875	167 032	2 938	362	997 188	273 724	1 270 912	299 347	–	971 565
2002	643 107	24 548	185 799	170 004	1 496	195	1 025 149	272 605	1 297 754	311 211	1 389	987 932
2003	661 289	25 765	189 626	174 353	1 540	–21	1 052 552	271 343	1 323 895	313 653	860	1 011 103†
Quarterly												
1998 Q1	136 298	5 368	41 431	37 275	427	31	221 423	58 221	279 669	59 146	–	220 584
Q2	137 464	5 433	42 245	38 029	230	7	223 461	58 967	282 474	60 854	–	221 598
Q3	138 653	5 476	42 646	38 621	1 990	9	227 037	58 413	285 441	61 377	–	224 047
Q4	139 771	5 436	42 763	39 223	2 266	10	229 148	58 381	287 496	62 023	–	225 455
1999 Q1	142 213	5 415	43 184	38 907	2 742	5	232 122	58 044	290 132	63 516	–	226 585
Q2	143 625	5 336	43 789	38 331	476	24	231 457	59 973	291 433	64 024	–	227 382
Q3	144 613	5 358	43 787	38 674	1 677	–15	233 974	62 579	296 598	66 678	–	229 864
Q4	147 214	5 434	43 685	39 664	1 531	14	237 824	63 389	301 247	68 383	–	232 808
2000 Q1	150 128	5 666	43 969	39 298	819	1	239 970	64 272	304 263	68 664	–	235 554
Q2	150 469	5 766	44 748	39 471	1 262	–	241 682	66 551	308 235	71 071	–	237 160
Q3	151 397	5 858	44 716	40 417	1 941	–3	244 269	67 103	311 366	72 467	–	238 914
Q4	151 355	5 898	44 361	42 024	1 249	5	244 894	69 081	313 958	74 355	–	239 637
2001 Q1	153 291	6 005	44 635	41 707	795	–34	246 399	70 235	316 634	75 053	–	241 581
Q2	153 965	5 964	44 541	42 069	1 806	251	248 596	69 074	317 670	75 211	–	242 459
Q3	156 368	5 945	45 489	41 974	355	33	250 164	67 340	317 504	74 287	–	243 218
Q4	158 512	5 931	46 210	41 282	–18	112	252 029	67 075	319 104	74 796	–	244 307
2002 Q1	158 674	6 064	46 878	41 206	736	59	253 617	66 875	320 492	75 740	137	244 888
Q2	160 450	6 087	46 029	42 702	–778	50	254 540	69 887	324 427	78 720	255	245 962
Q3	161 201	6 166	46 318	42 837	10	77	256 609	69 616	326 225	78 717	407	247 916
Q4	162 782	6 231	46 574	43 259	1 528	9	260 383	66 227	326 610	78 034	590	249 166
2003 Q1	162 754†	6 353†	47 083†	42 702†	981†	–1	259 871†	68 844†	328 715†	79 061†	245†	249 899†
Q2	164 349	6 378	47 177	43 376	–65	96	261 311	67 069	328 380	77 062	218	251 536
Q3	166 174	6 472	47 224	43 777	657	–62	264 242	67 108	331 350	77 915	202	253 636
Q4	168 012	6 562	48 142	44 498	–33	–54	267 128	68 322	335 450	79 615	195	256 032

Percentage change, latest quarter on corresponding quarter of previous year

1998 Q1	4.2	11.4	–1.8	14.9			5.2	5.2	5.2	11.5		3.4
Q2	3.4	5.2	2.0	13.6			4.3	4.1	4.3	9.5		2.8
Q3	4.2	8.1	3.0	13.3			5.8	1.2	4.8	9.2		3.5
Q4	3.6	3.8	2.2	9.3			4.6	0.6	3.7	7.0		2.8
1999 Q1	4.3	0.9	4.2	4.4			4.8	–0.3	3.7	7.4		2.7
Q2	4.5	–1.8	3.7	0.8			3.6	1.7	3.2	5.2		2.6
Q3	4.3	–2.2	2.7	0.1			3.1	7.1	3.9	8.6		2.6
Q4	5.3	0.0	2.2	1.1			3.8	8.6	4.8	10.3		3.3
2000 Q1	5.6	4.6	1.8	1.0			3.4	10.7	4.9	8.1		4.0
Q2	4.8	8.1	2.2	3.0			4.4	11.0	5.8	11.0		4.3
Q3	4.7	9.3	2.1	4.5			4.4	7.2	5.0	8.7		3.9
Q4	2.8	8.5	1.5	5.9			3.0	9.0	4.2	8.7		2.9
2001 Q1	2.1	6.0	1.5	6.1			2.7	9.3	4.1	9.3		2.6
Q2	2.3	3.4	–0.5	6.6			2.9	3.8	3.1	5.8		2.2
Q3	3.3	1.5	1.7	3.9			2.4	0.4	2.0	2.5		1.8
Q4	4.7	0.6	4.2	–1.8			2.9	–2.9	1.6	0.6		1.9
2002 Q1	3.5	1.0	5.0	–1.2			2.9	–4.8	1.2	0.9		1.4
Q2	4.2	2.1	3.3	1.5			2.4	1.2	2.1	4.7		1.4
Q3	3.1	3.7	1.8	2.1			2.6	3.4	2.7	6.0		1.9
Q4	2.7	5.1	0.8	4.8			3.3	–1.3	2.4	4.3		2.0
2003 Q1	2.6†	4.8†	0.4†	3.6†			2.5	2.9†	2.6†	4.4†		2.0†
Q2	2.4	4.8	2.5	1.6			2.7†	–4.0	1.2	–2.1		2.3
Q3	3.1	5.0	2.0	2.2			3.0	–3.6	1.6	–1.0		2.3
Q4	3.2	5.3	3.4	2.9			2.6	3.2	2.7	2.0		2.8

1 Estimates given to nearest million but cannot be regarded as accurate to the degree.
2 Non-profit making institutions serving households (NPISH).
3 Quarterly alignment adjustment included in this series.

Source: Office for National Statistics; Enquiries 020 7533 6031

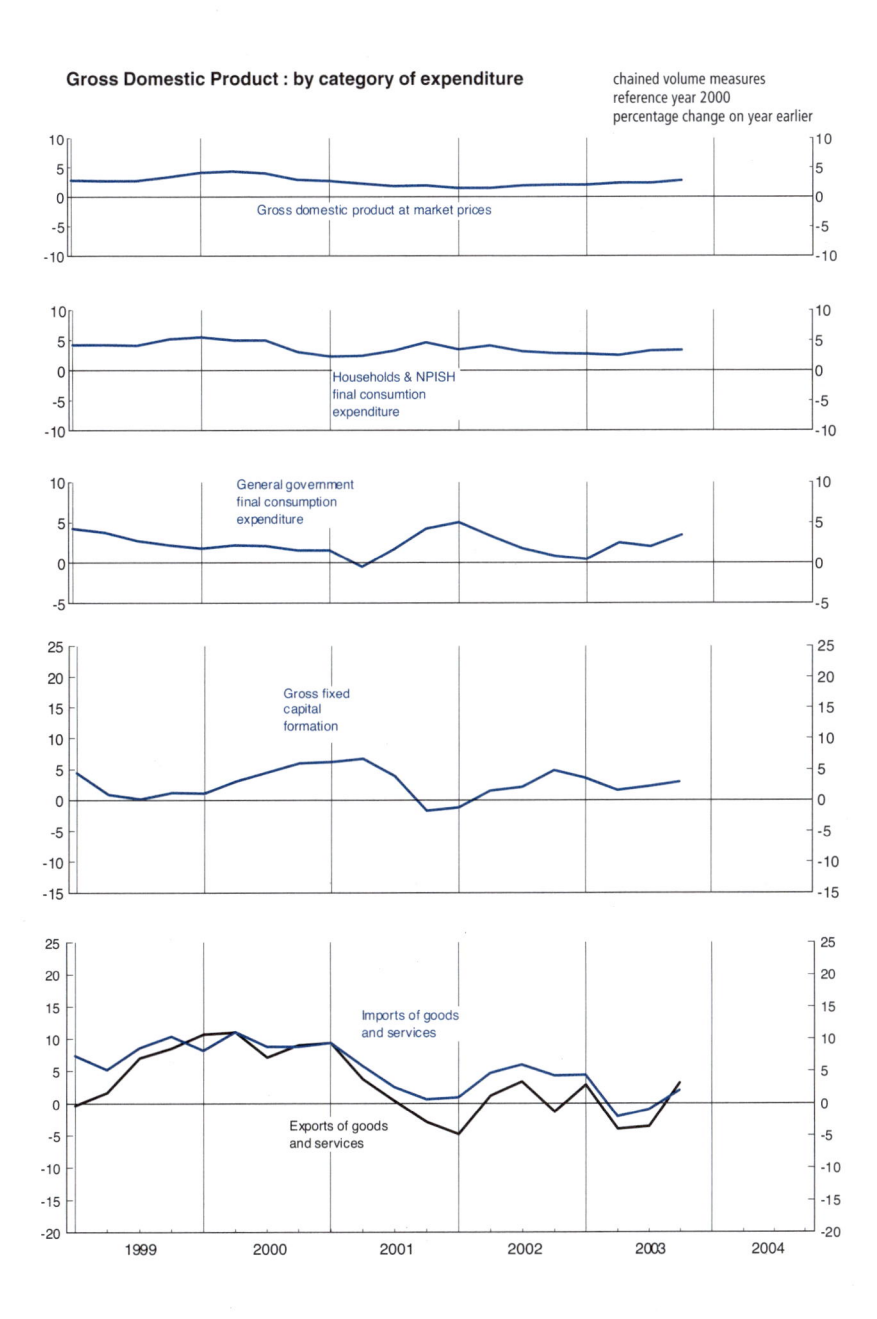

Gross Domestic Product : by category of expenditure

chained volume measures
reference year 2000
percentage change on year earlier

Gross domestic product at market prices

Households & NPISH final consumtion expenditure

General government final consumption expenditure

Gross fixed capital formation

Imports of goods and services

Exports of goods and services

2.3 Gross domestic product and shares of income and expenditure

	Gross domestic product at market prices	Gross final expenditure	Percentage share of gross final expenditure				Percentage share of GDP by category of income				
			Final consumption expenditure		Gross capital formation	Exports of goods and services	Gross operating surplus		Compensation of employees	Mixed income	Taxes on production and imports
			Household and NPISH	General govern-ment			Corporat-ions[1]	Other[2]			
	YBHA	ABMF	IHXI	IHXJ	IHXK	IHXL	IHXM	IHXO	IHXP	IHXQ	IHXR
Annual											
2000	951 265	1 237 822	50.6	14.4	13.4	21.5	21.9	2.6	56.0	6.0	13.5
2001	994 037	1 293 365	51.1	14.8	13.2	21.0	21.2	2.8	56.8	6.1	13.1
2002	1 042 908	1 346 155	51.3	15.6	12.8	20.3	21.5	3.0	56.3	6.1	13.1
2003	1 100 462	1 407 917	..	..	..	..	..	..	..	..	..
Quarterly											
2000 Q1	235 050	302 357	51.3	14.2	13.6	20.9	23.1	2.6	54.9	6.0	13.5
Q2	236 352	306 817	50.8	14.4	13.2	21.5	22.4	2.4	55.7	5.9	13.6
Q3	239 182	312 187	50.4	14.5	13.5	21.7	21.5	2.7	56.3	6.1	13.4
Q4	240 681	316 461	50.0	14.4	13.5	22.1	20.7	2.8	57.1	6.0	13.4
2001 Q1	245 227	321 527	50.2	14.4	13.4	22.1	21.2	2.7	56.9	6.0	13.1
Q2	247 908	324 212	50.4	14.5	13.6	21.5	21.0	3.4	56.5	6.1	13.1
Q3	248 578	322 409	51.7	14.9	13.2	20.2	21.3	2.5	56.8	6.2	13.2
Q4	252 324	325 217	52.0	15.3	12.5	20.3	21.3	2.8	56.8	6.2	12.9
2002 Q1	255 864	330 341	51.6	15.5	12.6	20.3	21.3	2.9	56.6	6.2	13.1
Q2	258 634	335 826	51.2	15.5	12.4	20.9	20.9	3.4	56.5	6.1	13.1
Q3	262 476	338 896	51.1	15.6	12.8	20.5	21.7	2.9	56.3	6.1	13.0
Q4	265 934	341 092	51.5	15.7	13.3	19.5	22.2	2.8	56.0	6.1	13.0
2003 Q1	269 771†	346 557†	51.1	16.2	12.8	19.9	22.5	2.7	55.9	6.1	12.9
Q2	273 027	348 509	51.3	16.6	12.8	19.2	22.3	2.8	56.0	6.1	12.9
Q3	276 879	353 673	51.4	16.5	12.9	19.2	22.4	2.7	56.0	6.1	13.0
Q4	280 785	359 178	..	..	..	..	..	..	..	..	..

1 Non-financial and financial corporations
2 Gross operating surplus of General government, and Households and NPISH plus the adjustment for financial services.

Source: Office for National Statistics; Enquiries 020 7533 6031

2.4 Income, product and spending per head

£

	At current prices				Chained volume measures (reference year 2000)		
	Gross national income at market prices	Gross domestic product at market prices	Household and NPISH final consumption expenditure	Households' gross disposable income	Gross domestic product at market prices	Household and NPISH final consumption expenditure	Real households' disposable income
	IHXS	IHXT	IHXU	IHXV	IHXW	IHXX	IHXZ
Annual							
2000	16 327	16 221	10 684	11 162	16 221	10 684	11 163
2001	17 059	16 839	11 188	11 867	16 459	10 943	11 609
2002	17 954	17 614	11 678	12 179	16 686	11 277	11 760
Quarterly							
2000 Q1	4 048	4 014	2 649	2 726	4 023	2 661	2 739
Q2	4 050	4 034	2 661	2 771	4 048	2 666	2 777
Q3	4 120	4 077	2 682	2 821	4 073	2 681	2 819
Q4	4 109	4 096	2 692	2 844	4 077	2 676	2 828
2001 Q1	4 217	4 165	2 740	2 925	4 103	2 705	2 889
Q2	4 253	4 202	2 771	2 923	4 110	2 711	2 860
Q3	4 272	4 207	2 820	2 974	4 116	2 747	2 897
Q4	4 317	4 265	2 857	3 045	4 130	2 780	2 963
2002 Q1	4 375	4 322	2 877	2 987	4 137	2 783	2 890
Q2	4 415	4 368	2 905	3 055	4 154	2 813	2 957
Q3	4 548	4 433	2 927	3 060	4 187	2 827	2 955
Q4	4 616	4 491	2 969	3 077	4 208	2 854	2 958
2003 Q1	4 670	4 541	2 974	3 082	4 204	2 844	2 948
Q2	4 655	4 598	3 002	3 141	4 229	2 867	2 999
Q3	4 704	4 656	3 039	3 183	4 263	2 892	3 029

Source: Office for National Statistics; Enquiries 020 7533 6031

Economic Trends 604 March 2004

Tables section

Shares of income and expenditure

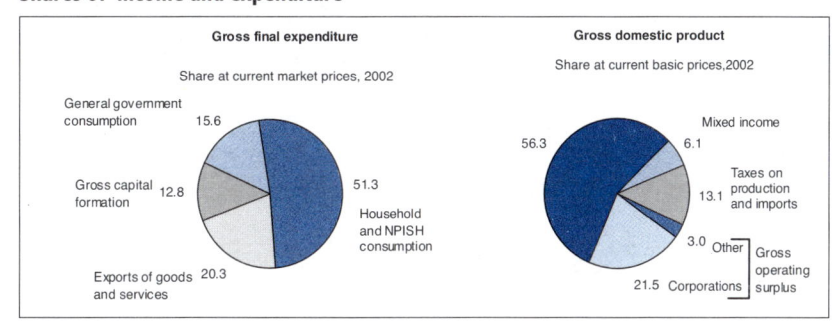

Gross final expenditure
Share at current market prices, 2002

- General government consumption: 15.6
- Gross capital formation: 12.8
- Exports of goods and services: 20.3
- Household and NPISH consumption: 51.3

Gross domestic product
Share at current basic prices, 2002

- Mixed income: 6.1
- Taxes on production and imports: 13.1
- Other: 3.0 — Gross operating surplus
- Corporations: 21.5 — Gross operating surplus
- 56.3

Income, product and spending per capita
chained volume measures, reference year 2000 — percentage change on year earlier

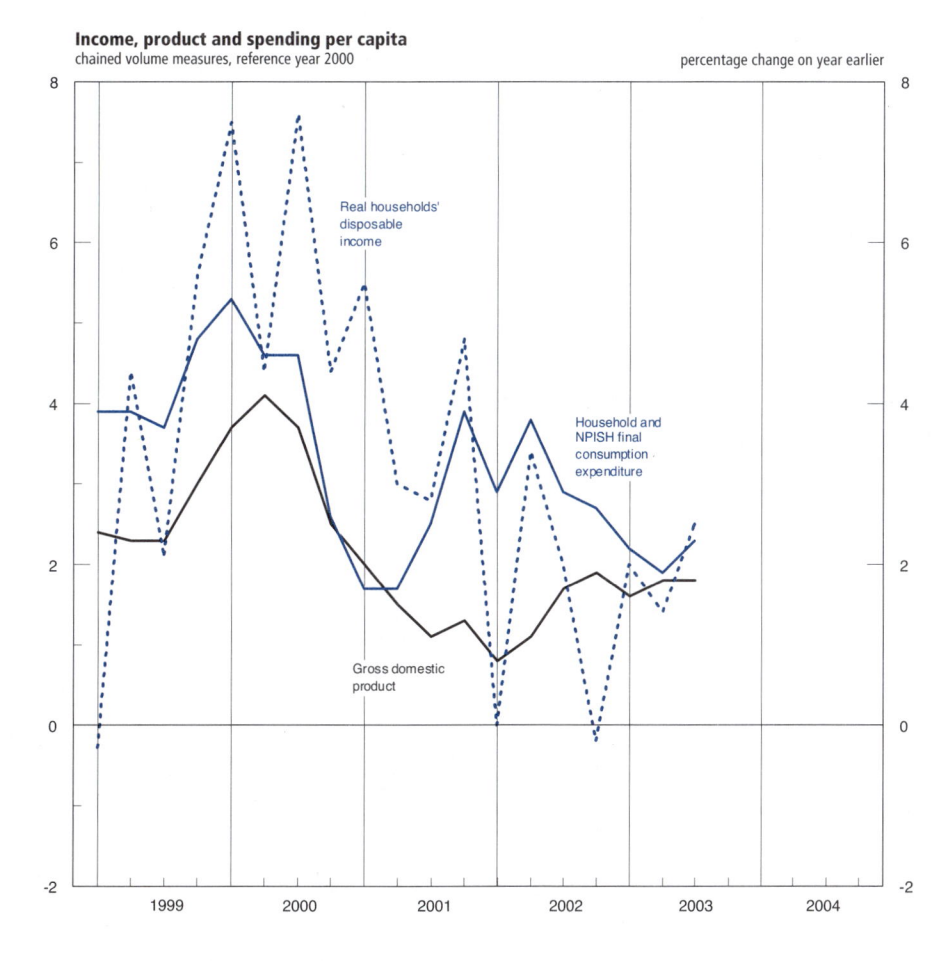

- Real households' disposable income
- Household and NPISH final consumption expenditure
- Gross domestic product

Office for National Statistics | 81

2.5 Households[1] disposable income and consumption

£ million, current prices | | | | | | | £ million, chained volume measures, reference year 2000 | | |

	Households income before tax Total	of which: Wages and salaries	Gross households' disposable income[2]	Adjustment for the change in net equity of households in pension funds	Households' Total resources	Households' final consumption expenditure	Households' saving ratio[3] (percentage)+	Real households' disposable income+[4]	Household final consumption expenditure+	Real households' disposable income (index 2000=100)
	RPHP	ROYJ	RPHQ	RPQJ	RPQK	RPQM	NRJS	NRJR	NPSP	OSXS
Annual										
2000	958 450	457 473	654 649	8 620	663 269	626 537	5.5	654 649	626 537	100.0
2001	1 011 310	484 906	700 538	7 453	707 991	660 380	6.7	685 263	645 981	104.6
2002	1 045 374	502 962	721 044	10 201	731 245	691 457	5.4	696 224	667 655	106.3
2003	..	..	..	..	..	721 928	..	..	687 054	..
Quarterly										
2000 Q1	230 454	111 597	159 378	2 296	161 674	155 089	4.1	160 106	155 791	97.8
Q2	237 963	113 150	162 435	1 022	163 457	155 917	4.6	162 773	156 235	99.5
Q3	242 703	115 371	165 558	2 120	167 678	157 366	6.1	165 450	157 257	101.1
Q4	247 330	117 355	167 278	3 182	170 460	158 165	7.2	166 320	157 254	101.6
2001 Q1	250 508	119 480	171 835	2 583	174 418	161 306	7.5	169 693	159 296	103.7
Q2	249 718	120 487	172 532	1 628	174 160	163 458	6.1	168 806	159 929	103.1
Q3	252 088	121 788	175 818	1 550	177 368	166 625	6.1	171 267	162 313	104.6
Q4	258 996	123 151	180 353	1 692	182 045	168 991	7.2	175 497	164 443	107.2
2002 Q1	256 999	124 025	176 825	3 038	179 863	170 302	5.3	171 046	164 738	104.5
Q2	261 223	125 623	180 860	1 880	182 740	172 025	5.9	175 088	166 537	107.0
Q3	263 082	126 043	181 170	2 488	183 658	173 303	5.6	174 963	167 367	106.9
Q4	264 070	127 271	182 189	2 795	184 984	175 827	5.0	175 127	169 013	107.0
2003 Q1	267 229	128 408	183 014	3 459	186 473	176 819†	5.3	175 039	169 107†	107.0
Q2	271 501	129 474	186 493	1 771	188 264	178 663	5.3	178 089	170 727	108.8
Q3	276 368	131 058	188 973	2 843	191 816	181 591	5.9	179 840	172 646	109.9
Q4	..	..	..	..	..	184 855	..	..	174 574	..

1 All households series include also Non-Profit Institutions Serving Households (NPISH).
2 Total household income *less* payments of income tax and other taxes, social contributions and other current transfers.
3 Households saving as a percentage of Total resources; this is the sum of Gross household disposable income and the Adjustment for the change in net equity of households in pension funds (D.8).
4 Gross household disposable income revalued by the implied Household and NPISH final consumption expenditure deflator (2000 = 100).

Sources: Office for National Statistics; Enquiries Column 1 020 7533 6005; Columns 2-5,7,8,10 020 7533 6027; Columns 6,9 020 7533 5999

2.6 Household final consumption expenditure[1,2]
Chained volume measures

Reference year 2000, £ million

UK National[4]
UK Domestic[5]

	Total	Net tourism	Total	Food & drink	Alcohol & tobacco	Clothing & footwear	Housing	Household goods & services	Health	Transport	Communication	Recreation & culture	Education	Restaurants & hotels	Miscellaneous
COICOP[3]	-	-	0	01	02	03	04	05	06	07	08	09	10	11	12
Annual															
	ABJR	ABTH	ZAKW	ZWUN	ZAKY	ZALA	ZAVO	ZAVW	ZAWC	ZAWM	ZAWW	ZAXA	ZWUT	ZAXS	ZAYG
2001	622 136	9 317	612 819	57 919	24 588	38 103	107 220	38 524	8 961	92 791	15 195	76 835	8 607	68 694	75 382
2002	643 107	10 491	632 616	58 395	25 198	41 506	108 652	42 581	9 381	95 782	15 805	80 329	7 522	70 449	77 016
2003	661 289	..	..	..	..	..	..	..	..	..	..	..	..	..	..
Quarters															
2001 Q1	153 291	1 944	151 347	14 612	6 059	9 119	26 691	9 297	2 337	22 840	3 712	18 605	2 274	17 162	18 639
Q2	153 965	2 391	151 574	14 146	6 137	9 379	26 757	9 439	2 226	22 840	3 784	19 072	2 209	17 003	18 582
Q3	156 368	2 484	153 884	14 328	6 193	9 675	26 868	9 725	2 188	23 453	3 802	19 393	2 128	17 310	18 821
Q4	158 512	2 498	156 014	14 833	6 199	9 930	26 904	10 063	2 210	23 658	3 897	19 765	1 996	17 219	19 340
2002 Q1	158 674	2 676	155 998	14 384	6 228	10 162	26 986	10 323	2 228	23 576	3 869	19 902	1 965	17 554	18 821
Q2	160 450	2 621	157 829	14 430	6 300	10 282	27 093	10 472	2 295	24 219	3 957	19 937	1 891	17 755	19 198
Q3	161 201	2 654	158 547	14 690	6 301	10 444	27 253	10 795	2 387	23 974	3 992	20 075	1 862	17 520	19 254
Q4	162 782	2 540	160 242	14 891	6 369	10 618	27 320	10 991	2 471	24 013	3 987	20 415	1 804	17 620	19 743
2003 Q1	162 754†	3 054†	159 700†	14 817†	6 275†	10 701†	27 466†	10 492†	2 506†	24 337†	3 993†	20 606†	1 836†	17 534†	19 137†
Q2	164 349	2 818	161 531	15 164	6 281	10 961	27 422	10 860	2 535	24 433	4 037	21 147	1 884	17 569	19 238
Q3	166 174	2 610	163 564	15 175	6 347	11 045	27 598	10 802	2 566	24 659	4 086	21 833	1 949	18 007	19 497
Q4	168 012	..	..	..	..	..	..	..	..	..	..	..	..	..	..

1 Estimates are given to the nearest £million but cannot be regarded as accurate to this degree.
2 More detailed estimates of Household Final Consumption Expenditure, expressed in both current prices and chained volume measures and both unadjusted and seasonally adjusted appear in the ONS publication *Consumer Trends*.
3 ESA 95 Classification of Individual Consumption by Purpose
4 Final consumption expenditure by UK households in the UK & abroad
5 Final consumption expenditure in the UK by UK & foreign households

Source: Office for National Statistics; Enquiries 020 7533 5999

Economic Trends 604 March 2004

Tables section

Household's Disposable Income and Consumption
Proportion of **Households' Income before tax** (Current Prices), per cent

Gross Household's disposable income

Household final consumption expenditure

Household final consumption expenditure – component categories
chained volume measures
reference year 2000, £ thousand million

Housing (LHS)

Food & drink (RHS)

Transport (LHS)

Office for National Statistics

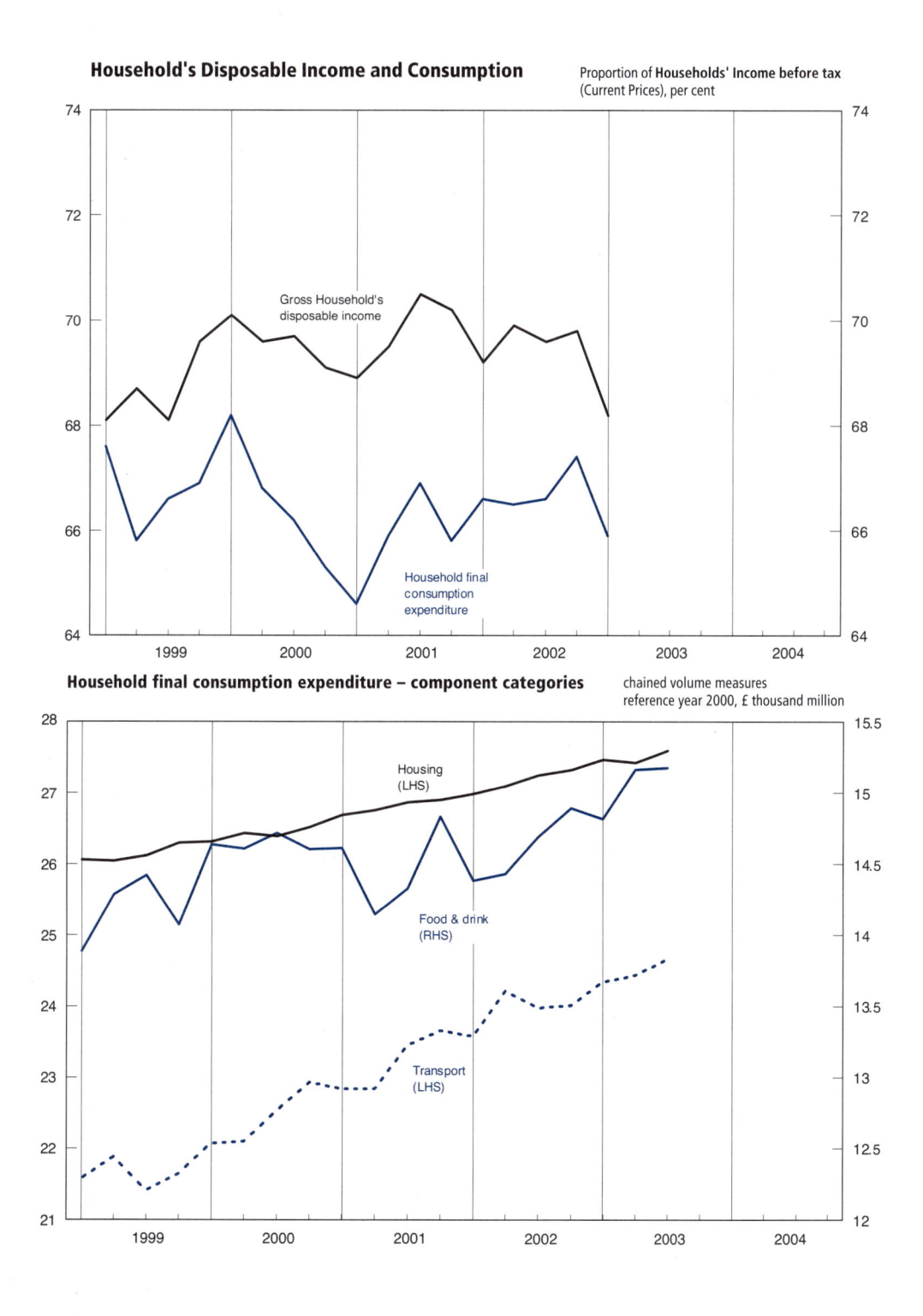

2.7 Gross fixed capital formation
Chained volume measures

Reference year 2000, £ million

	Analysis by sector							Analysis by asset				
			Public corporations[2]		Private sector							
	Business investment[1]	General government	NHS trusts	Transfer costs of non-produced assets	Dwellings	Transfer costs of non-produced assets	Total+	Transport equipment	Other machinery and equipment	Dwellings	Other building and structures[3]	Intangible fixed assets
	NPEL	DLWF	DFTI	DLWH	DFEA	DLWI	NPQT	DLWL	DLWO	DFEG	DLWT	EQDO
Annual												
1999	107 359	9 935	1 441	4	25 508	11 485	155 576	15 128	56 849	27 372	51 760	4 758
2000	112 302	10 412	1 680	6	25 604	11 206	161 210	13 444	62 698	27 394	52 708	4 966
2001	116 337	11 744	1 862	−55	25 937	11 207	167 032	15 296	65 290	27 999	53 524	4 923
2002	113 296	13 135	1 557	−14	30 026	12 004	170 004	16 183	61 739	32 825	53 858	5 399
2003	112 029	..	..	..	..	..	174 353	..	..	..	..	..
Quarterly												
1998 Q1	25 149	2 501	413	−78	6 574	2 448	37 275	4 036	12 808	7 085	12 517	1 103
Q2	25 667	2 291	385	−82	6 824	2 955	38 029	4 017	12 987	7 374	12 780	1 178
Q3	26 360	2 576	354	−76	6 532	2 772	38 621	4 137	13 352	7 125	12 886	1 264
Q4	27 209	2 718	370	−42	6 447	2 335	39 223	4 265	14 344	6 906	12 494	1 237
1999 Q1	27 146	2 512	363	−10	6 345	2 481	38 907	3 986	13 909	6 735	13 162	1 152
Q2	26 336	2 516	322	2	6 536	2 662	38 331	3 592	13 991	7 181	12 477	1 183
Q3	26 785	2 467	379	5	6 053	3 019	38 674	3 763	14 558	6 423	12 763	1 196
Q4	27 092	2 440	377	7	6 574	3 323	39 664	3 787	14 391	7 033	13 358	1 227
2000 Q1	26 931	2 243	457	6	6 638	3 126	39 298	3 364	14 508	7 016	13 301	1 203
Q2	27 299	2 607	366	2	6 511	2 684	39 471	3 276	15 163	6 970	12 826	1 253
Q3	28 317	2 555	409	−1	6 389	2 722	40 417	3 290	16 038	6 819	12 985	1 246
Q4	29 755	3 007	448	−1	6 066	2 674	42 024	3 514	16 989	6 589	13 596	1 264
2001 Q1	29 551	2 321	482	15	6 499	2 839	41 707	3 463	16 565	7 044	13 403	1 232
Q2	29 407	2 989	545	−13	6 327	2 814	42 069	3 911	16 257	6 769	13 910	1 222
Q3	29 156	3 129	414	−25	6 617	2 683	41 974	4 037	16 268	7 142	13 293	1 234
Q4	28 223	3 305	421	−32	6 494	2 871	41 282	3 885	16 200	7 044	12 918	1 235
2002 Q1	28 064	3 346	186	13	7 007	2 590	41 206	3 841	15 409	7 572	13 127	1 257
Q2	28 904	3 042	419	16	7 211	3 110	42 702	4 001	16 211	7 812	13 326	1 352
Q3	28 118	3 313	486	−20	7 697	3 243	42 837	4 188	15 164	8 401	13 721	1 363
Q4	28 210	3 434	466	−23	8 111	3 061	43 259	4 153	14 955	9 040	13 684	1 427
2003 Q1	27 636†	3 983†	386†	−33†	7 921†	2 809†	42 702†	4 046†	14 833†	8 617†	13 812†	1 394
Q2	28 023	3 903	438	−36	8 283	2 765	43 376	3 784	14 704	9 077	14 403	1 408
Q3	28 004	4 185	434	−76	8 523	2 707	43 777	3 863	14 652	9 379	14 475	1 408
Q4	28 366	..	..	..	..	..	44 498	..	..	..	..	..

Percentage change, latest quarter on corresponding quarter of previous year

1998 Q1	19.0	6.8	29.1		−0.2	3.2	14.9	16.2	28.0	−2.6	11.7	−5.4
Q2	18.0	21.5	11.9		10.4	−30.9	13.6	25.7	16.0	9.8	11.0	−6.1
Q3	19.9	4.1	−6.6		0.7	−8.9	13.3	22.9	22.6	1.9	5.4	7.4
Q4	15.8	10.0	3.9		−5.6	−16.3	9.3	25.7	24.3	−5.3	−4.8	7.2
1999 Q1	7.9	0.4	−12.1		−3.5	1.3	4.4	−1.2	8.6	−4.9	5.2	4.4
Q2	2.6	9.8	−16.4		−4.2	−9.9	0.8	−10.6	7.7	−2.6	−2.4	0.4
Q3	1.6	−4.2	7.1		−7.3	8.9	0.1	−9.0	9.0	−9.9	−1.0	−5.4
Q4	−0.4	−10.2	1.9		2.0	42.3	1.1	−11.2	0.3	1.8	6.9	−0.8
2000 Q1	−0.8	−10.7	25.9		4.6	26.0	1.0	−15.6	4.3	4.2	1.1	4.4
Q2	3.7	3.6	13.7		−0.4	0.8	3.0	−8.8	8.4	−2.9	2.8	5.9
Q3	5.7	3.6	7.9		5.6	−9.8	4.5	−12.6	10.2	6.2	1.7	4.2
Q4	9.8	23.2	18.8		−7.7	−19.5	5.9	−7.2	18.1	−6.3	1.8	3.0
2001 Q1	9.7	3.5	5.5		−2.1	−9.2	6.1	2.9	14.2	0.4	0.8	2.4
Q2	7.7	14.7	48.9		−2.8	4.8	6.6	19.4	7.2	−2.9	8.5	−2.5
Q3	3.0	22.5	1.2		3.6	−1.4	3.9	22.7	1.4	4.7	2.4	−1.0
Q4	−5.1	9.9	−6.0		7.1	7.4	−1.8	10.6	−4.6	6.9	−5.0	−2.3
2002 Q1	−5.0	44.2	−61.4		7.8	−8.8	−1.2	10.9	−7.0	7.5	−2.1	2.0
Q2	−1.7	1.8	−23.1		14.0	10.5	1.5	2.3	−0.3	15.4	−4.2	10.6
Q3	−3.6	5.9	17.4		16.3	20.9	2.1	3.7	−6.8	17.6	3.2	10.5
Q4	0.0	3.9	10.7		24.9	6.6	4.8	6.9	−7.7	28.3	5.9	15.5
2003 Q1	−1.5†	19.0†	+†		13.0†	8.5†	3.6†	5.3†	−3.7†	13.8†	5.2†	10.9
Q2	−3.0	28.3	4.5		14.9	−11.1	1.6	−5.4	−9.3	16.2	8.1	4.1
Q3	−0.4	26.3	−10.7		10.7	−16.5	2.2	−7.8	−3.4	11.6	5.5	3.3
Q4	0.6	..	..		..	..	2.9	..	..	..	..	..

1 Not including dwellings and costs associated with the transfer of ownership of non-produced assets.
2 Remaining investment by public non-financial corporations is included within business investment.
3 Including costs associated with transfer of ownership of non-produced assets.

Source: Office for National Statistics; Enquiries 020 7533 6010

Gross fixed capital formation-by sector

Chained volume measures, reference year 2000, £ million

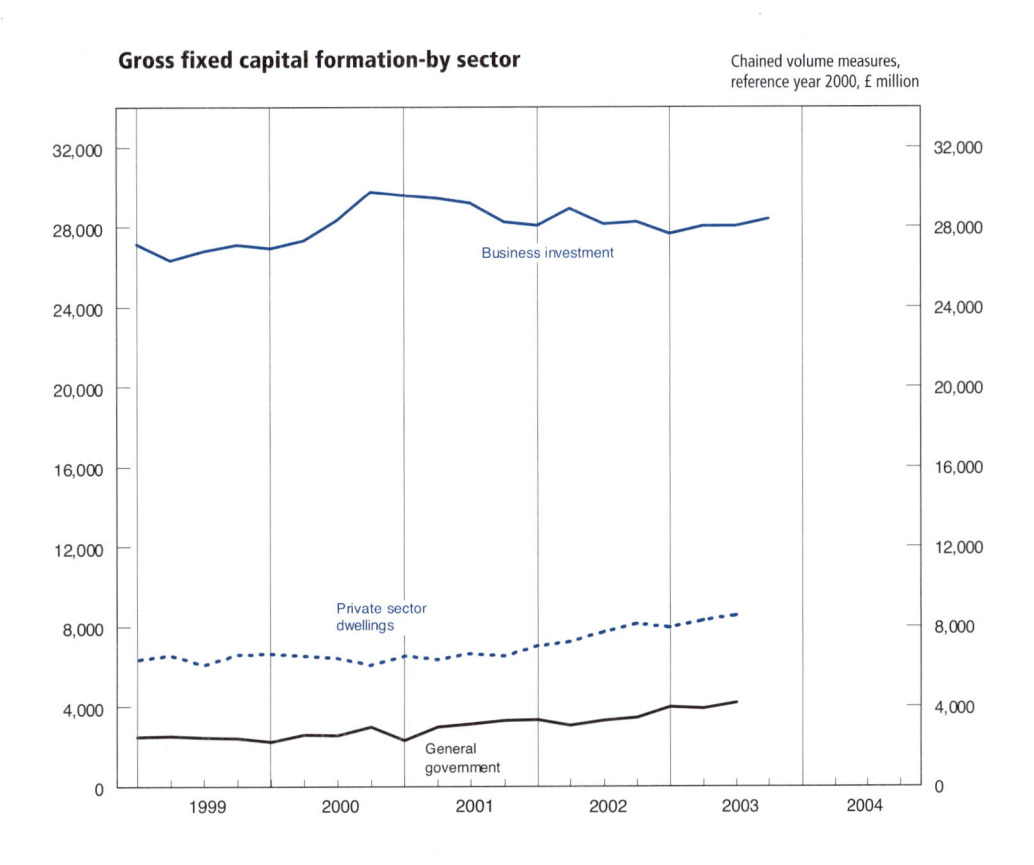

Gross fixed capital formation – by asset

Chained volume measures, reference year 2000, £ million

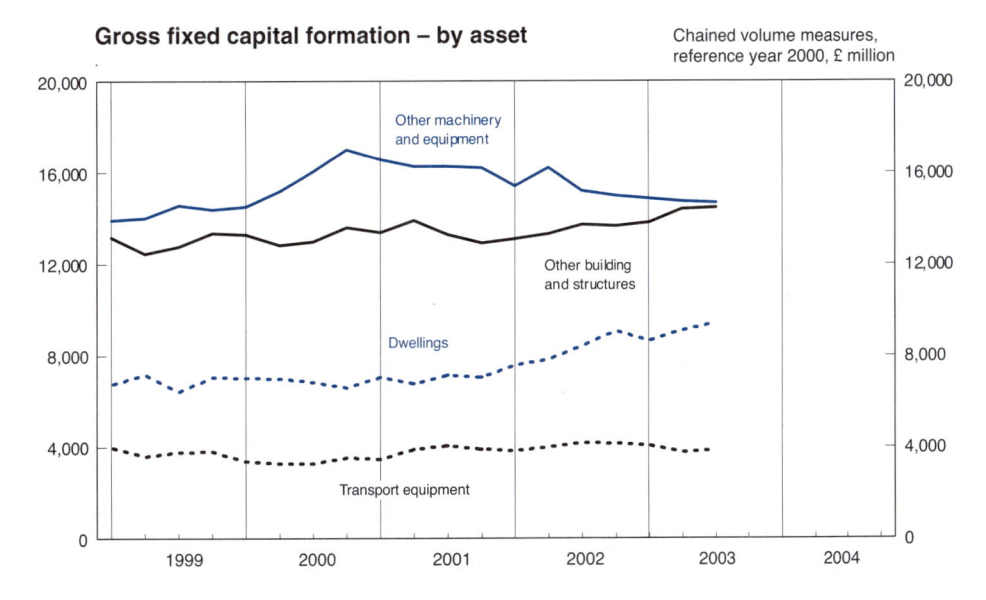

2.8 Gross value added, chained volume indices at basic prices, by category of output[1,3]

2000 = 100

	Production						Service industries						Gross value added at basic prices	Gross value added excluding oil
	Agriculture, forestry, and fishing	Mining and quarrying including oil and gas extraction	Manufacturing	Electricity gas and water supply	Total	Construction	Distribution hotels and catering; repairs	Transport storage and communication	Business services and finance	Government and other services	Total		
2000 Weights[2]	11	30	181	19	231	54	157	83	239	226	705	1000	973
	GDQA	CKYX	CKYY	CKYZ	CKYW	GDQB	GDQE	GDQH	GDQN	GDQU	GDQS	CGCE	JUNT
1999	100.6	103.3	97.6	97.9	98.1	98.7	97.3	91.2	95.6	97.1	95.9	96.3	96.2
2000	100.0	100.0	100.0	100.0	100.0	100.0	100.0	100.0	100.0	100.0	100.0	100.0	100.0
2001	89.9	94.5	98.7	102.4	98.4	103.4	101.8	104.0	103.9	101.4	102.6	101.9	102.1
2002	99.1	94.4	95.1	104.0	95.7	111.2	106.2	105.0	105.5	103.1	104.8	103.2	103.5
2003	97.1	88.6	95.0	105.1	95.0	118.2	108.9†	106.7	108.6	105.4	107.4†	105.2	105.7

Quarterly

1999 Q1	101.2	102.2	96.6	96.9	97.1	97.6	96.3	89.1	94.9	96.2	94.9	95.3	95.2
Q2	100.2	103.3	96.9	97.1	97.5	98.0	96.8	90.5	95.0	96.7	95.4	95.7	95.6
Q3	100.0	104.5	98.3	98.4	98.8	99.5	97.6	91.3	95.3	97.6	96.0	96.6	96.4
Q4	101.1	103.0	98.7	99.1	99.1	99.8	98.3	93.9	97.3	98.0	97.3	97.6	97.5
2000 Q1	100.7	103.8	99.2	98.7	99.6	102.3	99.0	97.0	98.0	99.0	98.4	98.9	98.8
Q2	100.1	102.4	99.8	101.0	100.2	100.0	99.6	99.2	99.2	99.8	99.5	99.7	99.6
Q3	101.4	98.9	100.0	99.9	99.9	98.3	100.9	101.4	100.9	100.7	100.9	100.6	100.6
Q4	97.8	94.9	100.9	100.3	100.3	99.4	100.5	102.4	101.9	100.5	101.2	100.9	101.0
2001 Q1	90.4	93.3	100.8	104.5	100.1	101.5	101.2	104.1	102.9	100.7	101.9	101.7	101.9
Q2	88.7	96.3	98.7	102.8	98.7	102.8	101.4	104.6	103.5	101.0	102.4	101.7	101.9
Q3	89.0	95.0	98.6	101.0	98.3	103.8	101.7	103.9	104.0	101.2	102.6	101.8	102.0
Q4	91.4	93.4	96.6	101.2	96.5	105.7	103.2	103.6	105.2	102.4	103.7	102.3	102.5
2002 Q1	98.4	94.2	95.8	101.5	96.1	108.8	104.5	104.3	104.3	102.7	103.8	102.5	102.8
Q2	98.7	99.1	94.6	104.6	96.0	110.0	105.6	103.9	104.8	102.8	104.2	102.8	102.9
Q3	99.9	90.2	95.5	106.2	95.7	112.0	106.9	105.3	106.2	103.1	105.3	103.5	104.0
Q4	99.4	94.0	94.5	103.6	95.2	114.0	107.9	106.6	106.7	104.0	106.1	104.0	104.3
2003 Q1	96.5†	92.4†	94.4†	102.9†	94.9†	112.7†	107.5†	106.0	107.8†	104.5†	106.4†	104.2†	104.5†
Q2	97.0	90.0	95.0	104.7	95.1	117.7	108.6	106.2†	107.1	105.1	106.7	104.7	105.2
Q3	97.1	87.3	95.3	105.9	95.1	120.1	109.5	106.9	108.9	105.6	107.8	105.6	106.1
Q4	97.8	84.5	95.5	106.8	95.0	122.1	110.1	107.8	110.4	106.4	108.8	106.4	107.0

Percentage change, latest quarter on corresponding quarter of last year

1999 Q1	4.7	4.4	−0.7	3.5	0.1	−3.5	3.2	7.9	5.8	2.1	4.3	2.7	
Q2	1.5	4.4	−0.3	2.0	0.3	0.4	3.4	7.1	4.4	2.0	3.7	2.5	
Q3	2.9	5.3	1.3	2.7	1.8	2.2	3.1	5.3	2.4	2.0	2.7	2.3	
Q4	4.4	2.6	2.6	2.6	2.6	2.4	2.4	5.9	2.3	2.3	2.7	2.6	
2000 Q1	−0.5	1.6	2.7	1.9	2.6	4.8	2.8	8.9	3.3	2.9	3.7	3.8	
Q2	−0.1	−0.9	3.0	4.0	2.8	2.0	2.9	9.6	4.4	3.2	4.3	4.2	
Q3	1.4	−5.4	1.7	1.5	1.1	−1.2	3.4	11.1	5.9	3.2	5.1	4.1	
Q4	−3.3	−7.9	2.2	1.2	1.2	−0.4	2.2	9.1	4.7	2.6	4.0	3.4	
2001 Q1	−10.2	−10.1	1.6	5.9	0.5	−0.8	2.2	7.3	5.0	1.7	3.6	2.8	
Q2	−11.4	−6.0	−1.1	1.8	−1.5	2.8	1.8	5.4	4.3	1.2	2.9	2.0	
Q3	−12.2	−3.9	−1.4	1.1	−1.6	5.6	0.8	2.5	3.1	0.5	1.7	1.2	
Q4	−6.5	−1.6	−4.3	0.9	−3.8	6.3	2.7	1.2	3.2	1.9	2.5	1.4	
2002 Q1	8.8	1.0	−5.0	−2.9	−4.0	7.2	3.3	0.2	1.4	2.0	1.9	0.8	
Q2	11.3	2.9	−4.2	1.8	−2.7	7.0	4.1	−0.7	1.3	1.8	1.8	1.1	
Q3	12.2	−5.1	−3.1	5.1	−2.6	7.9	5.1	1.3	2.1	1.9	2.6	1.7	
Q4	8.8	0.6	−2.2	2.4	−1.3	7.9	4.6	2.9	1.4	1.6	2.3	1.7	
2003 Q1	−1.9†	−1.9†	−1.5†	1.4†	−1.2†	3.6†	2.9†	1.6	3.4†	1.8†	2.5†	1.7†	
Q2	−1.7	−9.2	0.4	0.1	−0.9	7.0	2.8	2.2†	2.2	2.2	2.4	1.8	
Q3	−2.8	−3.2	−0.2	−0.3	−0.6	7.2	2.4	1.5	2.5	2.4	2.4	2.0	
Q4	−1.6	−10.1	1.1	3.1	−0.2	7.1	2.0	1.1	3.5	2.3	2.5	2.3	

1 Estimates cannot be regarded as accurate to the last digit shown.
2 Weights may not sum to the totals due to rounding. The weights shown are in proportion to total gross value added (GVA) in 2000, and are used to combine the industry output indices to calculate the totals for 2001 and 2002. For 2000 and earlier, totals are calculated using the equivalent weights for the previous year (e.g. totals for 2000 use 1999 weights).

3 Components of output are valued at basic prices, which excludes taxes and subsidies on production

Sources: Office for National Statistics; Enquiries Columns 1-11 020 7533 5969; Column 12 020 7533 6031

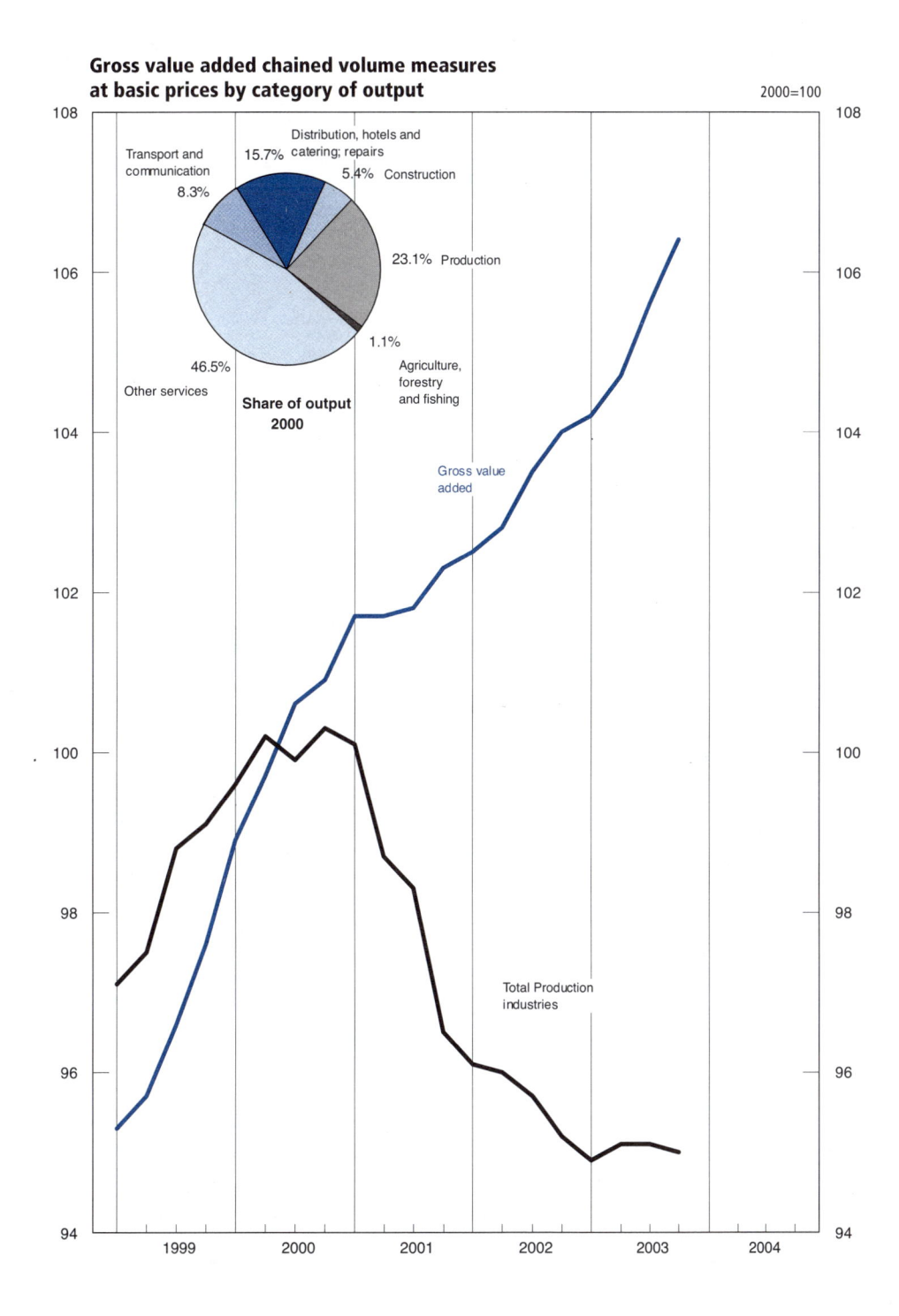

Gross value added chained volume measures at basic prices by category of output

2000=100

Share of output 2000:
- Transport and communication 8.3%
- Distribution, hotels and catering; repairs 15.7%
- Construction 5.4%
- Production 23.1%
- Agriculture, forestry and fishing 1.1%
- Other services 46.5%

Series shown: Gross value added; Total Production industries (1999–2003).

2.9 Gross value added chained volume indices at basic prices, by category of output: Service industries

2000 = 100

	Distribution hotels and catering; repairs		Transport, storage and communication		Business services and finance			Government and other services					
	Motor trades; wholesale and retail trade; repairs	Hotels and restaurants	Transport and storage	Post and telecommu-nication	Financial intermedi-ation[3]	Real estate, renting and business activities	Lettings of dwellings	PAD[1]	Education	Health and social work	Other services[2]	Adjustment for financial services[4]	Total services
2000 weights	123	33	51	32	55	154	75	56	57	62	51	-45	705
Annual													
	GDQC	GDQD	GDQF	GDQG	GDQI	GDQK	GDQL	GDQO	GDQP	GDQQ	GDQR	GDQJ	GDQS
1999	96.9	98.7	93.8	87.1	95.0	92.9	100.6	97.7	98.4	96.1	96.3	92.9	95.9
2000	100.0	100.0	100.0	100.0	100.0	100.0	100.0	100.0	100.0	100.0	100.0	100.0	100.0
2001	102.3	100.2	101.6	107.9	105.2	104.5	102.3	100.5	99.5	103.3	102.0	104.8	102.6
2002	107.1	102.9	103.1	108.0	104.8	107.6	103.7	102.3	99.7	107.7	102.3	108.9	104.8
2003	..	..	..	..	..	..	..	..	..	..	..	..	107.4†
Quarterly													
1999 Q1	96.2	96.9	93.5	82.4	93.1	92.0	101.0	97.1	97.3	95.8	94.6	91.8	94.9
Q2	96.5	98.2	93.1	86.4	95.4	91.4	101.5	97.5	98.3	95.4	95.6	93.3	95.4
Q3	97.2	99.3	93.3	88.1	94.4	92.7	100.6	98.1	99.4	96.1	96.9	93.6	96.0
Q4	97.8	100.2	95.5	91.4	97.0	95.4	99.2	98.0	98.6	97.1	98.2	93.1	97.3
2000 Q1	98.3	101.6	98.1	95.1	98.7	96.8	99.2	99.3	99.3	98.2	99.2	96.3	98.4
Q2	99.6	99.6	100.2	97.6	99.8	99.4	98.8	99.9	100.2	99.5	99.5	100.2	99.5
Q3	101.0	100.3	101.6	101.2	100.3	101.4	100.2	100.5	100.6	101.1	100.7	100.5	100.9
Q4	101.1	98.5	100.1	106.1	101.2	102.4	101.8	100.4	100.0	101.2	100.5	103.0	101.2
2001 Q1	101.5	99.8	101.2	108.5	104.1	103.6	101.8	100.1	99.7	101.7	101.3	105.3	101.9
Q2	101.7	100.0	101.7	109.0	104.3	103.9	102.1	100.2	99.1	102.8	101.9	103.5	102.4
Q3	102.0	100.5	101.8	107.4	105.1	104.5	102.5	100.4	99.2	103.4	101.8	104.7	102.6
Q4	104.0	100.4	101.7	106.5	107.3	105.7	103.0	101.2	100.1	105.2	103.1	105.8	103.7
2002 Q1	105.5	101.1	102.6	106.8	103.0	105.2	103.4	101.6	99.8	105.5	103.8	104.6	103.8
Q2	106.5	101.9	102.5	106.2	103.2	106.9	103.3	102.0	99.6	107.3	101.6	108.0	104.2
Q3	107.8	103.6	103.4	108.3	105.2	108.7	103.9	102.3	99.5	108.2	101.8	109.7	105.3
Q4	108.6	105.2	104.0	110.7	107.9	109.4	104.2	103.4	100.0	109.7	102.0	113.4	106.1
2003 Q1	107.9†	105.9†	102.3†	111.8	106.4	112.0†	104.6†	103.9†	100.6	110.7†	101.7†	115.0†	106.4†
Q2	108.8	107.8	102.0	112.9	107.7	111.9	105.1	104.4	101.0†	111.3	102.9	120.6	106.7
Q3	110.0	107.7	103.3	112.6	110.2†	114.6	105.5	104.9	101.2	111.8	103.9	124.2	107.8
Q4	..	..	..	..	..	..	..	..	..	..	..	..	108.8

Percentage change, quarter on corresponding quarter of previous year

Quarterly

1999 Q1	3.6	1.9	2.6	17.5	1.7	7.6	5.4	0.2	3.6	2.1	2.9	5.5	4.3
Q2	3.2	4.2	0.6	18.5	4.0	4.3	4.9	-0.2	4.1	1.8	2.4	4.1	3.7
Q3	2.4	6.0	-1.0	16.4	1.6	2.2	2.4	-0.2	4.0	2.0	2.0	0.3	2.7
Q4	2.0	3.8	0.7	14.7	6.4	1.8	-0.9	0.4	2.1	3.3	3.0	0.4	2.7
2000 Q1	2.2	4.9	4.9	15.4	6.0	5.2	-1.8	2.3	2.1	2.5	4.9	4.9	3.7
Q2	3.2	1.4	7.6	13.0	4.6	8.8	-2.7	2.5	1.9	4.3	4.1	7.4	4.3
Q3	3.9	1.0	8.9	14.9	6.3	9.4	-0.4	2.4	1.2	5.2	3.9	7.4	5.1
Q4	3.4	-1.7	4.8	16.1	4.3	7.3	2.6	2.4	1.4	4.2	2.3	10.6	4.0
2001 Q1	3.3	-1.8	3.2	14.1	5.5	7.0	2.6	0.8	0.4	3.6	2.1	9.3	3.6
Q2	2.1	0.4	1.5	11.7	4.5	4.5	3.3	0.3	-1.1	3.3	2.4	3.3	2.9
Q3	1.0	0.2	0.2	6.1	4.8	3.1	2.3	-0.1	-1.4	2.3	1.1	4.2	1.7
Q4	2.9	1.9	1.6	0.4	6.0	3.2	1.2	0.8	0.1	4.0	2.6	2.7	2.5
2002 Q1	3.9	1.3	1.4	-1.6	-1.1	1.5	1.6	1.5	0.1	3.7	2.5	-0.7	1.9
Q2	4.7	1.9	0.8	-2.6	-1.1	2.9	1.2	1.8	0.5	4.4	-0.3	4.3	1.8
Q3	5.7	3.1	1.6	0.8	0.1	4.0	1.4	1.9	0.3	4.6	0.0	4.8	2.6
Q4	4.4	4.8	2.3	3.9	0.6	3.5	1.2	2.2	-0.1	4.3	-1.1	7.2	2.3
2003 Q1	2.3†	4.7†	-0.3†	4.7	3.3	6.5†	1.2†	2.3†	0.8	4.9†	-2.0†	9.9†	2.5†
Q2	2.2	5.8	-0.5	6.3	4.4†	4.7	1.7	2.4	1.4†	3.7	1.3	11.7	2.4
Q3	2.0	4.0	-0.1	4.0	4.8†	5.4	1.5	2.5	1.7	3.3	2.1	13.2	2.4
Q4	..	..	..	..	..	..	..	..	..	..	..	..	2.5

1 Public administration and national defence; compulsory social security.
2 Comprising sections O, and P of the SIC(92).
3 Comprises section J of the SIC(92). This covers activities of institutions such as banks, building societies, securities dealers, insurance companies and pension funds. It also covers institutions whose activities are closely related to financial intermediation : for example fund managers and insurance brokers.
4 The weight and proxy series for financial intermediation are calculated before the deduction of interest receipts and payments to provide a better indication of the underlying activity for this section (see note 3). However, this overstates the contribution to GDP because interest flows should be treated as transfer payments rather than final consumption. The financial services adjustment, which has a negative weight, corrects for this.
5 See footnote 2 on Table 2.8

Source: Office for National Statistics; Enquiries 020 7533 5969

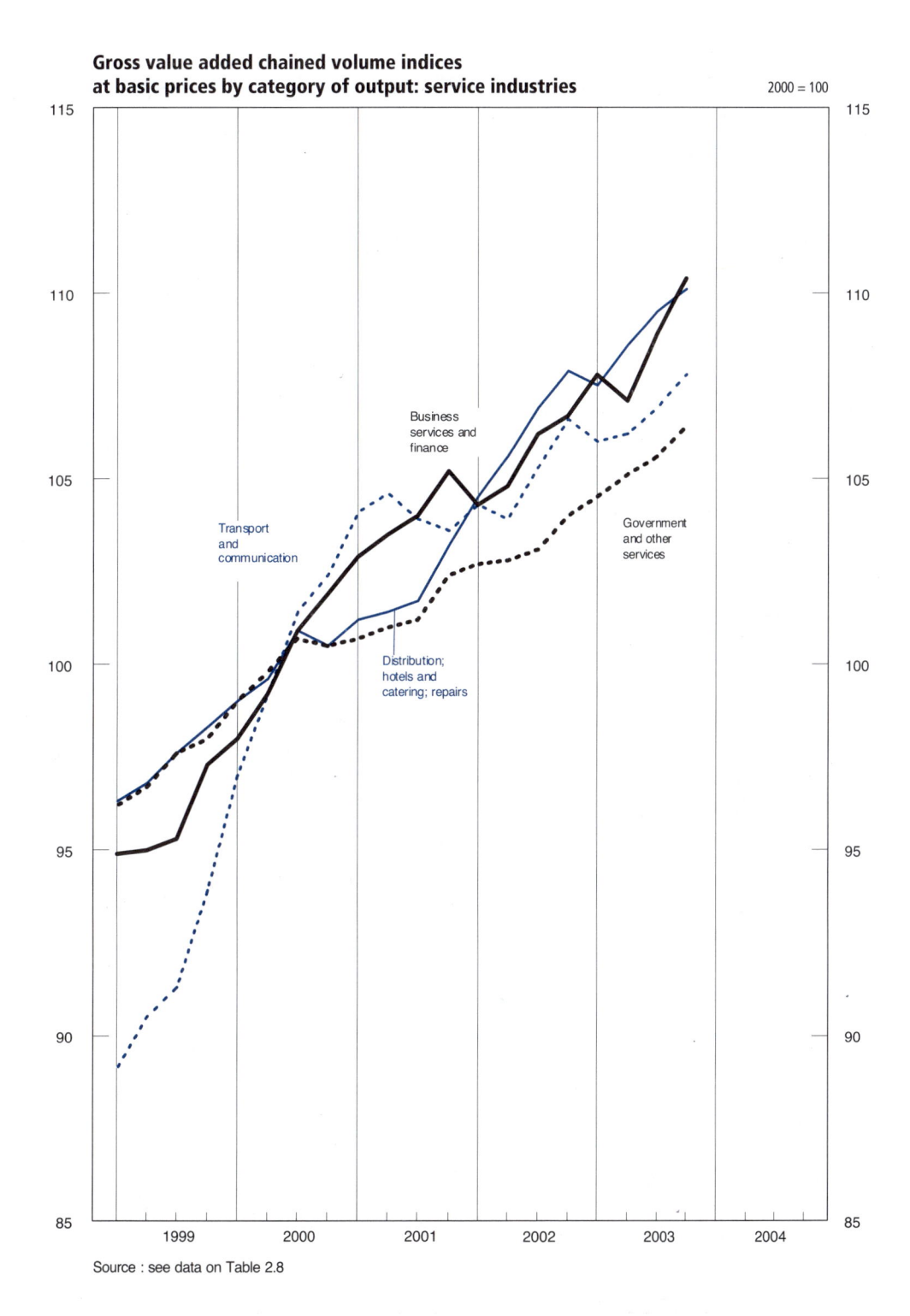

Gross value added chained volume indices at basic prices by category of output: service industries

2000 = 100

Source: see data on Table 2.8

2.10 Summary capital accounts and net lending/net borrowing

£ million

	Non-financial corporations				Financial corporations				General Government			
	Gross saving[1]	Capital transfers (net receipts)	Gross capital formation[2]	Net acquisition of non-financial assets	Gross saving[1]	Capital transfers (net receipts)	Gross capital formation[2]	Net acquisition of non-financial assets	Gross saving[1]	Capital transfers (net receipts)	Gross capital formation[2]	Net acquisition of non-financial assets
Annual	RPJV	GZQW	RQBZ	RQAX	RPPS	GZQE	RPYP	RPYO	RPQC	GZQU	RPZF	RPZE
1999	89 423	2 415	99 913	1 051	−8 863	−	8 073	−37	23 013	−4 014	9 867	−888
2000	95 286	1 638	101 766	856	−16 356	−	10 739	−37	26 728	−2 204	10 284	−776
2001	90 384	3 304	101 935	1 139	−15 068	−	7 255	25	23 652	−4 791	11 659	−915
2002	105 840	3 280	97 110	1 431	8 596	−	7 092	−36	1 788	−5 018	13 133	−1 087
Quarterly												
1999 Q1	26 492	685	25 503	284	−5 673	−	1 080	−2	4 253	−1 312	2 675	−256
Q2	18 715	483	23 343	299	−794	−	2 613	−8	4 554	−708	2 546	−224
Q3	20 956	676	25 692	233	982	−	2 265	−13	6 667	−1 005	2 368	−202
Q4	23 260	571	25 375	235	−3 378	−	2 115	−14	7 539	−989	2 278	−206
2000 Q1	22 912	588	25 326	208	275	−	2 151	−16	7 258	−922	2 161	−185
Q2	24 145	324	24 673	185	−4 631	−	2 416	−13	7 534	−139	2 554	−189
Q3	23 686	359	25 644	185	−4 071	−	3 170	−7	6 510	−575	2 563	−196
Q4	24 543	367	26 123	278	−7 929	−	3 002	−1	5 426	−568	3 006	−206
2001 Q1	23 178	599	26 317	253	−5 567	−	2 342	5	7 611	−776	2 251	−218
Q2	22 843	627	26 810	285	−2 431	−	2 232	8	6 442	−1 276	2 969	−220
Q3	21 791	719	25 159	314	−2 685	−	1 240	8	6 760	−1 142	3 112	−236
Q4	22 572	1 359	23 649	287	−4 385	−	1 441	4	2 839	−1 597	3 327	−241
2002 Q1	23 185	752	24 501	369	1 968	−	954	−3	1 353	−1 270	3 421	−282
Q2	24 370	635	23 322	330	140	−	1 252	−9	928	−972	3 079	−234
Q3	27 452	814	23 817	361	2 386	−	3 055	−12	1 442	−1 348	3 280	−238
Q4	30 833	1 079	25 470	371	4 102	−	1 831	−12	−1 935	−1 428	3 353	−333
2003 Q1	29 764	1 342	24 413	362	5 186	−	2 112	−8	−1 794	−2 319	3 895	−198
Q2	27 813	1 630	24 765	406	2 517	−	917	−3	−1 984	−2 090	4 092	−250
Q3	28 003	956	24 791	455	1 484	−	1 035	1	−1 707	−1 454	4 371	−252

	Households & NPISH				Net lending(+)/net borrowing(−)[3]					
	Gross saving[1]	Capital transfers (net receipts)	Gross capital formation[2]	Net acquisition of non-financial assets	Non-financial corporations	Financial corporations	General government	Households & NPISH	Rest of the world[4]	Statistical Discrepancy
Annual	RPQL	GZQI	RPZV	RPZU	RQAW	RPYN	RPZD	RPZT	RQCH	RVFE
1999	32 947	2 383	38 740	−138	−13 492	−16 899	10 020	−3 272	23 643	−
2000	36 732	2 300	39 249	−67	−10 375	−27 058	15 016	−150	22 567	−
2001	47 611	3 295	43 755	−152	−15 164	−22 348	8 117	7 303	22 092	−
2002	39 788	3 200	49 783	−176	5 460	1 540	−15 276	−6 619	16 941	−2 046
Quarterly										
1999 Q1	6 387	604	9 920	−27	176	−6 751	522	−2 902	8 955	−3 998
Q2	11 297	499	9 112	−36	−5 440	−3 399	1 524	2 720	4 595	−138
Q3	7 133	575	9 343	−40	−5 414	−1 270	3 496	−1 595	4 783	1 348
Q4	8 130	705	10 365	−35	−2 814	−5 479	4 478	−1 495	5 310	2 788
2000 Q1	6 585	553	10 410	−24	−3 089	−1 860	4 360	−3 248	3 837	−1 988
Q2	7 540	473	9 842	−16	−1 574	−7 034	5 030	−1 813	5 391	−2 588
Q3	10 312	616	9 585	−12	−2 982	−7 234	3 568	1 355	5 293	1 811
Q4	12 295	658	9 412	−15	−2 730	−10 930	2 058	3 556	8 046	2 765
2001 Q1	13 112	331	10 556	−25	−4 333	−7 914	4 802	2 912	4 533	−6 553
Q2	10 702	1 363	10 502	−36	−5 160	−4 671	2 417	1 599	5 815	−1 517
Q3	10 743	891	11 937	−44	−4 264	−3 933	2 742	−259	5 714	2 830
Q4	13 054	710	10 760	−47	−1 407	−5 830	−1 844	3 051	6 030	5 240
2002 Q1	9 561	682	11 834	−47	−2 046	1 017	−3 056	−1 544	5 862	−6 218
Q2	10 715	646	12 686	−45	21	−1 103	−2 889	−1 280	5 645	−4 246
Q3	10 355	948	11 929	−43	2 788	−657	−2 948	−583	1 992	6 874
Q4	9 157	924	13 334	−41	4 697	2 283	−6 383	−3 212	3 442	1 544
2003 Q1	9 898	1 230	13 068	−46	5 401	3 082	−7 810	−1 894	2 573	−2 484
Q2	10 035	835	13 509	−49	2 888	1 603	−7 916	−2 590	7 584	−3 858
Q3	11 359	1 147	14 052	−55	2 385	448	−7 280	−1 491	7 663	1 729

1 Before providing for depreciation, inventory holding gains.
2 Comprises gross fixed capital formation and changes in inventories and acquisitions less disposals of valuables.
3 This balance is equal to gross saving *plus* capital transfers *less* gross fixed capital formation, *less* Net acquisition of non-financial assets, *less* changes in inventories.
4 Equals, the current balance of payments accounts, *plus* capital transfers.

Sources: Office for National Statistics;
Enquiries Part 1 (Upper) Columns 1,3-5,7-9,11,12 020 7533 6031;
Columns 2,6,10 020 7533 5985;
Part2 (Lower) Columns 1, 3-10 020 7533 6031; Column 2 020 7533 5985

Sector net lending/net borrowing £ million

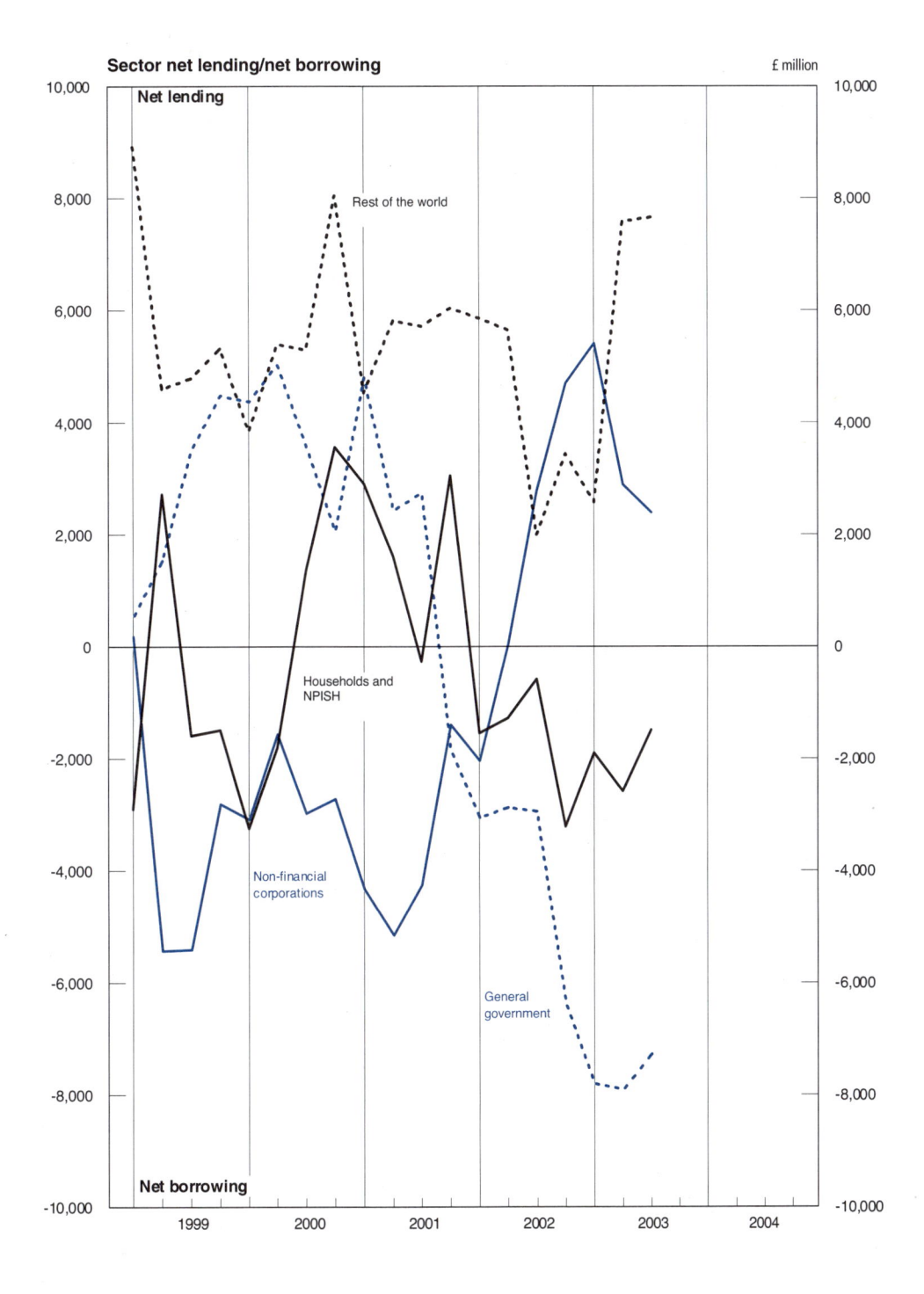

- Net lending
- Rest of the world
- Households and NPISH
- Non-financial corporations
- General government
- Net borrowing

2.11 Private Non-Financial Corporations: Allocation of Primary Income Account

£ million

	Resources						Uses				
	Gross operating surplus						Property income payments				
	Gross trading profits										
	Continental shelf companies	Others[1]	Rental of buildings	less Inventory holding gains	Gross operating surplus+[1]	Property income receipts	Total resources[1,2]	Total payments	of which Dividends	of which Interest	Gross balance of primary incomes[1]	Share of gross national income[1] (%)
	CAGD	CAED	FCBW	-DLRA	CAER	RPBM	RPBN	RPBP	RVFT	ROCG	RPBO	NRJL

Annual

1993	9 375	100 167	9 132	-2 392	116 282	29 773	146 055	72 847	32 250	21 755	73 208	11.4
1994	10 776	117 450	8 641	-3 830	133 037	36 090	169 127	80 872	36 365	21 057	88 255	12.9
1995	12 124	125 151	9 379	-4 489	142 165	42 948	185 113	95 631	46 218	24 098	89 482	12.5
1996	15 702	133 508	9 493	-958	157 745	45 695	203 440	101 125	51 609	23 490	102 315	13.4
1997	13 978	145 693	9 561	-361	168 871	47 954	216 825	107 623	56 253	25 822	109 202	13.4
1998	11 696	150 975	10 837	753	174 261	49 713	223 974	107 266	51 578	30 659	116 708	13.4
1999	13 864	153 954	11 435	-1 801	177 452	48 118	225 570	115 547	61 104	30 673	110 023	12.3
2000	21 333	153 142	12 271	-2 941	183 805	60 554	244 359	125 694	55 846	37 355	118 665	12.5
2001	19 822	153 445	12 999	-1 555	184 711	73 575	258 286	145 661	75 867	39 578	112 625	11.3
2002	18 742	160 241	13 318	-3 114	189 187	67 347	256 534	129 498	62 606	36 210	127 036	11.9

Quarterly

1993 Q1	2 171	25 292	2 259	-974	28 748	7 297	36 045	17 848	7 439	5 758	18 197	11.7
Q2	2 116	23 632	2 300	-359	27 689	7 190	34 879	18 617	9 185	5 385	16 262	10.3
Q3	2 456	25 593	2 305	-561	29 793	7 086	36 879	17 820	7 431	5 388	19 059	11.8
Q4	2 632	25 650	2 268	-498	30 052	8 200	38 252	18 562	8 195	5 224	19 690	12.0
1994 Q1	2 292	27 870	2 201	-443	31 920	9 245	41 165	19 053	8 537	5 276	22 112	13.2
Q2	3 050	29 556	2 148	-919	33 835	8 772	42 607	20 021	8 228	5 302	22 586	13.4
Q3	2 701	29 269	2 132	-1 109	32 993	8 423	41 416	21 013	9 459	5 163	20 403	11.9
Q4	2 733	30 755	2 160	-1 359	34 289	9 650	43 939	20 785	10 141	5 316	23 154	13.2
1995 Q1	2 966	31 234	2 264	-1 738	34 726	9 371	44 097	22 405	9 966	5 663	21 692	12.3
Q2	3 113	30 812	2 336	-1 588	34 673	9 963	44 636	22 201	9 264	6 057	22 435	12.7
Q3	2 934	31 531	2 379	-1 181	35 663	11 011	46 674	25 045	12 656	6 062	21 629	12.0
Q4	3 111	31 574	2 400	18	37 103	12 603	49 706	25 980	14 332	6 316	23 726	12.9
1996 Q1	3 523	32 645	2 386	-800	37 754	11 196	48 950	25 790	13 234	5 952	23 160	12.4
Q2	3 929	33 047	2 366	-102	39 240	12 391	51 631	23 978	12 135	5 759	27 653	14.5
Q3	4 081	33 895	2 362	-208	40 130	10 633	50 763	25 201	12 624	5 881	25 562	13.3
Q4	4 169	33 921	2 379	152	40 621	11 475	52 096	26 156	13 616	5 898	25 940	13.4
1997 Q1	3 885	36 710	2 337	-23	42 909	10 999	53 908	24 839	12 414	5 966	29 069	14.7
Q2	3 288	36 897	2 381	239	42 805	11 864	54 669	27 598	15 386	6 396	27 071	13.3
Q3	3 448	36 127	2 414	-506	41 483	14 105	55 588	27 741	15 588	6 497	27 847	13.6
Q4	3 357	35 959	2 429	-71	41 674	10 986	52 660	27 445	12 865	6 963	25 215	12.2
1998 Q1	3 160	36 913	2 629	107	42 809	13 933	56 742	29 295	15 180	7 405	27 447	13.1
Q2	3 103	36 759	2 670	53	42 585	11 731	54 316	25 942	11 931	7 517	28 374	13.2
Q3	2 779	39 114	2 727	315	44 935	11 776	56 711	26 104	11 712	7 916	30 607	13.8
Q4	2 654	38 189	2 811	278	43 932	12 273	56 205	25 925	12 755	7 821	30 280	13.6
1999 Q1	2 519	37 823	2 819	-302	42 859	8 254	51 113	19 597	8 789	7 482	31 516	14.5
Q2	3 293	39 464	2 832	-440	45 149	13 940	59 089	36 119	23 269	7 317	22 970	10.3
Q3	4 056	37 706	2 865	-645	43 982	11 367	55 349	29 019	14 358	7 712	26 330	11.6
Q4	3 996	38 961	2 919	-414	45 462	14 557	60 019	30 812	14 688	8 162	29 207	12.7
2000 Q1	4 695	39 079	2 914	-702	45 986	14 657	60 643	31 477	15 037	8 701	29 166	12.4
Q2	5 252	38 226	3 015	-830	45 663	13 987	59 650	29 757	12 305	9 297	29 893	12.7
Q3	5 580	37 789	3 135	-799	45 705	15 262	60 967	31 208	12 857	9 494	29 759	12.4
Q4	5 806	38 048	3 207	-610	46 451	16 648	63 099	33 252	15 647	9 863	29 847	12.4
2001 Q1	5 446	38 175	3 234	-1 070	45 785	19 062	64 847	36 104	16 558	10 277	28 743	11.6
Q2	5 407	38 252	3 250	-486	46 423	17 992	64 415	35 681	18 170	10 037	28 734	11.5
Q3	4 816	38 277	3 261	-97	46 257	21 374	67 631	40 629	23 666	10 078	27 002	10.8
Q4	4 153	38 741	3 254	98	46 246	15 147	61 393	33 247	17 473	9 186	28 146	11.1
2002 Q1	4 298	39 150	3 275	-669	46 054	18 402	64 456	36 377	19 536	9 084	28 079	10.8
Q2	4 663	39 811	3 301	-713	47 062	15 821	62 883	32 829	15 954	9 033	30 054	11.5
Q3	4 635	40 349	3 348	-800	47 532	16 386	63 918	31 032	14 949	8 991	32 886	12.2
Q4	5 146	40 931	3 394	-932	48 539	16 738	65 277	29 260	12 167	9 102	36 017	13.2
2003 Q1	5 237	41 744	3 446	-581	49 443†	18 368	68 214	33 308	16 904	9 024	34 906	12.6
Q2	4 100	42 555	3 474	292	49 991	16 237	66 658	34 002	17 279	9 164	32 656	11.8
Q3	4 646	43 205	3 483	249	51 210	18 130	69 713	36 420	19 173	9 161	33 293	11.9

1 Quarterly alignment adjustment included in this series.
2 Total resources equals total uses.

Source: Office for National Statistics; Enquiries 020 7533 6014

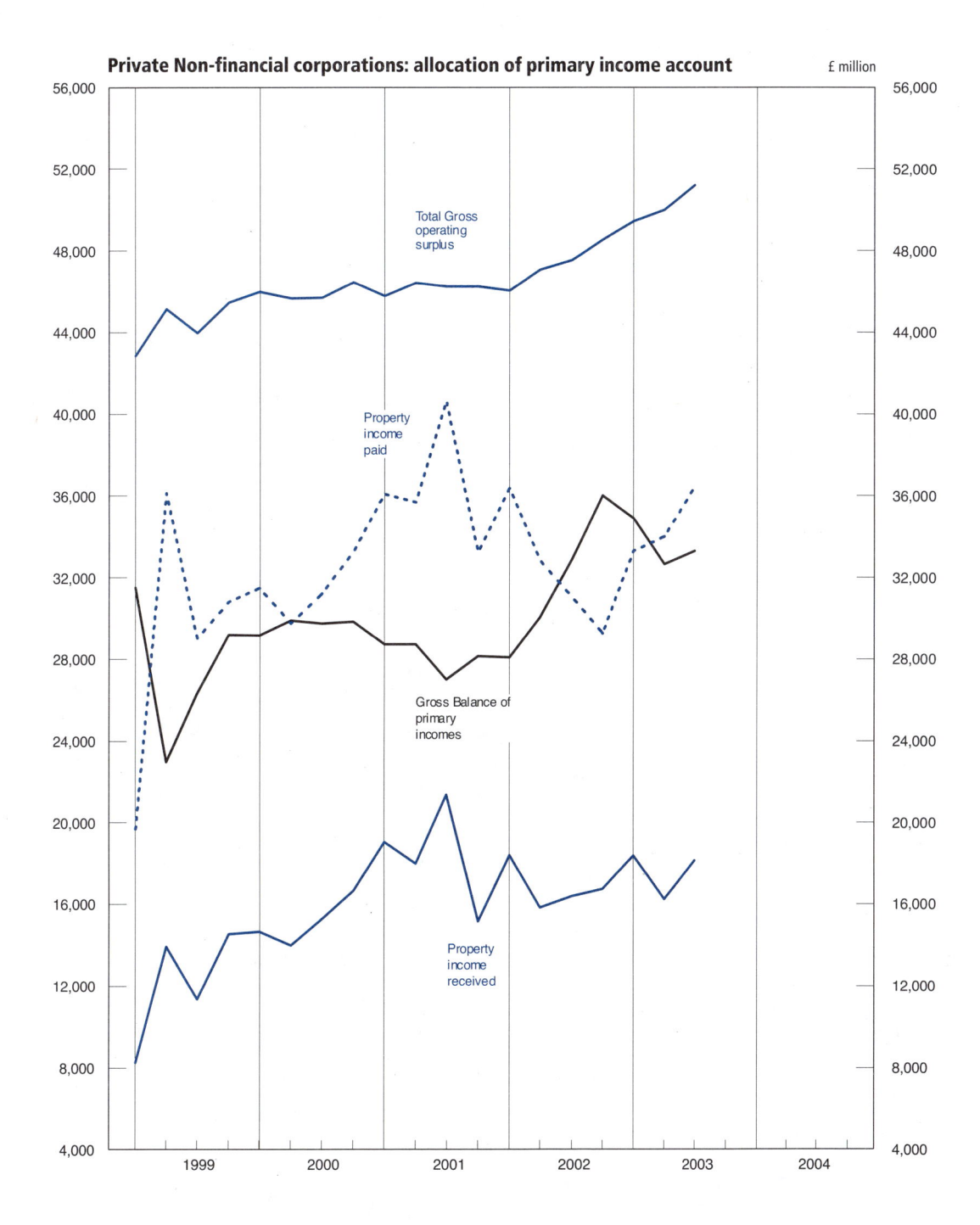

Private Non-financial corporations: allocation of primary income account £ million

2.12 Private Non-financial Corporations: Secondary Distribution of Income Account and Capital Account

£ million

| | Secondary Distribution of Income Account |||||| Capital Account |||||
| | Resources ||| Uses || Changes in liabilities & net worth | Changes in assets ||||
	Gross balance of primary incomes[1]	Other resources[2]	Total[1,3]	Taxes on income	Other uses[4]	Gross disposable income[1,5]	Net capital transfer receipts	Total[1]	Gross fixed capital formation	Changes in inventories[1]	Other changes in assets[6]	Net lending (+) or borrowing (-)[1,7]
Annual												
	RPBO	NROQ	RPKY	RPLA	NROO	RPKZ	NROP	RPXH	ROAW	DLQY	NRON	RQBV
1994	88 255	6 553	94 808	15 085	6 917	72 806	409	73 215	55 867	3 904	530	12 914
1995	89 482	7 704	97 186	18 953	8 104	70 129	433	70 562	64 444	4 542	388	1 188
1996	102 315	8 420	110 735	23 080	9 938	77 717	428	78 145	72 854	1 672	263	3 356
1997	109 202	7 097	116 299	28 558	7 576	80 165	671	80 836	81 317	3 949	401	−4 831
1998	116 708	8 390	125 098	26 877	8 834	89 387	1 081	90 468	89 848	4 533	1 287	−5 200
1999	110 023	7 875	117 898	22 608	8 444	86 846	958	87 804	93 756	6 174	1 036	−13 162
2000	118 665	9 990	128 655	26 188	10 403	92 064	405	92 469	96 329	5 512	768	−10 140
2001	112 625	10 218	122 843	25 367	10 629	86 847	1 633	88 480	99 045	2 890	1 069	−14 524
2002	127 036	12 866	139 902	23 697	13 288	102 917	2 095	105 012	95 594	1 559	1 212	6 647
Quarterly												
1994 Q1	22 112	1 673	23 785	3 206	1 759	18 820	82	18 902	13 699	160	136	4 907
Q2	22 586	1 686	24 272	3 887	1 778	18 607	96	18 703	13 120	2 024	119	3 440
Q3	20 403	1 498	21 901	4 076	1 591	16 234	120	16 354	14 130	193	124	1 907
Q4	23 154	1 696	24 850	3 916	1 789	19 145	111	19 256	14 918	1 527	151	2 660
1995 Q1	21 692	1 825	23 517	4 252	1 922	17 343	127	17 470	14 794	−496	121	3 051
Q2	22 435	1 936	24 371	5 420	2 032	16 919	98	17 017	16 117	2 111	125	−1 336
Q3	21 629	1 953	23 582	4 368	2 049	17 165	102	17 267	16 460	1 714	87	−994
Q4	23 726	1 990	25 716	4 913	2 101	18 702	106	18 808	17 073	1 213	55	467
1996 Q1	23 160	2 238	25 398	5 419	3 336	16 643	125	16 768	17 261	1 095	63	−1 651
Q2	27 653	2 219	29 872	5 148	2 369	22 355	102	22 457	17 599	837	71	3 950
Q3	25 562	1 994	27 556	6 334	2 124	19 098	96	19 194	18 566	127	57	444
Q4	25 940	1 969	27 909	6 179	2 109	19 621	105	19 726	19 428	−387	72	613
1997 Q1	29 069	1 771	30 840	6 642	1 888	22 310	233	22 543	19 359	1 357	64	1 763
Q2	27 071	1 757	28 828	7 363	1 901	19 564	164	19 728	20 439	1 046	94	−1 851
Q3	27 847	1 739	29 586	7 240	1 848	20 498	131	20 629	20 133	952	103	−559
Q4	25 215	1 830	27 045	7 313	1 939	17 793	143	17 936	21 386	594	140	−4 184
1998 Q1	27 447	2 225	29 672	6 607	2 336	20 729	343	21 072	22 016	468	256	−1 668
Q2	28 374	2 166	30 540	6 715	2 277	21 548	220	21 768	22 319	−187	380	−744
Q3	30 607	1 959	32 566	6 847	2 070	23 649	248	23 897	23 218	1 985	379	−1 685
Q4	30 280	2 040	32 320	6 708	2 151	23 461	270	23 731	22 295	2 267	272	−1 103
1999 Q1	31 516	2 037	33 553	5 484	2 264	25 805	344	26 149	23 139	2 370	301	339
Q2	22 970	1 925	24 895	4 846	2 038	18 011	199	18 210	22 928	403	314	−5 435
Q3	26 330	1 608	27 938	5 938	1 722	20 278	216	20 494	23 882	1 842	191	−5 421
Q4	29 207	2 305	31 512	6 340	2 420	22 752	199	22 951	23 807	1 559	230	−2 645
2000 Q1	29 166	2 472	31 638	6 998	2 589	22 051	315	22 366	23 685	1 646	193	−3 158
Q2	29 893	2 429	32 322	6 508	2 526	23 288	20	23 308	23 494	1 202	158	−1 546
Q3	29 759	2 735	32 494	6 572	2 834	23 088	34	23 122	24 044	1 629	156	−2 707
Q4	29 847	2 354	32 201	6 110	2 454	23 637	36	23 673	25 106	1 035	261	−2 729
2001 Q1	28 743	2 436	31 179	6 399	2 537	22 243	200	22 443	25 188	1 157	220	−4 122
Q2	28 734	2 529	31 263	6 560	2 632	22 071	443	22 514	24 969	1 807	306	−4 568
Q3	27 002	2 518	29 520	5 983	2 621	20 916	489	21 405	24 982	189	280	−4 046
Q4	28 146	2 735	30 881	6 425	2 839	21 617	501	22 118	23 906	−263	263	−1 788
2002 Q1	28 079	3 038	31 117	5 670	3 142	22 305	573	22 878	23 739	770	326	−1 957
Q2	30 054	3 068	33 122	6 294	3 173	23 655	436	24 091	24 247	−918	282	480
Q3	32 886	3 342	36 228	5 951	3 448	26 829	495	27 324	23 630	192	309	3 193
Q4	36 017	3 418	39 435	5 782	3 525	30 128	591	30 719	23 978	1 515	295	4 931
2003 Q1	34 906	3 124	38 030	5 737	3 231	29 062	871	29 933	23 032	1 404	278	5 219
Q2	32 656	3 425	36 081	5 513	3 532	27 036	787	27 823	24 412	353	338	2 720
Q3	33 293	3 619	36 912	6 087	3 727	27 098	782	27 880	23 744	1 084	344	2 708

1 Quarterly alignment adjustment included in this series.
2 Social contributions and other current transfers.
3 Total resources equals total uses.
4 Social benefits and other current transfers.
5 Also known as gross saving.
6 Acquisitions less disposals of valuables and non-produced non-financial assets.
7 Gross of fixed capital consumption.

Source: Office for National Statistics; Enquiries 020 7533 6014

Private Non-financial corporations : secondary distribution of income account £ million

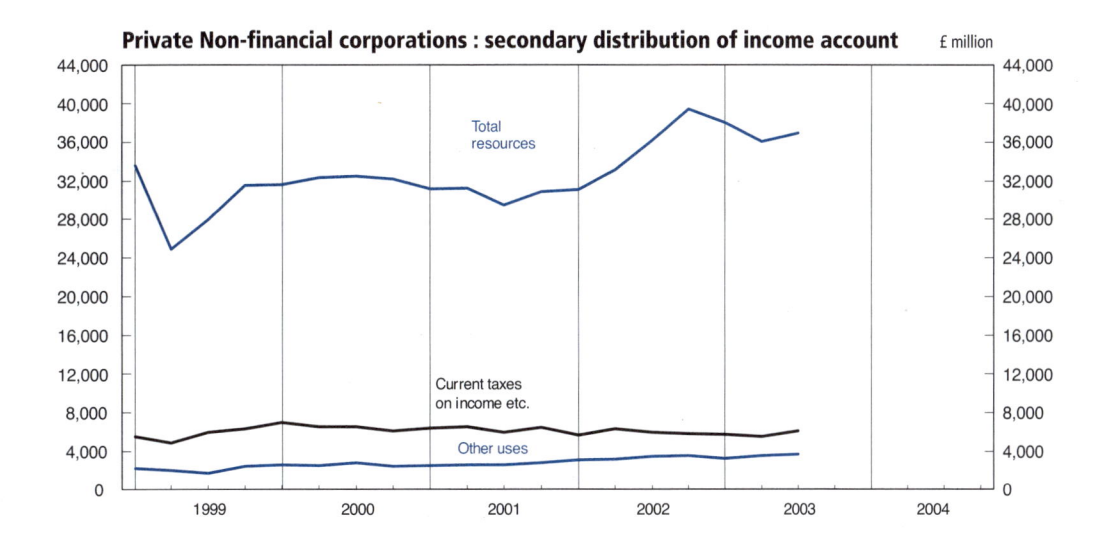

- Total resources
- Current taxes on income etc.
- Other uses

Private Non-financial corporations : capital account £ million

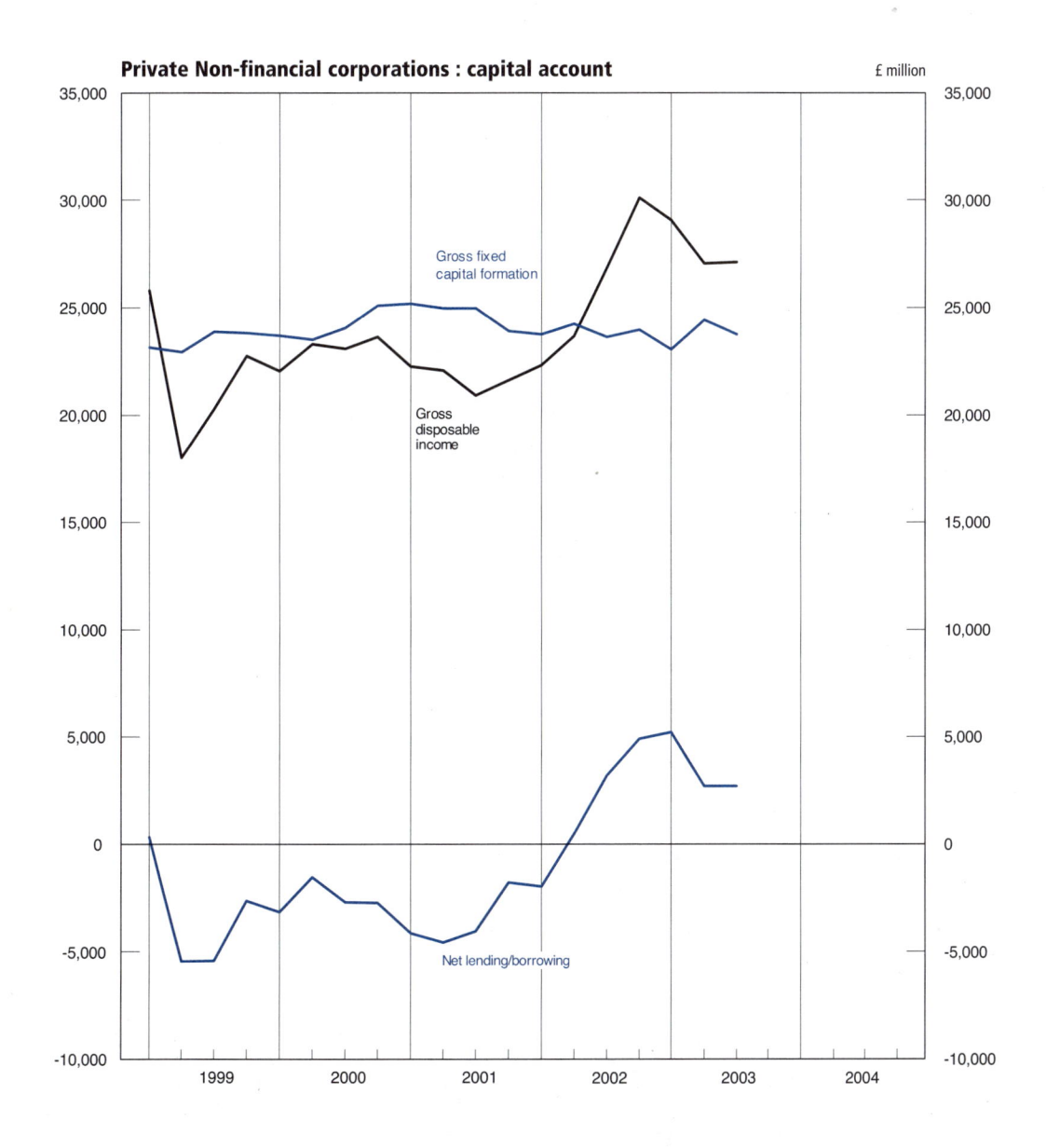

- Gross fixed capital formation
- Gross disposable income
- Net lending/borrowing

2.13 Balance of payments: current account

£ million

	Exports of goods+	Imports of goods+	Balance of trade in goods	Exports of services	Imports of services	Services balance	Income balance	Current transfers balance	Current balance
	BOKG	BOKH	BOKI	IKBB	IKBC	IKBD	HBOJ	IKBP	HBOP
Annual									
1999	166 166	195 217	−29 051	72 628	59 494	13 134	−1 116	−7 383	−24 416
2000	187 936	220 912	−32 976	79 071	65 645	13 426	5 208	−9 752	−24 094
2001	190 050	230 670	−40 620	81 658	68 658	13 000	10 723	−6 606	−23 503
2002	186 517	233 147	−46 630	86 753	71 572	15 181	22 152	−8 674	−17 971
2003	187 844	234 229	−46 385	87 362	74 162	13 200	..	..	..
Quarterly									
1999 Q1	38 959	46 893	−7 934	17 769	14 590	3 179	−2 256	−1 916	−8 927
Q2	40 378	46 976	−6 598	18 229	14 770	3 459	−155	−1 538	−4 832
Q3	43 582	50 180	−6 598	17 586	14 572	3 014	626	−2 087	−5 045
Q4	43 247	51 168	−7 921	19 044	15 562	3 482	669	−1 842	−5 612
2000 Q1	44 374	51 854	−7 480	18 914	15 453	3 461	1 983	−2 049	−4 085
Q2	46 851	54 256	−7 405	19 257	16 209	3 048	370	−2 020	−6 007
Q3	47 445	56 289	−8 844	20 166	16 716	3 450	2 410	−2 662	−5 646
Q4	49 266	58 513	−9 247	20 734	17 267	3 467	445	−3 021	−8 356
2001 Q1	49 554	58 824	−9 270	21 453	17 476	3 977	2 554	−1 875	−4 614
Q2	48 256	58 890	−10 634	21 497	17 414	4 083	2 653	−2 519	−6 417
Q3	46 539	56 715	−10 176	18 488	17 116	1 372	2 860	−119	−6 063
Q4	45 701	56 241	−10 540	20 220	16 652	3 568	2 656	−2 093	−6 409
2002 Q1	45 800	57 051	−11 251	21 209	17 569	3 640	4 116	−2 439	−5 934
Q2	49 380	59 657	−10 277	20 925	17 803	3 122	3 627	−2 311	−5 839
Q3	46 816	58 641	−11 825	22 761	18 210	4 551	6 497	−1 483	−2 260
Q4	44 521	57 798	−13 277	21 858	17 990	3 868	7 912	−2 441	−3 938
2003 Q1	47 580[†]	58 583[†]	−11 003[†]	21 960[†]	18 467[†]	3 493[†]	8 162	−2 411	−2 663
Q2	46 453	57 387	−10 934	21 558	18 332	3 226	3 882	−2 769	−7 782
Q3	46 426	58 126	−11 700	21 753	18 889	2 864	3 350	−2 418	−8 083
Q4	47 385	60 133	−12 748	22 091	18 474	3 617	..	..	..
Monthly									
2001 Jan	16 507	19 563	−3 056	7 010	5 751	1 259	..	..	..
Feb	16 819	19 722	−2 903	7 104	5 768	1 336	..	..	..
Mar	16 228	19 539	−3 311	7 339	5 957	1 382	..	..	..
Apr	15 880	19 468	−3 588	7 316	5 842	1 474	..	..	..
May	16 193	19 610	−3 417	7 197	5 832	1 365	..	..	..
Jun	16 183	19 812	−3 629	6 984	5 740	1 244	..	..	..
Jul	15 676	18 998	−3 322	6 992	5 726	1 266	..	..	..
Aug	15 403	19 353	−3 950	6 867	5 820	1 047	..	..	..
Sep	15 460	18 364	−2 904	4 629	5 570	−941	..	..	..
Oct	15 832	18 934	−3 102	6 278	5 514	764	..	..	..
Nov	15 208	18 620	−3 412	6 844	5 595	1 249	..	..	..
Dec	14 661	18 687	−4 026	7 098	5 543	1 555	..	..	..
2002 Jan	15 346	19 020	−3 674	7 272	5 755	1 517	..	..	..
Feb	15 259	18 974	−3 715	7 097	5 908	1 189	..	..	..
Mar	15 195	19 057	−3 862	6 840	5 906	934	..	..	..
Apr	16 319	20 110	−3 791	6 850	6 012	838	..	..	..
May	17 346	20 279	−2 933	6 907	5 814	1 093	..	..	..
Jun	15 715	19 268	−3 553	7 168	5 977	1 191	..	..	..
Jul	16 319	20 361	−4 042	7 465	6 003	1 462	..	..	..
Aug	14 871	19 025	−4 154	7 634	6 114	1 520	..	..	..
Sep	15 626	19 255	−3 629	7 662	6 093	1 569	..	..	..
Oct	15 121	19 517	−4 396	7 426	6 094	1 332	..	..	..
Nov	14 455	19 577	−5 122	7 212	5 824	1 388	..	..	..
Dec	14 945	18 704	−3 759	7 220	6 072	1 148	..	..	..
2003 Jan	15 873[†]	19 761[†]	−3 888[†]	7 078	6 190	888	..	..	..
Feb	16 074	19 242	−3 168	7 098	6 189	909	..	..	..
Mar	15 633	19 580	−3 947	7 038	6 148	890	..	..	..
Apr	16 541	19 018	−2 477	6 830	6 030	800	..	..	..
May	15 316	19 294	−3 978	6 856	6 125	731	..	..	..
Jun	14 596	19 075	−4 479	6 842	6 112	730	..	..	..
Jul	15 792	19 237	−3 445	6 939	6 214	725	..	..	..
Aug	15 388	18 926	−3 538	7 107	6 196	911	..	..	..
Sep	15 246	19 963	−4 717	7 087	6 083	1 004	..	..	..
Oct	15 814	20 047	−4 233	7 028	6 044	984	..	..	..
Nov	15 474	19 830	−4 356	7 076	5 969	1 107	..	..	..
Dec	16 097	20 256	−4 159	7 114	6 222	892	..	..	..

Sources: Office for National Statistics;
Enquiries Columns 1-3 020 7533 6064; Columns 4-6 & 8 020 7533 6090;
Columns 7 & 9 020 7533 6078.

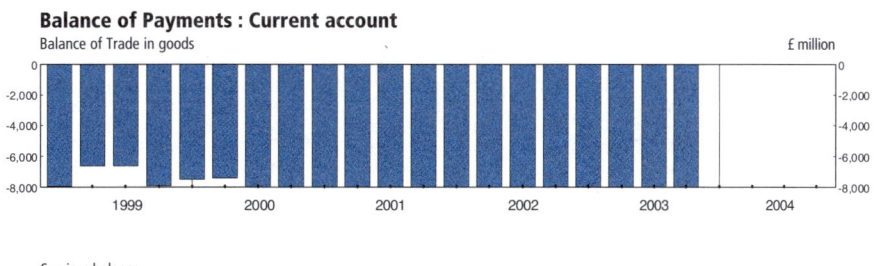

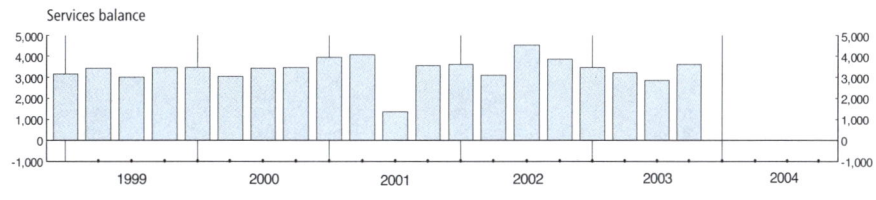

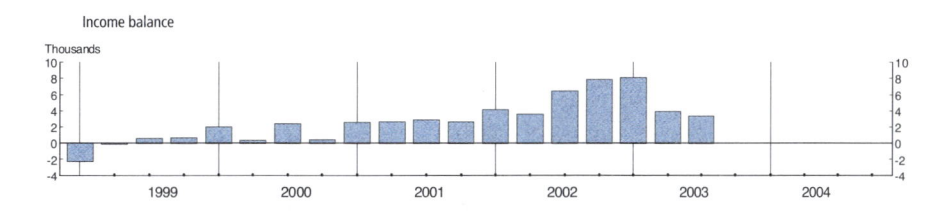

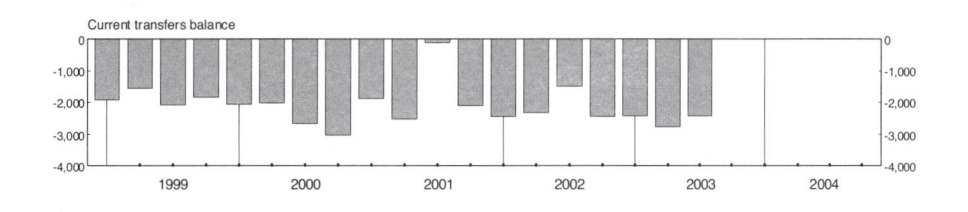

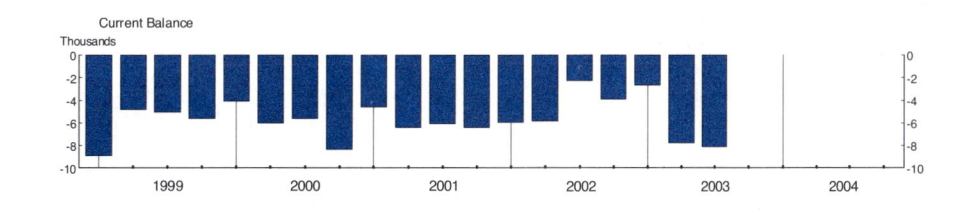

Balance of Payments : Current account

Balance of Trade in goods £ million

Services balance

Income balance

Current transfers balance

Current Balance

Tables section   Economic Trends 604 March 2004

2.14 Trade in goods (on a balance of payments basis)

2000 = 100

	Volume indices (SA)		Price indices (NSA)		
	Exports	Imports	Exports	Imports	Terms of trade[1]
Annual	BQKU	BQKV	BQKR	BQKS	BQKT
1999	89.2	91.5	98.9	96.8	102.2
2000	100.0	100.0	100.0	100.0	100.0
2001	102.7	105.4	98.3	99.1	99.2
2002	100.9	109.7	98.4	96.4	102.1
2003	100.2	110.8	100.2	95.8	104.6
Quarterly					
1999 Q1	83.5	88.3	98.9	95.8	103.2
Q2	86.7	88.7	98.9	96.1	102.9
Q3	93.6	93.9	99.0	97.7	101.3
Q4	92.9	95.0	98.8	97.8	101.0
2000 Q1	95.5	95.7	98.7	97.9	100.8
Q2	100.3	99.0	99.3	99.3	100.0
Q3	100.3	101.3	101.0	101.3	99.7
Q4	103.9	104.0	100.9	101.6	99.3
2001 Q1	105.1	105.4	99.8	101.2	98.6
Q2	102.6	105.7	100.1	101.1	99.0
Q3	101.7	104.4	97.6	98.2	99.4
Q4	101.1	106.2	95.8	96.0	99.8
2002 Q1	99.3	106.2	98.6	97.4	101.2
Q2	106.5	111.6	99.5	97.2	102.4
Q3	101.5	111.0	98.4	95.8	102.7
Q4	96.4	110.1	97.3	95.3	102.1
2003 Q1	101.5†	111.2†	100.1	96.1	104.2
Q2	99.2†	108.4	100.6†	95.6†	105.2†
Q3	98.9	109.7	100.5	96.1	104.6
Q4	101.1	113.8	99.4	95.6	104.0
Monthly					
2001 Jan	104.9	105.1	99.9	100.8	99.1
Feb	106.4	105.6	100.3	101.6	98.7
Mar	104.0	105.4	99.3	101.2	98.1
Apr	101.6	105.0	99.7	101.0	98.7
May	102.7	105.2	100.1	101.1	99.0
Jun	103.6	107.0	100.4	101.2	99.2
Jul	101.6	104.1	98.5	99.3	99.2
Aug	101.2	107.0	97.8	98.1	99.7
Sep	102.4	102.1	96.4	97.3	99.1
Oct	105.8	107.2	95.5	96.3	99.2
Nov	101.5	105.4	95.1	96.3	98.8
Dec	96.1	106.0	96.9	95.5	101.5
2002 Jan	99.6	105.9	97.5	97.1	100.4
Feb	99.7	106.3	98.4	97.1	101.3
Mar	98.5	106.3	99.9	97.9	102.0
Apr	105.0	112.8	100.2	97.5	102.8
May	112.7	114.0	99.2	97.0	102.3
Jun	101.8	108.0	99.0	97.1	102.0
Jul	106.2	116.3	98.6	95.7	103.0
Aug	95.9	107.3	98.8	95.9	103.0
Sep	102.3	109.3	97.7	95.8	102.0
Oct	98.2	111.1	97.4	95.6	101.9
Nov	94.3	112.4	96.8	95.0	101.9
Dec	96.8	106.7	97.8	95.2	102.7
2003 Jan	102.9†	113.0†	98.7	95.3	103.6
Feb	103.0	110.2	99.8	95.8	104.2
Mar	98.7	110.4	101.7	97.1	104.7
Apr	105.9	107.4	100.4†	96.2†	104.4†
May	97.6	109.0	101.3	95.7	105.9
Jun	94.1	108.8	100.1	95.0	105.4
Jul	101.4	109.0	100.2	95.6	104.8
Aug	98.0	106.9	101.1	96.3	105.0
Sep	97.3	113.1	100.3	96.3	104.2
Oct	101.3	113.5	99.9	95.9	104.2
Nov	98.6	112.3	99.3	95.8	103.7
Dec	103.3	115.6	99.0	95.2	104.0

1 Price index for exports expressed as a percentage of price index for imports.

Source: Office for National Statistics; Enquiries 020 7533 6064

Office for National Statistics

Trade in goods

At current prices (£ million)
- Imports (f.o.b.)
- Exports (f.o.b.)

Volume (2000=100)
- Imports
- Exports

Price index (2000=100)
- Exports
- Imports

2.15 Measures of UK competitiveness in trade in manufactures

1995=100

	Summary measures						Export unit value index[1,6]				
	Relative export prices[6]	Relative wholesale prices[5] (1990=100)	IMF index of relative unit labour costs[6] Actual	Normalised	Import price competi- tiveness[2,4]	Relative profit- ability of exports[2,4]	United Kingdom	United States	Japan	France	Germany[3]
	CTPC	CTPD	CTPE	CTPF	BBKM	BBKN	CTPI	CTPJ	CTPK	CTPL	CTPM
1997	111.4	114.7	130.4	123.6	105.9	97.4	98.7	101.2	83.8	86.0	80.3
1998	111.4	..	141.2	131.5	109.2	95.8	97.7	101.2	78.1	86.0	80.5
1999	114.2	..	141.7	133.9	109.7	94.4	97.4	101.1	82.7	81.4	76.7
2000	118.2	..	147.8	141.6	106.9	93.7	94.9	102.3	86.5	71.3	66.7
2001	117.0	..	143.9	141.4	105.6	95.8	90.7	102.3	78.3	69.5	64.7
2002	..	..	..	..	109.0	96.0	..	..	..	..	..
2000 Q1	119.4	..	149.4	142.1	108.7	92.0	99.3	102.1	86.2	76.0	71.5
Q2	118.2	..	148.9	141.2	108.6	93.2	95.8	102.5	86.2	72.1	67.5
Q3	116.7	..	146.2	140.2	107.0	94.6	93.0	102.6	87.2	70.1	65.4
Q4	117.9	..	146.8	142.7	105.4	94.9	91.4	102.3	86.5	67.6	62.8
2001 Q1	115.5	..	142.2	138.8	105.0	95.3	92.6	102.0	84.4	72.2	66.7
Q2	117.4	..	144.3	141.9	104.8	95.5	90.7	101.9	82.4	68.5	63.0
Q3	117.6	..	144.2	142.1	107.1	95.6	92.3	101.8	84.2	70.1	64.2
Q4	117.7	..	144.8	142.7	108.0	94.8	92.9	101.7	84.2	70.8	64.7
2002 Q1	..	..	..	..	109.2	95.9	..	..	..	..	..
Q2	..	..	..	..	109.4	96.8	..	..	..	..	..
Q3	..	..	..	..	108.0	95.7	..	..	..	..	..
Q4	..	..	..	..	109.3	94.6	..	..	..	..	..
2003 Q1	..	..	..	..	109.4	96.7	..	..	..	..	..

Percentage change, quarter on corresponding quarter of previous year

2001 Q2	−0.7	..	−3.1	0.5	−3.5	2.5	−5.3	−0.6	−4.4	−5.0	−6.7
Q3	0.8	..	−1.4	1.4	0.1	1.1	−0.8	−0.8	−3.4	0.0	−1.8
Q4	−0.2	..	−1.4	0.0	2.5	−0.1	1.6	−0.6	−2.7	4.7	3.0
2002 Q1	..	..	..	..	4.0	0.6	..	..	..	..	..
Q2	..	..	..	..	4.4	1.4	..	..	..	..	..
Q3	..	..	..	..	0.8	0.1	..	..	..	..	..
Q4	..	..	..	..	1.2	−0.2	..	..	..	..	..
2003 Q1	..	..	..	..	0.2	0.8	..	..	..	..	..

	Wholesale price index[1] (1990=100)					Unit labour costs index[1,6]				
	United Kingdom	United States	Japan	France	Germany[3]	United Kingdom	United States	Japan	France	Germany[3]
	CTPN	CTPO	CTPP	CTPQ	CTPR	CTPS	CTPT	CTPU	CTPV	CTPW
1998	116.5	106.8	102.7	..	..	118.6	95.6	70.5	82.8	77.1
1999	115.1	108.4	114.1	..	..	116.2	95.1	77.9	79.3	73.7
2000	..	..	..	..	..	108.0	94.9	77.5	68.2	61.6
2001	..	..	..	..	..	103.3	100.8	71.1	66.4	59.5
1999 Q4	116.8	109.7	123.4	..	..	116.8	94.6	82.2	77.1	70.5
2000 Q1	..	..	..	..	..	115.6	94.0	81.3	73.1	67.2
Q2	..	..	..	..	..	109.8	94.1	78.8	69.0	62.9
Q3	..	..	..	..	..	104.6	94.9	76.1	66.8	59.5
Q4	..	..	..	..	..	102.2	96.5	74.0	64.3	57.5
2001 Q1	..	..	..	..	..	104.3	99.2	72.5	68.5	61.5
Q2	..	..	..	..	..	101.6	100.8	70.7	64.8	58.0
Q3	..	..	..	..	..	103.2	101.4	71.3	66.1	59.1
Q4	..	..	..	..	..	104.2	101.7	70.1	66.4	59.5

Percentage change, quarter on corresponding quarter of previous year

1999 Q4	−0.6	2.7	12.2	..	..	−3.6	−1.0	5.8	−12.0	−15.3
2000 Q1	..	..	..	..	..	−2.3	−1.1	3.4	−12.6	−14.8
Q2	..	..	..	..	..	−5.3	−1.3	5.8	−12.3	−17.2
Q3	..	..	..	..	..	−8.3	−0.7	−0.8	−14.4	−16.8
Q4	..	..	..	..	..	−12.5	2.0	−10.0	−16.6	−18.4
2001 Q1	..	..	..	..	..	−9.8	5.5	−10.8	−6.3	−8.5
Q2	..	..	..	..	..	−7.5	7.1	−10.3	−6.1	−7.8
Q3	..	..	..	..	..	−1.3	6.8	−6.3	−1.0	−0.7
Q4	..	..	..	..	..	2.0	5.4	−5.3	3.3	3.5

1 All the indices are based on data expressed in US dollars.
2 Excludes erratics (ships, North sea installations, aircraft, precious stones and silver bullion).
3 Includes the former German Democratic Republic as from 1991 Q1.
4 These series are on a SIC 92 basis.
5 This series is calculated using UK producer prices. All other country indices are wholesale price indices.
6 Quarterly data have been obtained by interpolating the annuals.

Sources: International Monetary Fund;
Office for National Statistics; Enquiries 020 7533 5914

Measures of UK trade competitiveness

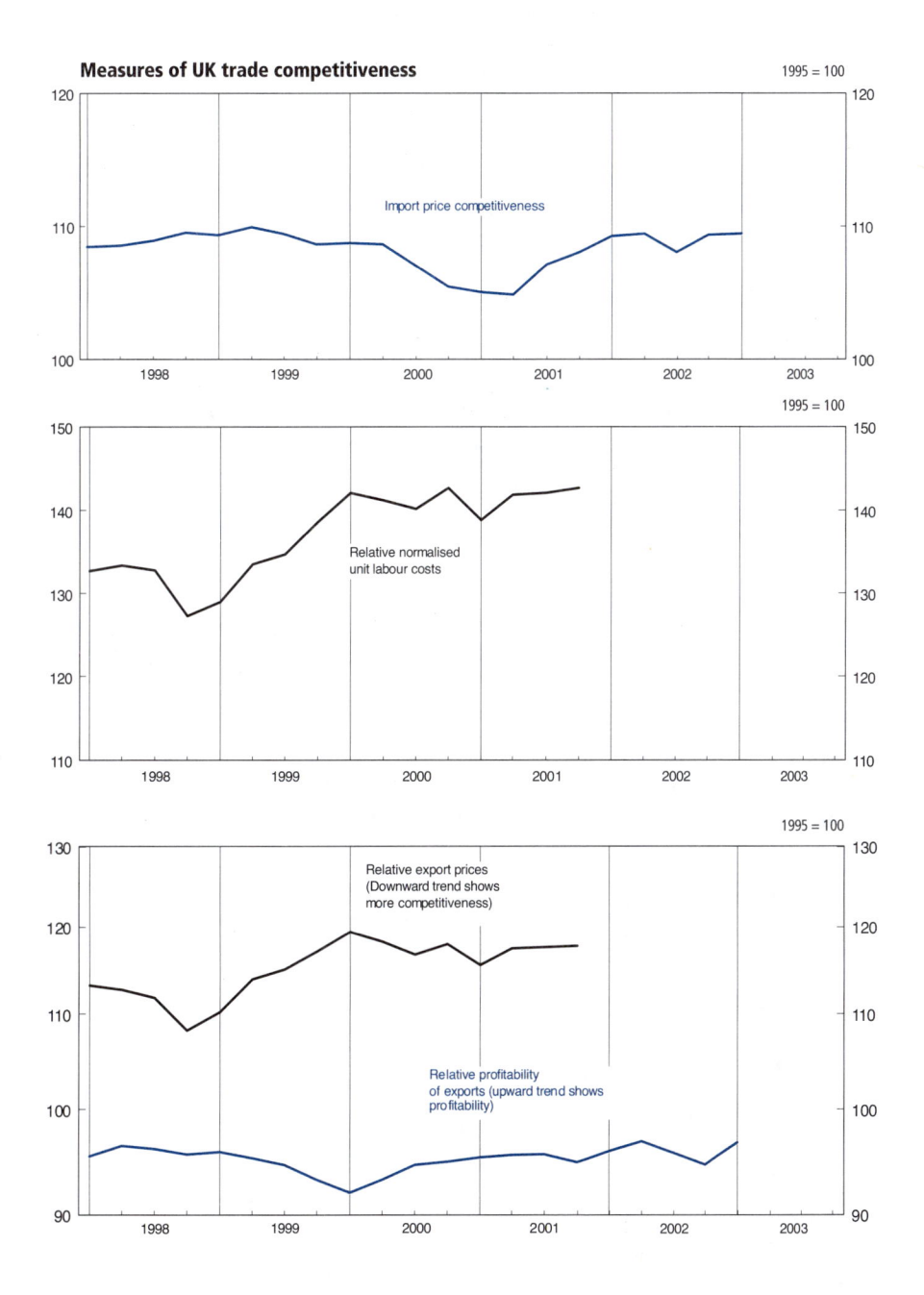

3.1 Prices

Not seasonally adjusted except series RNPE

	Producer price index (2000=100)		Consumer prices index[3,4] (1996=100)		Retail prices index (January 13, 1987=100)						Pensioner price index[6] (January 13, 1987=100)		
	Materials and fuel purchased by manufacturing industry (SA)[1,2]	Output: all manufactured products: home sales	All items		All items (RPI)		All items excluding mortgage interest payments (RPIX)		All items excluding mortgage interest payments & indirect taxes (RPIY)[5]		1-person household	2-person household	Purchasing power of the pound[7] (NSA) (1985=100)
			Index	% change on a year earlier	Index	% change on a year earlier	Index	% change on a year earlier	Index	% change on a year earlier			
	RNPE	PLLU	CHVJ	CJYR	CHAW	CZBH	CHMK	CDKQ	CBZW	CBZX	CZIF	CZIU	FJAK
Annual													
2000	100.0	100.0	105.6	0.8	170.3	3.0	167.7	2.1	159.9	1.8	150.8	156.1	56
2001	98.8	99.7	106.9	1.2	173.3	1.8	171.3	2.1	163.7	2.4	152.7	158.5	55
2002	94.4	99.8	108.3	1.3	176.2	1.7	175.1	2.2	167.5	2.3	155.5	160.9	54
2003	95.6	101.3	109.8	1.4	181.3	2.9	180.0	2.8	172.0	2.7	158.1	163.8	52
Quarterly													
2000 Q1	97.1	99.2	104.8	0.8	167.5	2.3	165.8	2.1	158.6	1.9	150.0	154.9	57
Q2	97.9	100.1	105.7	0.6	170.0	3.1	168.0	2.1	159.9	1.7	151.0	156.2	55
Q3	101.9	100.3	105.7	0.8	170.9	3.2	168.1	2.1	160.1	1.8	151.1	156.5	56
Q4	103.2	100.4	106.3	0.9	172.0	3.1	169.1	2.1	161.1	1.8	151.2	156.9	55
2001 Q1	100.8	99.7	105.7	0.9	171.8	2.6	168.9	1.9	161.1	1.6	150.6	156.5	55
Q2	101.6	100.1	107.3	1.5	173.9	1.9	171.8	2.3	164.1	2.6	153.3	159.3	54
Q3	98.3	99.8	107.3	1.5	174.0	1.8	172.1	2.4	164.6	2.8	153.0	158.9	54
Q4	94.4	99.3	107.4	1.0	173.8	1.0	172.4	2.0	165.0	2.4	153.9	159.3	55
2002 Q1	94.1	99.2	107.4	1.5	173.9	1.2	172.9	2.4	165.5	2.7	154.7	160.1	54
Q2	94.8	99.8	108.3	0.9	176.0	1.2	175.0	1.9	167.1	1.8	155.3	161.0	54
Q3	94.4	99.9	108.4	1.1	176.6	1.5	175.5	2.0	167.8	1.9	155.0	160.7	54
Q4	94.3	100.1	109.0	1.6	178.2	2.5	176.9	2.6	169.5	2.7	156.1	161.7	53
2003 Q1	95.7r†	100.9	109.0	1.5	179.2	3.0	177.9	2.9	170.6	3.1	156.7	162.6	53
Q2	94.3	101.1	109.7	1.3	181.3	3.0	180.1	2.9	171.8	2.8	157.9	163.7	52
Q3	95.5	101.3	109.9	1.4	181.8	2.9	180.5	2.8	172.3	2.7	158.3	164.0	52
Q4	96.9p	101.7p	110.5	1.3	182.9	2.6	181.5	2.6	173.2	2.2	159.4	165.0	52
Monthly													
2002 Jan	93.9	99.2	107.1	1.6	173.3	1.3	172.4	2.6	165.0	3.0	..	..	55
Feb	93.5	99.2	107.3	1.5	173.8	1.0	172.8	2.2	165.4	2.7	..	..	54
Mar	94.8	99.3	107.7	1.5	174.5	1.3	173.5	2.3	166.1	2.5	..	..	54
Apr	95.6	99.7	108.1	1.3	175.7	1.5	174.7	2.3	166.9	2.5	..	..	54
May	94.6	99.9	108.4	0.8	176.2	1.1	175.2	1.8	167.3	1.8	..	..	54
Jun	94.2	99.9	108.4	0.6	176.2	1.0	175.1	1.5	167.2	1.4	..	..	54
Jul	94.4	99.9	108.1	1.1	175.9	1.5	174.8	2.0	167.0	1.9	..	..	54
Aug	94.5	99.9	108.4	1.0	176.4	1.4	175.3	1.9	167.6	1.8	..	..	54
Sep	94.4	100.0	108.7	1.0	177.6	1.7	176.4	2.1	168.7	2.0	..	..	53
Oct	94.9	100.1	108.9	1.4	177.9	2.1	176.6	2.3	169.1	2.4	..	..	53
Nov	93.0	100.0	108.9	1.6	178.2	2.6	177.0	2.8	169.6	2.9	..	..	53
Dec	94.9	100.1	109.3	1.7	178.5	2.9	177.2	2.7	169.8	2.9	..	..	53
2003 Jan	95.7r†	100.5	108.6	1.4	178.4	2.9	177.1	2.7	169.8	2.9	..	..	53
Feb	95.8	100.7	109.0	1.6	179.3	3.2	177.9	3.0	170.6	3.1	..	..	53
Mar	95.6	101.4	109.4	1.6	179.9	3.1	178.7	3.0	171.4	3.2	..	..	53
Apr	94.6	101.3	109.7	1.5	181.2	3.1	180.0	3.0	171.8	2.9	..	..	52
May	94.1	101.0	109.7	1.2	181.5	3.0	180.2	2.9	171.9	2.7	..	..	52
Jun	94.2	101.0	109.6	1.1	181.3	2.9	180.0	2.8	171.7	2.7	..	..	52
Jul	95.3	101.2	109.5	1.3	181.3	3.1	179.9	2.9	171.6	2.8	..	..	52
Aug	96.2	101.4	109.9	1.4	181.6	2.9	180.4	2.9	172.2	2.7	..	..	52
Sep	95.1	101.4	110.2	1.4	182.5	2.8	181.3	2.8	173.2	2.7	..	..	52
Oct	96.9	101.6	110.4	1.4	182.6	2.6	181.3	2.7	173.1	2.4	..	..	52
Nov	97.0	101.7	110.3	1.3	182.7	2.5	181.4	2.5	173.1	2.1	..	..	52
Dec	96.7p	101.9p	110.7	1.3	183.5	2.8	181.8	2.6	173.5	2.2	..	..	52
2004 Jan	95.7p	102.1p	110.1	1.4	183.1	2.6	181.4	2.4	173.2	2.0	..	..	52

Note: Figures marked with a 'p' are provisional.
1 Minor revisions have been made to seasonally adjusted figures previously published. These reflect the routine updating of the seasonal adjustment factor.
2 Data now include the Climate Change Levy introduced in April 2001 and the Aggregates Levy introduced in April 2002.
3 Inflation rates prior to 1997 and index levels prior to 1996 are estimated. Further details are given in *Economic Trends* No.541 December 1998.
4 Prior to 10 December 2003, the consumer prices index (CPI) was published in the UK as the harmonised index of consumer prices (HICP).
5 The taxes excluded are council tax, VAT, duties, car purchase tax and vehicle excise duty, insurance tax and airport tax.
6 Pensioner price indices exclude housing costs, as these are often atypical for a pensioner household, based on RPI.
7 Movements in the purchasing power of the pound are based on movements in the retail prices index.

Sources: Office for National Statistics;
Enquiries Columns 1-2 01633 812106; Columns 3-13 020 7533 5853.

Economic Trends 604 March 2004

Tables section

Prices

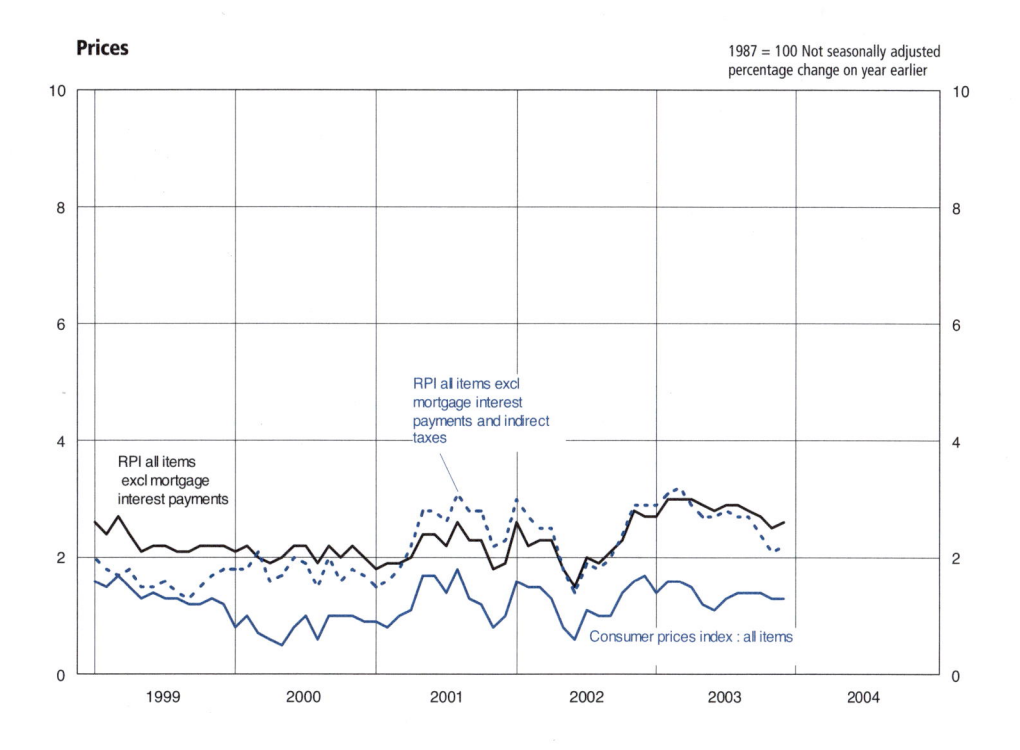

1987 = 100 Not seasonally adjusted
percentage change on year earlier

- RPI all items excl mortgage interest payments
- RPI all items excl mortgage interest payments and indirect taxes
- Consumer prices index : all items

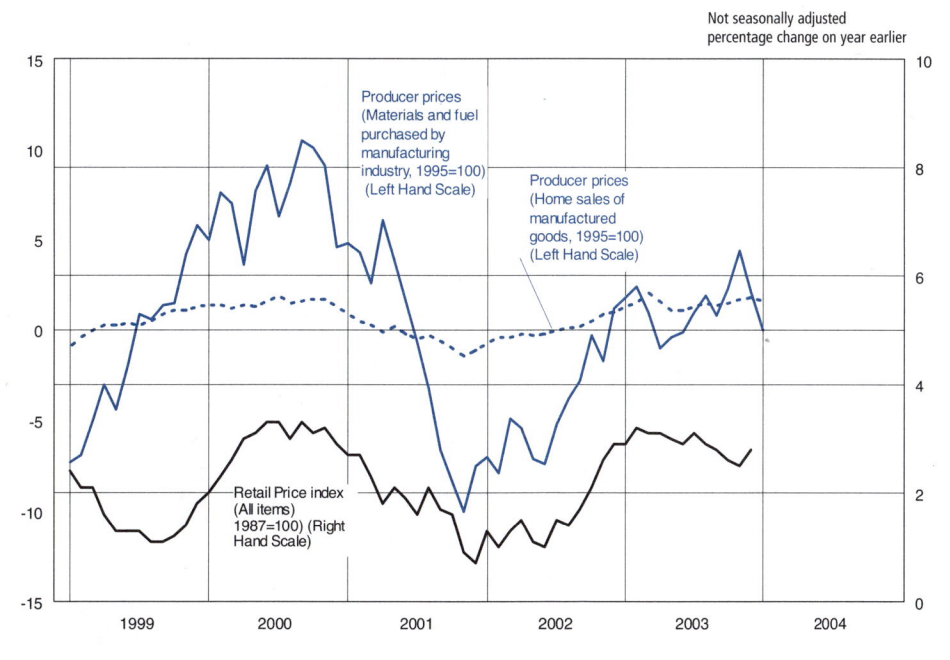

Not seasonally adjusted
percentage change on year earlier

- Producer prices (Materials and fuel purchased by manufacturing industry, 1995=100) (Left Hand Scale)
- Producer prices (Home sales of manufactured goods, 1995=100) (Left Hand Scale)
- Retail Price index (All items) 1987=100) (Right Hand Scale)

Office for National Statistics | 103

Tables section   Economic Trends 604 March 2004

4.1 Labour Market Activity[1,2]
United Kingdom

Thousands, seasonally adjusted[3]

	Employees	Self-employed	Unpaid family workers	Government training and employment programmes	Total employment	Unemployment	Total economically active	Economically inactive	Total aged 16 and over	Employment rate: age 16-59/64[4]
TOTAL										
	MGRN	MGRQ	MGRT	MGRW	MGRZ	MGSC	MGSF	MGSI	MGSL	MGSU
2001 Q1	24 244	3 104	98	147	27 592	1 475	29 067	17 231	46 298	74.5
Q2	24 346	3 097	95	141	27 679	1 463	29 142	17 235	46 377	74.6
Q3	24 313	3 129	95	121	27 658	1 489	29 147	17 304	46 451	74.3
Q4	24 392	3 117	104	119	27 732	1 518	29 249	17 268	46 517	74.4
2002 Q1	24 427	3 114	97	111	27 750	1 498	29 249	17 335	46 584	74.3
Q2	24 531	3 146	97	100	27 875	1 505	29 380	17 270	46 650	74.6
Q3	24 481	3 171	92	99	27 842	1 550	29 392	17 325	46 717	74.4
Q4	24 632	3 181	92	95	28 000	1 515	29 514	17 273	46 787	74.7
2003 Q1	24 629	3 245	87	91	28 052	1 510	29 562	17 295	46 857	74.7
Q2	24 583	3 366	88	86	28 122	1 468	29 591	17 336	46 927	74.7
Q3	24 490	3 453	103	105	28 151	1 481	29 631	17 365	46 997	74.6
Q4	24 482	3 474	96	103	28 156	1 459	29 615	17 452	47 067	74.5
Percentage change on quarter										
2003q3 to 2003q4	0.0	0.6	-7.1	-1.4	0.0	-1.4	-0.1	0.5	0.1	
Percentage change on year										
2002q4 to 2003q4	-0.6	9.2	4.3	8.8	0.6	-3.6	0.3	1.0	0.6	
MALE										
	MGRO	MGRR	MGRU	MGRX	MGSA	MGSD	MGSG	MGSJ	MGSM	MGSV
2001 Q1	12 581	2 279	35	95	14 991	891	15 882	6 441	22 323	79.5
Q2	12 599	2 267	33	93	14 992	879	15 871	6 499	22 370	79.3
Q3	12 611	2 300	30	79	15 020	899	15 919	6 494	22 414	79.3
Q4	12 631	2 302	33	74	15 040	907	15 947	6 503	22 450	79.2
2002 Q1	12 600	2 298	30	69	14 998	916	15 914	6 572	22 487	78.9
Q2	12 659	2 307	31	58	15 055	905	15 960	6 563	22 523	79.1
Q3	12 612	2 327	35	59	15 034	936	15 970	6 590	22 560	78.9
Q4	12 762	2 323	32	61	15 179	892	16 071	6 527	22 598	79.5
2003 Q1	12 721	2 357	28	54	15 160	917	16 077	6 558	22 636	79.2
Q2	12 705	2 463	32	50	15 250	888	16 138	6 536	22 674	79.5
Q3	12 621	2 527	38	59	15 245	880	16 126	6 586	22 711	79.4
Q4	12 555	2 549	35	58	15 196	883	16 079	6 670	22 750	79.0
Percentage change on quarter										
2003q3 to 2003q4	-0.5	0.8	-6.8	-2.7	-0.3	0.3	-0.3	1.3	0.2	
Percentage change on year										
2002q4 to 2003q4	-1.6	9.7	11.5	-5.1	0.1	-1.1	0.1	2.2	0.7	
FEMALE										
	MGRP	MGRS	MGRV	MGRY	MGSB	MGSE	MGSH	MGSK	MGSN	MGSW
2001 Q1	11 662	824	62	52	12 601	584	13 185	10 790	23 975	69.3
Q2	11 747	830	62	48	12 687	584	13 271	10 736	24 007	69.6
Q3	11 702	829	65	42	12 638	590	13 227	10 810	24 038	69.1
Q4	11 761	815	71	45	12 692	610	13 302	10 765	24 067	69.2
2002 Q1	11 827	816	68	42	12 752	582	13 334	10 763	24 097	69.4
Q2	11 872	839	67	43	12 820	600	13 420	10 707	24 126	69.7
Q3	11 868	844	56	39	12 808	615	13 422	10 734	24 157	69.6
Q4	11 870	857	60	34	12 821	622	13 443	10 746	24 189	69.6
2003 Q1	11 908	888	59	37	12 892	593	13 485	10 736	24 221	69.9
Q2	11 878	903	56	36	12 872	581	13 453	10 800	24 253	69.6
Q3	11 869	925	65	45	12 905	600	13 506	10 779	24 285	69.6
Q4	11 928	926	60	46	12 959	576	13 536	10 782	24 317	69.8
Percentage change on quarter										
2003q3 to 2003q4	0.5	0.0	-7.3	0.2	0.4	-4.0	0.2	0.0	0.1	
Percentage change on year										
2002q4 to 2003q4	0.5	8.0	0.4	33.8	1.1	-7.4	0.7	0.3	0.5	

1 The data in this table have been adjusted to reflect the 2001 Census population data.
2 Data are from the Labour Force Survey which uses the definitions recommended by the International Labour Organisation (ILO), an agency of the United Nations. For details see the *Guide to Labour Market Statistics Releases*.
3 Seasonally adjusted estimates are revised in April each year.
4 The employment rate equals those in employment aged 16-64 (male) and 16-59 (female), as a percentage of all in these age groups. The underlying data are available on request.

Source: Office for National Statistics; Enquiries 020 7533 6094

4.2 Labour Market Activity[1,2]
United Kingdom

Thousands, not seasonally adjusted

	Employees	Self-employed	Unpaid family workers	Government training and employment programmes	Total employment	Unemployment	Total economically active	Economically inactive	Total aged 16 and over	Employment rate: age 16-59/64[3]
TOTAL	MGTA	MGTD	MGTG	MGTJ	MGTM	MGTP	MGTS	MGTV	MGSL	MGUH
2001 Q1	24 121	3 103	95	150	27 468	1 488	28 957	17 341	46 298	74.2
Q2	24 280	3 085	93	144	27 601	1 419	29 021	17 356	46 377	74.4
Q3	24 449	3 138	100	112	27 799	1 559	29 358	17 093	46 451	74.7
Q4	24 459	3 125	105	121	27 810	1 476	29 285	17 232	46 517	74.6
2002 Q1	24 304	3 116	94	115	27 628	1 512	29 140	17 444	46 584	74.0
Q2	24 469	3 137	95	104	27 804	1 464	29 268	17 381	46 650	74.4
Q3	24 601	3 189	95	89	27 974	1 629	29 604	17 113	46 717	74.7
Q4	24 702	3 188	94	97	28 081	1 473	29 554	17 233	46 787	74.9
2003 Q1	24 490	3 247	83	97	27 916	1 520	29 436	17 421	46 857	74.3
Q2	24 534	3 365	86	89	28 074	1 411	29 485	17 442	46 927	74.6
Q3	24 569	3 481	109	99	28 259	1 567	29 826	17 171	46 997	74.9
Q4	24 556	3 467	99	107	28 229	1 418	29 647	17 420	47 067	74.7
Percentage change on year										
2002q4 to 2003q4	-0.6	8.8	5.3	10.3	0.5	-3.7	0.3	1.1	0.6	
MALE	MGTB	MGTE	MGTH	MGTK	MGTN	MGTQ	MGTT	MGTW	MGSM	MGUI
2001 Q1	12 500	2 281	36	97	14 914	904	15 817	6 506	22 323	79.1
Q2	12 566	2 255	32	95	14 949	859	15 808	6 562	22 370	79.1
Q3	12 714	2 304	29	75	15 123	927	16 050	6 363	22 414	79.8
Q4	12 652	2 312	34	73	15 071	883	15 955	6 496	22 450	79.4
2002 Q1	12 515	2 302	30	72	14 918	930	15 849	6 638	22 487	78.5
Q2	12 626	2 294	30	59	15 009	886	15 895	6 629	22 523	78.8
Q3	12 708	2 336	36	56	15 135	968	16 102	6 458	22 560	79.4
Q4	12 803	2 333	33	61	15 230	865	16 095	6 503	22 598	79.7
2003 Q1	12 624	2 363	27	58	15 072	935	16 007	6 629	22 636	78.7
Q2	12 677	2 455	31	51	15 213	860	16 073	6 601	22 674	79.3
Q3	12 684	2 546	40	57	15 326	916	16 242	6 469	22 711	79.8
Q4	12 592	2 550	37	60	15 239	851	16 090	6 660	22 750	79.2
Percentage change on year										
2002q4 to 2003q4	-1.6	9.3	12.1	-1.6	0.1	-1.6	0.0	2.4	0.7	
FEMALE	MGTC	MGTF	MGTI	MGTL	MGTO	MGTR	MGTU	MGTX	MGSN	MGUJ
2001 Q1	11 620	822	59	54	12 555	585	13 139	10 836	23 975	69.0
Q2	11 714	830	61	49	12 653	560	13 213	10 794	24 007	69.4
Q3	11 735	834	70	37	12 676	631	13 308	10 730	24 038	69.3
Q4	11 807	813	71	48	12 738	592	13 330	10 737	24 067	69.5
2002 Q1	11 789	813	64	43	12 710	581	13 291	10 806	24 097	69.2
Q2	11 843	842	65	45	12 795	578	13 374	10 753	24 126	69.6
Q3	11 893	853	60	33	12 840	662	13 501	10 655	24 157	69.8
Q4	11 900	854	61	36	12 851	607	13 459	10 730	24 189	69.8
2003 Q1	11 866	884	56	39	12 844	585	13 429	10 792	24 221	69.6
Q2	11 857	910	55	39	12 861	551	13 412	10 841	24 253	69.6
Q3	11 885	936	69	42	12 933	651	13 583	10 702	24 285	69.7
Q4	11 964	917	62	48	12 990	567	13 557	10 760	24 317	69.9
Percentage change on year										
2002q4 to 2003q4	0.5	7.4	1.6	33.3	1.1	-6.6	0.7	0.3	0.5	

1 The data in this table have been adjusted to reflect the 2001 Census population data.
2 Data are from the Labour Force Survey which uses the definitions recommended by the International Labour Organisation (ILO), an agency of the United Nations. For details see the *Guide to Labour market Statistics Releases*.
3 The employment rate equals those in employment aged 16-64 (male) and 16-59 (female), as a percentage of all in these age groups. The underlying data are available on request.

Source: Office for National Statistics; Enquiries 020 7533 6094

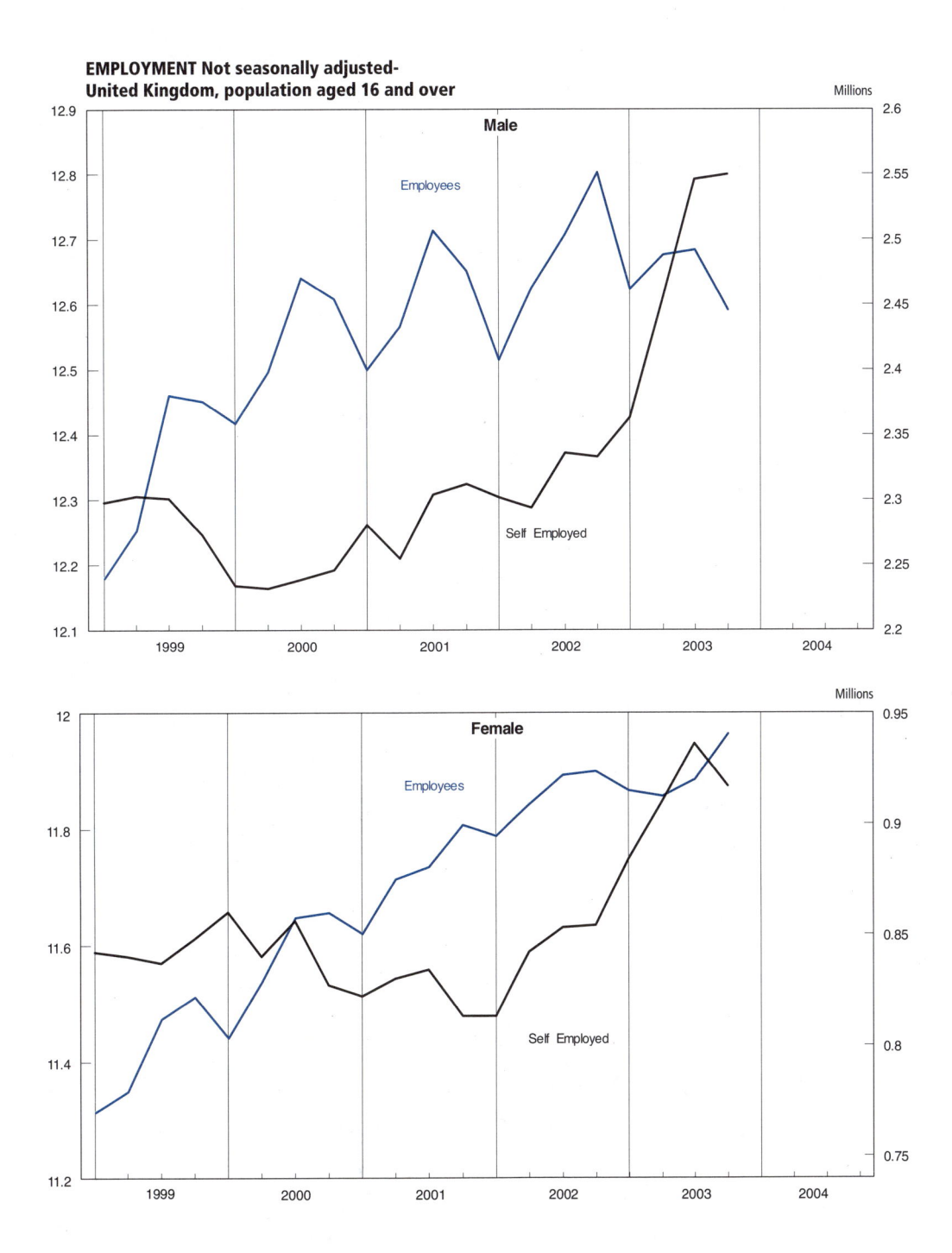

EMPLOYMENT Not seasonally adjusted - United Kingdom, population aged 16 and over

Male

Female

ECONOMICALLY ACTIVE POPULATION *(seasonally adjusted)*

Quarter on previous quarter percentage change

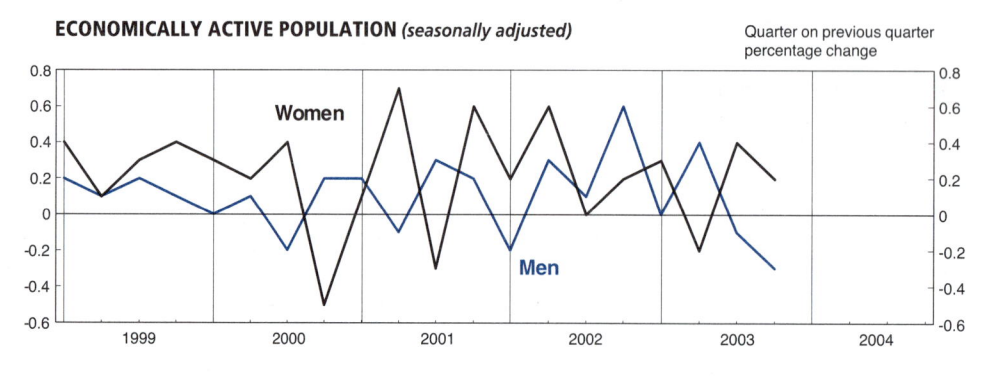

ECONOMIC ACTIVITY RATE *(seasonally adjusted)*

Quarter on previous quarter percentage change

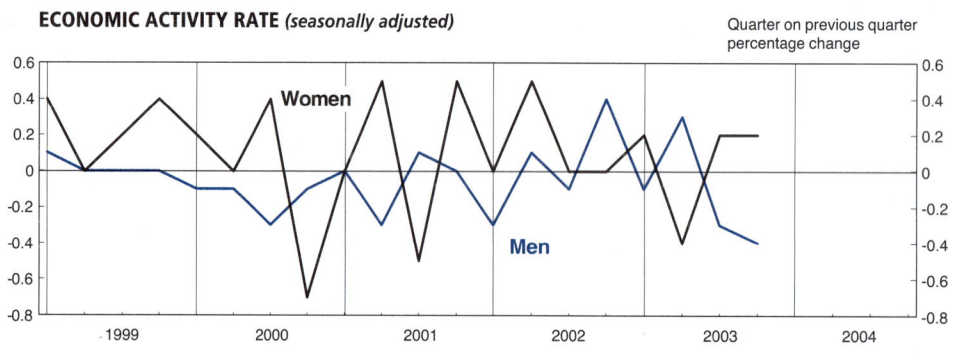

UNEMPLOYMENT *(seasonally adjusted)*

Quarter on previous quarter percentage change

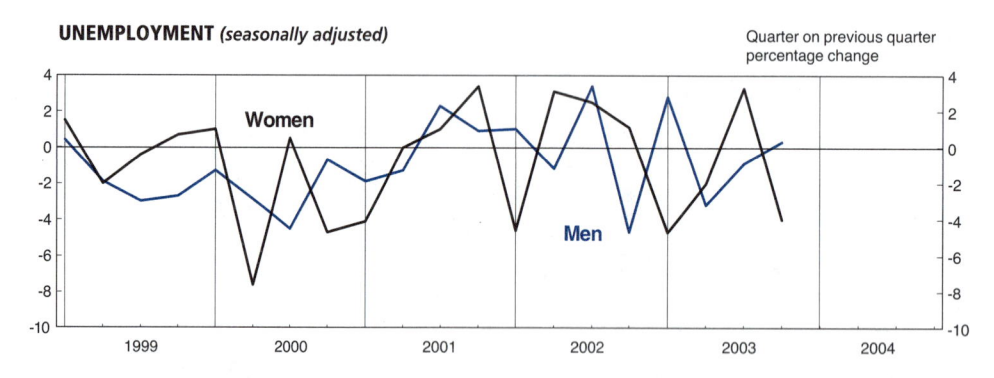

ECONOMICALLY INACTIVE POPULATION *(seasonally adjusted)*

Quarter on previous quarter percentage change

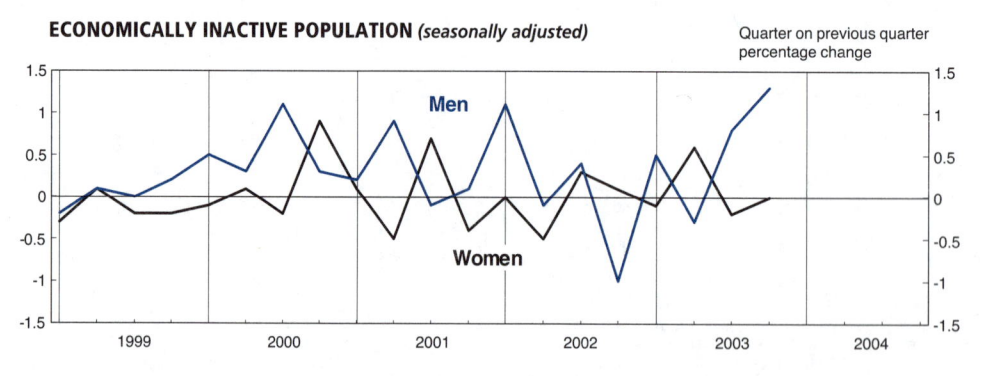

Economic Trends 604 March 2004

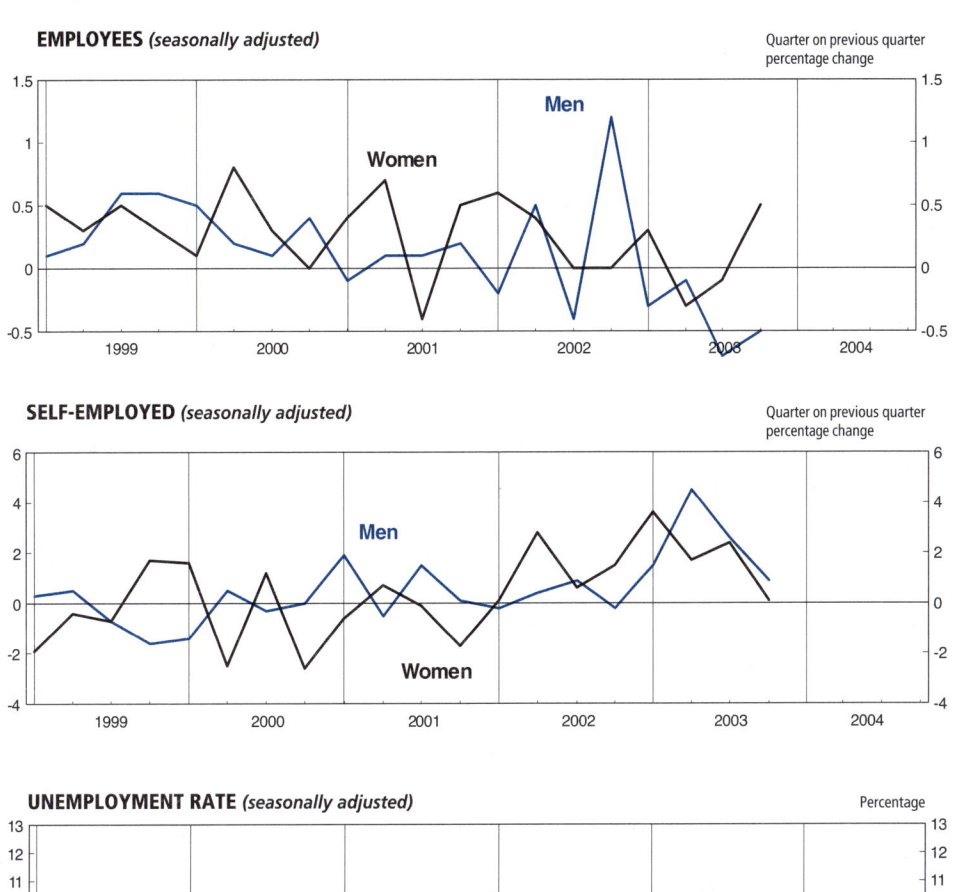

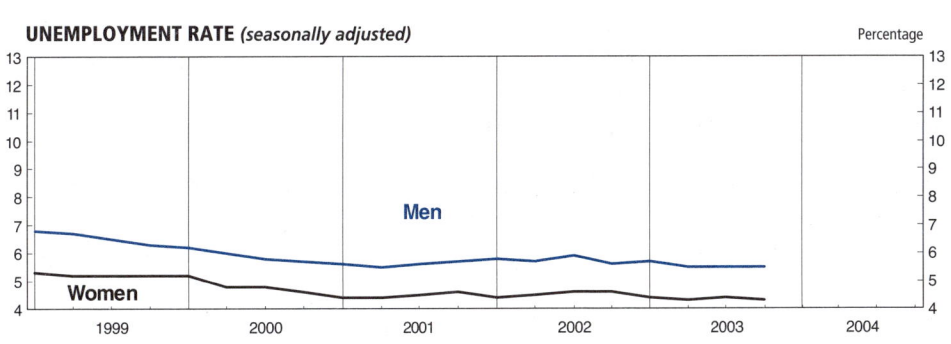

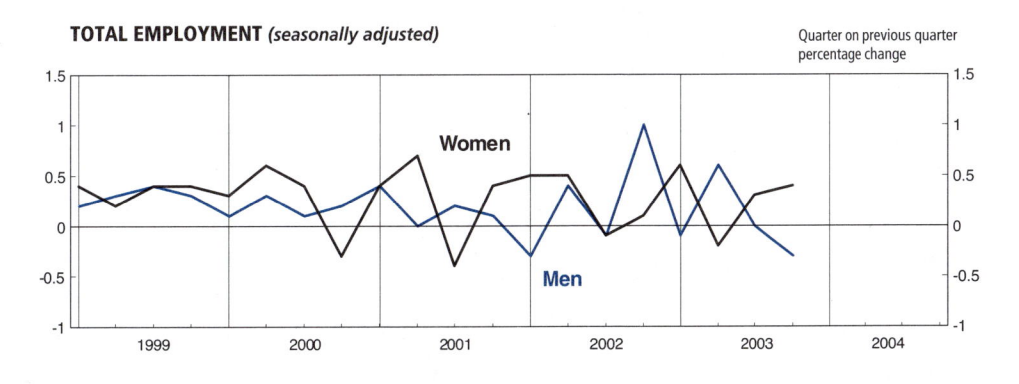

Tables section

EMPLOYEES *(seasonally adjusted)* — Quarter on previous quarter percentage change

SELF-EMPLOYED *(seasonally adjusted)* — Quarter on previous quarter percentage change

UNEMPLOYMENT RATE *(seasonally adjusted)* — Percentage

TOTAL EMPLOYMENT *(seasonally adjusted)* — Quarter on previous quarter percentage change

Office for National Statistics | 109

4.3 Labour Market Activity by age[1,2]
United Kingdom

Thousands, seasonally adjusted[3]

	Total aged 16 and over			Age groups[4]							
				16 - 24		25 - 49		50 - 59/64		60/65 and over	
	Total	Male	Female	Male	Female	Male	Female	Male	Female	Male	Female
In employment											
	MGRZ	MGSA	MGSB	MGUR	MGUS	MGUU	MGUV	MGUX	MGUY	MGVA	MGVB
2001 Q3	27 658	15 020	12 638	2 055	1 884	9 141	7 772	3 540	2 401	284	581
Q4	27 732	15 040	12 692	2 076	1 921	9 111	7 752	3 555	2 429	297	590
2002 Q1	27 750	14 998	12 752	2 063	1 923	9 105	7 798	3 543	2 434	287	597
Q2	27 875	15 055	12 820	2 077	1 940	9 123	7 824	3 560	2 462	295	594
Q3	27 842	15 034	12 808	2 045	1 943	9 109	7 787	3 582	2 484	299	593
Q4	28 000	15 179	12 821	2 101	1 952	9 135	7 792	3 633	2 491	310	586
2003 Q1	28 052	15 160	12 892	2 084	1 949	9 099	7 831	3 649	2 516	329	595
Q2	28 122	15 250	12 872	2 089	1 927	9 118	7 808	3 710	2 538	334	600
Q3	28 151	15 245	12 905	2 096	1 930	9 124	7 788	3 689	2 558	336	629
Q4	28 156	15 196	12 959	2 096	1 970	9 075	7 815	3 692	2 535	333	640
Unemployed											
	MGSC	MGSD	MGSE	MGVG	MGVH	MGVJ	MGVK	MGVM	MGVN	MGVP	MGVQ
2001 Q3	1 489	899	590	324	220	414	299	155	63	..	..
Q4	1 518	907	610	334	232	428	308	138	63	..	..
2002 Q1	1 498	916	582	338	222	431	288	138	65	..	..
Q2	1 505	905	600	327	215	419	304	150	69	..	12
Q3	1 550	936	615	335	225	430	309	161	68	10	13
Q4	1 515	892	622	338	224	396	313	152	72	..	13
2003 Q1	1 510	917	593	349	230	399	287	162	66	..	..
Q2	1 468	888	581	339	235	393	270	147	66	..	..
Q3	1 481	880	600	339	241	396	283	137	70	..	..
Q4	1 459	883	576	330	221	402	281	140	65	11	..
Economically inactive											
	MGSI	MGSJ	MGSK	MGVV	MGVW	MGVY	MGVZ	MGWB	MGWC	MGWE	MGWF
2001 Q3	17 304	6 494	10 810	806	1 074	806	2 482	1 351	1 261	3 531	5 993
Q4	17 268	6 503	10 765	794	1 040	815	2 493	1 364	1 246	3 530	5 986
2002 Q1	17 335	6 572	10 763	822	1 062	811	2 464	1 388	1 252	3 552	5 984
Q2	17 270	6 563	10 707	837	1 066	798	2 421	1 372	1 233	3 556	5 987
Q3	17 325	6 590	10 734	880	1 067	795	2 452	1 351	1 223	3 564	5 992
Q4	17 273	6 527	10 746	840	1 075	796	2 442	1 321	1 218	3 570	6 010
2003 Q1	17 295	6 558	10 736	866	1 087	821	2 428	1 307	1 206	3 565	6 016
Q2	17 336	6 536	10 800	890	1 121	801	2 467	1 272	1 190	3 572	6 022
Q3	17 365	6 586	10 779	901	1 127	786	2 474	1 314	1 172	3 584	6 007
Q4	17 452	6 670	10 782	926	1 118	826	2 453	1 321	1 204	3 597	6 007
Economic activity rate (per cent) [5]											
	MGWG	MGWH	MGWI	MGWK	MGWL	MGWN	MGWO	MGWQ	MGWR	MGWT	MGWU
2001 Q3	62.7	71.0	55.0	74.7	66.2	92.2	76.5	73.2	66.2	7.6	8.9
Q4	62.9	71.0	55.3	75.2	67.4	92.1	76.4	73.0	66.7	7.9	9.1
2002 Q1	62.8	70.8	55.3	74.5	66.9	92.2	76.6	72.6	66.6	7.7	9.2
Q2	63.0	70.9	55.6	74.2	66.9	92.3	77.1	73.0	67.2	7.9	9.2
Q3	62.9	70.8	55.6	73.0	67.0	92.3	76.8	73.5	67.6	8.0	9.2
Q4	63.1	71.1	55.6	74.4	66.9	92.3	76.8	74.1	67.8	8.2	9.1
2003 Q1	63.1	71.0	55.7	73.7	66.7	92.0	77.0	74.5	68.2	8.6	9.1
Q2	63.1	71.2	55.5	73.2	65.9	92.2	76.6	75.2	68.6	8.7	9.2
Q3	63.1	71.0	55.6	73.0	65.8	92.4	76.5	74.4	69.2	8.8	9.6
Q4	62.9	70.7	55.7	72.4	66.2	92.0	76.7	74.4	68.4	8.7	9.8
Unemployment rate (per cent) [6]											
	MGSX	MGSY	MGSZ	MGWZ	MGXA	MGXC	MGXD	MGXF	MGXG	MGXI	MGXJ
2001 Q3	5.1	5.6	4.5	13.6	10.5	4.3	3.7	4.2	2.6	..	..
Q4	5.2	5.7	4.6	13.9	10.8	4.5	3.8	3.7	2.5	..	..
2002 Q1	5.1	5.8	4.4	14.1	10.3	4.5	3.6	3.8	2.6	..	..
Q2	5.1	5.7	4.5	13.6	10.0	4.4	3.7	4.0	2.7	..	2.0
Q3	5.3	5.9	4.6	14.1	10.4	4.5	3.8	4.3	2.7	3.2	2.1
Q4	5.1	5.6	4.6	13.9	10.3	4.2	3.9	4.0	2.8	..	2.2
2003 Q1	5.1	5.7	4.4	14.3	10.6	4.2	3.5	4.2	2.6	..	..
Q2	5.0	5.5	4.3	14.0	10.9	4.1	3.3	3.8	2.6	..	..
Q3	5.0	5.5	4.4	13.9	11.1	4.2	3.5	3.6	2.6	..	..
Q4	4.9	5.5	4.3	13.6	10.1	4.2	3.5	3.6	2.5	3.2	..

1 The data in this table have been adjusted to reflect the 2001 Census population data.
2 Data are from the Labour Force Survey which uses the definitions recommended by the International Labour Organisation (ILO), an agency of the United Nations. For details see the *Guide to Labour Market Statistics Releases*.
3 Seasonally adjusted estimates are revised in April each year.
4 Data for more detailed age groups are published in *Labour Market Trends*.
5 The activity rate is the percentage of people in each age group who are economically active.
6 Unemployment rate is the percentage of economically active people who are unemployed on the ILO measure.

Source: Office for National Statistics; Enquiries 020 7533 6094

4.4 Jobs and claimant count
United Kingdom

Thousands

	Jobs[1]					Claimant count[5,6,9]			
		Employee jobs[3,4]					Percentage of workforce	Total Not	Job Centre
	Workforce jobs[2,3,4]	All industries	Manufacturing industry	Production industry	Service industries	Total	jobs and claimant count[7]	seasonally adjusted	vacancies+[8,10]
	DYDC	BCAJ	YEJA	YEJF	YEJC	BCJD	BCJE	BCJA	DPCB
Annual									
2000	29 271	25 626	3 960	4 159	19 962	1 088.4	3.6	1 102.3	358.3
2001	29 495	25 882	3 808	4 017	20 420	970.1	3.2	983.0	..
2002	29 491	25 829	3 628	3 836	20 613	946.8	3.1	958.8	..
2003	29 716	25 837	3 503	3 706	20 753	933.0†	3.1	945.9	..
Quarterly									
2000 Q1	29 104	25 453	3 990	4 187	19 784	1 153.0	3.8	1 219.2	342.2
Q2	29 271	25 626	3 960	4 159	19 962	1 103.9	3.6	1 109.2	355.7
Q3	29 314	25 692	3 918	4 119	20 105	1 060.0	3.5	1 073.6	363.4
Q4	29 390	25 774	3 889	4 096	20 230	1 036.7	3.4	1 007.1	371.8
2001 Q1	29 429	25 816	3 860	4 068	20 321	998.5	3.3	1 064.1	394.1
Q2	29 495	25 882	3 808	4 017	20 420	971.5	3.2	978.4	..
Q3	29 459	25 864	3 755	3 965	20 456	949.9	3.1	958.5	..
Q4	29 509	25 897	3 705	3 914	20 537	960.4	3.2	931.0	..
2002 Q1	29 524	25 918	3 666	3 876	20 612	951.0	3.1	1 014.6	..
Q2	29 491	25 829	3 628	3 836	20 613	952.3	3.1	958.1	..
Q3	29 517	25 806	3 593	3 797	20 657	945.3	3.1	951.8	..
Q4	29 564	25 825	3 561	3 765	20 698	938.6	3.1	910.6	..
2003 Q1	29 646	25 815	3 536	3 738	20 708	936.5	3.1	1 001.1	..
Q2	29 716	25 837	3 503	3 706	20 753	946.5	3.1	954.3	..
Q3	29 779	25 809	3 475	3 677	20 726	933.2	3.1	939.0	..
Q4	..	..	3 456	3 656	..	915.9†	3.0	889.2	..
Monthly									
2002 Jul	..	..	3 616	3 823	..	948.5	3.1	956.4	..
Aug	..	..	3 605	3 810	..	942.7	3.1	962.7	..
Sep	..	25 806	3 593	3 797	20 657	944.6	3.1	936.2	..
Oct	..	..	3 584	3 789	..	942.2	3.1	907.2	..
Nov	..	..	3 574	3 778	..	938.6	3.1	905.6	..
Dec	..	25 825	3 561	3 765	20 698	935.1	3.1	919.1	..
2003 Jan	..	..	3 554	3 756	..	932.4	3.1	998.0	..
Feb	..	..	3 546	3 748	..	938.1	3.1	1 012.8	..
Mar	..	25 815	3 536	3 738	20 708	939.0	3.1	992.3	..
Apr	..	..	3 523	3 725	..	941.1	3.1	966.1	..
May	..	..	3 515	3 717	..	950.3	3.1	957.8	..
Jun	..	25 837	3 503	3 706	20 753	948.0	3.1	939.2	..
Jul	..	..	3 488	3 691	..	937.7	3.1	946.3	..
Aug	..	..	3 479	3 682	..	931.7	3.1	948.6	..
Sep	..	25 809	3 475	3 677	20 726	930.2	3.1	922.1	..
Oct	..	..	3 468	3 669	..	925.7	3.0	893.2	..
Nov	..	..	3 461	3 661	..	916.5	3.0	884.6	..
Dec	..	..	3 456	3 656	..	905.5†	3.0	889.7	..
2004 Jan	..	..	..	..	..	892.1	2.9	952.4	..

1 Estimates of employee jobs and workforce jobs for Great Britain now use the Annual Business Inquiry as a benchmark on which quarterly movements are based. For further information see Labour Market Statistics First Release, April 2001 which is held on the National Statistics website www.statistics.gov.uk The Northern Ireland component of workforce jobs and employee jobs has not changed.
2 Workforce jobs comprise employee jobs, self-employed jobs, HM Forces and participants in work-related government supported training, which includes the Project Work Plan.
3 For all dates, individuals with two jobs as employees of different employers are counted twice.
4 Annual estimates relate to mid-year. Figures for the four quarters relate to March, June, September and December. For claimant count, unlike employment and workforce figures, the annual figure is an annual average.
5 Unadjusted claimant count figures have been affected by changes in the coverage. The seasonally adjusted figures however, as given in this table are estimated on the current basis, allowing for the discontinuities, except for the effect of the Jobseeker's Allowance introduced in October 1996 (see also below).
The seasonally adjusted figures now relate only to claimants aged 18 or over in order to maintain the consistent series, available back to 1971 (1974 for the regions), allowing for the effect of the change in benefit regulations for under 18 year olds from September 1988. (See pages 398 - 400 of November 1995 Labour Market Trends.)
6 Claimant count figures do not include students claiming benefit during a vacation who intend to return to full-time education.
7 The denominator used to calculate claimant count unemployment rates is comprised of the workforce jobs plus the claimant count.
8 Vacancies notified to Jobcentres and remaining unfilled. Jobcentre vacancies only account for *approximately* one third of all vacancies in the economy. *Note:* Quarter figures relate to the average for the three months in the quarter.
9 Quarterly and annual values are now the mean of the monthly and quarterly data respectively.
10 Publication of the job centre vacancy statistics has been deferred. Figures from May 2001 are affected by the introduction of Employer Direct. This major change involves transferring the vacancy taking process from job centres to regional Customer Service Centres, as part of Modernising the Employment Service. ONS and the Employment Service will continue to monitor and review the data with the aim of publishing the series fairly soon, as it is possible to produce a consistent measure.

Sources: Office for National Statistics;
Enquiries Columns 1-5 01633 812079; Columns 6,9 020 7533 6094;
also 24 hour recorded headline service on 020 7533 6176

Employee jobs & Claimant count (UK)

Percentage change on previous quarter

Total employment & unemployed (UK)

Percentage change on previous quarter

4.5 Regional claimant count rates[1,2]
by Government Office Region

Percentages

	North East	North West[3]	Yorkshire and the Humber	East Midlands	West Midlands	East	London	South East
Quarterly								
	DPDM	IBWC	DPBI	DPBJ	DPBN	DPDP	DPDQ	DPDR
1998 Q1	7.3	5.2	5.5	4.0	4.6	3.4	5.3	2.7
Q2	7.0	5.1	5.4	3.9	4.5	3.3	5.2	2.7
Q3	7.0	5.1	5.4	3.9	4.5	3.2	5.1	2.6
Q4	7.0	5.0	5.3	3.9	4.5	3.2	5.0	2.5
1999 Q1	7.4	4.8	5.3	3.8	4.6	3.0	4.7	2.4
Q2	7.3	4.7	5.1	3.7	4.6	3.0	4.6	2.3
Q3	7.1	4.6	5.0	3.6	4.5	2.9	4.5	2.2
Q4	6.7	4.4	4.8	3.5	4.3	2.7	4.3	2.1
2000 Q1	6.6	4.4	4.7	3.5	4.2	2.6	4.0	2.0
Q2	6.4	4.2	4.4	3.4	4.1	2.5	3.8	1.9
Q3	6.1	4.0	4.2	3.3	4.0	2.3	3.6	1.8
Q4	6.0	3.9	4.1	3.3	4.0	2.3	3.5	1.7
2001 Q1	5.9	3.8	4.1	3.2	3.9	2.1	3.3	1.6
Q2	5.7	3.8	4.0	3.2	3.8	2.1	3.2	1.5
Q3	5.5	3.7	3.9	3.0	3.7	2.0	3.2	1.5
Q4	5.6	3.7	3.8	3.0	3.6	2.1	3.4	1.6
2002 Q1	5.4	3.6	3.7	2.9	3.6	2.1	3.5	1.6
Q2	5.3	3.6	3.7	2.9	3.5	2.1	3.6	1.7
Q3	5.2	3.5	3.7	2.9	3.5	2.1	3.6	1.7
Q4	5.0	3.5	3.6	2.9	3.5	2.1	3.6	1.7
2003 Q1	4.9	3.5	3.6	2.8	3.6	2.1	3.6	1.7
Q2	4.8	3.4	3.5	2.9	3.6	2.2	3.7	1.8
Q3	4.7	3.4	3.4	2.9	3.6	2.2	3.7	1.8
Q4	4.6	3.3	3.3	2.9	3.5	2.1	3.6	1.8

	South West	England	Wales	Scotland	Great Britain	Northern Ireland	United Kingdom
Quarterly							
	DPBM	VASQ	DPBP	DPBQ	DPAJ	DPBR	BCJE
1998 Q1	3.5	4.4	5.6	5.5	4.6	7.6	4.7
Q2	3.4	4.3	5.5	5.4	4.5	7.4	4.6
Q3	3.4	4.3	5.4	5.5	4.4	7.3	4.5
Q4	3.3	4.2	5.4	5.4	4.4	7.2	4.5
1999 Q1	3.3	4.1	5.3	5.2	4.3	7.0	4.3
Q2	3.2	4.0	5.2	5.2	4.2	6.7	4.2
Q3	3.0	3.9	4.9	5.0	4.0	6.2	4.1
Q4	2.8	3.7	4.7	4.8	3.9	5.8	3.9
2000 Q1	2.7	3.6	4.5	4.8	3.8	5.5	3.8
Q2	2.6	3.5	4.4	4.6	3.6	5.3	3.6
Q3	2.4	3.3	4.4	4.4	3.5	5.2	3.5
Q4	2.3	3.2	4.3	4.3	3.4	5.3	3.4
2001 Q1	2.1	3.1	4.2	4.1	3.2	5.1	3.3
Q2	2.1	3.0	4.0	4.0	3.1	5.0	3.2
Q3	2.1	3.0	3.9	3.9	3.1	4.9	3.1
Q4	2.0	3.0	3.8	4.0	3.1	4.8	3.2
2002 Q1	2.0	3.0	3.7	3.9	3.1	4.7	3.1
Q2	2.0	3.0	3.7	3.9	3.1	4.6	3.1
Q3	2.0	3.0	3.6	3.8	3.1	4.4	3.1
Q4	1.9	2.9	3.6	3.8	3.0	4.4	3.1
2003 Q1	1.9	2.9	3.5	3.8	3.0	4.3	3.1
Q2	1.9	3.0	3.5	3.8	3.1	4.3	3.1
Q3	1.9	2.9	3.4	3.8	3.0	4.3	3.1
Q4	1.8	2.9	3.3	3.7[†]	3.0	4.3	3.0

Note: Quarterly claimant count figures relate to the average of the three months in each quarter.

1 Government Office Regions came into effect in April 1994. It was decided that from May 1997 sub-national data should be published for these areas rather than standard statistical regions (SSRs). Data by standard statistical regions are available on request.

2 The seasonally adjusted figures now relate only to claimants aged 18 or over in order to maintain the consistent series, available back to 1971 for Great Britain, Northern Ireland and the United Kingdom (1974 for Wales and Scotland; 1986 for the Government Office Regions), allowing for the effect of the change in benefit regulations for under 18 year olds from September 1988. (See pages 398 - 400 of the November 1995 *Labour Market Trends*.) The denominators used to calculate claimant count rates are the sum of the appropriate mid-year estimates of employee jobs, the self- employed, Government-supported trainees, HM Forces and claimants of unemployment-related benefits. The 2001 and 2002 rates are based on mid-2001 estimates and earlier years are based on the corresponding mid-year estimates.

3 Includes Merseyside.

Source: Office for National Statistics; Enquiries 020 7533 6094

Economic Trends 604 March 2004

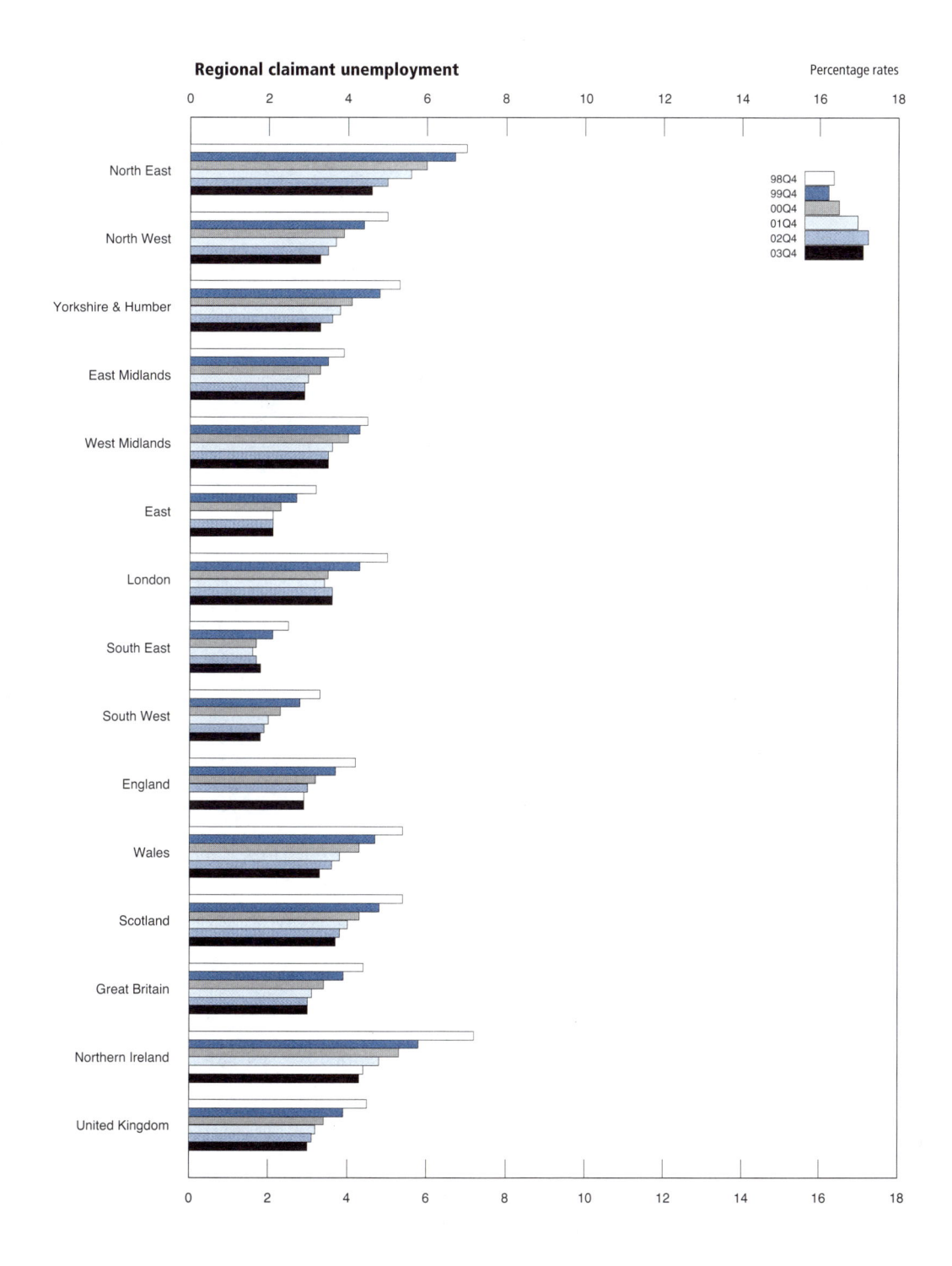

Tables section

Regional claimant unemployment

Percentage rates

Chart showing regional claimant unemployment percentage rates for 98Q4, 99Q4, 00Q4, 01Q4, 02Q4, 03Q4 across regions: North East, North West, Yorkshire & Humber, East Midlands, West Midlands, East, London, South East, South West, England, Wales, Scotland, Great Britain, Northern Ireland, United Kingdom.

Office for National Statistics

4.5A Unemployment rates[1,2] by Government Office Region

Percentages, seasonally adjusted [4]

	North East	North West[3]	Yorkshire and the Humber	East Midlands	West Midlands	East	London	South East
Quarterly	YCNC	YCND	YCNE	YCNF	YCNG	YCNH	YCNI	YCNJ
1998 Q1	8.4	6.7	7.1	5.2	6.2	5.4	8.1	4.4
Q2	8.2	6.9	7.3	4.9	5.9	4.9	8.4	4.4
Q3	8.3	6.7	7.1	5.4	6.1	4.5	7.7	4.5
Q4	9.7	7.0	7.0	4.9	6.5	4.3	7.5	3.9
1999 Q1	9.5	6.7	6.7	5.1	7.0	4.2	7.7	3.9
Q2	9.5	6.3	6.3	5.3	6.9	4.3	7.4	4.0
Q3	9.6	6.3	6.0	5.6	6.5	3.9	7.3	3.9
Q4	8.5	6.0	6.0	5.5	6.7	4.2	6.9	4.0
2000 Q1	8.9	6.1	6.4	5.1	6.1	3.9	7.5	3.5
Q2	8.8	5.4	6.1	4.8	6.1	3.6	7.3	3.3
Q3	8.8	5.4	5.9	4.8	5.8	3.7	6.9	3.1
Q4	7.9	5.3	6.1	4.7	5.9	3.6	6.7	3.4
2001 Q1	7.7	5.3	5.3	4.7	5.6	3.6	6.4	3.3
Q2	7.3	5.4	5.4	5.0	5.4	3.5	6.1	3.2
Q3	6.9	5.2	5.4	4.6	5.5	4.0	6.5	3.4
Q4	7.3	5.3	5.1	4.6	5.5	3.9	7.2	3.3
2002 Q1	7.3	5.4	5.0	4.7	5.6	3.7	6.8	3.5
Q2	6.3	5.6	5.2	4.5	5.5	3.7	6.7	3.8
Q3	6.2	5.5	5.5	4.6	6.0	3.8	7.0	4.0
Q4	7.5	5.0	5.1	4.8	5.6	3.9	6.5	4.0
2003 Q1	6.4	5.0	5.1	4.1	6.0	4.6	6.8	3.9
Q2	6.0	4.9	5.1	4.3	5.6	4.0	7.1	3.9
Q3	6.7	4.8	4.8	4.5	6.0	3.9	7.1	3.9
Q4	6.4	4.8	5.1	4.4	5.8	3.5	7.0	3.8

	South West	England	Wales	Scotland	Great Britain	Northern Ireland	United Kingdom
Quarterly	YCNK	YCNL	YCNM	YCNN	YCNO	ZSFB	MGSX
1998 Q1	4.6	6.1	7.2	7.6	6.3	8.5	6.3
Q2	4.7	6.1	7.1	7.4	6.2	6.8	6.3
Q3	4.9	6.0	7.4	7.6	6.2	7.9	6.2
Q4	4.5	5.9	7.1	7.7	6.1	6.9	6.1
1999 Q1	4.8	5.9	7.2	7.4	6.1	7.1	6.2
Q2	4.5	5.8	7.5	7.1	6.0	7.5	6.0
Q3	4.4	5.7	7.2	6.9	5.8	7.1	5.9
Q4	4.2	5.5	7.2	7.1	5.8	6.8	5.8
2000 Q1	4.2	5.5	6.7	7.6	5.7	6.5	5.8
Q2	4.3	5.3	6.1	7.0	5.5	6.6	5.5
Q3	4.0	5.1	6.6	6.7	5.3	5.6	5.3
Q4	3.9	5.1	5.8	6.3	5.2	6.2	5.2
2001 Q1	3.9	4.9	6.1	6.0	5.0	6.1	5.1
Q2	3.6	4.8	6.1	6.2	5.0	5.9	5.0
Q3	3.6	4.9	5.5	6.7	5.1	6.1	5.1
Q4	3.6	5.0	5.9	6.8	5.2	6.0	5.2
2002 Q1	3.4	4.9	5.7	6.6	5.1	6.0	5.1
Q2	3.7	5.0	5.7	6.4	5.1	5.4	5.1
Q3	3.9	5.1	5.2	6.4	5.3	6.3	5.3
Q4	4.0	5.0	5.3	6.2	5.1	5.6	5.1
2003 Q1	3.8	5.0	4.8	5.9	5.1	5.1	5.1
Q2	3.5	4.9	4.6	5.5	5.0	5.2	5.0
Q3	3.2	4.9	4.7	5.8	5.0	5.6	5.0
Q4	3.1	4.8	4.8	5.8	4.9	6.3	4.9

1 The data in this table have been adjusted to reflect the 2001 Census population data.
2 Data are from the Labour Force Survey. Unemployment rate is the percentage of economically active people who are unemployed on the ILO measure.
3 Includes Merseyside.
4 Seasonally adjusted estimates are revised in April each year.

Source: Office for National Statistics; Enquiries 020 7533 6094

Economic Trends 604 March 2004

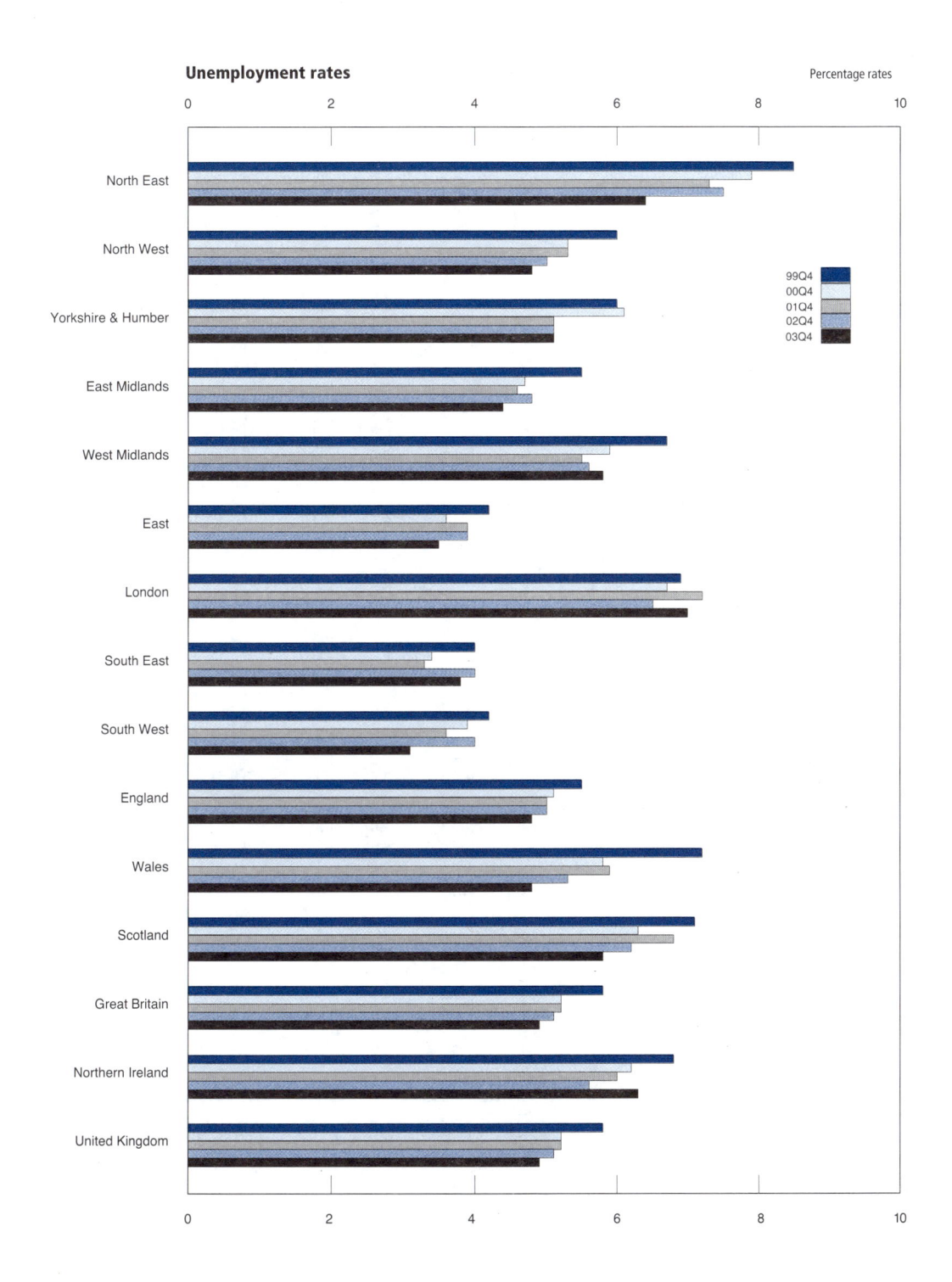

Tables section

Unemployment rates

Percentage rates

Legend:
- 99Q4
- 00Q4
- 01Q4
- 02Q4
- 03Q4

Regions shown: North East, North West, Yorkshire & Humber, East Midlands, West Midlands, East, London, South East, South West, England, Wales, Scotland, Great Britain, Northern Ireland, United Kingdom

Office for National Statistics

4.6 Average earnings (including bonuses)
Great Britain

2000 = 100

	Whole economy+	headline rate[2]	Private sector	headline rate[2]	Public sector	headline rate[2]	Manufacturing industries[3]	headline rate[2,3]	Production industries	headline rate[2]	Service industries	headline rate[2]	Private sector services	headline rate[2]
Annual														
	LNMQ		LNKY		LNNJ		LNMR		LNMS		LNMT		JJGH	
2000	100.0		100.0		100.0		100.0		100.0		100.0		100.0	
2001	104.4		104.3		105.0		104.3		104.2		104.4		104.2	
2002	108.2		107.9		109.3		108.0		107.9		108.1		107.7	
2003	111.8		111.1		114.8		111.9		111.7		111.8		110.7	
Monthly														
		LNNC		LNND		LNNE		LNNG		LNNF		LNNH		JJGJ
2000 Jan	98.8	5.8	98.8	6.3	98.9	4.0	98.9	5.4	99.2	5.1	98.9	6.1	99.0	6.7
Feb	98.7	5.9	98.7	6.3	99.5	4.3	98.2	5.3	98.5	5.1	98.9	6.1	98.9	6.8
Mar	98.9	5.5	98.9	5.9	98.9	4.2	98.4	4.9	98.4	4.7	98.9	5.7	99.0	6.3
Apr	98.7	5.0	98.5	5.2	99.2	4.1	98.7	4.5	98.6	4.1	98.6	5.1	98.4	5.4
May	98.8	4.5	98.6	4.7	99.2	3.7	99.5	4.6	99.5	4.2	98.6	4.4	98.4	4.7
Jun	99.2	4.1	99.0	4.2	100.0	3.6	99.3	4.6	99.3	4.2	99.0	3.9	98.8	4.0
Jul	99.5	3.9	99.4	4.0	99.8	3.4	99.9	4.6	99.8	4.3	99.4	3.5	99.2	3.6
Aug	100.3	4.0	100.3	4.1	100.1	3.4	100.1	4.3	100.1	4.0	100.4	3.8	100.4	3.9
Sep	100.7	4.1	100.8	4.3	100.4	3.4	100.9	4.3	100.8	4.0	100.7	4.0	100.7	4.3
Oct	101.3	4.2	101.4	4.4	100.8	3.4	101.3	4.3	101.2	4.0	101.4	4.2	101.4	4.5
Nov	101.9	4.3	101.9	4.4	101.4	3.6	102.2	4.6	102.1	4.3	101.9	4.2	101.9	4.4
Dec	103.3	4.5	103.7	4.6	101.7	3.9	102.7	4.7	102.6	4.4	103.4	4.5	103.9	4.7
2001 Jan	103.2	4.6	103.4	4.7	102.2	3.8	102.7	4.5	102.7	4.2	103.3	4.6	103.6	4.7
Feb	103.6	4.8	103.7	4.9	102.6	3.6	103.4	4.7	103.7	4.5	103.8	4.8	104.0	5.0
Mar	103.7	4.8	103.7	4.8	103.3	3.6	103.5	4.8	103.3	4.6	103.8	4.8	103.8	4.9
Apr	103.9	5.1	103.9	5.1	104.6	4.3	103.9	5.2	103.7	5.1	103.9	5.1	103.8	5.1
May	104.0	5.2	103.8	5.2	105.0	5.2	104.1	5.0	104.0	4.9	103.9	5.2	103.6	5.2
Jun	104.3	5.3	104.1	5.3	105.3	5.5	104.3	5.0	104.1	4.8	104.2	5.3	103.9	5.3
Jul	104.4	5.1	104.2	5.1	105.6	5.6	104.4	4.7	104.3	4.6	104.3	5.2	103.9	5.1
Aug	104.8	4.9	104.6	4.8	106.0	5.6	104.8	4.7	104.6	4.6	104.8	4.9	104.4	4.6
Sep	105.0	4.6	104.8	4.4	106.0	5.7	105.2	4.5	105.0	4.4	104.9	4.5	104.5	4.2
Oct	105.1	4.2	104.9	3.9	106.4	5.7	105.2	4.3	105.1	4.2	105.0	4.1	104.7	3.6
Nov	105.2	3.8	105.0	3.5	106.4	5.4	105.2	3.7	105.0	3.6	105.1	3.7	104.7	3.2
Dec	105.8	3.1	105.6	2.8	106.8	5.2	105.4	3.1	105.2	3.1	105.7	3.0	105.3	2.4
2002 Jan	106.3	2.9	106.1	2.5	107.0	4.9	105.9	2.9	105.8	2.8	106.3	2.7	106.0	2.1
Feb	106.9	2.8	106.7	2.4	107.2	4.7	106.0	2.8	106.0	2.6	107.1	2.8	107.0	2.2
Mar	106.7	3.0	106.4	2.7	107.9	4.5	106.4	2.8	106.5	2.8	106.6	2.9	105.9	2.4
Apr	108.0	3.3	108.1	3.2	108.3	4.1	107.4	2.9	107.2	2.9	108.0	3.3	108.1	3.0
May	107.9	3.5	107.8	3.5	108.7	3.8	107.7	3.2	107.6	3.3	107.9	3.5	107.7	3.4
Jun	108.2	3.8	108.0	3.9	109.0	3.5	108.1	3.5	108.0	3.5	108.2	3.9	108.0	4.0
Jul	108.4	3.8	108.2	3.8	109.6	3.6	108.3	3.6	108.2	3.7	108.3	3.9	108.0	3.9
Aug	108.6	3.7	108.5	3.8	109.1	3.4	108.8	3.7	108.7	3.8	108.5	3.7	108.2	3.8
Sep	108.8	3.7	108.5	3.7	110.1	3.5	108.8	3.6	108.7	3.7	108.7	3.7	108.2	3.7
Oct	109.0†	3.6	108.6†	3.6	110.9	3.7†	109.3	3.7	109.2	3.8	108.9†	3.6	108.3†	3.5†
Nov	109.6	3.8	109.1	3.7†	111.7†	4.4†	109.4†	3.8†	109.3	3.9	109.6	3.9†	108.9	3.7
Dec	109.5	3.8	108.9	3.6†	112.2†	4.7	109.8†	4.0†	109.8	4.1	109.2	3.8	108.3	3.4
2003 Jan	109.8	3.6	109.2	3.3	112.4	5.0	109.9	4.0	109.8	4.0†	109.6	3.6	108.6	3.1
Feb	109.9	3.2	109.3	2.8	112.8	5.1	110.7	4.1	110.6	4.1	109.8	3.0	108.7	2.3
Mar	111.4	3.5	110.8	3.2	113.4	5.1	113.3	4.9	113.1	4.8	110.9	3.2	109.8	2.6
Apr	110.8	3.3	110.2	2.8	113.9	5.1	110.2	4.5	110.2	4.5	110.9	3.1	110.0	2.3
May	111.3	3.4	110.7	3.0	113.7	4.9	111.1	4.1	111.0	4.1	111.5	3.3	110.7	2.7
Jun	111.6	3.0	110.9	2.4	114.8	5.1	111.3	2.9	111.3	3.0	111.8	3.1	110.8	2.4
Jul	112.3	3.3	111.7	2.9	115.4	5.1	111.8	3.1	111.6	3.1	112.5	3.5	111.6	2.9
Aug	112.4	3.4	111.5	2.9	115.9	5.6	111.9	3.0	111.8	3.0	112.6	3.7	111.5	3.0
Sep	112.8	3.6	112.0	3.1	116.1	5.6	112.5	3.2	112.3	3.1	112.9	3.8	111.8	3.2
Oct	113.0	3.6	112.3	3.2	116.1	5.4	112.8	3.2	112.6	3.1	113.0	3.8	111.9	3.2
Nov	113.1	3.5	112.3	3.2	116.4	4.8	113.3	3.4	113.1	3.3	113.0	3.5	111.7	3.1
Dec[1]	113.2	3.4	112.4	3.2	117.0	4.4	113.7	3.4	113.4	3.3	112.9	3.4	111.6	3.0

1 Provisional.
2 The headline rate is the change in the average seasonally adjusted index values for the last 3 months compared with the same period a year ago. Previously, the headline rate was centred on the middle month of the three under consideration. The new presentation aligns the average with the last month of the three.
3 ONS regrets that the series have been withdrawn for the period 1963-1982, owing to an irregularity.

Source: Office for National Statistics; Enquiries 01633 816024

Earnings, wages, retail prices and output

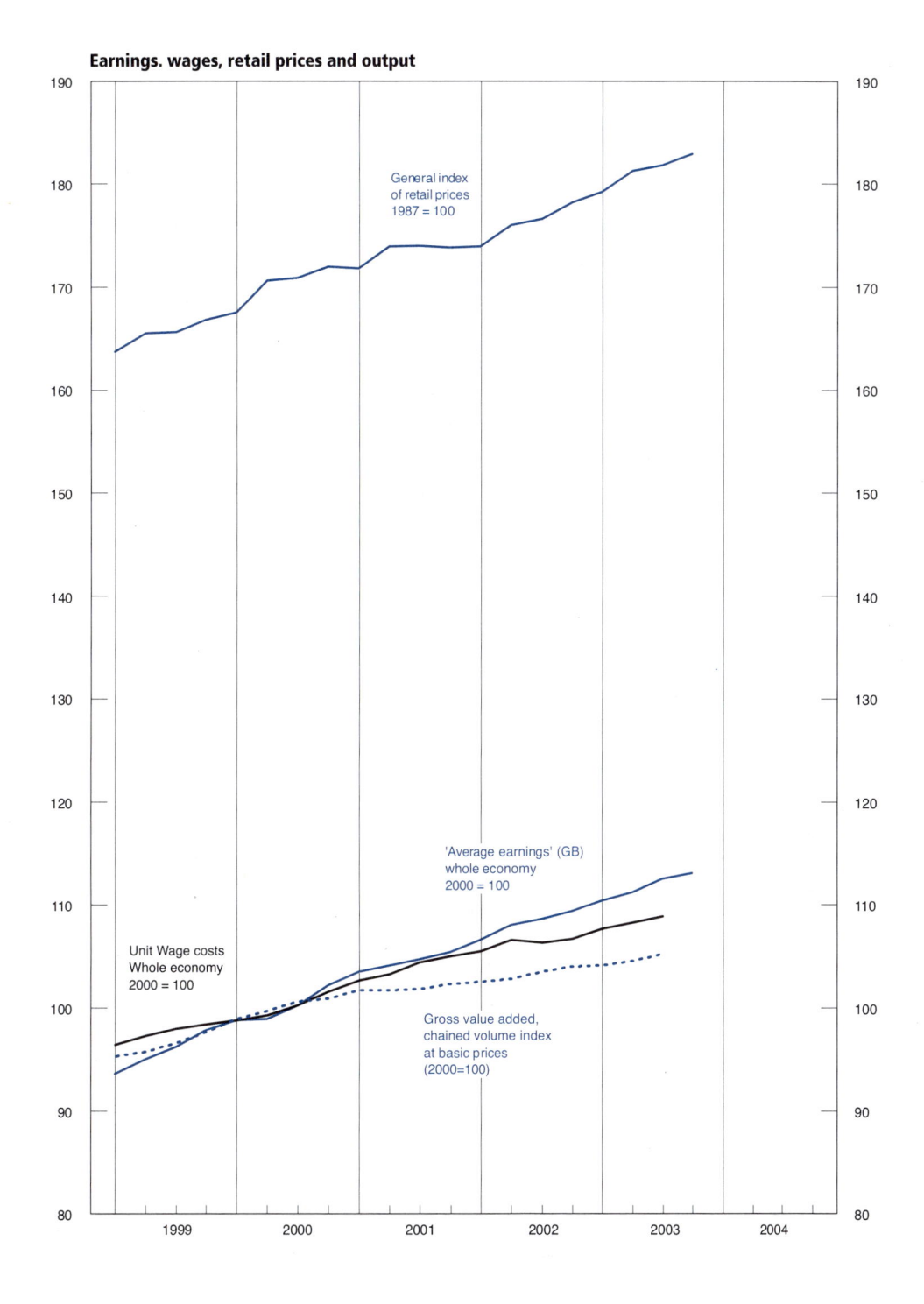

General index of retail prices 1987 = 100

'Average earnings' (GB) whole economy 2000 = 100

Unit Wage costs Whole economy 2000 = 100

Gross value added, chained volume index at basic prices (2000=100)

4.7 Productivity and Unit Wage costs[1]
United Kingdom

2000 = 100

	Productivity jobs			Output per filled job[2]			Output per hour worked[3]			Unit wage costs	
	Whole economy	Total production industries	Manufacturing industries	Whole economy	Total production industries	Manufacturing industries	Whole economy	Total production industries	Manufacturing industries	Whole economy	Manufacturing industries
Annual	LNNM	LNOJ	LNOK	LNNN	LNNW	LNNX	LZVB	LZVK	LZVF	LNNK	LNNQ
2001	100.8	96.0	95.5	101.1	102.5	103.3	100.9	103.1	103.7	103.8	101.0
2002	100.7	91.6	90.7	102.5	104.5	104.8	102.5	104.8	104.6	106.3	103.0
2003	..	..	86.5	..	..	109.9	..	..	..	..	101.8
Quarterly											
2001 Q1	100.6	97.6	97.3	101.1	102.5	103.5	100.8	103.2	104.1	102.7	99.7
Q2	100.8	96.6	96.2	100.8	102.2	102.6	100.4	102.2	102.5	103.3	101.5
Q3	100.8	95.3	94.8	101.0	103.1	104.0	100.8	102.8	103.4	104.4	100.7
Q4	100.9	94.4	93.8	101.4	102.2	102.9	101.8	104.4	104.7	105.0	102.3
2002 Q1	100.9	93.2	92.3	101.6	103.0	103.8	101.5	103.2	103.4	105.5	102.2
Q2	100.7	92.2	91.4	102.0	104.1	103.5	102.5	105.4	104.3	106.6	104.1
Q3	100.7	91.1	90.1	102.8	105.0	106.0	102.8	105.9	106.1	106.3	102.5
Q4	100.6	90.1	89.0†	103.4	105.7	106.1	103.4	104.7	104.6	106.7	103.2
2003 Q1	100.7	89.2	88.2	103.4	106.5	107.0†	103.1	105.5	105.6	107.7	104.0
Q2	100.8	88.0	86.8	103.7	108.2	109.4	103.5	109.0	109.5	108.3	101.3
Q3	100.8	86.8	85.8	104.3	109.6	111.0	104.0	108.6	109.7	108.9	100.9
Q4	..	..	85.0	..	..	112.3	..	..	..	..	100.9
Monthly											
2002 Jul	..	..	90.6	..	..	105.0	..	..	..	..	103.1
Aug	..	..	90.1	..	..	106.5	..	..	..	..	102.1
Sep	..	..	89.6	..	..	106.4	..	..	..	..	102.2
Oct	..	..	89.3	..	..	105.2	..	..	..	..	103.9
Nov	..	..	89.1	..	..	106.4	..	..	..	..	102.9
Dec	..	..	88.7†	..	..	106.7†	..	..	..	..	102.9
2003 Jan	..	..	88.6	..	..	106.4	..	..	..	..	103.3
Feb	..	..	88.2	..	..	107.3	..	..	..	..	103.2
Mar	..	..	87.9	..	..	107.3	..	..	..	..	105.6
Apr	..	..	87.3	..	..	108.7	..	..	..	..	101.3
May	..	..	86.8	..	..	109.3	..	..	..	..	101.6
Jun	..	..	86.4	..	..	110.2	..	..	..	..	101.0
Jul	..	..	86.1	..	..	111.0	..	..	..	..	100.7
Aug	..	..	85.8	..	..	110.8	..	..	..	..	101.0
Sep	..	..	85.5	..	..	111.3	..	..	..	..	101.1
Oct	..	..	85.3	..	..	112.5	..	..	..	..	100.3
Nov	..	..	85.0	..	..	112.1	..	..	..	..	101.1
Dec	..	..	84.8	..	..	112.3	..	..	..	..	101.2

Percentage change, quarter on corresponding quarter of previous year

Quarterly	LNNO	LNNR	LNNS	LNNP	LNNT	LNNU	LZVD	LZVM	LZVH	LOJE	LOJF
2001 Q1	1.2	−3.6	−4.1	1.7	4.3	5.9	0.9	5.2	6.7	3.9	−1.1
Q2	0.9	−3.9	−4.2	1.1	2.6	3.3	0.9	3.0	3.7	4.1	1.6
Q3	0.6	−4.3	−4.8	0.6	2.8	3.5	0.3	2.6	2.9	4.0	1.0
Q4	0.4	−4.2	−4.8	1.0	0.5	0.5	1.7	1.8	1.5	3.3	2.6
2002 Q1	0.3	−4.5	−5.2	0.5	0.5	0.3	0.8	−	−0.6	2.8	2.6
Q2	−0.1	−4.6	−5.1	1.2	1.9	0.9	2.1	3.1	1.8	3.2	2.6
Q3	−0.2	−4.4	−4.9	1.8	1.9	1.9†	2.0	3.0	2.7	1.8	1.7
Q4	−0.3	−4.6	−5.1†	2.0	3.3	3.1†	1.6	0.4	−0.1	1.6	0.9
2003 Q1	−0.2	−4.3	−4.4	1.8	3.3	3.1	1.5	2.2	2.1	2.1	1.8
Q2	0.1	−4.5	−5.0	1.6	3.9	5.7	0.9	3.5	5.0	1.6	−2.7
Q3	0.2	−4.7	−4.8	1.5	4.3	4.8	1.2	2.6	3.3	2.5	−1.5
Q4	..	..	−4.5	..	..	5.8	..	..	..	..	−2.3

1 The full productivity and unit wage costs data sets with associated articles can be found on the National Statistics web site at **www.statistics.gov.uk/productivity**
Contact the Labour Market Statistics helpline (020 7533 6094) for further information.

2 Output per filled job is the ratio of Gross value added at basic prices to productivity jobs.
3 Output per hour worked is the ratio of Gross value added at basic prices to productivity hours.

Source: Office for National Statistics; Enquiries 01633 812766

Economic Trends 604 March 2004

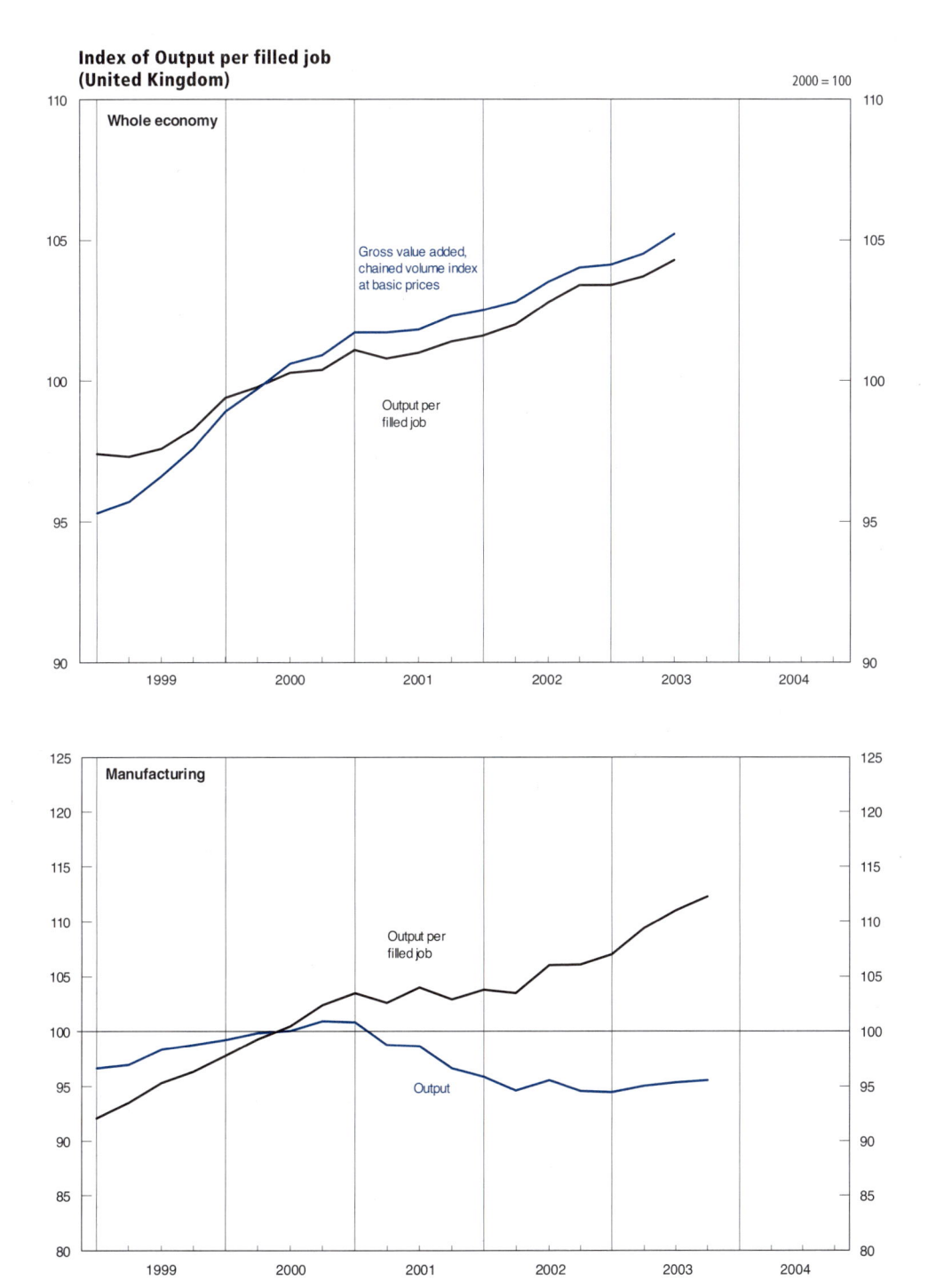

Index of Output per filled job (United Kingdom)

2000 = 100

Whole economy
- Gross value added, chained volume index at basic prices
- Output per filled job

Manufacturing
- Output per filled job
- Output

5.1 Output of production industries[1]

2000 = 100

	Broad industry groups				By main industrial groupings			
	Total production industries+	Mining and quarrying	Electricity, gas and water supply	Total manufacturing industries+	Consumer durables	Consumer non-durables	Capital goods	Intermediate goods and energy
2000 weights	1 000	130	83	786	37	258	221	485
Annual								
	CKYW	CKYX	CKYZ	CKYY	UFIU	UFJS	UFIL	JMOH
1999	98.1	103.3	97.9	97.6	98.4	99.6	96.5	98.2
2000	100.0	100.0	100.0	100.0	100.0	100.0	100.0	100.0
2001	98.4	94.5	102.4	98.7	102.5	101.2	98.4	96.6
2002	95.7	94.4	104.0	95.1	103.8	100.8	90.0	95.0
2003	95.0	88.6	105.1	95.0	102.2	100.2	91.9	93.2
Quarterly								
1999 Q1	97.1	102.2	96.9	96.6	96.3	98.5	94.7	97.7
Q2	97.5	103.3	97.1	96.9	97.3	99.4	95.4	97.6
Q3	98.8	104.5	98.4	98.3	99.5	100.2	97.6	98.6
Q4	99.1	103.0	99.1	98.7	100.4	100.3	98.3	98.8
2000 Q1	99.6	103.8	98.7	99.2	100.3	100.3	98.2	99.9
Q2	100.2	102.4	101.0	99.8	99.9	100.4	99.5	100.4
Q3	99.9	98.9	99.9	100.0	99.8	99.8	100.1	100.0
Q4	100.3	94.9	100.3	100.9	100.0	99.5	102.2	99.8
2001 Q1	100.1	93.3	104.5	100.8	102.8	101.2	103.2	97.9
Q2	98.7	96.3	102.8	98.7	101.9	100.8	98.5	97.5
Q3	98.3	95.0	101.0	98.6	102.3	101.4	98.1	96.5
Q4	96.5	93.4	101.2	96.6	103.2	101.4	93.8	94.7
2002 Q1	96.1	94.2	101.5	95.8	105.1	101.4	90.5	95.1
Q2	96.0	99.1	104.6	94.6	103.2	101.0	89.3	95.9
Q3	95.7	90.2	106.2	95.5	102.9	101.3	90.6	94.5
Q4	95.2	94.0	103.6	94.5	104.1	99.5	89.5	94.8
2003 Q1	94.9[†]	92.4[†]	102.9[†]	94.4[†]	99.6[†]	99.7[†]	90.2[†]	94.1
Q2	95.1	90.0	104.7	95.0	101.3	99.8	92.4	93.4[†]
Q3	95.1	87.3	105.9	95.3	103.8	100.5	92.3	92.9
Q4	95.0	84.5	106.8	95.5	104.3	100.7	92.7	92.3
Monthly								
2002 Jan	96.0	96.1	102.3	95.3	104.3	100.2	90.5	95.6
Feb	95.9	92.8	99.8	95.9	104.7	102.4	90.0	94.4
Mar	96.3	93.8	102.4	96.1	106.3	101.5	91.1	95.2
Apr	96.5	96.0	102.8	95.9	106.1	102.3	90.0	95.7
May	98.2	101.0	106.3	96.8	105.8	102.1	92.9	97.9
Jun	93.4	100.3	104.6	91.0	97.7	98.6	85.1	94.0
Jul	95.3	87.6	109.2	95.1	101.0	101.4	89.7	94.2
Aug	96.0	88.0	108.0	96.0	104.0	101.4	92.1	94.2
Sep	95.8	95.1	101.5	95.4	103.9	101.3	90.1	94.9
Oct	95.0	95.8	104.1	94.0	103.2	99.5	88.3	95.1
Nov	95.1	93.0	102.1	94.7	104.4	99.7	89.6	94.5
Dec	95.4	93.2	104.7	94.7	104.5	99.2	90.6	94.7
2003 Jan	94.5	92.0[†]	100.4[†]	94.2[†]	101.3[†]	99.2[†]	89.8[†]	93.5
Feb	95.3[†]	92.9	105.2	94.6	99.6	99.8	90.7	94.7[†]
Mar	94.9	92.4	103.2	94.4	97.8	100.0	90.2	94.0
Apr	94.8	89.9	102.3	94.9	100.7	99.1	93.0	93.0
May	94.9	89.7	103.0	94.9	100.3	100.6	91.3	93.0
Jun	95.7	90.3	108.9	95.3	103.0	99.8	92.9	94.3
Jul	95.6	90.2	104.3	95.6	104.2	100.6	92.8	93.5
Aug	94.8	86.6	104.7	95.1	102.3	100.4	91.5	92.8
Sep	95.0	85.1	108.8	95.2	104.7	100.4	92.5	92.4
Oct	95.6	85.7	107.7	95.9	104.8	101.5	92.9	92.9
Nov	94.7	84.4	105.8	95.3	104.6	100.2	92.7	92.1
Dec	94.6	83.5	106.9	95.2	103.6	100.5	92.4	91.9

1 The figures contain, where appropriate, an adjustment for stock changes.

Source: Office for National Statistics; Enquiries 01633 812786

Economic Trends 604 March 2004   Tables section

Index of output of the production industries
By broad industry group   2000 = 100

Share of output in 2000

- Manufacturing 78.7%
- Mining and quarrying 13.0%
- Energy and water supply 8.3%

By main industrial groupings   2000 = 100

Share of output in 2000

- Capital goods 22.1%
- Durable & Non-durable goods 29.5%
- Intermediate goods and energy 48.5%

Office for National Statistics | 123

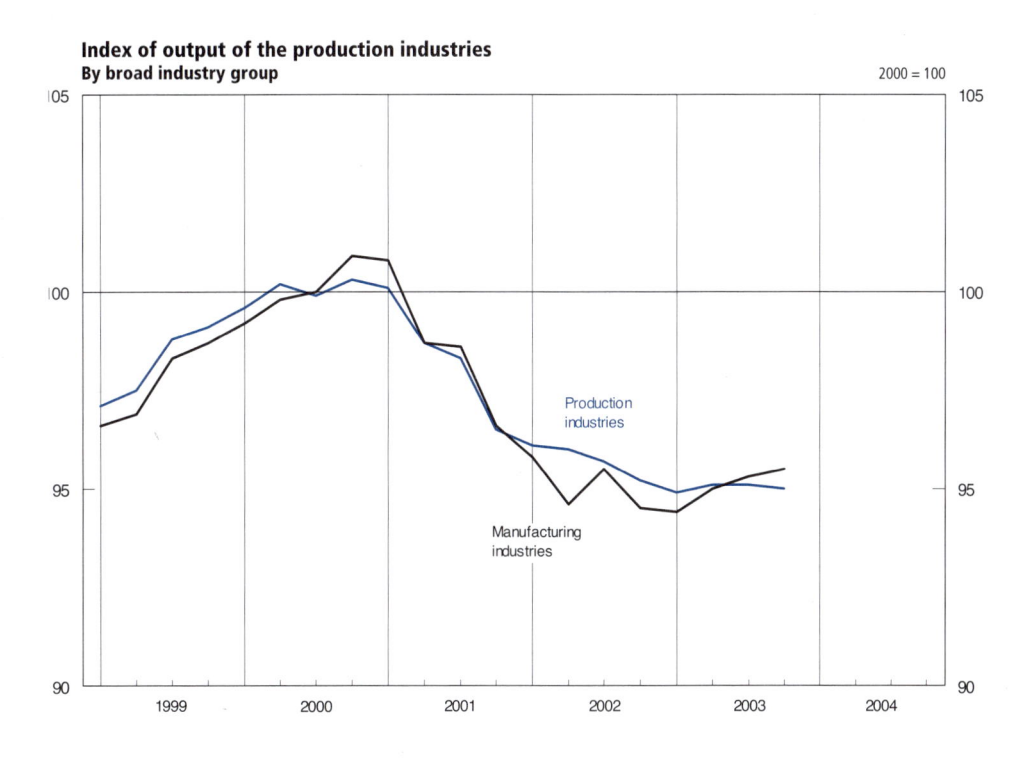

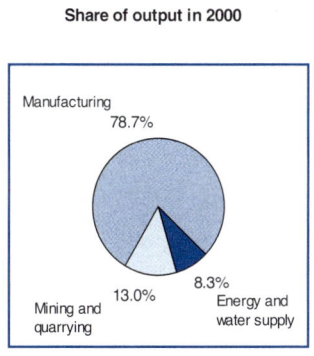

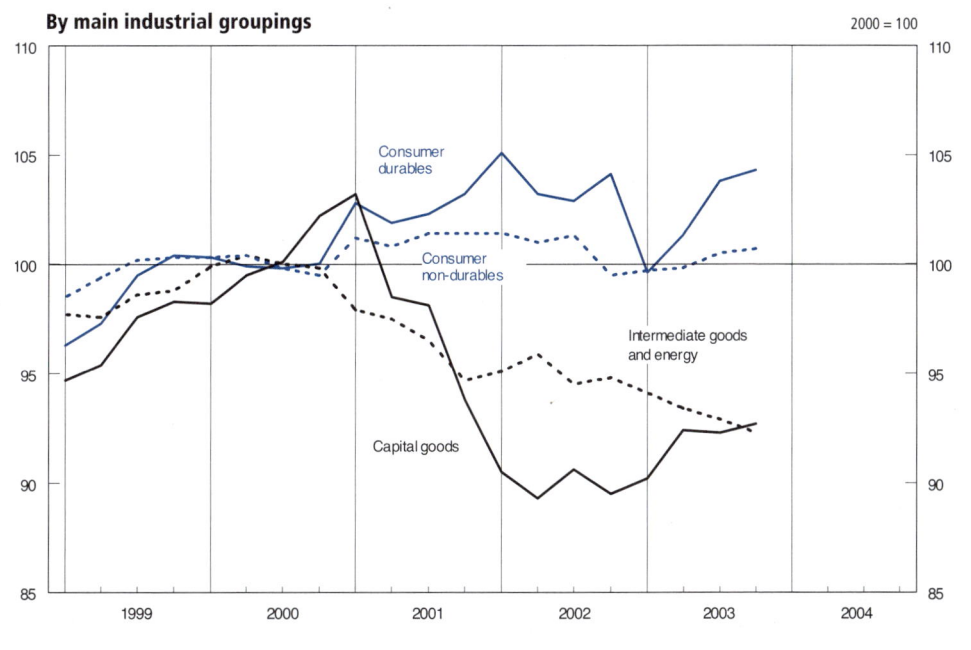

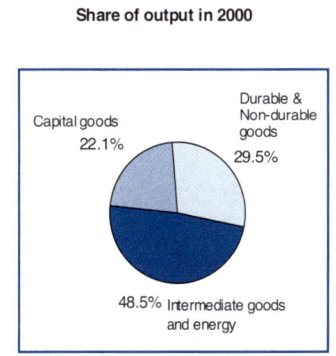

5.2 Engineering and construction : output and orders
Seasonally adjusted Index numbers at constant prices[1]

| | Engineering (2000 =100) ||||||||| Construction(GB) (2000=100) ||
| | Total ||| Home ||| Export ||| | |
	Orders[2] on Hand	New[3] Orders	Turnover	Orders[2] on Hand	New[3] Orders	Turnover	Orders[2] on Hand	New[3] Orders	Turnover	Gross output+[4]	Orders received
	JIQI	JIQH	JIQJ	JIQC	JIQB	JIQD	JIQF	JIQE	JIQG	SFZX	SGAA
Annual											
1999	92.0	91.8	91.9	92.8	94.2	93.5	90.8	88.6	89.9	93.2†	98.5
2000	103.4	100.0	100.0	104.9	100.0	100.0	100.8	100.0	100.0	100.0	100.0
2001	94.4	89.5	95.3	104.6	94.5	98.4	77.2	82.9	91.2	99.5	99.2
2002	91.7	80.4	84.1	104.2	87.3	91.1	70.5	71.2	74.8	104.2	102.2
2003	90.8	80.1	83.4	106.5	90.3	93.6	64.2	66.5	69.9	..	98.2
Quarterly											
1999 Q1	83.1	88.6	90.2	79.9	88.5	91.1	88.5	88.6	89.0	89.3†	..
Q2	82.4	86.8	90.6	80.6	88.7	91.3	85.3	84.2	89.8	92.4	..
Q3	86.8	95.0	93.0	85.3	98.1	95.9	89.3	90.8	89.0	95.3	..
Q4	92.0	96.9	93.9	92.8	101.5	95.6	90.8	90.8	91.7	95.9	..
2000 Q1	96.2	95.9	94.1	96.6	96.2	95.1	95.7	95.5	92.8	101.8	..
Q2	100.6	101.6	99.9	100.2	101.0	100.3	101.3	102.4	99.3	100.3	..
Q3	102.7	100.7	101.5	101.8	99.2	101.0	104.4	102.8	102.2	98.9	..
Q4	103.4	101.8	104.5	104.9	103.6	103.6	100.8	99.4	105.7	99.0	..
2001 Q1	104.4	102.1	104.4	106.2	102.2	104.7	101.3	102.0	104.2	97.8	..
Q2	102.0	91.0	97.1	108.2	97.8	99.0	91.3	81.9	94.5	98.9	..
Q3	99.9	86.6	92.0	107.6	91.5	96.0	86.9	79.9	86.6	99.7	103.1
Q4	94.4	78.5	87.8	104.6	86.4	93.9	77.2	67.8	79.6	101.5	90.2
2002 Q1	95.1	82.1	84.4	105.5	87.9	90.8	77.4	74.2	76.0	103.0	108.0
Q2	93.9	80.2	84.4	105.8	88.1	91.3	73.8	69.6	75.1	103.6	89.5
Q3	93.7	81.5	84.6	106.2	88.5	91.7	72.6	72.2	75.2	104.4	109.2
Q4	91.7	77.9	83.0	104.2	84.5	90.7	70.5	69.0	72.9	105.8	102.1
2003 Q1	90.3†	77.5†	82.5†	102.9†	86.9†	93.5†	69.1†	64.8†	68.1†	103.1	104.7
Q2	91.5	82.0	83.5	104.7	92.2	93.7	69.1	68.3	70.0	108.9	95.7
Q3	91.1	80.2	83.5	105.4	90.7	93.5	66.9	66.2	70.2	111.0	98.7
Q4	90.8	80.8	84.0	106.5	91.4	93.7	64.2	66.7	71.2	..	93.6
Monthly											
2002 Jan	94.7	81.5	84.1	104.3	84.2	90.0	78.5	78.0	76.3	..	94.1
Feb	95.9	85.7	84.3	105.6	92.1	90.7	79.5	77.2	75.9	..	104.6
Mar	95.1	79.0	84.8	105.5	87.5	91.6	77.4	67.5	75.7	..	125.2
Apr	94.7	81.4	85.6	105.4	89.1	93.3	76.7	71.2	75.3	..	82.2
May	94.3	82.5	87.0	105.9	92.5	94.1	74.6	69.2	77.5	..	96.0
Jun	93.9	76.6	80.6	105.8	82.8	86.6	73.8	68.3	72.6	..	90.4
Jul	94.4	83.8	84.8	106.0	88.3	91.0	74.8	77.8	76.6	..	113.3
Aug	94.8	81.9	83.6	107.9	95.2	91.6	72.5	64.1	73.0	..	99.9
Sep	93.7	78.8	85.4	106.2	82.0	92.4	72.6	74.6	76.1	..	114.4
Oct	93.9	80.5	82.5	105.5	83.5	89.8	74.4	76.5	72.9	..	92.6
Nov	91.3	71.1	83.0	102.7	76.1	90.2	71.9	64.4	73.6	..	92.0
Dec	91.7	82.0	83.4	104.2	94.0	92.0	70.5	66.0	72.1	..	121.7
2003 Jan	91.4†	77.0†	82.8†	102.4†	79.4†	93.8†	72.9†	73.7†	68.4†	..	110.4
Feb	91.2	79.6	83.2	103.2	94.6	95.2	70.8	59.4	67.4	..	112.9
Mar	90.3	75.9	81.6	102.9	86.6	91.6	69.1	61.4	68.4	..	90.6
Apr	93.8	93.2	83.9	108.1	110.3	94.3	69.7	70.3	70.2	..	111.2
May	92.4	76.2	83.9	105.9	83.0	95.1	69.6	67.2	69.0	..	89.5
Jun	91.5	76.6	82.6	104.7	83.3	91.6	69.1	67.5	70.8	..	86.3
Jul	92.0	84.0	85.0	104.6	91.2	95.5	70.8	74.3	71.1	..	111.8
Aug	91.8	78.8	82.3	106.0	93.5	91.9	67.9	59.1	69.5	..	80.9
Sep	91.1	77.9	83.2	105.4	87.3	93.1	66.9	65.2	70.1	..	103.6
Oct	91.7	84.1	85.1	106.3	95.4	95.9	66.9	69.0	70.8	..	88.9†
Nov	93.1	85.6	83.3	109.1	100.0	93.1	66.1	66.1	70.3	..	102.4
Dec	90.8	72.8	83.7	106.5	78.7	92.2	64.2	64.9	72.4	..	89.7

1 The figures shown represent the output of United Kingdom based manufacturers classified to Subsections DK and DL of the Standard Industrial Classification (2003).
2 For Orders on Hand, the annual and quarterly index values represent the value at the end of the period in question, rather than the average value for that period, so the annual value shown for 2000 may not equal 100.
3 Net of cancellations.
4 This index is based upon a gross output series which includes repair and maintenance estimates, unrecorded output by self-employed workers and small firms and output by the direct labour departments of the public sector.

Sources: Office for National Statistics; Enquiries Columns 1-9 01633 812540;
Department of Trade and Industry;
Enquiries Columns 10-11 020 7944 5583

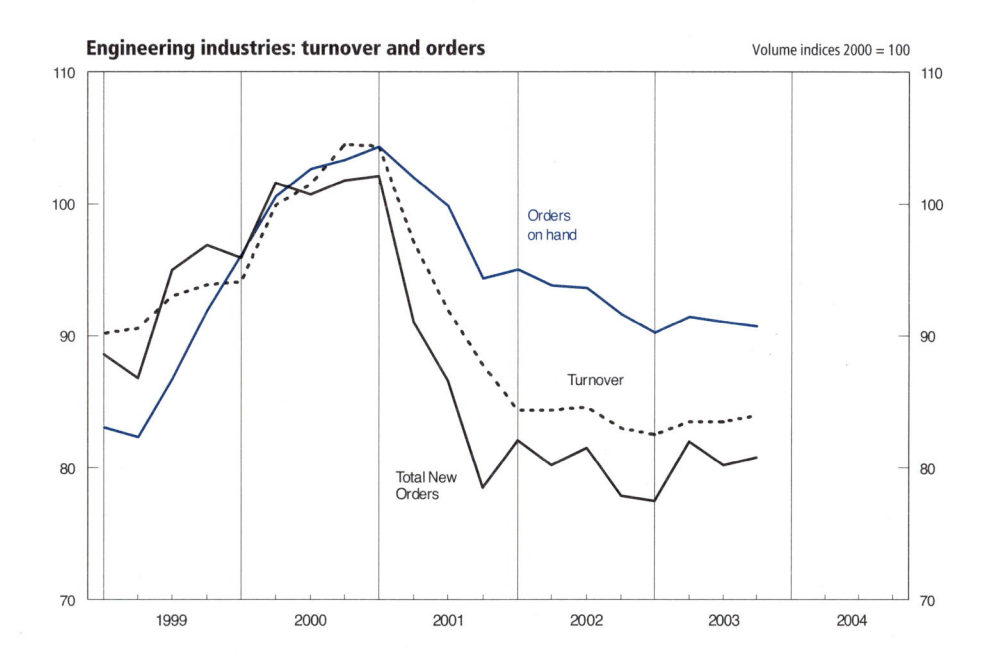

Economic Trends 604 March 2004

Tables section

Engineering industries: turnover and orders

Volume indices 2000 = 100

- Orders on hand
- Turnover
- Total New Orders

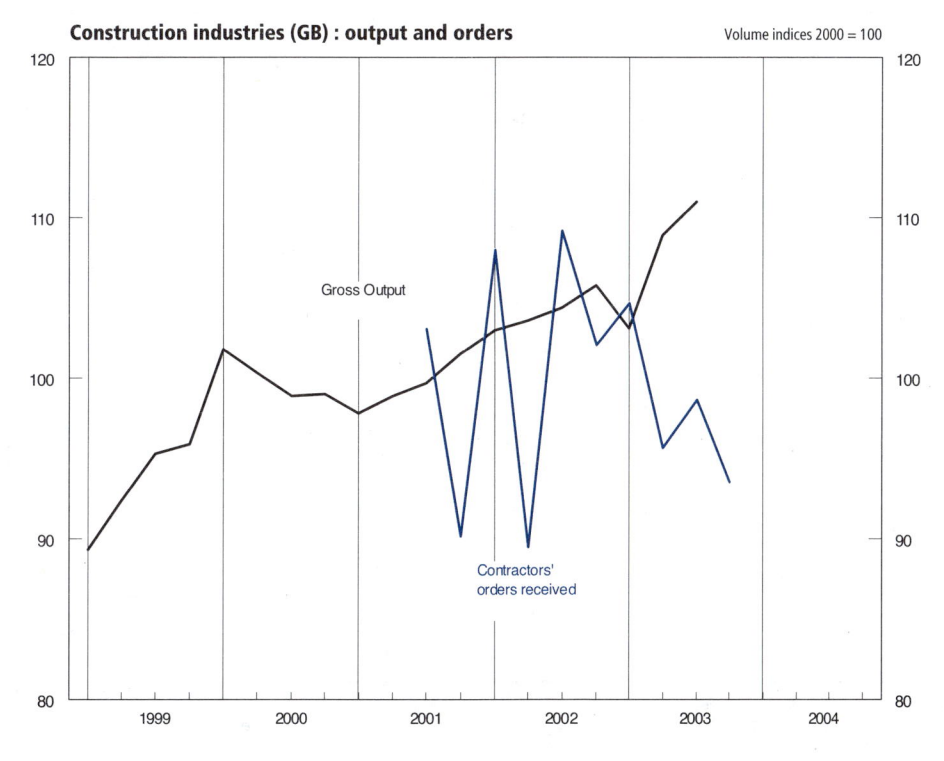

Construction industries (GB): output and orders

Volume indices 2000 = 100

- Gross Output
- Contractors' orders received

Office for National Statistics | 125

5.3 Motor vehicle and steel production

| | Passenger cars[1] |||| Commercial vehicles[1] |||| Crude steel production (NSA)[2] (thousand tonnes) |
| | Not seasonally adjusted || Seasonally adjusted[4] || Not seasonally adjusted || Seasonally adjusted[4] || |
	Total production (thousands)	of which for export (thousands)	Total production (thousands)	of which for export (thousands)	Total production (thousands)	of which for export (thousands)	Total production (thousands)	of which for export (thousands)	
Annual	FFAA	FFAB	FFAO	FFAP	FFAC	FFAD	FFAQ	FFAR	BCBS
1999	148.9	94.9	148.9	94.9	15.5	6.2	15.5	6.2	16 283.8
2000	136.8	88.6	136.8	88.6	14.3	6.3	14.4	6.3†	15 154.6
2001	124.4	74.5	124.4	74.5	16.1	8.0	16.1	8.0	13 542.7
2002	135.7	87.3†	135.8†	87.3†	15.9	9.5	15.9	9.5	11 667.1
2003	138.1	95.3	138.1	95.3	15.7	8.6	15.8†	8.6	13 268.0†
Quarterly									
1999 Q1	153.5	97.6	142.8	93.6†	17.8	7.5	16.7	6.9	4 126.5
Q2	149.6	97.7	144.8†	91.7	16.8	6.6	16.0†	6.3†	4 376.9
Q3	135.9	76.7	149.7	94.6	12.1	4.4	14.3	5.5	4 054.9
Q4	156.5	107.5	158.3	99.6	15.3	6.4	15.0	6.2	3 725.5
2000 Q1	164.8	105.0	151.8	100.4	16.7	8.4	15.3	7.8	4 442.5
Q2	144.4	97.6	140.9	91.5	17.3	8.2	16.7	7.9	4 019.8
Q3	111.7	63.2	126.2	79.1	9.5	3.5	11.9	4.6	3 288.7
Q4	126.3	88.6	128.2	83.3	13.7	5.2	13.6	5.0	3 403.6
2001 Q1	129.0	75.5	119.8	73.0	17.2	6.6	15.6	6.0	3 651.7
Q2	124.1	76.5	119.5	70.9	16.6	7.7	15.4	7.2	3 729.6
Q3	111.9	61.0	125.2	75.3	14.5	7.4	17.9	9.3	3 205.5
Q4	132.4	85.1	133.0	78.9	16.1	10.3	15.4	9.5	2 955.9
2002 Q1	149.9	85.0	138.8	82.0	16.7	8.4	15.2	7.9	3 046.3
Q2	133.5	94.0†	128.3	85.4	14.8	9.4	14.2	9.0	3 060.0
Q3	130.6	80.7	146.8	98.2	14.9	9.3	17.6	11.1	2 801.9
Q4	128.7	89.3	129.4	83.5	17.3	10.9	16.8	10.1	2 758.9
2003 Q1	141.4†	91.5	131.7	88.3	16.5	9.3	15.1	8.9	3 115.9
Q2	144.4	101.3	138.9	93.5	15.5	8.3	14.8	8.0	3 293.6
Q3	130.4	85.8	143.6	102.0	13.4	6.9	15.6	8.1	3 299.2†
Q4	136.2	102.7	138.3	97.4	17.6	9.7†	17.4	9.2	3 559.3
Monthly									
2002 Jan	154.4	84.9	144.5†	83.2†	16.7	8.4	15.0†	8.4†	1 119.7*
Feb	147.6	81.8	140.5	84.4	17.4	7.4	15.9	7.0	960.5
Mar	147.8	88.4	131.3	78.4	15.9	9.5	14.6	8.3	966.1
Apr	129.5	93.6†	136.7	90.7	16.5	11.1	16.2	10.3	1 003.4
May	158.2	109.5	145.0	90.6	15.8	9.9	15.8	9.9	1 204.9*
Jun	112.8	78.9	103.2	74.8	12.2	7.3	10.5	6.7	851.7
Jul	134.5	84.9	134.9	89.9	15.2	9.9	16.2	10.7	1 082.0
Aug	112.8	67.0	170.4	118.5	9.8	6.1	17.8	11.1	805.4
Sep	144.5	90.3	135.1	86.3	19.8	11.9	18.7	11.5	914.5
Oct	149.7	98.0	133.8	84.4	19.8	12.5	17.9	11.2	1 116.5*
Nov	138.8	98.7	129.3	84.0	18.8	11.2	17.0	9.7	846.0
Dec	97.5	71.2	125.2	82.2	13.4	9.0	15.6	9.4	796.4
2003 Jan	136.1	85.8	127.4	82.2	15.8	8.3	14.8	8.7	1 107.1*
Feb	136.3†	86.2	130.6	89.4	16.3	8.9	15.0	8.8	994.6
Mar	151.9	102.4	137.1	93.2	17.3	10.7	15.5	9.2	1 014.2
Apr	144.8	100.8	148.9	96.3	14.6	8.0	14.7	8.1	1 230.5*
May	133.1	97.6	127.8	86.8	14.0	7.5	14.4	7.6	1 034.9
Jun	155.4	105.6	140.1	97.3	18.0	9.5	15.4	8.4	1 028.2
Jul	146.3	93.1	144.5	100.7	15.2	7.6	16.1	8.6	1 257.4*
Aug	91.4	57.5	143.9	103.6	7.8	3.8	15.2	7.3	989.5
Sep	153.5	106.8	142.4	101.8	17.1	9.2	15.6	8.5	1 052.3†
Oct	153.4	113.8	137.0	96.6	16.8	9.5	15.6	8.6	1 209.7*
Nov	142.9	110.5	137.9	100.7	19.0	9.8	17.6	9.0	1 129.4
Dec	112.4	83.8	140.1	95.0	17.0	9.9†	19.1	10.1	1 220.2*
2004 Jan	141.3	96.4	140.2	100.0	20.5	9.6	19.6	10.1	1 077.6[3]

1 Annual and quarterly figures are monthly averages.
2 The totals are for 'usable steel' in accordance with the system used by the EC and the IISI, **but** in a change from previous publications, figures are actual production totals based on a four or five week period (not seasonally adjusted).
3 Provisional.
4 A seasonally adjusted series, based on the seasonal patterns of production from January 1999, has now been re-introduced. This affects the series from January 1999 only. Earlier data is based on previous production patterns.

Sources: Office for National Statistics; Enquiries Columns 1-8 01633 812810; ISSB Ltd; Enquiries Column 9 020 7343 3900

Economic Trends 604 March 2004

Tables section

Production of passenger cars – Seasonally adjusted Thousands

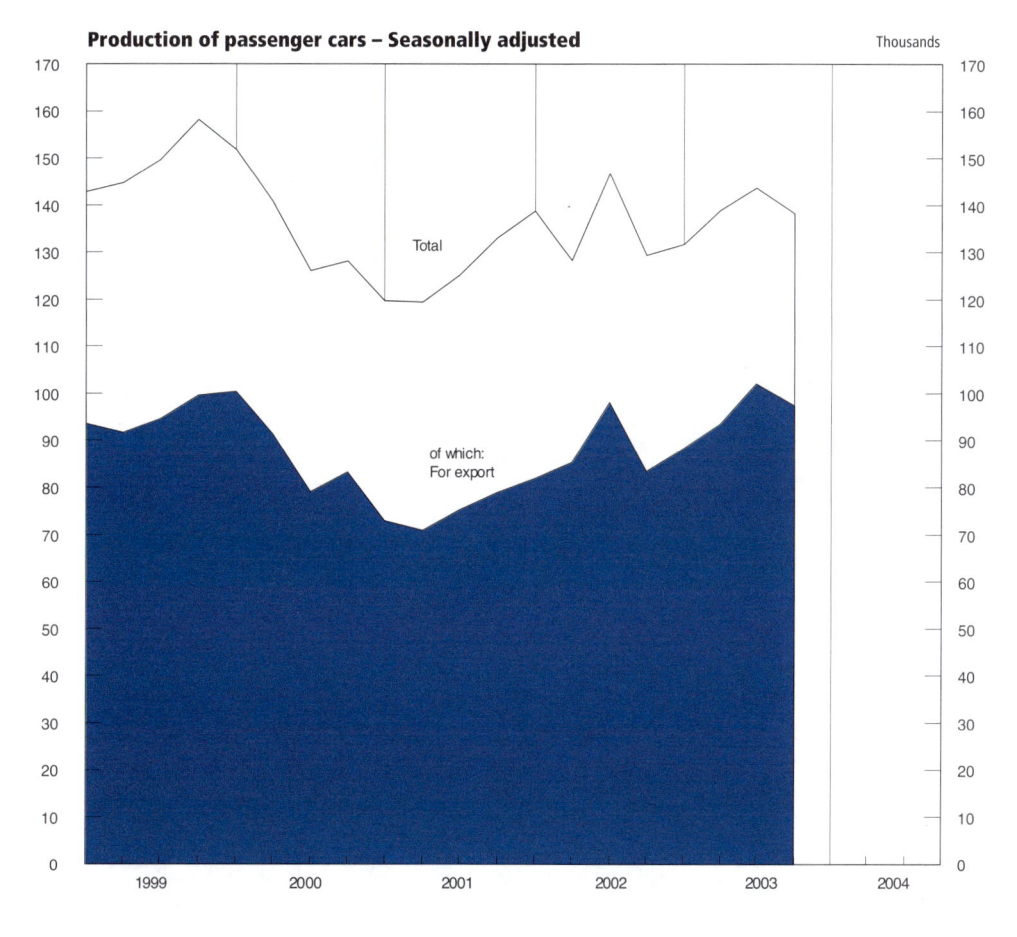

Production of commercial vehicles – Seasonally adjusted Thousands

Office for National Statistics | 127

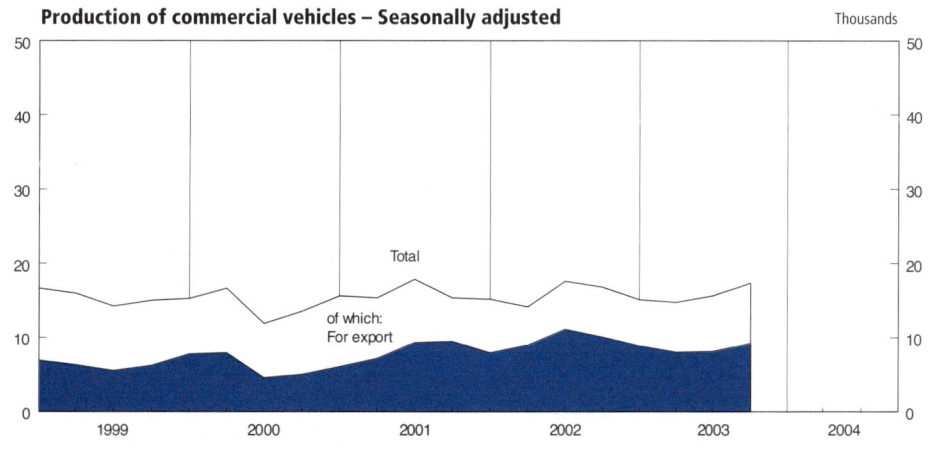

5.4 Indicators of fixed investment in dwellings

	Fixed investment in dwellings (£ million, chained volume measures, reference year 2000))	Orders received by contractors for new houses (GB) (£ million, 2000 prices)	Housing starts[1,2,3] (GB)+ Private enterprise (thousands)	Housing starts[1,2,3] (GB)+ Registered Social Landlords[4,5] (thousands)	Housing starts[1,2,3] (GB)+ Local Authorities (NSA) (thousands)	Housing completions[1,2,3] (GB)+ Private enterprise (thousands)	Housing completions[1,2,3] (GB)+ Registered Social Landlords[4,5] (thousands)	Housing completions[1,2,3] (GB)+ Local Authorities (NSA) (thousands)	Mix-adjusted price of new dwellings at mortgage completion stage(NSA)[6] (£)
Annual	DFEG	SGAB	FCAT	CTOQ	CTOU	FCAV	CTOS	CTOW	WMPS
2000	27 394	7 005	158.3	18.9	0.3	144.1	22.9	0.3	127 728
2001	27 999	7 084	162.9	16.9	0.3	140.3	21.2	0.5	134 234
2002	32 825	7 697	165.1	17.6	0.3	150.3	19.7	0.4	161 533
2003	..	8 070	..	..	..	..	..	..	186 485
Quarterly									
2000 Q1	7 016	..	41.6	5.1	0.1	37.7	5.6	–	118 944
Q2	6 970	..	39.5	4.9	–	36.8	5.9	0.1	125 917
Q3	6 819	..	40.0	4.3	0.1	35.3	4.7	0.1	130 215
Q4	6 589	..	36.7	4.5	0.1	35.5	6.6	0.1	135 936
2001 Q1	7 044	..	38.3	5.7	0.2	34.7	5.7	0.3	130 771
Q2	6 769	..	40.4	4.2	–	34.6	4.7	–	130 774
Q3	7 142	1 813	41.9	3.3	–	36.0	4.7	0.1	135 507
Q4	7 044	1 746	42.9	3.8	0.1	35.0	6.2	0.1	137 368
2002 Q1	7 572	1 905	41.0	5.5	0.1	36.4	5.2	–	143 996
Q2	7 812	1 754	39.6	4.2	0.1	38.1	4.6	0.2	157 646
Q3	8 401	2 000	42.7	4.3	–	36.3	4.5	–	164 293
Q4	9 040	2 039	42.6	3.7	0.1	39.4	5.5	0.1	173 254
2003 Q1	8 617[†]	2 059	44.6	4.6	0.1	38.2	5.0	0.2	175 947
Q2	9 077	2 078	..	..	..	..	..	..	187 676
Q3	9 379	1 857[†]	..	..	..	..	..	..	188 711[†]
Q4	..	2 076	..	..	..	..	..	..	193 605
Monthly									
2002 Jan	..	731	13.4	1.6	0.1	12.2	1.7	–	..
Feb	..	552	13.4	1.7	–	12.4	1.7	–	147 989
Mar	..	622	14.2	2.1	–	11.8	1.7	–	153 792
Apr	..	619	15.6	1.7	–	12.3	1.7	0.1	153 366
May	..	544	12.6	1.4	–	13.4	1.3	0.1	157 653
Jun	..	591	11.4	1.0	0.1	12.4	1.7	–	161 917
Jul	..	673	13.6	1.1	–	11.3	1.4	–	156 787
Aug	..	715	13.5	1.7	–	12.2	1.3	–	165 201
Sep	..	612	15.6	1.5	–	12.8	1.8	–	170 891
Oct	..	655	13.9	1.5	–	12.5	1.8	–	168 194
Nov	..	658	13.9	1.2	–	13.0	1.8	–	171 984
Dec	..	726	14.7	1.1	–	14.0	1.8	–	179 585
2003 Jan	..	773	14.6	1.4	–	11.4	1.5	–	175 758
Feb	..	636	16.0	1.5	–	13.7	1.6	–	174 039
Mar	..	649	14.0	1.8	0.1	13.1	1.9	0.1	178 045
Apr	..	745	..	..	..	..	..	..	188 126
May	..	689	..	..	..	..	..	..	187 498
Jun	..	644	..	..	..	..	..	..	187 403
Jul	..	677	..	..	..	..	..	..	186 807
Aug	..	587	..	..	..	..	..	..	191 100
Sep	..	593[†]	..	..	..	..	..	..	188 227[†]
Oct	..	727	..	..	..	..	..	..	195 551
Nov	..	715	..	..	..	..	..	..	189 913
Dec	..	634	..	..	..	..	..	..	193 352

1 Monthly data collection ceased after March 2003. Only quarterly data are now collected. Great Britain data for Q2 2003 is not yet available. Data for England, Scotland and Wales are available from the website of the Office of the Deputy Prime Minister: www.odpm.gov.uk
2 Data includes estimates for Scotland monthly, quarterly from Q4 2002, and annually from 2002.
3 The annual totals shown do not equal the equivalent non-seasonally adjusted annual totals because the adjustment was based on financial years.
4 Includes registered and non-registered social landlords.
5 The Registered social landlords series is seasonally adjusted to March 2000 only for England, to December 1996 only for Scotland, and unadjusted for Wales.
6 Series based on mortgage lending by all financial institutions rather than building societies only, as previously published. This change has been made necessary because of the mergers. takeovers and conversions to plc status affecting the building society sector. The series is based on the Office of the Deputy Prime Ministers' 5% Survey of Mortgage Lenders (at completion stage) up to 2003q2. From 2003q3, quarterly data are based on monthly data from the significantly enlarged Survey of Mortgage Lenders.

Sources: Office for National Statistics;
Enquiries Column 1 01633 812537;
Department of Trade and Industry ; Column 2 020 7944 5583;
Office of the Deputy Prime Minister;
Columns 3-8 0117 372 8055; Column 11 020 7944 3325

Fixed investment in dwellings £ million

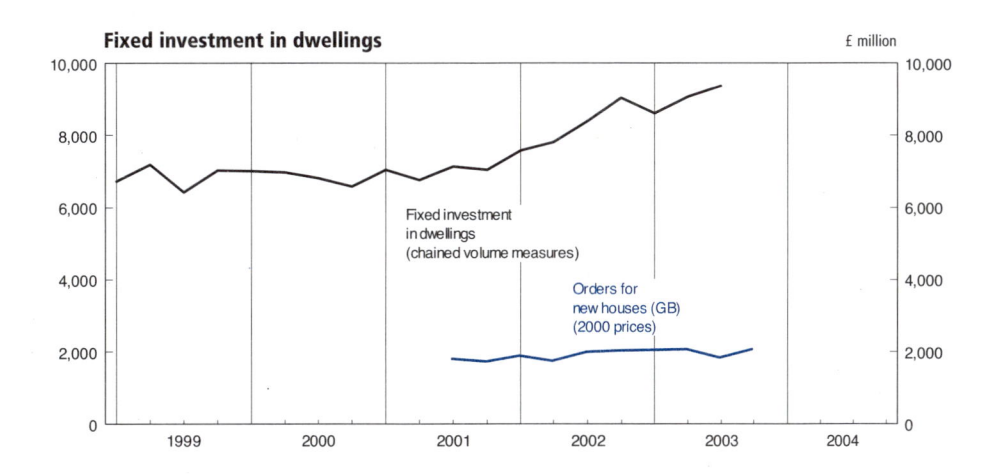

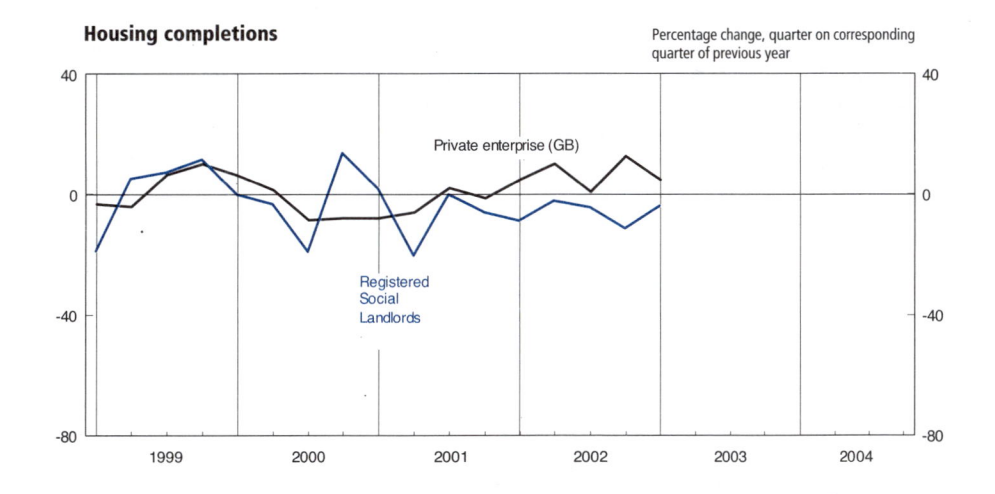

Housing completions Percentage change, quarter on corresponding quarter of previous year

5.5 Number of property transactions[1]

Thousands

	Number of property transactions				Number of property transactions		
	Not seasonally adjusted England & Wales	Seasonally adjusted England & Wales[2,3]	Not seasonally adjusted England, Wales & N. Ireland		Not seasonally adjusted England & Wales	Seasonally adjusted England & Wales[2,3]	Not seasonally adjusted England, Wales & N. Ireland
	FTAP		FTAR	Sep	140	125	145
1998	1 347		1 384	Oct	134	130	137
1999	1 469		1 511	Nov	141	129	144
2000	1 433		1 471	Dec	122	128	125
2001	1 458		1 497				
2002	1 586		1 627	2000 Jan	137	136	140
				Feb	112	128	116
2003	1 333		1 385	Mar	118	128	122
				Apr	97	114	100
		FTAQ		May	122	120	126
1998 Q1	317	344	327	Jun	129	122	130
Q2	317	332	327				
Q3	377	345	386	Jul	127	117	130
Q4	335	326	345	Aug	134	117	137
				Sep	117	112	121
1999 Q1	316	345	325	Oct	123	112	127
Q2	342	358	354	Nov	117	111	121
Q3	414	379	425	Dec	98	114	101
Q4	397	388	407				
				2001 Jan	123	113	127
2000 Q1	367	392	379	Feb	99	117	102
Q2	348	356	356	Mar	105	116	108
Q3	379	346	388	Apr	101	115	105
Q4	339	338	349	May	121	122	126
				Jun	125	125	128
2001 Q1	327	346	337				
Q2	347	363	360	Jul	132	120	135
Q3	396	369	405	Aug	140	125	143
Q4	387	379	396	Sep	124	124	127
				Oct	140	125	143
2002 Q1	342	374	351	Nov	137	131	141
Q2	395	410	404	Dec	110	123	112
Q3	457	417	468				
Q4	392	385	404	2002 Jan	131	120	134
				Feb	108	127	110
2003 Q1	340	361	359	Mar	104	127	106
Q2	306	323	320	Apr	129	135	132
Q3	358	327	369	May	137	140	140
Q4	329	322	337	Jun	129	135	132
1998 Jan	119	114	122	Jul	152	134	154
Feb	94	114	97	Aug	166	149	171
Mar	104	116	108	Sep	139	134	144
Apr	103	110	106	Oct	147	131	151
May	96	109	99	Nov	127	124	131
Jun	119	113	122	Dec	118	131	122
Jul	129	113	132	2003 Jan	131	121	137
Aug	119	116	121	Feb	103	120	109
Sep	129	116	133	Mar	106	119	113
Oct	119	109	122	Apr	101	113	108
Nov	110	106	113	May	101	106	105
Dec	107	111	110	Jun	103	105	107
1999 Jan	112	115	116	Jul	132	115	135
Feb	96	116	99	Aug	112	106	116
Mar	108	115	110	Sep	114	106	118
Apr	110	122	114	Oct	120	108	124
May	106	117	110	Nov	110	109	113
Jun	126	119	130	Dec[4]	99	105	101
Jul	140	129	144	2004 Jan[4]	117	110	120
Aug	134	125	137				

1 The figures are based on counts of the relevant administrative forms processed each month. Because of the time lags involved, the series above should be lagged by one month to give a broad representation of transactions occurring in the month, although this relationship will be weaker in the second quarter of 2002 because of the operational pressures in the network of Stamp Offices which delayed the processing of a proportion of property transactions.

2 The Jubilee celebrations meant that the late May bank holiday was taken in June 2002. Seasonal features in the data arising from the May Bank holiday will therefore not automatically be removed by the process of seasonal adjustment. Caution should therefore be taken when interpreting monthly movements involving May or June 2002 data.

3 The sum of seasonally adjusted components does not exactly match the unadjusted (definitive) annual total.

4 Because of the change in processing arrangements associated with the introduction of stamp duty land tax, the numbers recorded for December and January are slightly depressed compared to previous months.

Source: Board of Inland Revenue; Enquiries 020 7438 6314

5.6 Change in inventories
Chained volume measures[1]

Reference year 2000, £ million

	Mining and quarrying	Manufacturing industries				Electricity, gas and water supply	Distributive trades		Other industries[3]	Change in inventories
		Materials and fuel	Work in progress	Finished goods	Total		Wholesale[2]	Retail[2]		
Level of inventories at end-December 2002	930	20 845	16 155	19 806	56 806	1 219	27 064	22 024	37 223	145 266
Quarterly										
	FAEA	FBNF	FBNG	FBNH	DHBM	FAEB	FAJX	FBYN	DLWX	CAFU
1999 Q1	22	216	−230	−4	−16	−36	156	442	2 176	2 742
Q2	−86	−29	−32	−481	−541	−3	407	600	105	476
Q3	−94	158	257	22	437	−101	387	321	729	1 677
Q4	−62	344	−113	−2	231	−23	742	129	506	1 531
2000 Q1	−36	139	400	102	640	71	620	599	−1 069	819
Q2	1	375	−91	114	399	37	440	363	17	1 262
Q3	−34	293	−80	67	282	78	750	320	538	1 941
Q4	−108	−76	291	188	401	99	93	−13	783	1 249
2001 Q1	−3	150	2	426	578	−355	266	235	74	795
Q2	−5	−241	−84	110	−215	164	458	118	1 286	1 806
Q3	32	−409	43	−172	−538	80	339	152	290	355
Q4	−3	−104	−264	47	−321	30	−584	9	851	−18
2002 Q1	236	538	99	−90	547	−276	−1 670	521	1 378	736
Q2	−74	−507	−476	−334	−1 317	51	712	848	−998	−778
Q3	−84	−436	−60	−212	−708	84	212	397	109	10
Q4	−87	−252	−145	−92	−489	103	543	92	1 366	1 528
2003 Q1	−30	−42	20	−149	−171	−203	−153	−4	1 542†	981†
Q2	60	−380	64	82	−234	82	−52	247	−168	−65
Q3	−13	53	87	361	501	−37	366	205	−365	657
Q4	−19	−74	−138	−115	−327	−30	−159	117	385	−33

1 Estimates are given to the nearest £ million but cannot be regarded as accurate to this degree.
2 Wholesaling and retailing estimates exclude the motor trades.
3 Quarterly alignment adjustment included in this series. For description see notes to the *Economic Trends Annual Supplement*. For details of adjustments, see notes section in the Sector and Financial Accounts article in *UK Economic Accounts*.

Sources: Office for National Statistics; Enquiries Columns 1-8 01633 812351;
Columns 9-10 020 7533 5949

5.7 Inventory ratios

	Manufacturers' inventories[1] to manufacturing production				Retail inventories[1] to retail sales[2]	Total inventories[1,3] to gross value added
	Materials and fuel	Work in progress	Finished goods	Total inventories		
Quarterly						
	FAPG	FAPH	FAPI	FAPF	FAPC	FDCA
1999 Q1	99.8	99.6	104.6	101.3	96.3	100
Q2	99.3	99.1	101.7	100.1	98.6	100
Q3	98.6	99.2	100.4	99.4	99.0	101
Q4	99.9	98.1	100.0	99.4	98.5	101
2000 Q1	100.0	100.0	100.0	100.0	100.0	100
Q2	101.1	98.9	100.0	100.1	101.8	100
Q3	102.3	98.2	100.1	100.4	102.1	101
Q4	101.0	99.0	100.2	100.1	101.1	101
2001 Q1	101.8	99.1	102.4	101.2	100.6	101
Q2	102.8	100.7	105.1	103.0	99.1	102
Q3	101.0	101.1	104.3	102.2	98.2	102
Q4	102.6	101.6	106.7	103.7	97.0	102
2002 Q1	106.1	103.0	107.2	105.6	97.4	102
Q2	105.0	101.4	106.8	104.5	99.6	101
Q3	101.8	100.0	104.5	102.2	100.6	101
Q4	101.4	99.9	104.9	102.2	99.5	101
2003 Q1	101.3	100.1	104.2	102.0	100.2	101
Q2	98.9	100.0	104.1	101.0	99.8	100
Q3	99.0	100.3	105.8	101.7	99.1	99
Q4	..	..	..	..	..	98

1 Chained volume measure: reference year 2000
2 Classes 64-65 excluding activity headings 6510 and 6520, retail distribution of motor vehicles and parts, and filling stations.
3 Including quarterly alignment adjustment. For details of adjustments see notes section in the Sector and Financial Accounts article in *UK EconomicAccounts*.

Source: Office for National Statistics; Enquiries Columns 1-6 01633 812351

Inventory ratios

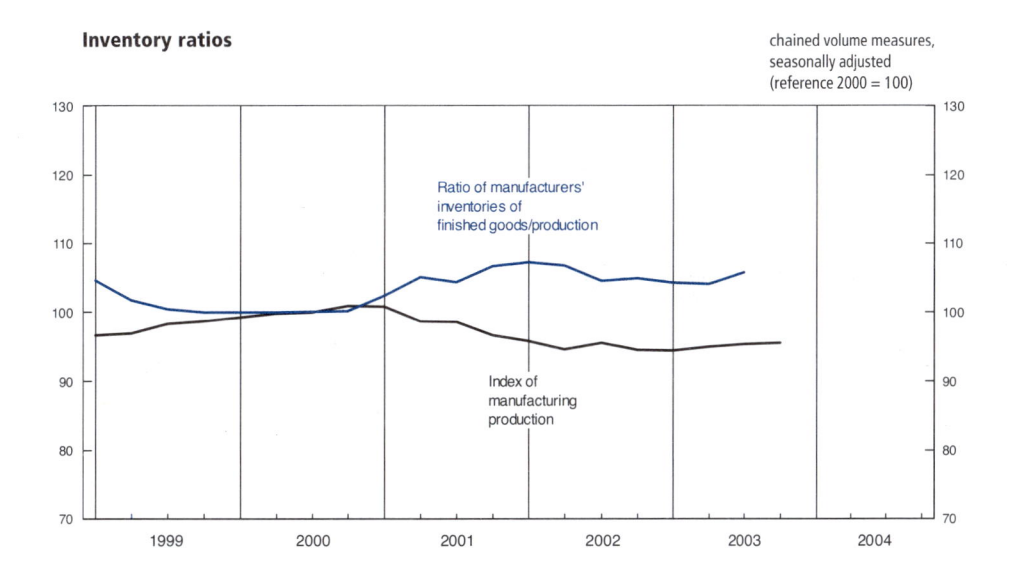

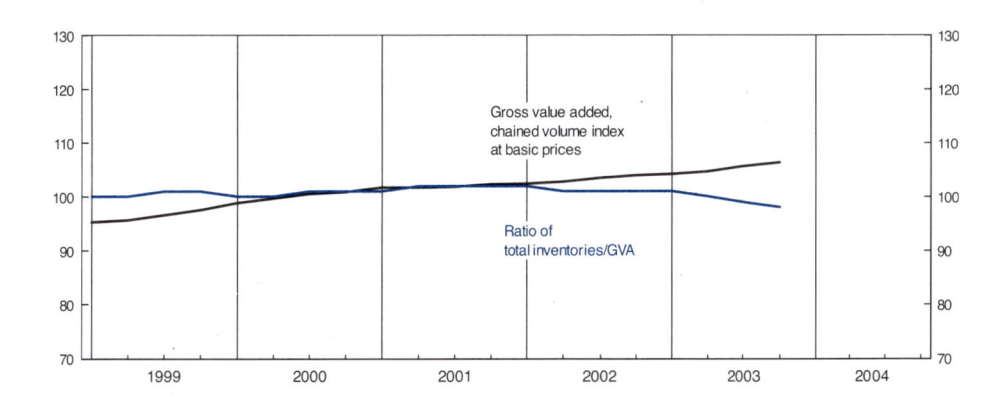

chained volume measures, seasonally adjusted (reference 2000 = 100)

5.8 Retail sales, new registrations of cars and credit business (Great Britain)

	Value of retail sales per week: total (average 2000=100)[1,2]	Volume of retail sales per week+(average 2000=100)[1,2]								New registrations of cars (NSA, thousands)[5]	Total consumer credit: Net lending (£ million)[3,4]	of which	
		All retailers	Predominantly food stores	Predominantly non-food stores								Credit cards[6]	Other[6]
				Total	Non-specialist stores	Textile, clothing and footwear	Household goods stores	Other stores	Non-store and repair				

Sales in 2000 £ million	207 149	207 149	89 041	106 359	18 781	27 880	27 699	31 999	11 749				
Annual													
	EAQV	EAPS	EAPT	EAPV	EAPU	EAPX	EAPY	EAPW	EAPZ	BCGT	RLMH	VZQX	VZQY
2000	100.0	100.0	100.0	100.0	100.0	100.0	100.0	100.0	100.0	2 337.3	14 149†	6 619†	7 525†
2001	105.9	106.1	104.1	107.7	105.9	109.4	110.9	104.6	106.1	2 577.5	17 611	6 248	11 446
2002	111.2†	112.7†	108.2†	116.4†	110.4†	120.9	120.9	112.2†	113.4	2 682.0	21 050	7 566	13 529
2003	114.0†	116.6†	111.8†	121.6†	113.7†	129.3	126.4†	115.4†	107.9	2 646.2	19 055	8 112	10 943
Quarterly													
2000 Q1	99.0	99.0	99.3	98.6	100.6	96.1	99.6	98.8	100.3	682.4	4 127†	1 741†	2 539†
Q2	99.1	99.1	99.4	98.8	98.4	98.3	99.0	99.5	99.2	581.4	3 525	1 799	1 713
Q3	100.3	100.5	100.3	100.8	99.4	101.5	100.5	101.1	99.5	612.5	2 911	1 542	1 398
Q4	101.6	101.4	101.0	101.8	101.7	104.1	100.9	100.6	101.0	461.0	3 586	1 537	1 875
2001 Q1	102.8	103.1	102.8	103.7	104.1	104.9	107.1	99.3	100.5	704.2	3 330	1 350	2 147
Q2	105.5	105.3	103.7	106.6	106.0	107.4	110.6	102.6	106.8	617.7	4 605	1 752	2 835
Q3	107.0	107.1	104.6	109.0	106.8	111.0	111.5	106.2	109.6	725.6	4 131	1 226	2 920
Q4	108.0	108.4	105.6	110.9	107.3	113.3	113.8	108.3	107.7	530.0	5 545	1 920	3 544
2002 Q1	110.1	110.8	106.7	114.7	108.9	118.2	117.7	112.5	106.1	758.7	5 144	1 982	3 206
Q2	111.2	112.8	108.0	116.7	109.7	121.2	119.6	114.4	113.2	650.0	4 791	1 774	3 066
Q3	111.9	113.7	109.1	117.2	112.2	122.4	121.6	111.6	117.5	744.6	5 939	2 001	3 879
Q4	113.3	115.4	110.8	118.9	113.3	122.7	124.3	114.1	119.1	528.7	5 176	1 809	3 378
2003 Q1	112.3†	114.4†	110.2†	119.0†	111.8†	125.8†	122.8†	114.0†	105.1†	737.6	5 028	2 203	2 805
Q2	113.5	116.1	112.1	120.7	112.7	128.2	126.4	113.9	105.3	642.7	5 251	2 416	2 915
Q3	114.8	117.5	113.1	122.8	114.7	130.4	128.7	115.8	103.8	742.8	4 855	1 997	2 763
Q4	116.5	119.6	113.9	126.0	117.7	131.6	132.0	120.9	105.6	523.1	3 921	1 496	2 460
Monthly													
2002 Jan	109.1	109.4	106.3	112.4	108.4	114.4	114.9	110.7	106.8	213.5	1 862†	738†	1 124†
Feb	110.6	111.5	107.0	115.7	109.6	119.6	118.0	113.8	107.4	98.9	2 139	955	1 184
Mar	110.9	111.6	106.9	116.3	108.7	120.8	120.2	113.3	104.3	446.3	1 371	375	996
Apr	112.7	113.9	107.3	119.6	111.3	126.6	119.4	118.5	112.8	214.0	1 874	662	1 212
May	111.2	112.6	108.2	116.5	111.2	117.7	120.9	114.6	111.2	219.0	1 696	405	1 292
Jun	110.2	111.9	108.3	114.6	107.2	119.7	118.8	110.9	115.2	217.0	1 201	554	648
Jul	111.7	113.4	109.1	116.8	112.7	122.2	120.6	111.1	116.0	204.7	1 885	664	1 222
Aug	111.8	113.8	109.2	117.0	111.3	124.0	120.4	111.3	119.1	93.0	2 043	775	1 268
Sep	112.0	113.9	109.1	117.6	112.4	121.4	123.3	112.3	117.5	446.9	1 872	721	1 152
Oct	113.1	114.9	110.0	118.6	113.5	123.2	123.9	113.0	119.0	193.0	2 134	486	1 648
Nov	112.8	114.9	110.4	118.4	113.7	118.6	125.6	114.9	117.6	182.9	1 263	606	656
Dec	113.9	116.2	111.8	119.5	112.8	125.6	123.7	114.3	120.5	152.8	1 738	587	1 150
2003 Jan	111.6†	113.8†	109.0†	118.7†	112.3†	124.1†	123.1†	114.0†	104.8†	193.4	1 435	810	625
Feb	112.4	114.3	110.4	118.7	111.0	125.7	122.7	113.5	105.3	92.2	1 822	749	1 073
Mar	112.9	115.0	111.1	119.4	112.0	127.2	122.6	114.2	105.3	452.0	1 692	779	912
Apr	113.4	115.8	112.0	119.9	111.5	127.4	125.5	113.5	107.0	196.3	1 440	620	819
May	113.0	115.6	111.7	120.1	112.3	125.9	127.3	113.3	104.5	202.6	1 991	850	1 142
Jun	113.9	116.8	112.4	121.8	113.9	130.7	126.4	114.6	104.7	243.8	1 749	728	1 021
Jul	114.1	116.8	112.5	121.7	113.8	129.4	127.5	114.4	104.6	201.1	1 716	674	1 042
Aug	114.8	117.4	113.5	122.3	114.8	128.7	128.5	115.7	103.0	94.2	1 596	731	865
Sep	115.4	118.3	113.3	124.0	115.2	132.5	129.7	116.9	103.8	447.5	1 735	831	905
Oct	116.1	119.0	113.6	125.0	117.3	132.1	130.2	119.0	104.6	186.6	1 640	664	976
Nov	116.2	119.4	113.5	125.7	116.7	131.0	131.5	121.3	106.8	175.7	1 467	475	992
Dec	117.0	120.4	114.3	127.1	118.7	131.6	133.9	122.1	105.5	160.8	873	166	707
2004 Jan	118.0	121.0	114.4	127.9	116.2	134.7	132.9	124.4	109.8	..	1 928	744	1 184

1 Great Britain only. The motor trades are excluded. Information for periods earlier than those shown is available from ONS Newport (tel 01633 812509).
2 The retail sales index has been rebased using detailed information from the 2000 Annual Business inquiry. Further information is available via the National Statistics website: www.statistics.gov.uk
3 Net lending equals changes in amounts outstanding adjusted to remove distortions arising from revaluations of debt such as write-offs.
4 Covers all institutions providing finance for consumers; including loans by banks on personal accounts and on bank credit cards and charge cards, by insurance companies, retailers and other specialist lenders, but excluding loans for house purchase.
5 Seasonally adjusted data are not published in Economic Trends at present. Series DKBY ends in 1998 because seasonal adjustment has ceased; the existing model is not applicable to the new bi-annual registration system. It is published in the Economic Trends Annual Supplement.
6 See Table 6.6, note 2.

Sources: Office for National Statistics;
Enquiries Columns 1-9 01633 812713; Columns 12-14 01633 812782.;
Department of Transport;
Enquiries Column 10,11 020 7944 3077.

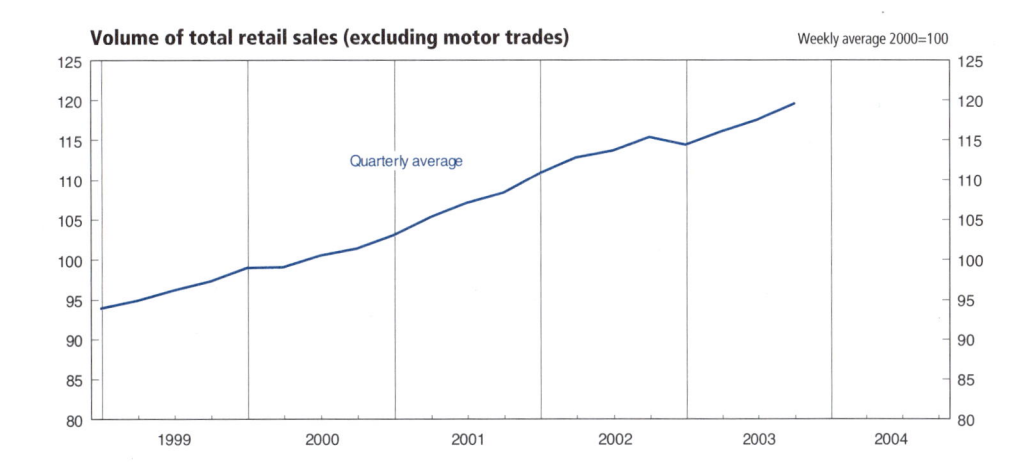

Economic Trends 604 March 2004

Tables section

Volume of total retail sales (excluding motor trades) — Weekly average 2000=100

Quarterly average

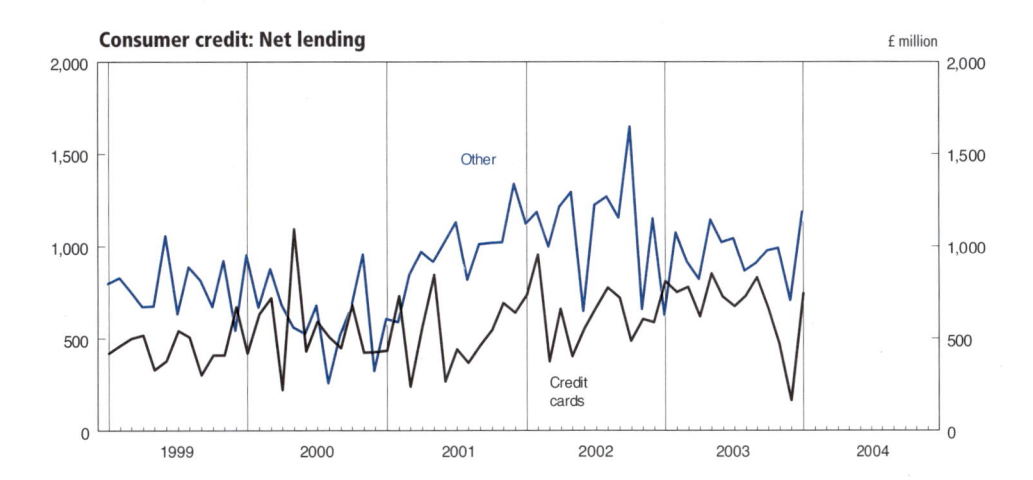

Consumer credit: Net lending — £ million

Other

Credit cards

5.9 Inland energy consumption: primary fuel input basis

Million tonnes of oil equivalent

Seasonally adjusted and temperature corrected[7] (annualised rates)

	Coal[1]	Petroleum[2]	Natural gas[3]	Nuclear	Primary electricity[5] Natural flow Hydro[4]	Net imports[6]	Total
Annual	FDAI	FDAJ	FDAK	FDAL	FDAM	FDAW	FDAH
1998	43.6	76.8	90.4	23.4	0.5	1.1	235.8
1999	38.1†	77.7†	95.8	22.2	0.5	1.2	235.7†
2000	40.0	77.8	98.8	19.7	0.5	1.2	238.0
2001	43.0	76.0	96.9	20.8	0.4	0.9	238.1
2002	39.8	73.5	99.5	20.1	0.6	0.7	234.2
Quarterly							
1998 Q1	43.9	76.5	97.6	23.4	0.5	1.4	243.4
Q2	46.3	79.7	87.7	22.3	0.5	1.4	237.9
Q3	45.2	77.2	79.8	23.1	0.6	0.3	226.2
Q4	38.9	73.9	96.6	24.7	0.4	1.2	235.7
1999 Q1	37.4†	80.4†	104.9	23.4	0.5	1.2	247.9†
Q2	37.5	79.6	90.1	23.1	0.6	1.3	232.3
Q3	38.2	77.2	84.9	21.6	0.5	1.1	223.6
Q4	39.4	73.8	103.4	20.8	0.5	1.2	239.1
2000 Q1	39.0	80.2	110.5	20.2	0.6	1.1	251.6
Q2	40.2	75.6	95.2	19.8	0.5	1.3	232.5
Q3	39.9	80.3	86.5	19.5	0.5	1.3	227.8
Q4	40.9	75.1	103.1	19.2	0.5	1.2	240.0
2001 Q1	45.9	74.2	108.2	20.0	0.3	1.1	249.8
Q2	43.7	73.8	93.1	19.0	0.4	0.9	230.9
Q3	41.9	81.5	86.0	22.0	0.5	0.9	232.9
Q4	40.4	74.6	100.3	22.4	0.5	0.7	238.9
2002 Q1	42.4	74.0	108.1	21.4	0.6	0.6	247.2
Q2	34.9	76.1	96.6	20.0	0.7	1.0	229.3
Q3	37.8	77.2	90.5	20.1	0.5	0.2	226.4
Q4	46.3	66.8	102.8	18.8	0.4	1.1	234.1
2003 Q1	43.6	70.6	107.7	21.6	0.3	0.3	244.2
Q2	43.2	82.1	93.3	21.1	0.5	0.1	240.2
Q3	43.6	70.6	107.7	21.6	0.3	0.3	244.2

Percentage change, quarter on corresponding quarter of previous year

	FDAP	FDAQ	FDAR	FDAS	FDAT	FDAX	FDAO
Quarterly							
1998 Q1	-3.6	1.7	4.7	2.9	..	-1.3	2.2
Q2	15.7	4.3	4.3	-2.7	..	-2.0	5.8
Q3	3.9	5.8	-0.5	5.8	..	-78.8	-1.7
Q4	-13.6	-2.3	5.3	20.3	..	-19.4	-1.6
1999 Q1	-13.9†	6.1†	7.5	-0.2	-0.1	-14.1	2.3†
Q2	-18.6	–	2.8	3.6	22.2	-6.8	-2.3
Q3	-14.9	0.2	6.4	-6.5	-9.8	–	-0.9
Q4	1.6	0.3	7.0	-15.6	4.7	5.6	1.5
2000 Q1	4.2	-0.2	5.3	-13.7	11.7	-10.6	1.5
Q2	7.0	-5.1	5.6	-14.5	-25.2	1.9	0.1
Q3	4.4	4.0	1.8	-9.8	-13.0	12.9	1.9
Q4	3.7	1.8	-0.3	-7.8	5.9	-5.1	0.3
2001 Q1	17.5	-7.5	-2.0	-0.9	-43.9	–	-0.7
Q2	8.8	-2.4	-2.2	-4.0	-9.2	-30.3	-0.7
Q3	5.2	1.5	-0.5	13.0	5.0	-29.0	2.2
Q4	-1.2	-0.7	-2.7	16.4	6.1	-45.0	-0.5
2002 Q1	-7.5	-0.3	-0.1	7.0	74.1	-43.7	-1.0
Q2	-20.1	3.1	3.8	5.6	73.7	5.5	-0.7
Q3	-9.9	-5.2	5.1	-8.7	12.2	-75.5	-2.8
Q4	9.7	-10.5	2.4	-15.9	-32.1	67.6	-2.0
2003 Q1	2.9	-4.6	-0.4	0.9	-44.4	-56.2	-1.2
Q2	23.9	7.9	-3.4	5.1	-32.0	-89.0	4.8
Q3	15.5	-8.5	19.0	7.3	-39.0	23.7	7.9

1 Includes solid renewable sources (wood, straw, waste), and net foreign trade and stock changes in other solid fuels.
2 Excludes non-energy use.
3 Includes gas used during production, colliery methane, landfill gas and sewage gas. Excludes gas flared or re-injected and non energy-use of gas.
4 Includes generations at wind stations. Excludes generation from pumped storage stations.
5 Not temperature corrected.
6 Not seasonally adjusted.
7 For details of temperature correction see DTI energy statistics website at **www.dti.gov.uk/energy/inform/dukes/dukes2002/01longterm.pdf**

Source: Department of Trade and Industry; Enquiries 020 7215 2698

Economic Trends 604 March 2004

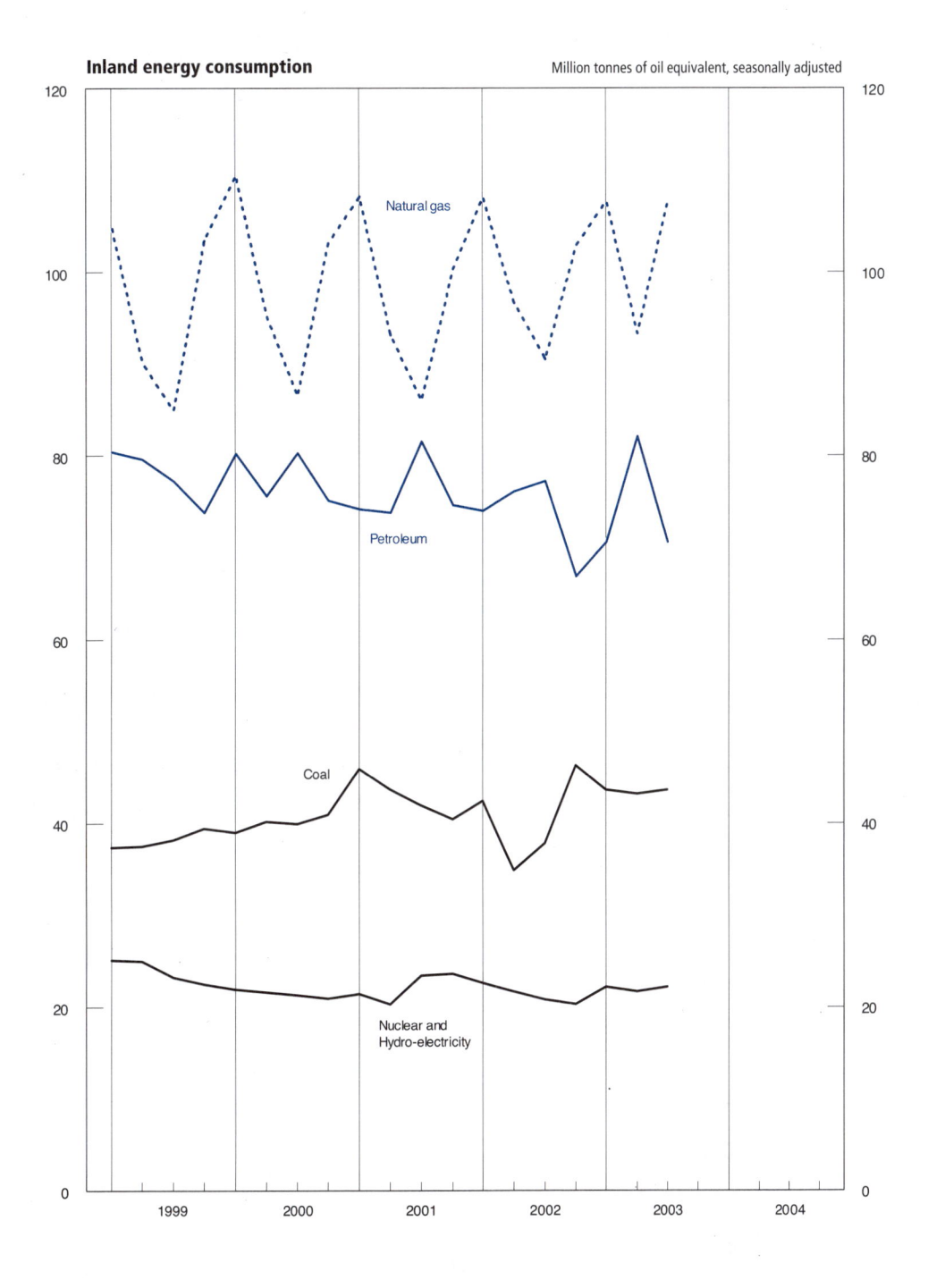

Tables section

Inland energy consumption — Million tonnes of oil equivalent, seasonally adjusted

- Natural gas
- Petroleum
- Coal
- Nuclear and Hydro-electricity

Office for National Statistics | 137

6.1 Sterling exchange rates and UK reserves[4]

Not seasonally adjusted

	Japanese yen	US dollar	Swiss franc	Euro[2]	Danish kroner	Norwegian kroner	Swedish kronor	Hong Kong dollar	UK international reserves[3] at end of period (£ million)	Sterling exchange rate index 1990 = 100
	AJFO	AUSS	AJFD	THAP	AJFK	AJFJ	AJFI	AJFU	THFE	AGBG
Annual										
1999	184.01	1.6183	2.430	1.5192	11.296	12.619	13.373	12.5541	25 938	103.8
2000	163.40	1.5162	2.558	1.6422	12.240	13.324	13.870	11.8057	32 227	107.5
2001	174.90	1.4400	2.430	1.6087	11.987	12.944	14.886	11.2312	27 773	105.8
2002	187.84	1.5026	2.334	1.5909	11.821	11.953	14.570	11.7265	26 566	106.0
2003	189.34	1.6346†	2.197	1.4456	10.742	11.562	13.189	12.7337	25 677	100.2
Quarterly										
1999 Q1	190.19	1.6335	2.328	1.4574	10.8368	12.514	13.059	12.6531	..	101.1
Q2	194.13	1.6070	2.432	1.5209	11.3044	12.527	13.539	12.4547	..	104.1
Q3	181.35	1.6021	2.446	1.5271	11.3547	12.561	13.304	12.4369	21 447	103.8
Q4	170.35	1.6306	2.515	1.5712	11.6851	12.874	13.588	12.6721	25 938	105.9
2000 Q1	171.99	1.6067	2.617	1.6286	12.1257	13.206	13.835	12.4926	22 090	108.4
Q2	163.52	1.5334	2.568	1.6398	12.2271	13.466	13.584	11.9236	26 898	107.7
Q3	159.19	1.4784	2.522	1.6336	12.1862	13.232	13.726	11.5304	28 818	106.4
Q4	158.89	1.4464	2.523	1.6670	12.4250	13.394	14.333	11.2735	32 227	107.6
2001 Q1	172.26	1.4584	2.424	1.5814	11.7988	12.965	14.230	11.3765	30 457	104.5
Q2	174.19	1.4208	2.487	1.6280	12.1436	13.039	14.847	11.0866	30 632	106.4
Q3	174.67	1.4380	2.432	1.6152	12.0231	12.928	15.203	11.2092	29 662	106.1
Q4	178.45	1.4428	2.375	1.6111	11.9887	12.845	15.264	11.2548	27 773	106.1
2002 Q1	188.79	1.4260	2.396	1.6263	12.0863	12.700	14.895	11.1230	28 053	106.9
Q2	185.29	1.4630	2.329	1.5923	11.8379	11.956	14.564	11.4015	28 623	105.3
Q3	184.85	1.5495	2.305	1.5747	11.6973	11.662	14.538	12.0871	27 950	105.7
Q4	192.42	1.5720	2.304	1.5716	11.6733	11.494	14.285	12.2547	26 566	106.0
2003 Q1	190.67	1.6017†	2.189	1.4937	11.0987	11.313	13.709	12.5030	26 349	102.3
Q2	191.90	1.6194	2.163	1.4256	10.5851	11.344	13.032	12.6352	25 147	99.1
Q3	189.14	1.6108	2.209	1.4300	10.6264	11.794	13.103	12.5605	26 909	99.2
Q4	185.64	1.7065	2.228	1.4334	10.6591	11.796	12.913	13.2305	25 677	100.2
Monthly										
2001 Jul	176.07	1.4139	2.487	1.6433	12.234	13.095	15.225	11.0279	29 187	107.2
Aug	174.42	1.4365	2.416	1.5955	11.878	12.853	14.844	11.2038	29 669	105.1
Sep	173.53	1.4635	2.394	1.6060	11.951	12.837	15.540	11.4144	29 662	106.1
Oct	176.14	1.4517	2.371	1.6024	11.917	12.813	15.338	11.3230	28 090	105.8
Nov	175.67	1.4358	2.370	1.6166	12.036	12.813	15.233	11.1984	28 733	106.1
Dec	183.55	1.4409	2.384	1.6151	12.021	12.908	15.220	11.2375	27 773	106.5
2002 Jan	190.01	1.4323	2.392	1.6222	12.057	12.844	14.972	11.1705	27 089	106.9
Feb	190.11	1.4231	2.415	1.6348	12.146	12.731	15.013	11.0993	27 940	107.4
Mar	186.26	1.4225	2.381	1.6224	12.059	12.525	14.700	11.0946	28 053	106.5
Apr	188.50	1.4434	2.386	1.6282	12.104	12.415	14.878	11.2581	28 191	107.1
May	184.26	1.4593	2.318	1.5914	11.833	11.963	14.676	11.3814	28 055	105.3
Jun	183.10	1.4863	2.284	1.5515	11.532	11.491	14.137	11.5934	28 623	103.6
Jul	183.50	1.5546	2.290	1.5665	11.640	11.615	14.528	12.1261	27 649	105.3
Aug	182.97	1.5377	2.302	1.5723	11.677	11.698	14.550	11.9944	28 208	105.4
Sep	188.07	1.5561	2.323	1.5861	11.780	11.672	14.537	12.1370	27 950	106.5
Oct	192.90	1.5574	2.325	1.5868	11.790	11.645	14.450	12.1464	28 322	106.7
Nov	190.99	1.5723	2.303	1.5694	11.654	11.484	14.237	12.2624	28 972	105.9
Dec	193.36	1.5863	2.284	1.5566	11.560	11.354	14.167	12.3711	26 566	105.5
2003 Jan	192.07	1.6169	2.226	1.5222	11.314	11.172	13.964	12.6105	24 708	104.0
Feb	192.12	1.6046	2.189	1.4893	11.091	11.262	13.652	12.5450	26 140	102.4
Mar	187.82	1.5836	2.152	1.4649	10.880	11.506	13.511	12.3503	26 349	100.6
Apr	188.79	1.5747	2.170	1.4505	10.771	11.347	13.279	12.2817	25 232	99.8
May	190.42	1.6230	2.125	1.4030	10.417	11.047	12.840	12.6579	25 371	97.9
Jun	196.49	1.6606	2.193	1.4234	10.569	11.638	12.978	12.9502	25 147	99.6
Jul	192.72	1.6242	2.209	1.4277	10.613	11.828	13.130	12.6671	25 736	99.4
Aug	189.42	1.5950	2.200	1.4286	10.617	11.800	13.186	12.4395	26 511	99.0
Sep	185.29	1.6131	2.219	1.4338	10.649	11.755	12.994	12.5590	26 909	99.2
Oct	183.76	1.6787	2.220	1.4334	10.651	11.807	12.917	12.9962	26 092	99.8
Nov	184.47	1.6901	2.250	1.4426	10.729	11.832	12.973	13.1201	26 572	100.4
Dec	188.70	1.7507	2.214	1.4246	10.602	11.749	12.850	13.5923	25 677	100.3
2004 Jan	193.82	1.8234	2.262	1.4447	10.760	12.425	13.203	14.1598	..	102.4

1 Average of daily Telegraphic Transfer rates in London.
2 Prior to January 1999, a synthetic Euro has been calculated by geometrically averaging the bilateral exchange rates of the 11 Euro-area countries using "internal weights" based on each country's share of the extra Euro-area trade.
3 International reserves data are all valued at end-period market prices and exchange rates. They additionally include other reserve assets such as repos (sale and purchase agreements) and derivatives. Full details are shown in Table 1.2I of *Financial Statistics*.
4 These figures fall outside the scope of National Statistics.

Source: Bank of England: Enquiries 020 7601 4342

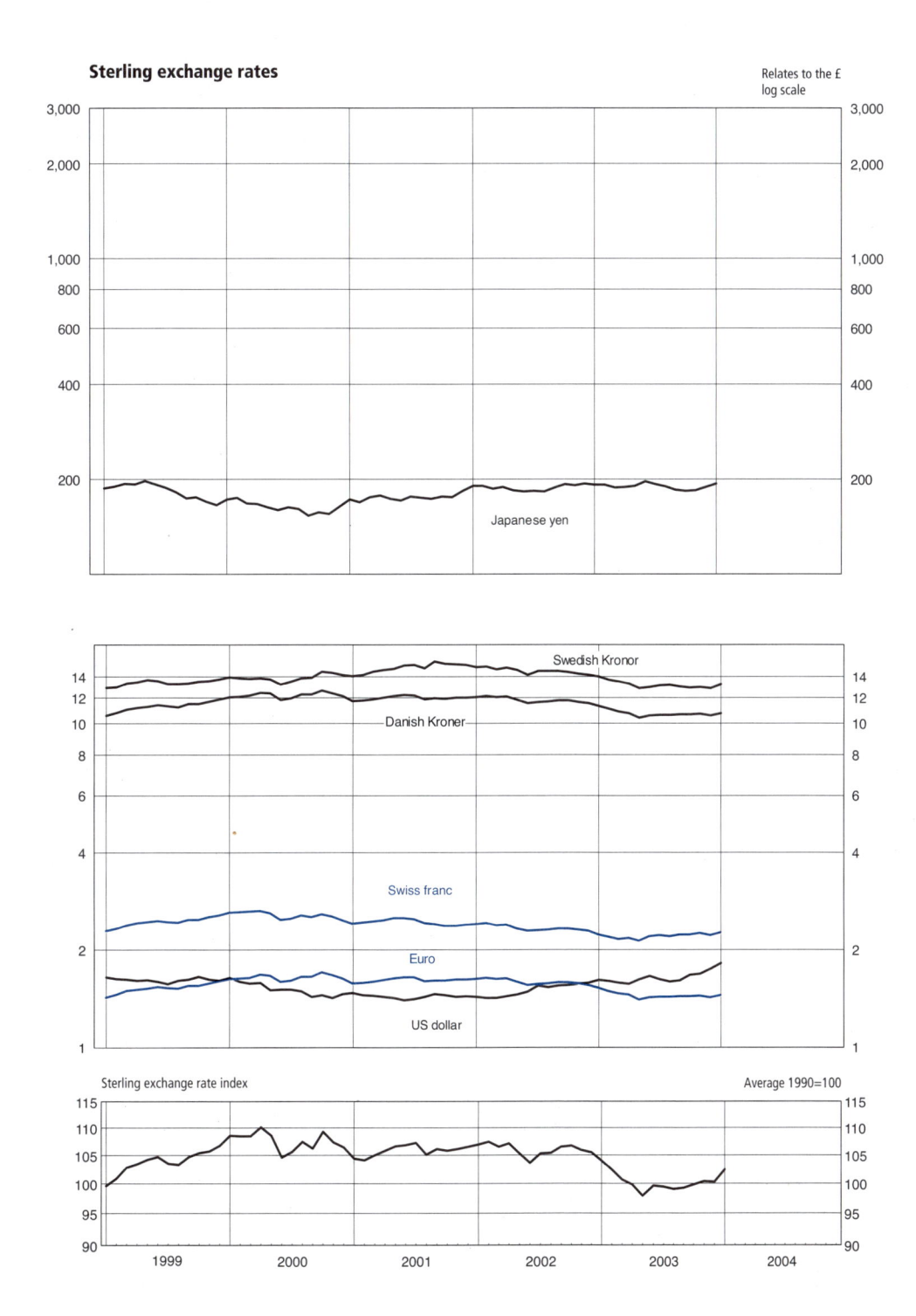

Sterling exchange rates

Relates to the £ log scale

Japanese yen

Swedish Kronor
Danish Kroner
Swiss franc
Euro
US dollar

Sterling exchange rate index — Average 1990=100

6.2 Monetary aggregates[1,3]

	M0				M4			
	Amount outstanding[2] (NSA)				Amount outstanding (NSA)			
	£ million	Annual percentage change	Amount outstanding (£ million) +	Velocity of circulation: ratio	£ million	Annual percentage change	Amount outstanding (£ million) +	Velocity of circulation: ratio
	AVAD	VQNB	AVAE	AVAM	AUYM	VQLC	AUYN	AUYU
Annual								
1999	32 768	11.7	30 916	31.23†	816 545	4.3	817 524†	1.13†
2000	34 566	5.5	32 320	30.36	884 839	8.2	885 736	1.12
2001	37 319	8.0	34 981	29.67	942 433	6.7	943 195	1.08
2002	39 540†	6.0	37 039†	28.82	1 008 707	7.3	1 009 290	1.08
2003	42 319	7.0	39 773	..	1 068 302	6.8	1 068 681	..
Quarterly								
1999 Q1	27 830	6.5	28 160	31.64†	792 903	7.1	791 256†	1.12
Q2	28 884	8.0	28 932	31.38	800 698	5.7	798 561	1.13
Q3	29 477	7.1	29 398	31.12	793 684	3.0	796 268	1.14†
Q4	32 768	11.7	30 916	30.78	816 545	4.3	817 524	1.15
2000 Q1	29 968	7.7	30 462	30.46	836 240	5.4	835 073	1.15
Q2	30 896	7.0	31 158	30.62	856 220	6.9	853 807	1.12
Q3	31 821	8.0	31 941	30.42	866 379	9.0	868 802	1.11
Q4	34 566	5.5	32 320	29.95	884 839	8.2	885 736	1.10
2001 Q1	32 489	8.4	32 986	29.86	905 800	8.3	905 349	1.10
Q2	32 896	6.5	33 243	29.99	921 571	7.6	918 675	1.09
Q3	33 797	6.2	33 964	29.59	937 071	8.4	939 382	1.07
Q4	37 319	8.0	34 981	29.24	942 433	6.7	943 195	1.07
2002 Q1	35 157	8.2	35 479†	28.92	954 972	5.7	955 242	1.08
Q2	36 225†	10.1	36 344†	28.86	974 562	6.0	971 228	1.08
Q3	36 511	8.0	36 660	28.77	988 716	5.8	990 926	1.07
Q4	39 540	6.0	37 039	28.74	1 008 707	7.3	1 009 290	1.07
2003 Q1	37 184	5.8	37 749	28.73	1 014 270	7.1	1 015 217	1.07
Q2	38 403	6.0	38 800	28.27	1 041 890	8.1	1 038 084	1.07
Q3	39 348	7.8	39 496	28.15	1 043 502†	6.6	1 045 750	1.07
Q4	42 319	7.0	39 773	..	1 068 302	6.8	1 068 681	..
Monthly								
2001 Jul	33 272	6.8	33 494	..	918 688	7.8	921 530†	..
Aug	33 881	7.1	33 754	..	930 373	7.3	929 125	..
Sep	33 797	6.2	33 964	..	937 071	8.4	935 384	..
Oct	33 978	7.0	34 175	..	942 388	8.4	942 781	..
Nov	34 883	8.1	34 666	..	945 995	8.3	942 916	..
Dec	37 319	8.0	34 981	..	942 433	6.7	938 965	..
2002 Jan	35 799	8.9	35 302	..	930 915	6.1	943 988	..
Feb	34 750	7.4	35 327	..	941 288	6.6	949 424	..
Mar	35 157	8.2	35 479	..	954 972	5.7	950 400	..
Apr	35 369	7.1	35 610	..	954 581	5.7	952 916	..
May	35 661	8.5	35 904†	..	958 400	5.7	956 364	..
Jun	36 225†	10.1	36 344	..	974 562	6.0	965 972	..
Jul	36 052	8.4	36 252	..	970 055	5.8	973 875	..
Aug	36 690	8.3	36 483	..	981 498	5.9	980 938	..
Sep	36 511	8.0	36 660	..	988 716	5.8	987 415	..
Oct	36 751	8.2	36 976	..	994 112	5.8	993 147	..
Nov	37 167	6.6	37 005	..	1 002 418	6.2	998 695	..
Dec	39 540	6.0	37 039	..	1 008 707	7.3	1 004 466	..
2003 Jan	37 230	4.0	37 137	..	994 196	6.7	1 007 146	..
Feb	36 946	6.3	37 541	..	1 004 384	6.7	1 012 308	..
Mar	37 184	5.8	37 749	..	1 014 270	7.1	1 011 594	..
Apr	38 590	9.1	38 688	..	1 023 815	8.2	1 022 499	..
May	38 827	8.9	38 777	..	1 028 393	8.4	1 027 309	..
Jun	38 403	6.0	38 800	..	1 041 890	8.1	1 033 444	..
Jul	38 938	8.0	39 198	..	1 029 651	7.4	1 032 740	..
Aug	39 579	7.9	39 366	..	1 033 045	6.3	1 033 173	..
Sep	39 348	7.8	39 496	..	1 043 502†	6.6	1 041 203	..
Oct	39 416	7.3	39 671	..	1 045 987	6.3	1 043 710	..
Nov	40 149	8.0	40 034	..	1 059 629	6.8	1 055 389	..
Dec	42 319	7.0	39 773	..	1 068 302	6.8	1 063 945	..

1 A fuller range of monetary aggregates is published monthly in the ONS publication *Financial Statistics*.
2 The monthly figures for M0 give the average of the amounts outstanding each Wednesday during the calendar month.
3 These figures fall outside the scope of National Statistics.

Source: Bank of England; Enquiries 020 7601 5467

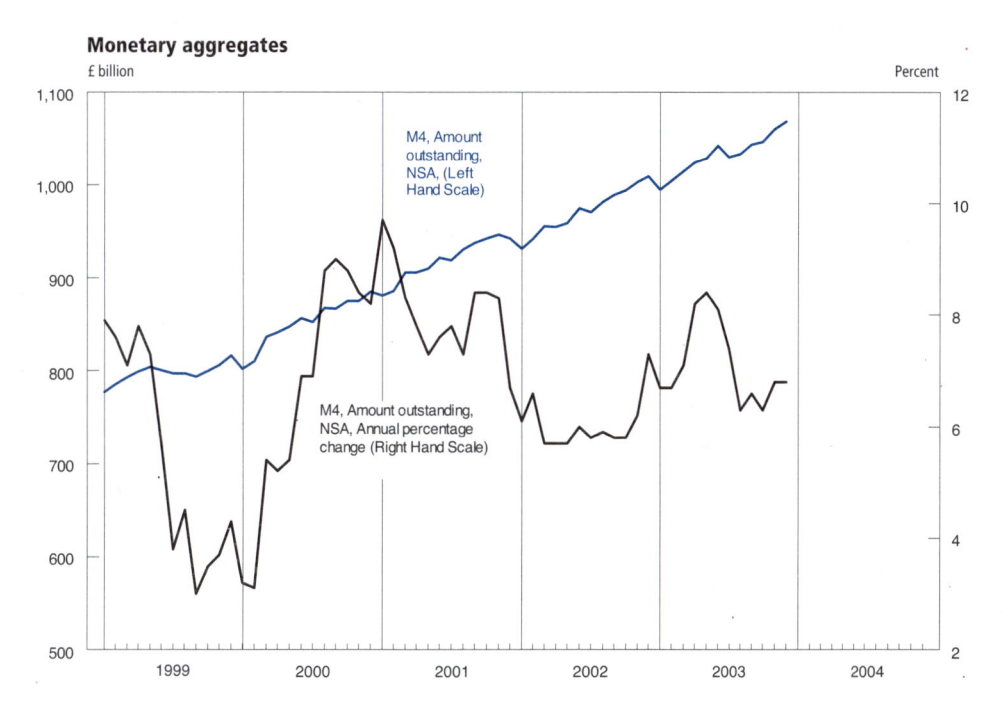

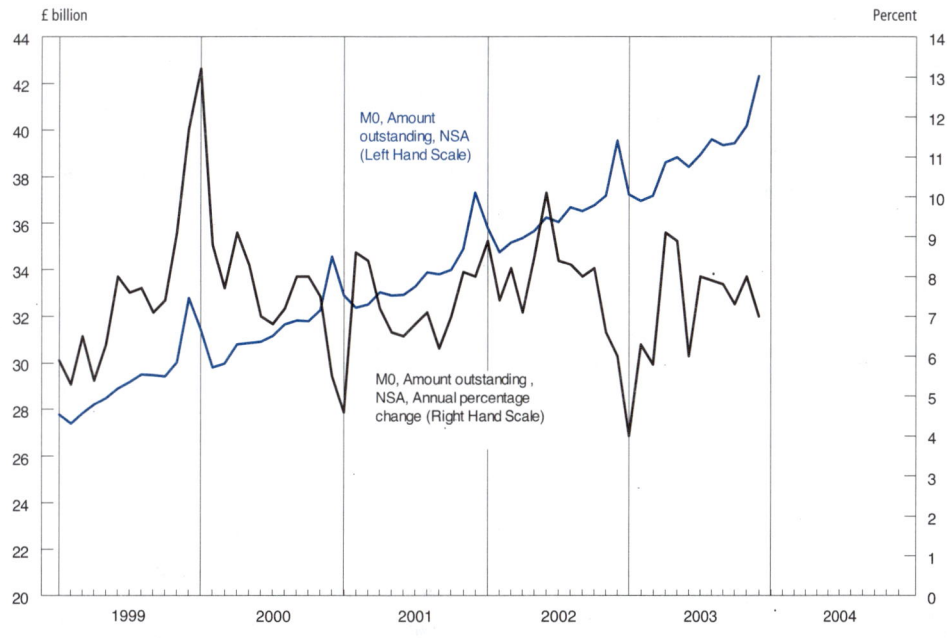

Monetary aggregates

6.3 Counterparts to changes in money stock M4[1,4]

£ million, not seasonally adjusted

	Public Sector Net Cash Requirement+[3]	Purchases by the M4[2] private sector of: Central government debt British government stocks	Other	Other public sector debt	External and foreign currency financing of public sector Purchase of British government stocks by overseas sector	Other	Banks' and Building Societies' sterling lending to the M4 private sector	External and foreign currency transactions of UK banks and building societies	Net non-deposit sterling liabilities of UK banks and building societies	Domestic counterparts	External and foreign currency counterparts	M4
	1	2	3	4	5	6	7	8	9	10	11	12
	RURQ	AVBY	AVBU	AVBV	AVBZ	AQGA	AVBS	AVBW	AVBX	AVBN	VQLP	AUZI
Annual												
1999	−1 296	−4 182†	1 803	1 115	−4 906	1 294	78 088	−44 743	−3 103	75 033	−38 544	33 386
2000	−37 562	11 388	1 825	375	4 040	7 657	111 230	7 072	−30 949	87 480	10 688	67 220
2001	−2 921	−9 671	−2 422	191	−19 361	4 195	82 446	−21 637	−10 785	67 732	1 920	58 868
2002	17 165	−8 383	879	−597	−897	1 588†	107 654	−25 050	−25 291	116 711	−22 564	68 858
2003	38 300†	−18 495	−9 699	−502	14 400	−2 959	126 292	−29 562	−21 926	136 498	−46 921	67 653
Quarterly												
1999 Q1	−5 641	4 127†	−478	341	8	419	21 386	−9 294	−952	19 550	−8 884	9 714
Q2	5 334	−4 957	157	226	790	511	18 342	−9 120	−2 353	19 110	−9 399	7 358
Q3	−3 185	−2 684	1 658	−92	−5 497	108	12 703	−11 829	−9 399	8 386	−6 224	−7 237
Q4	2 196	−668	466	640	−207	256	25 657	−14 500	9 601	27 987	−14 037	23 551
2000 Q1	−12 886	5 013	−1 257	−336	2 141	2 577	36 677	−2 568	−5 927	27 432	−2 133	19 372
Q2	−11 831	−4 104	6 729	147	−1 017	3 301	25 254	278	−1 472	16 198	4 596	19 323
Q3	−16 499	5 653	−177	269	540	1 281	27 255	5 374	−13 189	16 491	6 115	9 417
Q4	3 654	4 826	−3 470	295	2 376	498	22 044	3 988	−10 361	27 359	2 110	19 108
2001 Q1	−12 573	163	−1 093	−268	−6 682	3 734	31 075	−7 738	1 273	17 317	2 677	21 267
Q2	6 317	−12 059	−474	233	−10 982	1 000	21 194	−7 294	−4 293	15 289	4 689	15 685
Q3	−6 138	1 267	3 408	95	−2 709	1 288	15 710	7 251	−8 866	14 361	11 249	16 744
Q4	9 473	958	−4 263	131	1 012	−1 827	14 467	−13 856	1 101	20 765	−16 695	5 172
2002 Q1	−6 334	−679	3 710	−261	−1 045	2 398†	24 732	−7 337	−3 149	21 165	−3 894	14 123
Q2	7 056	−1 330	−2 970	101	−266	−1 001	24 507	809	−8 178	27 429	75	19 325
Q3	665	−2 432	335	−190	−1 960	208	34 214	−8 307	−11 055	32 586	−6 139	15 393
Q4	15 778	−3 942	−196	−247	2 374	−17	24 201	−10 215	−2 909	35 531	−12 606	20 017
2003 Q1	−1 035	−3 092	−269	−107†	1 934	431	21 514	2 432	−4 465	16 979	929	13 444
Q2	16 197†	−4 909	−4 378†	−106	2 035	−2 087	35 394	−987	−7 208	42 192	−5 109	29 875
Q3	6 024	−11 759	1 129	−257	979	−1 224	29 542	−3 164	−17 357	24 689†	−5 367	1 966†
Q4	17 114	1 265	−6 181	−32	9 452	−79	39 842	−27 843	7 104	52 638	−37 374	22 368
Monthly												
2002 Jan	−11 995	−1 443	1 204	−295	−2 433	2 210	9 432	−1 145	−8 736	−3 101	3 498	−8 339
Feb	−2 108	105	2 863	−116	60	897	5 446	1 919	330	6 188	2 757	9 275
Mar	7 769	659	−357	150	1 328	−709	9 854	−8 111	5 257	18 078	−10 148	13 186
Apr	−3 038	725	−411	100	−1 098	−560	−1 380	2 150	857	−3 989	2 688	−444
May	2 748	−1 438	−358	19	573	−49	14 719	−10 011	−1 236	15 691	−10 632	3 823
Jun	7 346	−617	−2 201	−17	259	−392	11 168	8 670	−7 799	15 727	8 018	15 947
Jul	−6 806	−3 287	2 756	−78	−460	−267	−1 554	13 335	−9 460	−8 964	13 528	−4 896
Aug	2 134	3 647	−858	58	902	548	14 719	−11 159	5 200	19 699	−11 514	13 385
Sep	5 337	−2 793	−1 563	−170	−2 402	−73	21 049	−10 482	−6 794	21 851	−8 153	6 904
Oct	−2 448	−1 713	2 479	−178	339	−154	14 738	−8 403	1 515	12 873	−8 896	5 491
Nov	6 616	−2 217	−549	24	570	731	10 941	−993	−5 692	14 757	−832	8 233
Dec	11 610	−12	−2 126	−94	1 465	−594	−1 477	−819	1 269	7 901	−2 878	6 292
2003 Jan	−11 863	−4 053	1 889	−199†	1 138	761	4 739	10 236	−15 022	−9 533	9 859	−14 695
Feb	−182	−870	509	189	−1 402	−245	11 019	−12 390	10 836	10 669	−11 233	10 272
Mar	11 010	1 831	−2 667	−96	2 198	−85	5 756	4 585	−280	15 843	2 303	17 866
Apr	261†	−6 125	1 608†	−220	−1 969	−927	10 964	2 037	3	6 487	3 079	9 569
May	5 791	4 496	−4 981	151	4 611	−234	10 688	5 760	−10 945	16 134	915	6 104
Jun	10 145	−3 280	−1 005	−37	−607	−926	13 742	−8 784	3 734	19 571	−9 103	14 202
Jul	−6 063	−5 777	3 202	−141	−1 339	879	6 723	−711	−11 403	−2 050	1 507	−11 946
Aug	3 520	−4 143	−1 533	−18	227	−771	5 462	−10 595	11 699	3 294	−11 592	3 401
Sep	8 567	−1 839	−540	−98	2 091	−1 332	17 357	8 142	−17 653	23 445†	4 719	10 511†
Oct	−1 673	−7 308†	2 033	−47	−1 161	3 050†	23 147†	−22 674†	5 073†	16 149	−18 463†	2 759
Nov	5 710	6 269	−5 460	83	7 050†	−19	9 348	8 190	−3 334	15 853	1 122	13 641
Dec	13 077	2 305	−2 754	−69	3 563	−3 110	7 346	−13 360	5 365	20 636	−20 033	5 968
2004 Jan	−14 364	..	..	..	..	..	..	..	..	..	..	..

For most periods the relationships between the columns are as follows: 11 = 5 + 6 + 8; 12 = 9 + 10 + 11. Due to the inclusion of Public Sector Net Cash Requirement (PSNCR) information on a ESA95 basis, 10 = 1 + 2 + 3 + 4 + 7 from 1994/95 only. Because the latest available PSNCR information is included figures for more recent periods may not add exactly.

1 A wider range of figures is published monthly in *Financial Statistics*.
2 The M4 private sector comprises all UK residents other than the public sector, banks and building societies.
3 Formerly called the Public Sector Borrowing Requirement.
4 Columns 2 -12 do not contain National Statistics data.

Sources: Office for National Statistics; Enquiries Column 1 020 7533 5984;
Bank of England; Columns 2-12 020 7601 5467

Counterparts to change in money stock M4

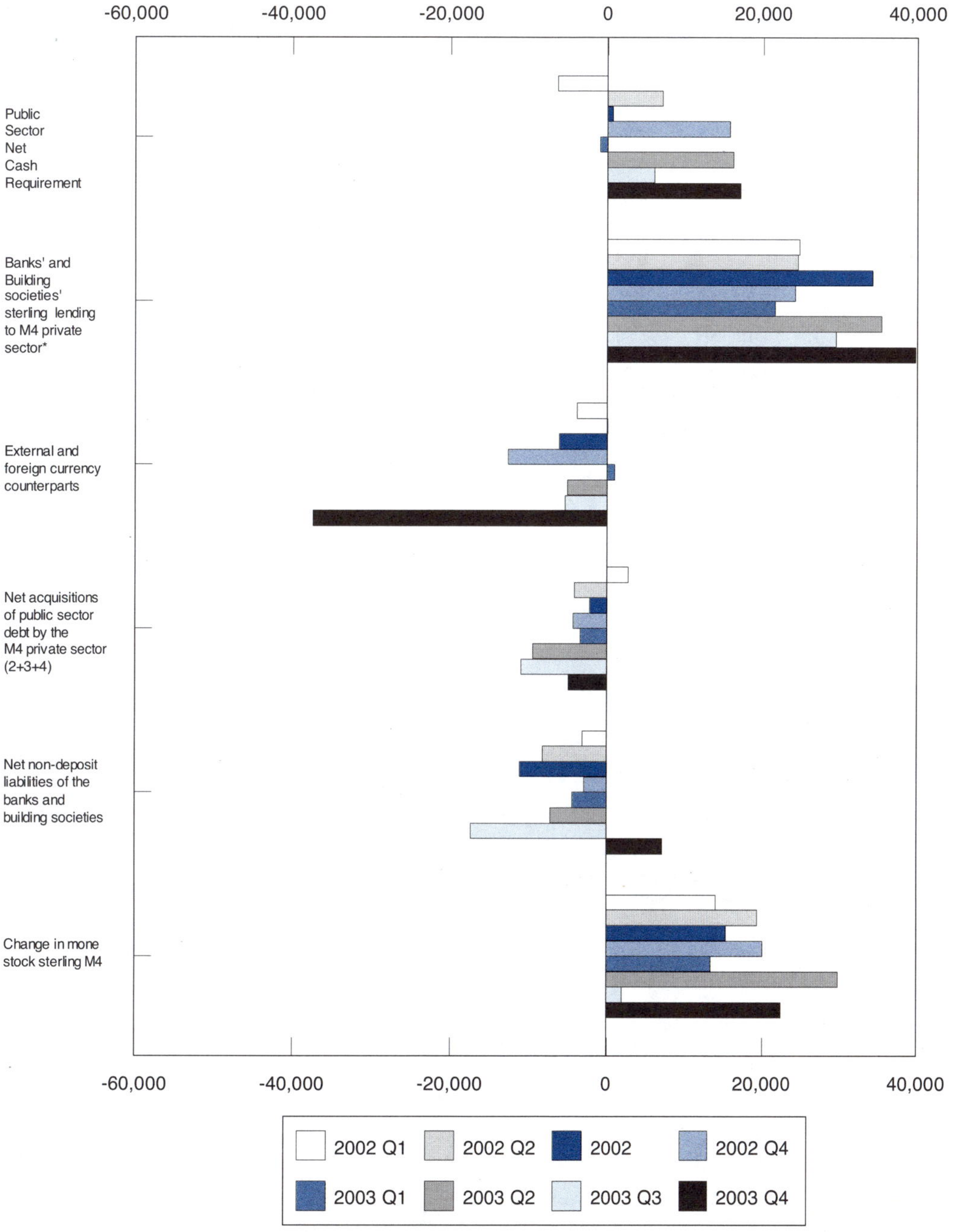
£ million
-60,000
-40,000
-20,000
0
20,000
40,000
Public Sector Net Cash Requirement
Banks' and Building societies' sterling lending to M4 private sector*
External and foreign currency counterparts
Net acquisitions of public sector debt by the M4 private sector (2+3+4)
Net non-deposit liabilities of the banks and building societies
Change in mone stock sterling M4
2002 Q1
2002 Q2
2002
2002 Q4
2003 Q1
2003 Q2
2003 Q3
2003 Q4

*Private sector other than banks and building societies

6.4 Public sector receipts and expenditure

£ million, not seasonally adjusted

	Public sector current expenditure						Public sector current receipts							
	Current expenditure on goods and services	Subsidies	Net Social Benefits	Net current grants abroad	Other current grants	Interest paid to private sector and RoW	Total current expenditure	Operating surplus	Taxes on production	Taxes on income and wealth	Taxes on capital	Other Current taxes	Compulsory social contributions	Interest/dividend from private/RoW	Rent and other current transfers	Total current receipts
	GZSN	NMRL	ANLY	GZSI	NNAI	ANLO	ANLT	ANBP	NMYE	ANSO	NMGI	NVCM	ANBO	ANBQ	ANBS	ANBT
Annual																
2000	177 740	5 058	114 986	334	18 638	26 122	342 878	17 814	129 716	140 088	2 215	18 223	60 284	5 433	2 130	375 043
2001	191 171	6 405	123 574	–2 134	18 899	23 618	361 533	18 681	133 111	147 521	2 396	19 168	62 887	5 395	2 879	391 118
2002	209 461	6 281	126 881	–539	22 840	21 392	386 316	18 424	140 570	142 121	2 381	20 286	63 381	4 370	2 815	393 408
Quarterly																
2000 Q1	42 447	1 283	27 452	219	4 230	6 047	81 678	4 378	31 319	43 124	548	4 350	16 173	1 091	540	101 306
Q2	44 496	1 213	28 054	–163	4 575	6 700	84 875	4 363	32 830	26 834	566	4 605	14 588	1 263	363	85 198
Q3	45 285	1 208	28 369	73	4 695	6 359	85 989	4 345	32 368	34 721	579	4 692	14 337	1 532	716	93 075
Q4	45 512	1 354	31 111	205	5 138	7 016	90 336	4 728	33 199	35 409	522	4 576	15 186	1 547	511	95 464
2001 Q1	45 932	1 410	29 293	–261	4 945	6 331	87 650	4 473	31 508	47 192	569	4 620	17 957	1 699	909	108 712
Q2	47 201	1 685	29 913	–259	4 757	5 990	89 287	4 497	33 134	29 131	612	4 907	14 518	1 283	560	88 407
Q3	48 218	1 704	31 068	–1 294	4 312	5 329	89 337	4 616	34 098	35 513	617	4 865	15 064	1 276	853	96 667
Q4	49 820	1 606	33 300	–320	4 885	5 968	95 259	5 095	34 371	35 685	598	4 776	15 348	1 137	557	97 332
2002 Q1	51 300	1 225	30 233	12	5 513	5 238	93 521	4 574	33 098	44 693	556	4 806	18 231	1 018	808	107 549
Q2	52 068	1 606	31 144	–126	5 640	5 432	95 764	4 460	34 627	28 649	607	5 158	14 703	1 074	596	89 639
Q3	52 571	1 674	31 802	–375	6 271	4 643	96 586	4 516	36 300	35 682	619	5 185	14 900	1 116	826	98 909
Q4	53 522	1 776	33 702	–50	5 416	6 079	100 445	4 874	36 545	33 097	599	5 137	15 547	1 162	585	97 311
2003 Q1	56 453	1 832	31 761	–75	6 038	5 244	101 253	4 530	34 618	45 425	545	5 132	18 407	1 118	752	110 292
Q2	58 451	1 965	33 107	–184	6 094	5 905	105 338	4 652	37 397	29 995	607	5 668	17 071	1 034	397	96 584
Q3	57 533	1 856	33 777	–266	5 177	5 471	103 548	4 821	37 000	36 810	631	5 689	17 596	1 028	403	103 741

Sources: Office for National Statistics;
Enquiries 020 7533 5987

6.5 Public sector key fiscal indicators[1]

£ million[5], not seasonally adjusted

	Surplus on current budget[2]		Net investment[3]		Net borrowing[4]		Net cash requirement		Public sector net debt	
	General Government	Public Sector	General Government	Public Sector	General Government	Public Sector	General Government	Public Sector	£ billion[6]	% of GDP[7]
	ANLW	ANMU	-ANNV	-ANNW	NNBK	ANNX	RUUS	RURQ	RUTN	RUTO
Annual										
2000	20 377	19 086	5 361	4 305	15 016	14 781	–38 282	–37 562	317.4	32.6
2001	17 146	15 948	9 029	8 471	8 117	7 477	–3 462	–2 921	318.8	31.4
2002	–5 133	–7 140	10 143	9 323	–15 276	–16 463	16 486	17 165	335.9	31.4
2003	..	–21 428†	..	13 916†	–34 010†	–35 344†	..	38 300†	375.0†	33.3
Quarterly										
2000 Q1	17 443	16 405	2 958	2 722	14 485	13 683	–14 336	–12 886	340.9	36.2
Q2	–3 023	–2 931	–1	–344	–3 022	–2 587	–11 602	–11 831	329.1	34.6
Q3	4 456	3 802	910	655	3 546	3 147	–16 913	–16 499	313.6	32.6
Q4	1 501	1 810	1 494	1 272	7	538	4 569	3 654	317.4	32.6
2001 Q1	18 688	17 706	3 310	3 411	15 378	14 295	–13 826	–12 573	306.9	31.2
Q2	–4 259	–4 266	951	1 018	–5 210	–5 284	6 636	6 317	314.3	31.6
Q3	4 533	3 910	1 725	1 589	2 808	2 321	–6 538	–6 138	308.2	30.7
Q4	–1 816	–1 402	3 043	2 453	–4 859	–3 855	10 266	9 473	318.8	31.4
2002 Q1	11 554	10 526	4 620	4 468	6 934	6 058	–6 958	–6 334	311.2	30.2
Q2	–9 445	–9 669	1 055	960	–10 500	–10 629	7 435	7 056	318.2	30.5
Q3	–430	–1 255	2 129	1 865	–2 559	–3 120	–257	665	320.4	30.3
Q4	–6 812	–6 742	2 339	2 030	–9 151	–8 772	16 266	15 778	335.9	31.4
2003 Q1	6 623	5 411	6 338	5 779	285	–368	–1 933	–1 035	334.1	30.8
Q2	–12 146	–12 407	3 363	2 640	–15 509	–15 047	16 845	16 197†	349.9	31.9
Q3	–2 970	–3 483	2 899	2 785	–5 869	–6 268	5 905	6 024	355.5	32.0
Q4	..	–10 949†	..	2 712†	–12 917†	–13 661†	..	17 114	375.0†	33.3

1 National accounts entities as defined under the European System of Accounts 1995 (ESA95).
2 Net saving, plus capital taxes.
3 Gross capital formation, plus payments less receipts, of investment grants less depreciation.
4 Net borrowing = surplus on current budget minus net investment.
5 Unless otherwise stated
6 Net amount outstanding at end of period.
7 Net debt at end of the month, Gross domestic product at market prices for 12 months centred on the end of the month.

Sources: Office for National Statistics;
Enquiries 020 7533 5984

Public sector finances

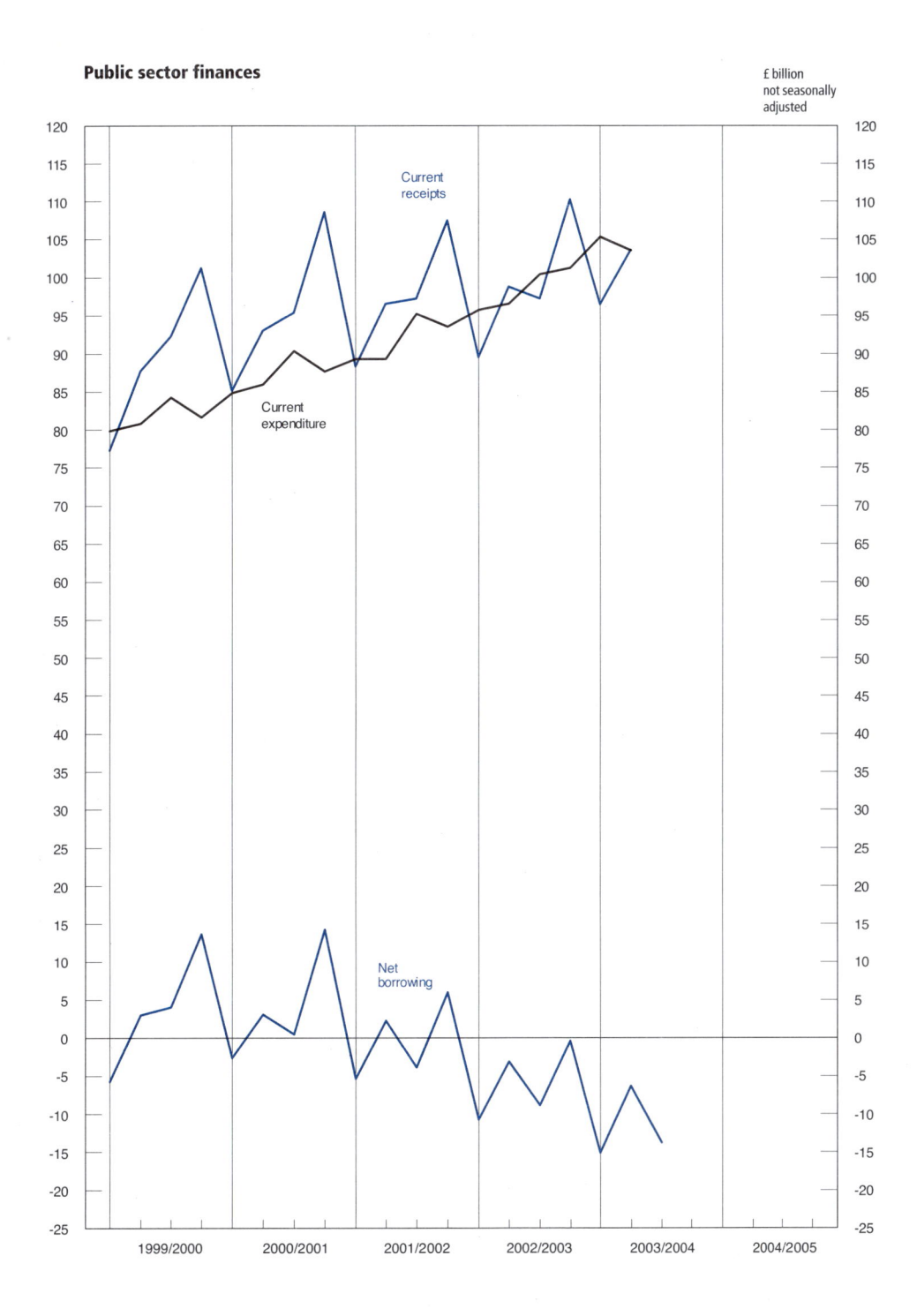

£ billion
not seasonally adjusted

6.6 Consumer credit and other household sector borrowing

£ million

	Total consumer credit[1]	of which credit cards[1,2]	of which other[1,2]	Banks[1]	Building Societies' Class 3 Loans[1]	Other specialist lenders	Retailers	Insurance companies	Loans secured on dwellings (NSA[†])
	VZRI	VZRJ	VZRK	VRVV	VZRG	VZRH	RLBO	VZQZ	AMWT
Amounts outstanding: quarterly									
1999 Q1	105 894[†]	28 430[†]	77 506[†]	75 736[†]	298[†]	25 845[†]	2 698[†]	1 320[†]	463 303
Q2	109 044	29 672	79 398	77 810	312	26 773	2 693	1 384	472 729
Q3	112 309	30 761	81 600	80 462	329	27 499	2 655	1 400	484 269
Q4	115 473	32 084	83 277	82 669	297	28 305	2 775	1 462	494 199
2000 Q1	119 266	33 440	85 861	86 077	315	28 826	2 663	1 415	503 559
Q2	122 037	34 941	87 118	88 733	315	28 945	2 614	1 310	514 840
Q3	124 328	36 307	88 072	91 035	349	29 147	2 553	1 273	525 842
Q4	127 274	37 600	89 553	94 223	392	29 015	2 504	1 197	535 751
2001 Q1	129 073	37 986	91 122	95 903	412	29 074	2 523	1 229	546 485
Q2	133 005	39 448	93 574	100 311	424	28 356	2 510	1 221	561 443
Q3	136 045	40 031	96 046	103 433	447	28 494	2 519	1 206	577 424
Q4	140 839	41 704	99 086	107 691	436	29 108	2 482	1 178	591 466
2002 Q1	144 317	43 372	100 943	111 151	463	29 110	2 502	1 183	606 459
Q2	147 321	43 500	103 864	113 189	460	29 699	2 575	1 193	625 890
Q3	152 988	45 982	106 989	118 327	523	30 442	2 557	1 196	648 587[†]
Q4	156 855	47 137	109 719	120 773	610	31 804	2 539	1 182	670 858
2003 Q1	160 532	48 608	111 899	116 965	625	39 366	2 516	1 138	690 824
Q2	164 752	50 409	114 397	119 763	672	40 781	2 201	1 111	713 299
Q3	167 808	52 239	115 528	121 861	736	41 975	2 196	1 092	740 283
Q4	169 593	52 399	117 202	122 629	766	42 987	2 219	1 066	..
Amounts outstanding: monthly									
2001 Jul	134 219[†]	39 629[†]	94 591[†]	101 632[†]	444[†]	28 366[†]	2 512[†]	1 213[†]	..
Aug	135 202	39 899	95 303	102 355	444	28 336	2 501	1 209	..
Sep	136 073	39 921	96 152	103 620	444	28 448	2 511	1 206	..
Oct	137 425	40 419	97 006	104 832	456	28 398	2 496	1 198	..
Nov	138 870	41 008	97 862	106 069	413	28 676	2 482	1 187	..
Dec	140 571	41 547	99 025	107 571	420	29 261	2 484	1 178	..
2002 Jan	142 119	42 170	99 948	109 032	429	29 232	2 478	1 174	..
Feb	143 573	43 050	100 523	110 252	439	29 198	2 475	1 177	..
Mar	144 282	43 305	100 976	111 233	469	29 037	2 488	1 183	..
Apr	145 707	43 860	101 847	112 532	469	29 213	2 488	1 188	..
May	147 143	44 153	102 989	113 296	471	29 217	2 543	1 191	..
Jun	147 269	43 286	103 983	113 487	470	29 672	2 577	1 193	..
Jul	148 709	43 721	104 988	114 587	482	29 732	2 556	1 194	..
Aug	151 235	45 195	106 040	116 991	497	29 701	2 526	1 195	..
Sep	152 795	45 924	106 871	118 098	516	30 408	2 552	1 196	..
Oct	154 463	46 149	108 314	118 683	533	31 684	2 546	1 195	..
Nov	155 387	46 626	108 762	119 456	541	31 795	2 553	1 191	..
Dec	156 620	46 941	109 679	120 855	587	31 938	2 535	1 182	..
2003 Jan	157 574	47 454	110 120	121 132	603	32 033	2 537	1 169	..
Feb	158 935	47 939	110 997	119 778	616	34 501	2 528	1 153	..
Mar	160 222	48 558	111 664	116 558	632	39 261	2 499	1 138	..
Apr	161 106	48 830	112 276	116 915	652	40 034	2 477	1 126	..
May	162 809	49 599	113 211	118 261	659	40 039	2 441	1 117	..
Jun	164 371	50 141	114 230	119 562	687	40 748	2 208	1 111	..
Jul	165 818	50 983	114 835	120 877	701	41 016	2 202	1 105	..
Aug	167 036	51 567	115 468	121 735	715	40 972	2 222	1 099	..
Sep	167 620	52 210	115 409	121 805	725	41 979	2 192	1 092	..
Oct	168 660	52 489	116 171	121 837	731	42 720	2 183	1 084	..
Nov	169 782	52 824	116 958	122 741	732	43 344	2 226	1 075	..
Dec	169 471	52 172	117 299	122 698	737	43 139	2 211	1 066	..
2004 Jan	170 807	52 756	118 051	125 289	752	41 513	2 192	1 057	..

1 These figures fall outside the scope of National Statistics.
2 From January 1999 onwards, a more accurate breakdown between credit card and 'other lending' is available.

Credit card lending by other specialist lenders can now be separately identified and is included for the first time within the credit card component. Hence, data from January 1999 onwards are not directly comparable with earlier periods.

Sources: Bank of England; Enquiries Columns 1-5, 9 020 7601 5468; Office for National Statistics; Enquiries Columns 6-8 020 7 533 6046

Economic Trends 604 March 2004 — Tables section

Consumer credit and other Household sector borrowing — Percentage change on year earlier

Consumer credit: amounts outstanding — £ million

Legend: 2002 Q4, 2003 Q1, 2003 Q2, 2003 Q3, 2003 Q4

Categories: Banks, Other specialist lenders, *Other

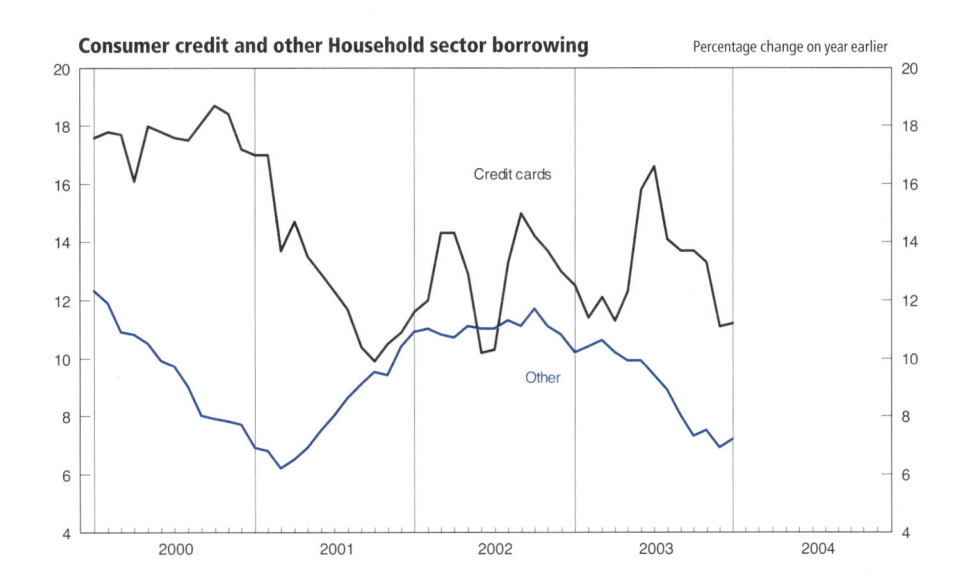

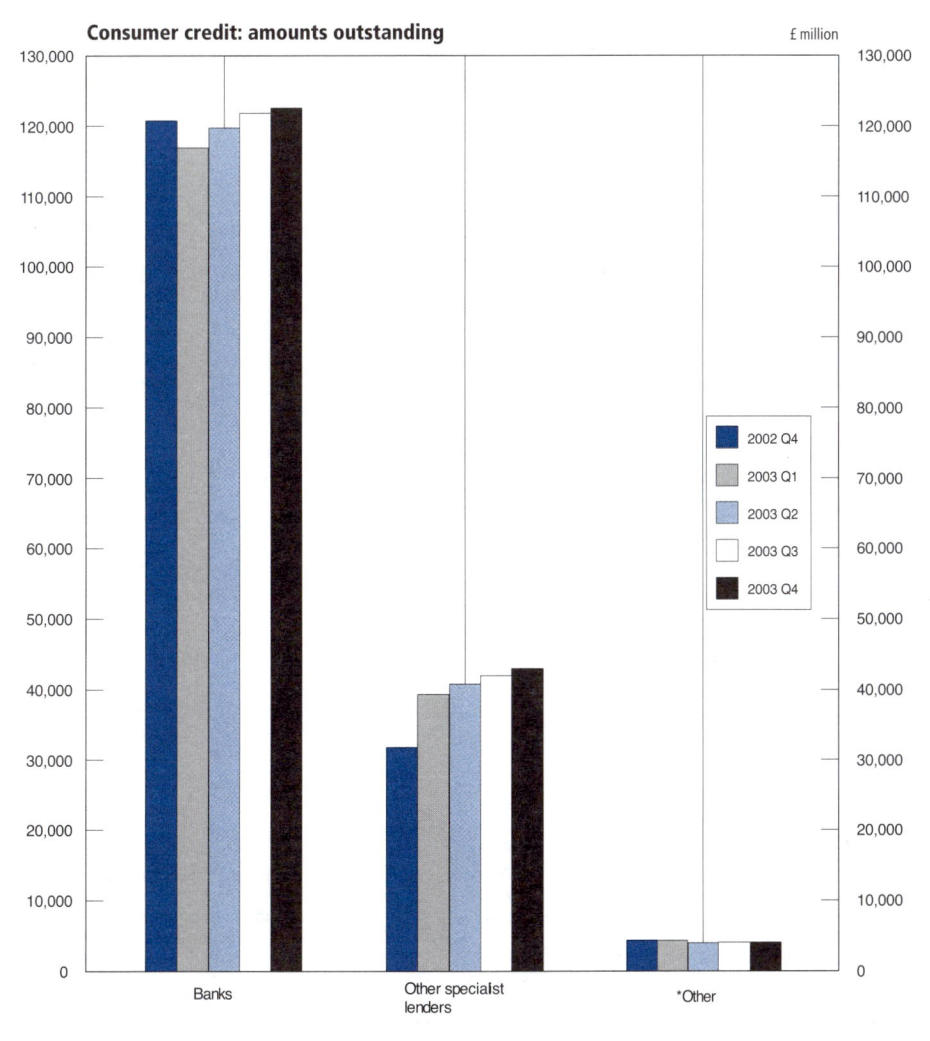

*Other is the sum of Retailers, Insurance companies and Building society class 3 loans

Office for National Statistics

6.7 Analysis of bank lending to UK residents[1,2,4,5,6]
Amounts outstanding

£ million, not seasonally adjusted

	Manufacturing[3]	Other production	Financial	Services	Persons	Total loans, advances and acceptances
Total Loans, Advances, Acceptances and Sterling Commercial paper						
	TBSF	BCEX	BCFH	BCFR	TBTW	TBSA
2002 Q3	53 142	34 454	338 483	223 171	560 584	1 209 833
Q4	51 708	35 004	338 353	236 069	576 315	1 237 449
2003 Q1	50 875	35 255	360 829	240 309	573 875	1 261 143
Q2	49 483	35 355	360 586	248 528	588 463	1 282 415
Q3	47 320	34 662†	382 603†	247 501†	606 819	1 318 905
Q4	43 102	32 944	398 616	251 701	620 815	1 347 178
Of which in sterling						
	TBUF	BCEY	BCFI	BCFS	TBVW	TBUA
2002 Q3	34 462	30 937	180 673	204 287	560 146	1 010 505
Q4	34 231	31 477	174 298	215 949	575 819	1 031 774
2003 Q1	32 532	31 752	181 717	219 366	573 342	1 038 710
Q2	32 436	31 862	182 826	226 680	587 926	1 061 730
Q3	30 839	31 411†	192 842†	226 445†	606 197	1 087 734
Q4	29 850	30 197	195 691	233 123	620 255	1 109 116
Changes in total lending (sterling)						
	TBWF	BCEZ	BCFJ	BCFT	TBXW	TBWA
2002 Q3	−211	−213	6 714	7 745	19 662	33 697
Q4	−249	540	−6 357	11 638	16 832	22 404
2003 Q1	−1 451	371	2 587	4 425	4 997	10 929
Q2	−61	224	3 230	7 109	16 473	26 974
Q3	−1 589	−443†	10 040†	155†	22 071†	30 234†
Q4	−989	−1 215	3 211	7 156	17 706	25 870
Changes in total lending (foreign currencies)						
	TBYF	BCFA	BCFK	BCFU	TBZW	TBYA
2002 Q3	376	−450	−8 385	−675	−13	−9 147
Q4	−1 359	17	4 462	1 181	60	4 361
2003 Q1	214	−134	10 441	116	22	10 659
Q2	−967	76	12 236	1 356	21	12 722
Q3	−649†	−253†	10 718†	193†	86†	10 094†
Q4	−2 759	−381	4 685	−1 812	−36	−303
Facilities granted						
	TCAF	BCFB	BCFL	BCFV	TCBW	TCAA
2002 Q3	95 975	65 006	387 612	321 029	620 172	1 489 793
Q4	96 946	63 765	384 484	330 529	631 881	1 507 605
2003 Q1	97 860	64 422	408 170	337 951†	639 426	1 547 829†
Q2	93 240	65 963	407 773	343 472	661 318	1 571 766
Q3	91 556	65 423†	430 778†	345 908	681 360	1 615 025
Q4	85 063	63 557	448 352	350 461	700 354	1 647 787
Of which in sterling						
	TCCF	BCFC	BCFM	BCFW	TCDW	TCCA
2002 Q3	57 928	49 216	212 141	276 475	619 516	1 215 275
Q4	57 848	49 349	205 087	287 157	631 178	1 230 620
2003 Q1	56 944	49 334	212 398	294 815†	638 662	1 252 154†
Q2	54 711	50 685	215 042	301 434	660 540	1 282 412
Q3	54 779	50 738†	226 080†	303 030	680 456	1 315 082
Q4	52 679	49 996	230 710	311 550	699 570	1 344 505
Changes in sterling (facilities granted)						
	TCEF	BCFD	BCFN	BCFX	TCFW	TCEA
2002 Q3	−1 148	−1 752	6 977	6 315	17 551	27 944
Q4	−97	133	−7 036	10 521	12 821	16 342
2003 Q1	−657	82	2 478	8 670†	15 070	25 643†
Q2	−2 183	1 473	4 787	6 461	23 778	34 315
Q3	76	60†	11 062†	1 986	23 716†	36 900
Q4	−2 100	−742	4 993	8 998	22 762	33 911
Changes in foreign currencies (facilities granted)						
	TCGF	BCFE	BCFO	BCFY	TCHW	TCGA
2002 Q3	595	−1 758	−9 040	2 793	37	−7 373
Q4	989	−1 225	2 274	−895	51	1 193
2003 Q1	575	287	11 315	−1 513	39	10 703
Q2	−1 321	697†	11 044	100†	37	10 558
Q3	−1 891†	−636†	10 643†	1 820†	128†	10 064†
Q4	−2 834	−341	5 255	−2 092	−85	−96

1 Comprises loans advances (including under reverse repos), finance leasing, acceptances, facilities and holdings of sterling commercial paper issued by UK residents, provided by reporting banks to their UK resident non-bank and non-building society customers. This analysis is based on Standard Industrial Classification of 1992 and excludes lending to residents in the Channel Islands and the Isle of Man which are classified as non-residents for statistical purposes from end-September 1997. Holdings of investments and bills and adjustments for transit items are no longer included. For a more detailed breakdown of these data, see *Financial Statistics* Table 4.5B.
2 Changes in the reporting population in the quarter to end-December 1997, including the entry of Northern rock plc, account for an increase of £12.8bn in total sterling lending. Other currency lending was unchanged. Changes data have been adjusted to reflect only the new business undertaken by Northern Rock plc during the quarter.
3 Includes lending under DTI special scheme for domestic shipbuilding.
4 In the quarter to end-June 1999, Halifax plc acquired Birmingham Midshires Building Society; adjustments have been applied so that only the growth in the latter's business in the quarter is included in the aggregate flows.
5 Data for amounts outstanding to end-Q4, 2000 reflect the entry of Bradford and Bingley plc to the banking sector in December 2000. Changes data have been adjusted to reflect only the net business undertaken by Bradford and Bingley plc during December.
6 These figures fall outside the scope of National Statistics.

Source: Bank of England; Enquiries 020 7601 5360

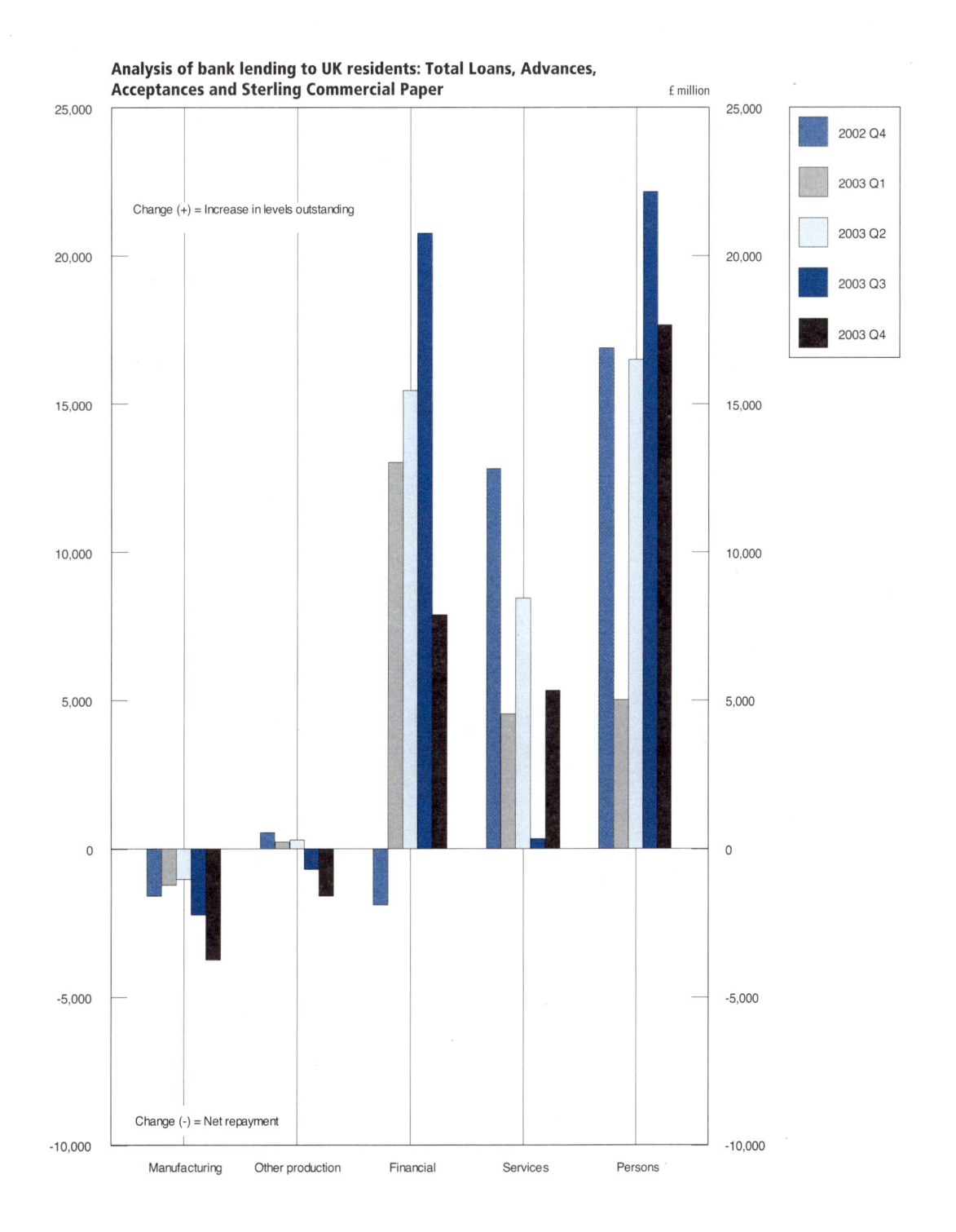

Analysis of bank lending to UK residents: Total Loans, Advances, Acceptances and Sterling Commercial Paper

£ million

Change (+) = Increase in levels outstanding

Change (-) = Net repayment

Legend: 2002 Q4, 2003 Q1, 2003 Q2, 2003 Q3, 2003 Q4

Categories: Manufacturing, Other production, Financial, Services, Persons

6.8 Interest rates, security prices and yields[5]

Percentage rate

	Last Friday							Last working day	Average of working days
	Treasury bill yield[1]	Deposits with local authorities - 3 months[2]	Inter-bank 3 months bid rate[3]	Inter-bank 3 months offer rate[3]	Sterling certificates of deposit 3 months bid rate	Sterling certificates of deposit 3 months offer rate	Selected retail banks: base rate	Euro-dollar 3 month rate	British government securities: long dated[4] - 20 years
	AJRP	AJOI	HSAJ	HSAK	HSAL	HSAM	ZCMG	AJIB	AJLX
Annual									
2000	5.69	5.84	5.81	5.84	5.75	5.81	..	6.35	4.68
2001	3.87	4.00	4.03	4.06	3.98	4.02	..	1.83	4.78
2002	3.92	..	3.94	3.96	3.90	3.94	..	1.35	4.83
Monthly									
2000 Jan	5.85	6.25	6.09	6.16	6.03	6.09	5.75	6.05	4.82
Feb	5.93	6.06	6.16	6.22	6.09	6.16	6.00	6.08	4.71
Mar	5.93	6.13	6.16	6.22	6.13	6.16	6.00	6.29	4.56
Apr	6.05	6.22	6.25	6.31	6.22	6.25	6.00	6.44	4.63
May	6.04	6.13	6.19	6.22	6.13	6.16	6.00	6.82	4.69
Jun	5.93	6.06	6.13	6.16	6.06	6.13	6.00	6.76	4.63
Jul	5.93	6.03	6.16	6.19	6.13	6.16	6.00	6.71	4.64
Aug	5.95	6.06	6.16	6.19	6.09	6.13	6.00	6.64	4.74
Sep	5.85	6.03	6.09	6.13	6.03	6.09	6.00	6.74	4.86
Oct	5.81	6.00	6.03	6.06	6.00	6.03	6.00	6.71	4.81
Nov	5.72	5.88	5.94	5.97	5.91	5.97	6.00	6.64	4.59
Dec	5.69	5.84	5.81	5.84	5.75	5.81	6.00	6.35	4.49
2001 Jan	5.57	5.63	5.69	5.72	5.66	5.72	6.00	5.35	4.51
Feb	5.46	5.53	5.53	5.56	5.50	5.53	5.75	5.01	4.57
Mar	5.29	5.38	5.44	5.47	5.40	5.43	5.75	4.86	4.56
Apr	5.11	5.13	5.25	5.28	5.23	5.25	5.50	4.27	4.86
May	5.02	5.13	5.16	5.19	5.16	5.17	5.25	3.95	4.99
Jun	5.10	5.06	5.19	5.25	5.18	5.18	5.25	3.80	5.07
Jul	5.04	5.13	5.16	5.22	5.16	5.17	5.25	3.60	5.03
Aug	4.71	4.75	4.84	4.88	4.83	4.84	5.00	3.43	4.81
Sep	4.33	4.38	4.41	4.47	4.41	4.51	4.75	2.52	4.93
Oct	4.16	4.06	4.13	4.19	4.10	4.13	4.50	2.15	4.80
Nov	3.81	3.94	3.94	4.00	3.92	3.96	4.00	2.00	4.51
Dec	3.87	4.00	4.03	4.06	3.98	4.02	4.00	1.83	4.75
2002 Jan	3.90	3.94	3.97	4.03	3.97	3.99	4.00	1.86	4.81
Feb	3.91	3.88	3.97	4.00	3.91	3.95	4.00	1.85	4.83
Mar	4.04	4.09	4.09	4.16	4.09	4.11	4.00	2.00	5.11
Apr	3.98	4.00	4.06	4.13	4.05	4.06	4.00	1.86	5.13
May	4.04	4.03	4.09	4.13	4.09	4.11	4.00	1.82	5.18
Jun	3.97	4.03	4.06	4.09	4.05	4.07	4.00	1.83	5.02
Jul	3.75	..	3.94	3.97	3.92	3.94	4.00	1.75	4.90
Aug	3.86	..	3.91	3.97	3.91	3.93	4.00	1.80	4.64
Sep	3.81	..	3.88	3.91	3.85	3.86	4.00	1.74	4.45
Oct	3.73	..	3.88	3.91	3.85	3.87	4.00	1.64	4.59
Nov	3.86	..	3.94	3.98	3.94	3.95	4.00	1.42	4.64
Dec	3.92	..	3.94	3.96	3.90	3.94	4.00	1.35	4.62
2003 Jan	3.79	..	3.88	3.91	3.88	3.89	4.00	1.29	4.44
Feb	3.49	..	3.59	3.64	3.60	3.62	3.75	1.30	4.39
Mar	3.51	..	3.57	3.61	3.57	3.59	3.75	1.25	4.54
Apr	3.47	..	3.55	3.58	3.54	3.56	3.75	1.28	4.67
May	3.44	..	3.54	3.57	3.55	3.55	3.75	1.22	4.46
Jun	3.50	..	3.55	3.59	3.55	3.56	3.75	1.09	4.39
Jul	3.32	..	3.36	3.40	3.36	3.38	3.50	1.06	4.65
Aug	3.53	..	3.54	3.57	3.54	3.56	3.50	1.11	4.68
Sep	3.59	..	3.66	3.67	3.63	3.65	3.50	1.13	4.76
Oct	3.81	..	3.86	3.90	3.85	3.87	3.50	1.13	4.88
Nov	3.86	..	3.90	3.94	3.90	3.92	3.75	1.12	4.95
Dec	3.77	..	3.95	3.98	3.95	3.98	3.75	1.10	4.83
2004 Jan	3.86	..	4.05	4.10	4.06	4.08	3.75	1.08	4.75

1 Average discount rate expressed as the rate at which interest is earned during the life of the bills.
2 For a minimum term of 3 months and thereafter at 7 days' notice.
3 Spread of rates over the day in the inter-bank sterling market; from June 1982 rates are the spread at 10.30 am.
4 Averages of Wednesdays until February 1980; from March 1980 figures are the average of all observations (3 a week); from January 1982 average of working days. Calculated gross redemption yields - see *Financial Statistics Explanatory Handbook*.
5 These figures fall outside the scope of National Statistics.

Sources: Bank of England;
Enquiries 020 7601 4342.

Economic Trends 604 March 2004

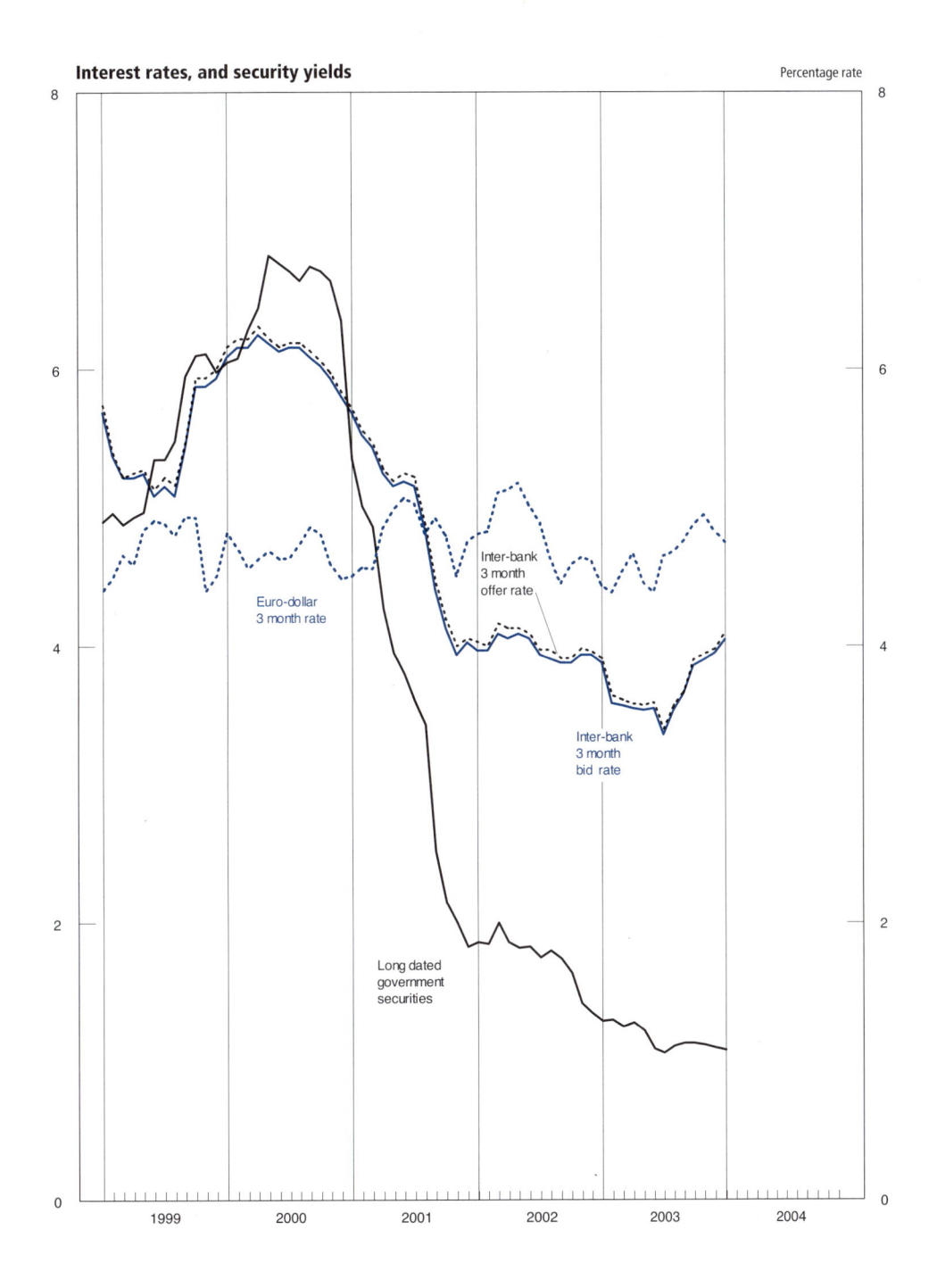

Interest rates, and security yields

Percentage rate

- Euro-dollar 3 month rate
- Inter-bank 3 month offer rate
- Inter-bank 3 month bid rate
- Long dated government securities

6.9 A selection of asset prices

	Producer price indices (NSA) (2000 = 100)		Housing: ODPM all lenders mix adjusted house price index (NSA) (2002 = 100)			
	Plant and machinery bought as fixed assets by Motor vehicle industry	Manufactured output Motor vehicle industry	New dwellings[1]	Secondhand dwellings[1]	All dwellings[1]	Average price of agricultural land in England (NSA)(1995 = 100)[2]
	PVJL	PQIR	WMPN	WMPP	WMPQ	BAJI
Annual						
2000	100.0	100.0	84.6	88.0	87.7	..
2001	102.0	95.4	90.3	95.7	95.1	..
2002	100.2	95.2	108.7	111.6	111.2	..
2003	99.6	94.6	126.4	129.0	128.7	..
Quarterly						
2000 Q1	99.0	102.0	81.3	83.9	83.6	142[3]
Q2	99.4	101.8	86.0	88.5	88.2	142[3]
Q3	100.1	99.9	89.0	89.9	89.9	159[3]
Q4	101.4	96.3	92.9	92.3	92.5	144[3]
2001 Q1	102.9	95.4	90.8	92.1	92.1	156[3]
Q2	103.1	95.5	90.8	96.0	95.4	146[3]
Q3	101.2	95.4	94.1	99.4	98.8	161[3]
Q4	101.1	95.4	95.4	96.9	96.8	154[3]
2002 Q1	101.0	95.6	100.0	100.0	100.0	130[3]
Q2	100.5	95.5	106.5	108.4	108.2	139[3]
Q3	100.0	94.9	111.0	116.1	115.5	154[3]
Q4	99.2	94.9	117.1	121.8	121.3	154[3]
2003 Q1	99.1	94.6	119.3	124.0	123.4	145[3]
Q2	99.7	94.1	127.2†	127.3	127.2	..
Q3	99.9p	94.5r†	127.9†	131.1	130.7	..
Q4	99.6p	95.1p	131.3	133.7	133.4	..
Monthly						
2002 Jan	100.9	95.6	..	..	..	..
Feb	101.1	95.6	100.0	100.0	100.0	..
Mar	101.1	95.6	103.9	103.5	103.5	..
Apr	100.8	95.6	103.6	105.1	104.9	..
May	100.1	95.6	106.5	107.8	107.6	..
Jun	100.5	95.4	109.4	112.4	112.0	..
Jul	100.2	94.9	105.9	113.8	112.9	..
Aug	100.4	94.9	111.6	115.9	115.4	..
Sep	99.4	94.9	115.5	118.6	118.2	..
Oct	99.2	94.9	113.7	119.9	119.1	..
Nov	99.2	95.0	116.2	120.9	120.3	..
Dec	99.1	94.9	121.4	124.7	124.3	..
2003 Jan	98.5	94.7	119.2	124.0	123.4	..
Feb	99.0	94.6	118.0	122.7	122.1	..
Mar	99.7	94.6	120.7	125.2	124.7	..
Apr	99.9	94.2	127.5	127.8	127.7	..
May	99.8	93.9	127.1	126.8	126.8	..
Jun	99.4	94.2	127.1	127.2	127.1	..
Jul	99.7	94.2	126.6	129.7	129.3	..
Aug	100.0	94.5†	129.6	131.9	131.6	..
Sep	100.0p	94.7r†	127.6	131.7	131.2	..
Oct	99.5p	95.1	132.6	133.7	133.5	..
Nov	99.6p	95.1	128.8	132.4	132.0	..
Dec	99.6p	95.1p	132.4	135.0	134.6	..
2004 Jan	..	95.0p	..	..	..	..

1 Series based on mortgage lending by all financial institutions rather than building societies only, as previously published. This change has been made necessary because of the mergers, takeovers and conversions to plc status affecting the building society sector. The series is based on the Office of the Deputy Prime Ministers' 5% survey of mortgage lenders (at completion stage), but now includes all mortgage lenders rather than building societies only. From February 2002, monthly data has been obtained from the enlarged survey and quarterly data from 2002q2 are based on monthly indices.

2 Please note that because of some changes in coverage, the revised series from Q1 1993 is not directly comparable with the old series. From Q1 1993 prices of all sales of agricultural land exclude some transfers in order to come closer to estimates of market determined prices. However the new series does not represent exactly competitive open market values. Sales are now analysed and recorded on the basis of when the transactions actually took place. Further information is available on the DEFRA Website (www.defra.gov.uk/esg/default.htm) accessible through the Internet and by a faxback facility (Fax No 0906 711 0396 charged at 50 pence per minute). Data prior to 1993 remains on the previous basis.

3 Provisional estimates.

Sources: Office for National Statistics, Enquiries Columns 1-2 01633 812106 or 813390;
Office of the Deputy Prime Minister, Enquiries Columns 3-5 020 7944 3325;
Department of Environment, Food and Rural Affairs;
Enquiries Column 6 01904 455083

Economic Trends 604 March 2004   Tables section

Measures of variability of selected economic series[1]

	Table	Period covered	$\overline{CI}$	$\overline{I}$	$\overline{C}$	$\overline{I}/\overline{C}$	MCD or QCD	$\overline{I}/\overline{C}$ for MCD (or QCD) span
Quarterly series								
National income and components:chained volume measures, reference year 2000								
Gross Value Added (GVA) at Basic Prices	2.1	Q1 1985 to Q3 2003	0.7	0.2	0.7	0.3	1	0.3
Households' Final Consumption Expenditure	2.5	Q1 1985 to Q3 2003	0.9	0.3	0.9	0.4	1	0.4
Gross fixed capital formation	2.2, 2.7	Q1 1985 to Q3 2003	2.1	1.2	1.5	0.8	1	0.8
Exports: goods and services	2.2	Q1 1985 to Q3 2003	2.0	1.1	1.4	0.8	1	0.8
Imports: goods and services	2.2	Q1 1985 to Q3 2003	2.1	1.0	1.7	0.6	1	0.6
Real Households' disposable income	2.5	Q1 1985 to Q3 2003	1.2	1.0	0.9	1.1	2	0.3
Gross operating surplus of private non-financial corporations	2.11	Q1 1985 to Q3 2003	3.1	2.1	2.0	1.1	2	0.4
Other quarterly series								
Households' saving ratio[3]	2.5	Q1 1985 to Q3 2003	0.9	0.9	0.4	2.1	2	0.7
Monthly series								
Retail sales (volume per week)								
Predominantly food stores	5.8	Jan 1986 to Sep 2003	0.6	0.6	0.2	2.4	3	0.8
Predominantly non-food stores	5.8	Jan 1986 to Sep 2003	1.1	1.0	0.4	2.5	3	0.8
Non-store and repair	5.8	Jan 1986 to Sep 2003	1.8	1.7	0.5	3.6	4	1.0
Housing starts[2]:								
Private enterprise	5.4	Jan 1985 to Mar 2003	7.0	6.8	1.5	4.4	5	0.9
Registered Social Landlords	5.4	Jan 1985 to Mar 2003	14.9	14.8	1.6	9.1	6	1.0
Housing completions[2]								
Private enterprise	5.4	Jan 1985 to Mar 2003	5.7	5.7	0.7	8.6	6	1.0
Registered Social Landlords	5.4	Jan 1985 to Mar 2003	14.1	14.0	1.6	8.8	6	1.0
Index of industrial production								
Production industries	5.1	Jan 1985 to Sep 2003	0.7	0.7	0.2	3.1	4	0.9
Manufacturing industries	5.1	Jan 1985 to Sep 2003	0.7	0.7	0.3	2.5	3	0.8
Average earnings: whole economy	4.6	Jan 1990 to Sep 2003	0.4	0.3	0.4	0.7	1	0.7
Exports: value, f.o.b.[4]	2.13	Jan 1985 to Sep 2003	2.9	2.7	0.8	3.2	4	0.8
Imports: value, f.o.b.[4]	2.13	Jan 1985 to Sep 2003	2.3	2.2	0.8	2.7	3	0.8
Money stock - M0[5]	6.2	Jan 1985 to Sep 2003	0.5	0.3	0.5	0.6	1	0.6
Money stock - M4[5]	6.2	Jan 1985 to Sep 2003	0.8	0.3	0.7	0.4	1	0.4

1 For a fuller description of these measures see article 'Measuring variability in economic time series' in *Economic Trends*, No 226, August 1972.
The following are brief definitions of the measures.
$\overline{CI}$ is the average month to month (quarter to quarter for quarterly series) percentage change without regard to sign in the seasonally adjusted series.
$\overline{C}$ is the same for the trend component.
$\overline{I}$ is the same for the irregular component, obtained by dividing the trend component into the seasonally adjusted series, except for those series which are seasonally adjusted using an additive model, see footnotes 3 and 5.
$\overline{I}/\overline{C}$ is therefore a measure of the size of the relative irregularity of the seasonally adjusted series.
The average changes $\overline{I}$ and $\overline{C}$ can also be computed successively over spans of increasing numbers of months (quarters). MCD (QCD), months (quarters) for cyclical dominance, is the shortest span of months (quarters) for which $\overline{I}/\overline{C}$ is less than 1 and therefore represents the minimum period over which changes in the trend, on average, exceed the irregular movement.
MCD cannot exceed 6 even if $\overline{I}/\overline{C}$ exceeds 1 for 6-month periods.

2 Series relate to Great Britain.
3 The figures in the tables were obtained from an additive analysis of the households' saving ratio so $\overline{CI}$, $\overline{I}$ and $\overline{C}$ are differences in percentage points.
4 The figures have been updated as described in an article in *Economic Trends*, No 320, June 1980.
5 As the irregular component for M0 and M4 is obtained by subtraction of the trend rather than by division, the figures for $\overline{CI}$, $\overline{I}$ and $\overline{C}$ are expressed as percentages of the trend level in the preceding month.

Source: Office for National Statistics: Enquiries 020 7533 6243

Index of sources

Abbreviations

DEFRA – Department for Environment, Food and Rural Affairs.
ODPM – Office of the Deputy Prime Minister.

	Table	Source	Further statistics (where available)
Asset prices	6.9	Office for National Statistics DEFRA ODPM Bank of England	Financial Statistics (for financial assets)
Average earnings	1.1, 4.6	Office for National Statistics	First Release Labour Market Trends Monthly Digest of Statistics
Balance of payments (current account)	2.13	Office for National Statistics	First Release Financial Statistics UK Economic Accounts
Banking		Bank of England	Financial Statistics
Banking loans, advances and acceptances	6.7		
British government sucurities (long dated) 20 years yield	6.8	Bank of England	
Building societies			Financial Statistics
Advances on new dwellings	5.4	Building Societies Association	
Average prices of new dwellings on mortgage completion (see also Housing)	5.4	ODPM Housing Statistics	
Commitments on new dwellings	5.4	Building Societies Association	
Capital account summary, analysis by sector	2.10	Office for National Statistics	
Cars (see also Motor Vehicles)			
Production	1.1, 5.3	Office for National Statistics	News Release
Registration	5.8	Department of Transport	
Change in inventories			
By industry	5.7	Office for National Statistics	First Release
Manufacturing	1.1		Monthly Digest of Statistics
Ratios	5.7		
Total	2.2		
Claimant count (see Unemployment)			
Coal (see also Energy)	5.9	Department of Trade and Industry	Energy Trends
Consumer prices index	1.1, 3.1	Office for National Statistics	First Release Focus on consumer price indices Labour Market Trends
Commercial vehicles, production (see also Motor vehicles)	5.3	Office for National Statistics	News Release
Construction industry			
Index of output (see also) Industrial production)	1.1, 2.8	Office for National Statistics	
Orders received	5.2, 5.4	Department of Trade and Industry	Construction Statistics
Output	5.2	Department of Trade and Industry	
Corporations		Office for National Statistics	
Financial corporations			Financial Statistics
Capital transfers	2.10		UK Economic Accounts
Gross saving	2.10		
In relation to gross domestic product	2.3		Monthly Digest of Statistics
Non-financial corporations			First Release
Allocation of primary income account	2.11		Financial Statistics
Capital account, net lending/net borrowing	2.12		UK Economic Accounts
Gross operating surplus	2.11		
Gross saving	2.10		
Property income received/paid	2.11		
Resources	2.11, 2.12		
Secondary distribution of income account	2.12		
Security prices and yields (see also Interest rates)	6.8	Bank of England	
Uses	2.11, 2.12	Office for National Statistics	

Economic Trends 604 March 2004   Index of sources

Consumer credit	5.8, 6.6	Office for National Statistics	Consumer Trends Financial Statistics
Counterparts to changes in money stock M4	6.3	Bank of England	Financial Statistics Press Notice
Credit business (see also Hire purchase)	5.8	Office for National Statistics	Financial Statistics
Current balance (see also Balance of payments)	2.13	Office for National Statistics	First Release Financial Statistics UK Economic Accounts
Dwellings (see also Housing)	5.4	Office for National Statistics ODPM	
Earnings (average)	1.1, 4.6	Office for National Statistics	First Release Labour Market Trends Monthly Digest of Statistics
Economic activity (Labour Force Survey)	4.1, 4.2, 4.3	Office for National Statistics	First Release Labour Market Trends
Electricity (see also Energy)	5.9	Department of Trade and Industry	Energy Trends
Employees in employment	4.1, 4.2, 4.3, 4.4	Office for National Statistics	First Release Labour Market Trends Monthly Digest of Statistics
Energy	5.9	Department of Trade and Industry	Energy Trends UK Energy Statistics
Household final consumption expenditure on energy products	2.6	Office for National Statistics	Monthly Digest of Statistics
Output index for energy and water supply	5.1		Monthly Digest of Statistics
Primary fuel input: total, coal, petroleum, natural gas and primary electricity	5.9	Department of Trade and Industry	Energy Trends
Engineering industries Sales and orders: total, home market and export	1.1, 5.2	Office for National Statistics	News Release Monthly Digest of Statistics
Eurodollar-3-month rate (see also Interest rates)	6.8	Bank of England	Financial Statistics
Exchange rates	1.1, 6.1	Bank of England	First Release Financial Statistics
Expenditure (see also Total final expenditure)	2.2, 2.3	Office for National Statistics	Monthly Digest of Statistics UK Economic Accounts
Exports		Office for National Statistics	
Of goods	1.1, 2.13		First Release Monthly Digest of Statistics
Price index	1.1, 2.14		First Release UK Economic Accounts
Volume indices	2.14		First Release UK Economic Accounts
Of goods and services	2.2, 2.3		First Release UK Economic Accounts
Of passenger cars, commercial vehicles	5.3		News Release
Orders; engineering industries	5.2		News Release
Price indices	2.14		First Release UK Economic Accounts
Price index for manufactures (international comparisons)	2.15	International Monetary Fund	
Relative prices (as measure of trade competitiveness)	2.15		
Relative profitability (as measure of trade competitiveness)	2.15	International Financial Statistics	
Unit value index	2.15		
Final expenditure (see also Total final expenditure)	2.2, 2.3	Office for National Statistics	First Release Monthly Digest of Statistics UK Economic Accounts
Financial corporations (see also corporations)	2.10	Office for National Statistics	Financial Statistics UK Economic Accounts
Fixed investment			
By sector and by type of asset	2.7	Monthly Digest of Statistics	
Dwellings (see also Housing)	2.7, 5.4	Office for National Statistics	
Gas (see also Energy)	5.9	Department of Trade and Industry	Energy Trends
General government final consumption expenditure	2.2, 2.3	Office for National Statistics	Financial Statistics Monthly Digest of Statistics UK Economic Accounts

Index of sources

Gross disposable income: non-financial corporations	2.12	Office for National Statistics	First Release Financial Statistics
Gross domestic product	2.1	Office for National Statistics	First Release Monthly Digest of Statistics UK Economic Accounts
At basic prices	1.1, 2.1, 2.3, 2.4		
At market prices	2.1, 2.2		
By category of expenditure	2.2		
In relation to output	2.8		
In relation to stocks	5.7		
Per head	2.4		UK Economic Accounts
Gross fixed capital formation (see also Fixed investment)	2.2	Office for National Statistics	First Release Monthly Digest of Statistics UK Economic Accounts
By sector and type of asset	2.7		
Dwellings	2.7		
Gross household disposable income	2.4, 2.5	Office for National Statistics	First Release Monthly Digest of Statistics UK Economic Accounts
Gross national income (per head)	2.4	Office for National Statistics	
Gross operating surplus of non-financial corpoirations	2.11	Office for National Statistics	First Release Financial Statistics UK Economic Accounts
Gross saving (corporations)	2.10	Office for National Statistics	First Release Financial Statistics UK Economic Accounts
Household final consumption expenditure		Office for National Statistics	First Release Consumer Trends Monthly Digest of Statistics
Component categories	2.6		
In relation to personal income	2.5		
In relation to total final expenditure	2.3		
Per head	2.4		
Households' income before tax	2.4, 2.5	Office for National Statistics	Monthly Digest of Statistics
Housing			
Average price of new dwellings at mortgage completion stage	5.4	ODPM	Housing Statistics
Commitments and advances on new dwellings	5.4	Building Societies Association	Financial Statistics Press Notice
Fixed investment in dwellings	2.7, 5.4	Office for National Statistics	
Orders received by contractors for new houses	5.4	Department of Trade and Industry	Monthly Digest of Statistics Press Notice
Starts and completions	1.1, 5.4	ODPM The Scottish Executive National Assembly for Wales	Housing Statistics
Imports			
Of goods	1.1, 2.13	Office for National Statistics	First Release Monthly Digest of Statistics
Price index	1.1, 2.14		
Volume indices	2.14		
Of goods and services	2.2		First Release Monthly Digest of Statistics UK Economic Accounts
Price competitiveness (manufactures)	2.15	Office for National Statistics	
Incomes		Office for National Statistics	
Households' gross disposable income	2.5		First Release Monthly Digest of Statistics UK Economic Accounts
Households' income before tax	2.5		First Release Monthly Digest of Statistics UK Economic Accounts
Income from employment as a percentage of gross domestic product (see also Wages: Earnings)	2.3		Monthly Digest of Statistics
Inventory holding gains (non-financial corporations)	2.11	Office for National Statistics	First Release Financial Statistics UK Economic Accounts

Economic Trends 604 March 2004　　　Index of sources

Industrial production: index of output	5.1	Office for National Statistics	First Release Monthly Digest of Statistics
By main industrial groupings	5.1		
By selected industries	5.1		
In relation to output (gross domestic product)	2.8		
In relation to stocks (manufacturing industries)	5.7		
Inter-bank 3-month rate (see also Interest rates)	6.8	Bank of England	Monetary and Financial Statistics
Interest rates	6.8	Bank of England	Financial Statistics
Eurodollar 3-month rate			
Inter-bank 3-month bid and offer rates			Bank of England
Local authorities 3-month deposit rate			
Selected retail banks base rate			
Sterling certificates of deposit 3-month bid and offer rates			
Treasury bill yield			
International Reserves	6.1	Bank of England	Financial Statistics
Key fiscal indicators	6.5	Office for National Statistics	
Labour Force Survey	4.1, 4.2, 4.3, 4.5a	Office for National Statistics	First Release Labour Market Trends
Local authorities 3-month deposit rate (see also Interest rates)	6.8	Bank of England	
Housing starts and completions (see also Housing)	5.4	ODPM	Housing Statistics Press Notice
Manufacturing industries		Office for National Statistics	Monthly Digest of Statistics
Change in inventories	1.1, 5.7		
Inventory ratios	5.8		First Release Monthly Digest of Statistics
Output (constant prices)	5.1		
in constant prices	1.1		
per filled job, per hour worked	4.7		
Money stock	1.1, 6.2	Bank of England	Financial Statistics Press Notice
Motor vehicles			
New car registrations	1.1, 5.8	Department of Transport	
Production of passenger cars and commercial vehicles: total and for export	1.1, 5.3	Office for National Statistics	News Release Monthly Digest of Statistics
National accounts	2.1 - 2.15	Office for National Statistics	First Release Financial Statistics UK Economic Accounts
National disposable income at market prices	2.1	Office for National Statistics	
Non-financial corporations (see also Corporations)	2.10, 2.11, 2.12	Office for National Statistics	First Release Financial Statistics UK Economic Accounts
Operating surplus (see also Corporations)	2.3, 2.11	Office for National Statistics	First Release Financial Statistics UK Economic Accounts
Orders received			
By construction industry (see also Construction)	5.2	Department of Trade and Industry	Construction Statistics
By engineering industries (see also Engineering)	5.2	Office for National Statistics	News Release Monthly Digest of Statistics
Output			
By construction industry (see also Construction)	1.1, 2.8, 5.2	Office for National Statistics Department of Trade and Industry	Construction Statistics
By engineering industries (see also Engineering)	5.2	Office for National Statistics	News Release Monthly Digest of Statistics
Gross value added by category of	2.8		First Release Monthly Digest of Statistics
Gross value added at basic prices service inds.	2.9		
Per filled job (see also Productivity)	4.7		
Overseas trade (see Exports; Imports; Trade in goods)			
Petroleum (see also Energy)	5.9	Department of Trade and Industry	Energy Trends
Population			
Estimates per capita, income, product and spending	2.4	Office for National Statistics	

Office for National Statistics | 157

Index of sources

Prices			
Asset prices	6.9	Office for National Statistics DEFRA ODPM Bank of England	Financial Statistics (for financial assets)
Average price of new dwellings at mortgage completion (see also Housing)	5.4	ODPM	Housing Statistics
Consumer prices index	1.1, 3.1	Office for National Statistics	First Release Focus on Consumer price indices Labour Market Trends
Pensioner price index	3.1	Office for National Statistics	Labour Market Trends
Producer input and output prices	1.1		
Producer price index	3.1	Office for National Statistics	First Release Monthly Digest of Statistics
Retail prices index	1.1, 3.1		First Release Labour Market Trends Focus on Consumer price indices Monthly Digest of Statistics
Productivity (see Output per filled job)	4.7		First Release Labour Market Trends Monthly Digest of Statistics
Private sector			
Capital account, net lending/net borrowing	2.10	Office for National Statistics	Financial Statistics
Gross fixed investment	2.3, 2.7		Monthly Digest of Statistics
Housing starts and completions (see also Housing)	5.4	ODPM	Housing Statistics Press Notice
Producer price index (see also Prices)	3.1	Office for National Statistics	First Release Monthly Digest of Statistics
Production (see Industrial production; Motor vehicles; Output; Steel)		Office for National Statistics	
Productivity	1.1, 4.7	Office for National Statistics	Monthly Digest of Statistics
Profits (see also Companies)	2.3, 2.11	Office for National Statistics	First Release Financial Statistics UK Economic Accounts
Property income received/paid; non-financial corporations	2.11	Office for National Statistics	First Release Financial Statistics UK Economic Accounts
Property transactions	5.5	Board of Inland Revenue	
Public sector			
Expenditure and receipts	6.4	Office for National Statistics	
Fiscal indicators	6.5	Office for National Statistics	
Gross fixed capital formation	2.7		
Index numbers of output	2.9	Office for National Statistics	
Net cash requirement (PNSCR)	6.3, 6.5		First Release
Net borrowing	1.1, 6.5		Financial Statistics
Purchasing power of the pound	3.1	Office for National Statistics	
Regional claimant unemployment rates (see also Unemployment)	4.5	Office for National Statistics	First Release Labour Market Trends
Retail prices index (see also Prices)	1.1, 3.1	Office for National Statistics	First Release Monthly Digest of Statistics Focus on consumer prices indices Labour Market Trends
Retail sales			
Value index numbers	5.8	Office for National Statistics	First Release Monthly Digest of Statistics
Volume index numbers	1.1, 5.8		
Ratio of distributors' stocks to retail sales	5.7		
Savings ratio, household	2.5	Office for National Statistics	First Release Financial Statistics Monthly Digest of Statistics UK Economic Accounts
Selected retail banks' rates (see also Interest rates)	6.8	Bank of England	
Service industries			
Gross value added	2.8, 2.9	Office for National Statistics	First Release

Steel, production	5.3	Iron and Steel Statistics Bureau Ltd.	Monthly Digest of Statistics
Sterling certificates of deposit (see also Interest rates)	6.8	Bank of England	Financial Statistics
Sterling			
Exchange rate index	1.1, 6.1	Bank of England	Financial Statistics
Exchange rates against major currencies	6.1		
Taxes		Office for National Statistics	Financial Statistics
Public sector receipts of	6.4		
Payment of taxes by non-financial corporations	2.12		First Release Financial Statistics UK Economic Accounts
Total final expenditure on goods and services	2.2	Office for National Statistics	First Release Monthly Digest of Statistics UK Economic Accounts
Trade competitiveness measures	2.15	Office for National Statistics International Monetary Fund	International Financial Statistics
Trade in goods	1.1, 2.13, 2.14	Office for National Statistics	First Release Monthly Digest of Statistics UK Economic Accounts
Transfers (see also Balance of payments)	2.13	Office for National Statistics	First Release UK Economic Accounts
Treasury bill yield (see also Interest rates)	6.8	Bank of England	Financial Statistics
Unemployed (ILO)	4.1, 4.2, 4.3		First Release (Labour Force Survey)
Unemployment		Office for National Statistics	First Release Labour Market Trends Monthly Digest of Statistics
Regional claimant count	4.5		
Total claimant count	1.1, 4.4		
Unit labour costs index (international comparisons)	2.15	International Monetary Fund	International Financial Statistics
Unit wage costs	4.7		
Vacancies	1.1, 4.2	Office for National Statistics	First Release Labour Market Trends Monthly Digest of Statistics
Wages and salaries			
Unit costs - manufacturing	1.1, 4.7	Office for National Statistics	First Release Labour Market Trends Monthly Digest of Statistics
Unit costs - whole economy	1.1, 4.7		
In relation to gross household disposable income	2.5	Office for National Statistics	Monthly Digest of Statistics First Release Labour Market Trends
Per unit of output (see Unit wage costs)			
Wholesale price index for manufactures (international comparisons)	2.15	International Monetary Fund	International Financial Statistics
Workforce Jobs	4.4	Office for National Statistics	First Release Labour Market Trends Monthly Digest of Statistics

Portofolio of ONS macro-economic statistics   Economic Trends 604 March 2004

United Kingdom macro-economic statistics

Published by ONS

Annual publications

Economic Trends Annual Supplement

Input-Output Analyses

Overseas Direct Investment

Financial Statistics Explanatory Handbook

Share Ownership

UK Balance of Payments (Pink Book)

UK National Accounts (Blue Book)

First releases

- UK Balance of Payments
- UK National Accounts
- UK Output, Income & Expenditure
- GDP Preliminary estimate
- Business investment

Recent editions

All editions are downloadable from the National Statistics website www.statistics.gov.uk

Economic Trends annual supplement 2003. TSO, ISBN 011 621591 7. Price £30
www.statistics.gov.uk/products/p311.asp

Financial Statistics explanatory handbook 2004. TSO, ISBN 0 11 621604 2. Price £39.50. www.statistics.gov.uk/products/p4861.asp

Quarterly publications

UK Economic Accounts

Consumer Trends

Overseas Trade analysed in terms of industry

First releases

- UK Balance of Payments
- UK National Accounts
- UK Output, Income & Expenditure
- GDP Preliminary estimate
- Business investment
- Institutional Investment
- Govt Deficit & Debt under the Treaty
- Public Sector Accounts
- Profitability of UK companies
- Productivity

Consumer Trends 2003 quarter 3
www.statistics.gov.uk/products/p242.asp

United Kingdom Economic Accounts: 2003 quarter 3. TSO, ISBN 0 11 621727 8. Price £27.
www.statistics.gov.uk/products/p1904.asp

UK Trade in Goods analysed in terms of industry (MQ10): 2003 quarter 4
www.statistics.gov.uk/products/p731.asp

Monthly publications

Consumer Price Indices

Economic Trends

Producer Price Indices

Financial Statistics

Monthly Review of External Trade Statistics

First releases

- UK Trade
- Public Sector Finances
- Consumer Price indices
- Producer Prices
- Retail Sales Index
- Institutional Investment
- Index of Production

Financial Statistics: February 2004. TSO, ISBN 0 11 621683 2. Price £24.50.

Focus on Consumer Price Indices: January 2004. www.statistics.gov.uk/products/p867.asp

Monthly review of External Trade Statistics (MM24): January 2004
www.statistics.gov.uk/products/p613.asp

Other publications
- Retail Prices 1914–1990
- Labour Market Trends
- National Accounts Concepts Sources and Methods -
- Sector Classification Guide for the National Statistics